The ACT™ For Dummies®, 2nd Edition

Important Things You Should Know about the ACT

- The ACT has no penalty for wrong answers. *Never* leave any answer blank: *guess, guess, guess!*
- The ACT features four tests: English, Mathematics, Reading, and Science Reasoning.
- The ACT does *not* have a verbal portion that specifically tests vocabulary.
- You are allowed to use a calculator on the Mathematics Test.
- Many colleges accept either the ACT or the SAT I (Scholastic Assessment Tests). You may want to take both exams to maximize your chances of college admission.
- The ACT does not require an essay.
- All questions on the ACT have multiple-choice answers.
- Mark answers in the booklet and on the grid. When you answer a question, circle the answer in your test booklet first and then shade in the appropriate circle on your test grid. Doing so can be your salvation if you make a mistake in your numbering on the grid and have to erase and start over again. This technique also helps you when you double-check your work.

The English Test Do's and Don'ts

When rushed for time . . .

- *Do* look for diction (choosing between two words, such as *lie* and *lay* or *affect* and *effect*) and grammar (choosing the proper verb, adjective, or adverb) questions. They are usually the easiest to answer quickly.
- *Don't* get trapped by time-consuming, potentially difficult box questions that require you to understand the passage as a whole.
- *Don't* choose the OMIT option every time you see it.
- *Don't* automatically choose the "other" word in a diction or grammar question (choosing *lie* when *lay* is given or *whom* when *who* is given).

The Mathematics Test Do's and Don'ts

Remember the following as you get ready to take the Mathematics Test:

- *Do* start in the middle when plugging in answer choices; you'll know whether your answer needs to be larger or smaller.
- *Do* work forward and backward: Double-check the problem with your answer inserted.
- *Don't* mess up on the answer sheet. The math questions are the only questions on the ACT with five answer choices rather than four.
- *Don't* forget your calculator and extra batteries for it.

The ACT™ For Dummies®, 2nd Edition

The Reading Test Do's and Don'ts

Keep this information in mind when you encounter the Reading Test:

- *Do* preview the passages, decide on a strategy (reading quickly to finish all passages or going more slowly and carefully through only three out of the four passages), and pay special attention to the first and last paragraphs.
- *Do* summarize the information in your mind, looking for relationships and connections.
- *Don't* expect to have to know specific information; the passages give or imply all the information you need in order to answer the questions. You do not need specific background knowledge.
- *Don't* memorize the information; you may go back to the passage as often as you'd like.

The Science Reasoning Test Do's and Don'ts

Knowing these do's and don'ts will help you to do your best on the Science Reasoning Test:

- *Do* note any trends or significant shifts in the data presented in the introductory text, tables, diagrams, or graphs.
- *Do* make sure that you can identify the purpose of the study, the experimental design, and the results in Research Summary passages.
- *Do* identify the viewpoint of each scientist, his or her main idea, and the evidence that supports or contradicts each point of view in the Conflicting Viewpoints questions.
- *Don't* attempt to answer questions based on your own background knowledge; all necessary information is stated or implied in the passages, tables, or graphs.

The ACT in a Nutshell

Test	*Minutes*	*Questions*	*Topics*
English	45	75	Run-ons, fragments, grammar, usage, punctuation, organization, style, and strategy.
Mathematics	60	60	Geometry, algebra, mathematics, and only four questions on trigonometry. The test does *not* cover calculus.
Reading	35	40	Humanities, social studies, natural sciences, and prose fiction.
Science Reasoning	35	40	Science reasoning; all questions may be answered by reading the information stated or implied in the passages, graphs, or tables; no specific background knowledge is required.

****Warning:*** The ACT is rated PG: Proctor Guarded. Proctors have been genetically altered to have eyes in the backs of their heads, and they'll catch you if you peek at this sheet during the ACT. Learn it, and then burn it.

Cheat Sheet $2.95 value. Item 5210-4.
For more information about Hungry Minds, call 1-800-762-2974.

For Dummies: Bestselling Book Series for Beginners

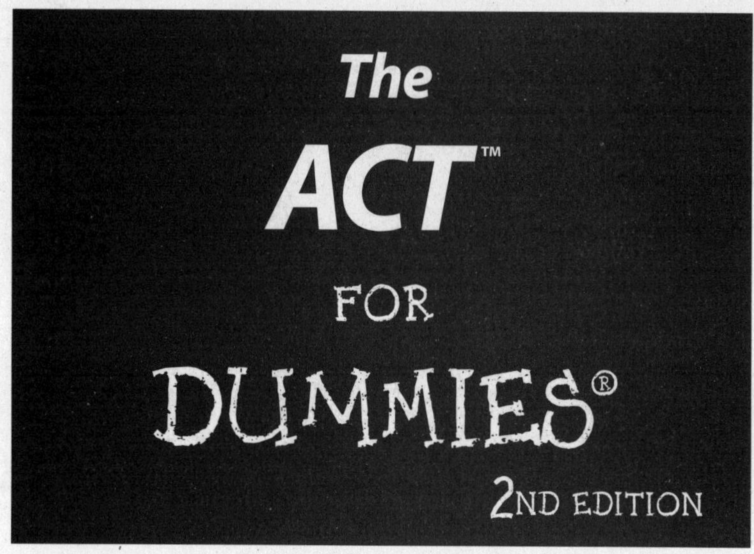

by Suzee Vlk

Hungry Minds™

Best-Selling Books • Digital Downloads • e-Books • Answer Networks • e-Newsletters • Branded Web Sites • e-Learning

New York, NY ◆ Cleveland, OH ◆ Indianapolis, IN

The ACT™ For Dummies,® 2nd Edition

Published by
Hungry Minds, Inc.
909 Third Avenue
New York, NY 10022
www.hungryminds.com
www.dummies.com

Library of Congress Catalog Card No.: 99-66375

ISBN: 0-7645-5210-4

Printed in the United States of America

10 9 8 7 6 5

2B/QW/RR/QR/IN

Distributed in the United States by IDG Books Worldwide, Inc.

Distributed by CDG Books Canada Inc. for Canada; by Transworld Publishers Limited in the United Kingdom; by IDG Norge Books for Norway; by IDG Sweden Books for Sweden; by IDG Books Australia Publishing Corporation Pty. Ltd. for Australia and New Zealand; by TransQuest Publishers Pte Ltd. for Singapore, Malaysia, Thailand, Indonesia, and Hong Kong; by Gotop Information Inc. for Taiwan; by ICG Muse, Inc. for Japan; by Intersoft for South Africa; by Eyrolles for France; by International Thomson Publishing for Germany, Austria and Switzerland; by Distribuidora Cuspide for Argentina; by LR International for Brazil; by Galileo Libros for Chile; by Ediciones ZETA S.C.R. Ltda. for Peru; by WS Computer Publishing Corporation, Inc., for the Philippines; by Contemporanea de Ediciones for Venezuela; by Express Computer Distributors for the Caribbean and West Indies; by Micronesia Media Distributor, Inc. for Micronesia; by Chips Computadoras S.A. de C.V. for Mexico; by Editorial Norma de Panama S.A. for Panama; by American Bookshops for Finland.

For general information on IDG Books Worldwide's books in the U.S., please call our Consumer Customer Service department at 800-762-2974. For reseller information, including discounts and premium sales, please call our Reseller Customer Service department at 800-434-3422.

For information on where to purchase IDG Books Worldwide's books outside the U.S., please contact our International Sales department at 317-596-5530 or fax 317-596-5692.

For consumer information on foreign language translations, please contact our Customer Service department at 1-800-434-3422, fax 317-596-5692, or e-mail rights@idgbooks.com.

For information on licensing foreign or domestic rights, please phone +1-650-655-3109.

For sales inquiries and special prices for bulk quantities, please contact our Sales department at 650-655-3200 or write to the address above.

For information on using IDG Books Worldwide's books in the classroom or for ordering examination copies, please contact our Educational Sales department at 800-434-2086 or fax 317-596-5499.

For press review copies, author interviews, or other publicity information, please contact our Public Relations department at 650-655-3000 or fax 650-655-3299.

For authorization to photocopy items for corporate, personal, or educational use, please contact Copyright Clearance Center, 222 Rosewood Drive, Danvers, MA 01923, or fax 978-750-4470.

About the Author

"I'm not a complete idiot. Parts of me are missing."

Although more likely to admit to being a mortician, used-car salesperson, or guinea pig for Army experiments, Suzee Vlk has been a test prep specialist since 1975, working her way through graduate business school and law school teaching courses in ACT, SAT I, GRE, GMAT, and LSAT preparation. She found the paranoia and take-no-prisoners mindset required for doing well on the ACT a big help in developing cutthroat tactics to use in the boardroom or courtroom.

Today, Suzee is president of Suzee Vlk Test Prep (no ego involved in *that* company name!) and has taught thousands of students in dozens of courses at universities and private corporations, including "mature" adults who have been out of school for a decade (or two or three) and international students from countries all over the world. (All victims have, so far, survived.) She has written material used in SAT and GRE preparation software and videos (starring in one set of videos when she was younger and blonder). Her prep books for the ACT and other standardized exams have been published worldwide.

Suzee currently specializes in one-on-one tutorials and teaches ACT prep tricks and traps to all levels of students, from those who are struggling to remember the basics ("Let's see: A triangle, that's three sides, or is it four?") to whiz kids who will probably be her boss one day. Her students have not only been accepted at colleges and universities nationwide, including such dream schools as Harvard and Stanford, but have done well enough on the ACTs to be awarded scholarships—to the unbounded joy of their parents, who can now spend what's left of their kids' education fund on sailboats, flashy sports cars, and other midlife crisis toys.

Suzee lives by the following motto, which she is delighted to share with you:

> Madness takes its toll. Please have exact change ready.

Dedication

This book is cheerfully dedicated to Kathy and Ron Drake, the World's Greatest Neighbors.

Author's Acknowledgments

After years of having California students groan at my puns (they frequently remind me of the Fred Allen joke that "hanging is too good for a person who makes puns; he should be drawn and quoted"), make rude hand gestures in response to my scintillatingly clever quips, and threaten to storm out of the room if I tell my geometry jokes one more time, it's wonderful to get the chance to inflict my dysfunctional sense of humor on a worldwide, unsuspecting audience. The decline of civilization begins here.

Thanks to my agents, Bill Gladstone and Matt Wagner of Waterside Productions in Cardiff, California, for getting me this opportunity. Extreme gratitude is due to Paul Dickstein for his expertise and assistance during my calls for aid, and especially for his understanding and empathy during my (many) calls of exasperation. A thousand thanks to Dani Grubbs for her quick response to my desperate pleas for help and for all her input.

Special thanks to Kathy Welton, Mark Butler, Diane Steele, Kristin Cocks, and Mary Corder. Many thanks also go to this book's cast of long-suffering editors: Pam Mourouzis, Tina Sims, Barb Terry, Kathy Cox, Suzanne Thomas, Diana Conover, Kelly Ewing, and Greg Robertson. Thanks to Dr. Cary Wintz, Marcy Denmark Manning, Dr. Della Bell, Richard Menke, and Dr. John Sapp, who reviewed the manuscript for technical accuracy.

It's important for me to acknowledge one of the most underused and underappreciated resources today's students have: high school counselors. Thanks to all of you who go out of your way to help students to do their best to prepare for that rite of passage known as the ACT.

And finally, thanks go to my students over the years, those wonderful kids and adults who have had enough faith in me to use my tricks and tips . . . and enough kindness to let me share their joy in the good scores that result.

You all keep this fun.

Publisher's Acknowledgments

We're proud of this book; please register your comments through our Online Registration Form located at `www.dummies.com`.

Some of the people who helped bring this book to market include the following:

Acquisitions, Development, and Editorial

Senior Project Editor: Pamela Mourouzis
(Previous Edition: Barb Terry, Colleen Totz Rainsberger, Kathleen M. Cox)

Senior Acquisitions Editor: Mark Butler

Copy Editor: Tina Sims

Technical Reviewers: Dr. Cary Wintz, Marcy Denmark Manning, Dr. Della Bell, Dr. John Sapp, Richard Menke

Editorial Manager: Seta Frantz

Production

Project Coordinator: Maridee V. Ennis

Layout and Graphics: Brian Drumm, Angela F. Hunckler, Brent Savage, Janet Seib, Michael A. Sullivan, Dan Whetstine

Proofreaders: Laura Albert, John Greenough, Nancy Price, Marianne Santy, Rebecca Senninger, Susan Sims

Indexer: Johnna VanHoose

Hungry Minds Consumer Reference Group

Business: Kathleen A. Welton, Vice President and Publisher; Kevin Thornton, Acquisitions Manager

Cooking/Gardening: Jennifer Feldman, Associate Vice President and Publisher

Education/Reference: Diane Graves Steele, Vice President and Publisher

Lifestyles/Pets: Kathleen Nebenhaus, Vice President and Publisher; Tracy Boggier, Managing Editor

Travel: Michael Spring, Vice President and Publisher; Suzanne Jannetta, Editorial Director; Brice Gosnell, Publishing Director

Hungry Minds Consumer Editorial Services: Kathleen Nebenhaus, Vice President and Publisher; Kristin A. Cocks, Editorial Director; Cindy Kitchel, Editorial Director

Hungry Minds Consumer Production: Debbie Stailey, Production Director

Contents at a Glance

Cartoons at a Glance

By Rich Tennant

The 5th Wave
By Rich Tennant
THEY'RE MOVING ON TO THE READING QUESTIONS. THAT SHOULD DAZE AND CONFUSE THEM ENOUGH FOR US TO FINISH CHANGING THE TIRE AND GET THE HECK OUT OF HERE.
ACT TEST BOOK PUBLISHERS

page 123

The 5th Wave
By Rich Tennant
ACT Testing Center
Ready? Begin the test.
THE MIGHTY TUBAS
Jazz Ensemble
Ready? "Flight of the Bumble Bee."

page 5

The 5th Wave
By Rich Tennant
ACT overload
We can't eat the pizza until Lamar determines the relationship of the 3 small wedges to the 2 larger ones.

page 47

The 5th Wave
By Rich Tennant
Igor prepares for the Science Reasoning portion of the ACT.
OK, CAREFUL NOW. THIS IS WHERE IT GETS TRICKY. YOU'VE DROPPED THE NORMAL BRAIN, BUT THE ABNORMAL BRAIN REMAINS INTACT IN THE JAR. YOU SHOULD; Ⓐ SCOOP THE NORMAL BRAIN UP IN A HANKY AND RETURN TO THE CASTLE WITH IT IN YOUR POCKET; Ⓑ RETURN TO THE CASTLE WITH THE ABNORMAL BRAIN AND HOPE FOR THE BEST; Ⓒ TAKE NEITHER BRAIN AND RETURN TO THE CASTLE EXPLAINING YOU GOT LOST IN THE STORM.
ABNORMAL BRAIN

page 137

The 5th Wave
By Rich Tennant
IT SAYS, "BREAK GLASS," BUT IT DOESN'T SAY WHAT GLASS!
TRY THE DOOR AGAIN!
MAYBE THE WHOLE THING IS SUPPOSED TO COME OFF THE WALL.
"AIM THE HOSE?" AIM IT AT WHAT?!
LET'S GO OVER IT ONCE MORE—SLOWLY!
I COULD BREAK A WINDOW! THAT'S GLASS!
FIRE
ACT

page 31

The 5th Wave
By Rich Tennant
Jimmy spent all day concentrating on his upcoming ACT. This proved an excellent study habit up until he tried milking his father's prize bull.

page 63

The 5th Wave
By Rich Tennant
It didn't help that the ACT proctor also happened to be Kevin's dentist.
Well, I don't like the looks of that. You keep working—I'm going out to the car for some Novocaine.

page 335

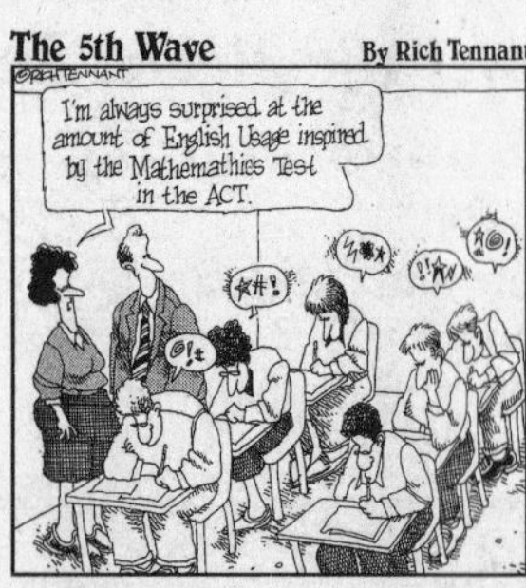

The 5th Wave
By Rich Tennant
I'm always surprised at the amount of English Usage inspired by the Mathematics Test in the ACT.

page 15

The 5th Wave
By Rich Tennant
SHERLOCK HOLMES TAKES THE ACT
Hmm... ELEMENTARY! Ah, yes... ummm... AHA! ELEMENTARY! ELEMENTARY! Now, let's see. Ahhhhh HA! ELEMENTARY INDEED!!
Gimme a break.

page 159

Fax: 978-546-7747

E-mail: richtennant@the5thwave.com

World Wide Web: www.the5thwave.com

Table of Contents

Part V: More Fun Than a Root Canal: The Dreaded Math Review 63

Part VIII: I'd Rather Wait for the Movie: Full-Length Practice ACTs 159

Introduction

Putting on a Good ACT

Welcome to *The ACT For Dummies,* 2nd Edition. This is a nondiscriminatory, equal-opportunity book. You're welcome to participate whether you are a genius or (like me) you need a recipe to make ice. Besides, the title is not a slam at you. *You're* not the dummy; the test is (and I've heard it called worse, believe me — especially the Friday night before the exam). The goal of this book is to show you exactly how to survive this ridiculous situation. No matter how excellent your high school teachers are (or were), they prepared you for the Real World, a world that, alas, has very little connection to the ACT. High school teachers can give you a good foundation in grammar, reading, science, and math skills (the areas tested on the ACT), but think of them as the friendly old GPs, the general practitioners whose job is to keep you well or handle the little day-to-day problems. What do you do when you have a crisis that's making you really sick, like the ACT? I like to think of *The ACT For Dummies,* 2nd Edition, as a loony but gifted specialist you can call in when the situation is desperate.

No one wants to deal with the eccentric specialist for too terribly long. The goal of this book, just like the goal of the expert, is to come in with the Code Blue crash cart, deal with the situation, and then leave rapidly with as few lives destroyed as possible. This book has one goal: to prepare you for the ACT — period. It is not my heart's desire to teach you every grammar rule ever created or every math formula Einstein knew. No extra "filler" material is included in this book to make it look fat and impressive on bookstore shelves. If you want a thick book to use as a booster seat for the vertically challenged, go find *War and Peace.* If you're looking for something that you can use to prepare you for the ACT as quickly and painlessly as possible, again I say to you, welcome to *The ACT For Dummies,* 2nd Edition.

You Can Run, but You Can't Hide

There is no escaping the ACT. Many colleges require that you take this entrance exam before they will even look at your application. Some colleges will accept scores from either the ACT or the SAT. (It just so happens that Hungry Minds publishes an *SAT I For Dummies* book as well, should you choose to take that exam.) Many students decide to take both tests to see which one they do better on. Is that a good idea? Absolutely. If you have the option of taking either the ACT or the SAT, take both. (I'll discuss the similarities and differences of these exams later.)

Many schools emphasize the ACT scores to compensate for grade inflation. That is, some high schools may give you an A for doing the same level work that would gain you a C in other high schools. It's certainly not fair that a person at an "easy" high school has a 4.0 while a student at a more demanding high school has a 3.0 for doing the same work. Because the ACT is the same for everyone (students nationwide take the exact same exam), colleges can use the scores to get inside your head and see what's really there. Think of this as an opportunity, not a crisis: A good ACT score can overcome a low GPA. In just a few hours one fine Saturday morning, you can make up a little for years of messing up in school.

In *The ACT For Dummies,* 2nd Edition, you learn what types of questions are on the exam, which questions to work on carefully, and which to guess at quickly (good news: The ACT has **no penalty for wrong answers;** you should guess at absolutely every question you don't know), the approach to each type of question, and, perhaps most important, some traps that are built into each question style. I have been a test-prep tutor since the Jurassic age and have developed a list of the "gotchas" that have trapped thousands of students over the years. Let me see whether I can make them trap you as well.

This book is also full of the substantive information that you need to know, including grammar rules and geometry, algebra, and arithmetic formulas. Naturally, I include some truly sick humor, on the principle that, as you're groaning at my jokes, you won't notice that you're suffering from the questions. (Hey, as the mushroom said to his friends, "Of course, everyone likes me. I'm a fun-gi!")

Note to nontraditional students: The days of high school may be just a fading memory for you (along with your thin waistline and full head of hair). I recognize that not everyone taking the ACT is a high school junior or senior. Maybe you took a few years off to build your career or to nurture a family (or to pay your debt to society) and are now having to go back and review what you thought you had left behind years ago. As the Walrus said, "I weep with you; I deeply sympathize." It can be totally frustrating to have to deal with the subjunctive or pluperfect or quadratic equations all over again. Postpone your nervous breakdown. Things aren't as dismal as they look. You will be surprised how quickly material comes back to you as you go through this book. If you need more hands-on instruction such as private tutoring, call a high school or community college. Someone there will almost certainly be able to recommend a low-cost course or a tutor. The local library can also give you some help.

Using This Book Efficiently

You've probably heard the joke about the student who was debating over whether to buy a book at the bookstore. The sales clerk, eager to make his commission, proclaims, "Buy this book — it'll do half the work for you!" The student brightens up and exclaims, "Great! I'll take two!"

As much as I wish I could simply transfer this material into your brain in one dump, I realize that learning it takes effort on your part. Meet me halfway. I've done my job by showing you what and how to learn; now it's your turn. I suggest two ways to use this book:

- **First, fine-tune your skills.** Maybe you're already a math whiz and just need help with the English grammar. Go right to the English portion. Maybe you're a grammar guru who wouldn't know a nonagon if you met one in a dark alley. The math review is for you.
- **Second, start from scratch.** Lock yourself into your room, lay in a sack of food and some sharpened pencils, and go through this book word for word. Don't worry; it's not as bad as it seems. Actually, starting from scratch is the preferred method. Many students make what I call the "mediocre" mistake: They are good at one section, mediocre at a second, and dismal at the third. They spend all their time in their worst section and barely look at the sections that they're mediocre or good in. *Big* mistake! If you spend two hours studying something that's totally incomprehensible to you, you may improve your score a few points. If you spend two hours studying your mediocre material, you may improve your score by 10 or 20 points (scoring is discussed in detail in a future section). Twenty points that you gain in your mediocre section are just as valuable — and a heck of a lot easier to gain — than 20 points you gain in your weakest section. Humor me and read the book from cover to cover. You'll pick up some great material . . . and a few new jokes along the way.

Some stuff in this book is really, really important. I flag it by using an icon (and if Icon, hey, anyone con . . .). For example, if I know of a particular trap that most students fall for, I put a Traps & Tricks icon next to the explanation. If I have some time-saving tips, an icon goes next to them as well. Here are the examples of the icons:

This icon marks the sample problems in the lectures.

Follow the arrow to score a bull's-eye by using these shortcut tips.

These are the "gotchas" that can kill you before you know that you're dead. Pay special attention to the cheesy things marked with this mousetrap.

You should burn this stuff into your brain or carve it into your heart; it's the really important material. If you skip or ignore the Heads Up icons, you won't get your money's worth out of this book.

This icon points out information pertaining to international students — which questions are worth doing and which ones are "guess and go on."

Making a Commitment

In the real world, you have classes, family obligations, sports practices, and, if you're lucky, a social life. How on earth are you going to fit studying for the ACT into your schedule? The answer is that you have to commit to this project and make it a priority. How many hours exactly should you carve out of your schedule? Here is what I suggest.

This book features two full-length ACTs. Each ACT takes 2 hours and 55 minutes, not including breaks. You may take about an hour to review your errors on each exam. (Not that *you'll* make that many mistakes, but I'd like you to review the answer explanations to every question, not just to the ones you miss. Doing so provides you with yet another opportunity to see shortcuts you may not have noticed, or traps you luckily avoided.)

Basically, therefore, each exam should take you 4 hours, for a total of 8 hours. In addition, this book has four general chapters (English, math, reading, and science), each of which should take you about an hour. At the end of each chapter is a short practice exam requiring about 30 minutes to take and review. Therefore, each of these chapters is an hour and a half, for a total of 6 hours.

This book features a very important grammar review that I strongly suggest you spend at least two hours on. Even if you are good at grammar, this section features all sorts of persnickety grammar rules, just the type that (with your luck) you'd get caught on during the ACT. And finally, the book features three math reviews: geometry, algebra, and arithmetic, each of which should take you about an hour. Here's the final timetable:

Activity	*Time*
Four chapters and sets of practice questions at $1\frac{1}{2}$ hours per chapter/set	6 hours
Two practice exams at 4 hours per exam	8 hours
Three math review chapters at 1 hour per chapter	3 hours
One grammar review chapter at 2 hours	2 hours
Time spent groaning in pain at author's lame jokes	10 minutes
Time spent firing off letter complaining about author's lame jokes (or sending me your better ones!)	10 minutes
TOTAL TIME	**19 hours, 20 minutes**

Fear not: You do not have to do all 19 hours at once. The book is designed so that you can start at any unit at any time. You do not have to have finished the general math chapter, for example, before you go through the general reading chapter.

Okay, are you ready? Are you quivering with anticipation, living for the moment when you can pick up your yellow No. 2 pencil and head for the thrills of a lifetime? (Or are you thinking, "This author's got to get a life!"?) Listen, you're going to take the ACT anyway, so you may as well have a good time learning how to do so. Laughing while learning is the whole purpose of this book. Take a deep breath, rev up the brain cells, and go for it! Good luck. Just remember that for you, ACT can come to stand for Ace Conquers Test!

Part I

Coming to Terms with Reality: An Overview of the ACT

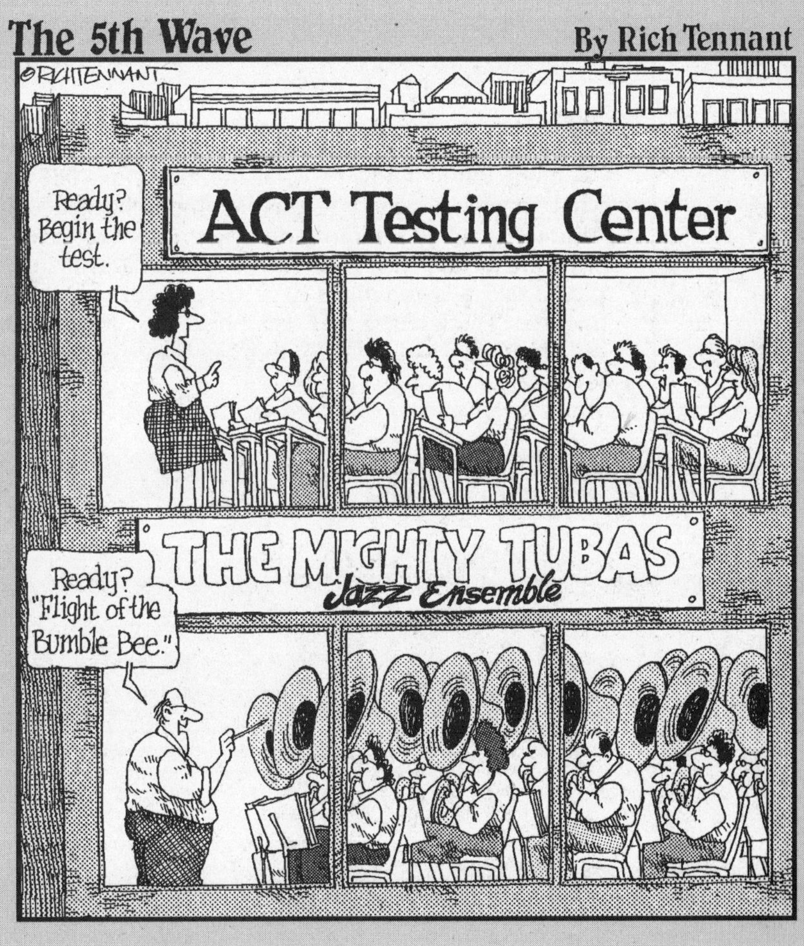

In this part . . .

The reality is that you have to take the ACT. Reality bites. But by knowing what the ACT looks like and what you can expect, you may be able to bite back. Although you are undoubtedly eager to get right to studying for the ACT (Hello, what planet am *I* from?), please take a few minutes to go through this introductory material. Think of the ACT as a blind date: Knowing a little bit about what you'll encounter can lower your anxiety level at least a smidgen.

Chapter 1

Getting Your ACT Together: The Format

In This Chapter

- Packed bags: What to take to the ACT
- Dead weight: What not to take to the test
- Unusual circumstances: What to do if you're someone special
- Sophisticated scoring: What's that about dumb-luck guessing?
- Right before your eyes: What's on the ACT
- Strange but true: Horrible (but hilarious) tales of the ACT

Are you the type who jumps in the cold water all at once instead of just dipping your toe in a little at a time? If so, do I have a table for you. Table 1-1 gives an overview of the ACT and shocks you with the entire kit and caboodle all at once.

Table 1-1 ACT Breakdown by Section

Test	*Number of Questions*	*Time Allotted*
English	75	45 minutes
Mathematics	60	60 minutes
Reading	40	35 minutes
Science Reasoning	40	35 minutes

If you add up the numbers, you find that you have 215 questions to answer in 175 minutes; 175 minutes is 2 hours and 55 minutes, or nearly 3 hours. You get one ten-minute break between tests two and three (the Mathematics and the Reading tests). If you include the time in the classroom spent giving out the tests, explaining the directions, checking ID, and so on, your whole morning is shot. You may as well figure on giving up 4 to $4^1/_2$ hours for this test.

I'd Forget My Head if It Weren't Attached: What to Take to the ACT

If you can't borrow the brain of that whiz kid in your calculus class, you're stuck taking your own. In addition, be sure that you have the following with you:

- **Admission ticket:** By about two weeks before the exam, you should have received your ticket in the mail. If you don't have the ticket by then or if you got it but lost it, call the ACT at 319-337-1270.
- **Pencils:** Take a bunch of sharpened No. 2 pencils with you. You may also want to take a big eraser (nothing personal, everyone makes mistakes) and a small pencil sharpener.

- **Map or directions:** Go to the test center a few days before the actual exam, and scope out your driving route and parking area. Often the ACT is given at colleges that have parking lots far, far from the test room. Drive to the college a few days in advance, park your car, and see just how long it takes you to get to the room. You don't need the stress of having to run to the test room at the last minute.
- **Clothing:** Rumor has it some weird kids are lobbying for a special Nude ACT. Until it becomes available, you need to have some sort of external covering. Take a few extra layers. Many classrooms turn off the heating on the weekend (the ACT is usually offered on a Saturday), and the room is freezing cold. Alternately, in the summer, schools turn off the air conditioning, making the room boiling hot. Dress in layers and be prepared for anything.
- **Photo ID:** Showing the birthmark your boyfriend thinks is so cute isn't going to cut it with the proctor. You need to bring a photo ID (student ID, driver's license, passport, military ID, FBI Most Wanted mug shot, whatever). If you don't have a photo ID, you can bring a letter of identification from your school. (The ACT registration booklet goes into detail about what this letter entails; I won't bore you with that information here.)
- **Eyeglasses:** Students forget their reading glasses at home and then squint for the next four hours. The ACT itself is enough of a headache; you don't need eyestrain as well. And if you wear contacts, be sure to bring cleaning/wetting solution in case you have to take the lenses out and reinsert them. (Hey, all those tears can really mess up your lenses!)
- **A snack:** True, your break is only ten minutes between tests two and three, but that's enough time to gobble down something to jump-start your brain. I often take an energy bar or some peanuts, something with protein and carbohydrates. Scarfing down a candy bar is actually counterproductive; your sugar levels rise only momentarily and then drop down below where they were before you had your chocolate fix.
- **A watch:** If your watch has an alarm, turn it off so that you don't disturb the other students. If you don't know how to do so, borrow another watch. The proctor *will* take a beeping watch away from you.
- **A calculator:** The ACT gurus finally joined the 20th century and agreed to allow students to use calculators. Although the ACT information bulletin has an entire quarter page detailing which calculators can and cannot be used, for all practical purposes, you can use any calculator (yes, even a graphing calculator) as long as it doesn't make a noise. You may not use a laptop computer (don't laugh; you'd be surprised at how many of my students want to bring one to the test!) or a pocket organizer.

What Not to Take to the ACT

Believe it or not, you shouldn't take some things to the test, such as the following:

- **Books and notes:** Last-minute studying will not do you much good. Forget the books; you will not be allowed to take them into the test room with you. (Just be sure to tell this to your parents. I once had a student whose mother drove all the way to the test center with her daughter's ACT prep book, thinking the girl needed it for the test. The mom actually pulled the girl out of the test to give her the book, resulting in the girl's nearly being disqualified from continuing.)
- **Scratch paper:** You may not bring your own scratch paper, and no scratch paper will be given to you during the exam. Fortunately, the exam booklet has plenty of blank space on which you may do your calculations.

The Watch Game: Using your watch to simplify the test

Here's the deal. The proctor — whom you're pretty sure you saw on *America's Most Wanted* last week — tells you at 8:47 that you may begin a 45-minute section. You have 75 questions. The time is now 9:29, and you're on question 30. How are you doing for time? Can you relax and slow down, or are you entering Panic City?

Who needs this kind of stress? It's like adding on another whole math problem. Don't strain your brain; make life easier by resetting your watch. What's your lucky number? Three? When the proctor tells you to begin, set your watch for 2:15. That way, you're counting down the minutes to your lucky number. A glance at your watch tells you how many minutes you have left. Who cares what the time is outside in the Real World? You can use your watch as a stopwatch for the exam, not as a timepiece.

Normal Is Boring: Unusual Circumstances

Not everyone takes the ACT under the same conditions. You may have a special circumstance that can allow you to change the date of the ACT or the way you take your exam. Here is a brief list of special circumstances and how they affect your ACT.

- **Learning disabilities:** If you have a diagnosed learning disability, you may be able to get special accommodations. You may have extended time, but you must specifically request this on your application form. Please note that in order to get special testing you must have been diagnosed LD professionally and must have a current, individualized plan at school. Talk to your counselor for further information.
- **Physical disabilities:** If you have a physical disability, you may be allowed to take a test in a special format — in Braille, large print, or on audiocassette. If your disability is physical, do not complete a registration folder; write to the ACT Universal Testing and receive a form called "Request for ACT Assessment: Special Testing." This booklet explains your options.
- **Religious obligations:** If your religion prohibits you from testing on a Saturday, you may test on an alternate date. The ACT registration bulletin specifies dates and locations in each state.
- **Military duty:** If you are an active military person, you do not complete the normal registration form. Instead, ask your Educational Services Officer about testing through DANTES (Defense Activity for NonTraditional Educational Support).

Anything's Better than Nothing: Guessing for Points

Scoring on the ACT is very straightforward:

- You get one point for every answer you get right.
- You get zero points for every answer you omit.
- You get zero points for every wrong answer.

The ACT is absolutely wonderful in that it does *not* penalize you for wrong answers. The SAT subtracts a fraction of a point for every question you miss. The ACT does not. Therefore, guessing on the ACT obviously works to your advantage. Never leave anything blank. I suggest that you save a couple of minutes at the end of each section just to go through the test and make sure that you've filled in an answer for every single question.

Your number's up: Scoring

I once had a frustrated student tell me that the scores on the ACT looked like measurements to him: 34, 29, 36. However, the ACT has *four* scores, which would be a very strange set of measurements! The ACT scores are nothing like high school scores based on percentages. They are not even like the more familiar SAT scores that range from 200 to 800. The ACT scores are as follows:

- Each test (English, Mathematics, Reading, and Science Reasoning) goes from 1 (low) to 36 (high).
- You also have a composite score, which is the average of the four test scores.

- Three of the tests have subscores. The subscores in English, Mathematics, and Reading range from 1 to 18. Don't assume that the subscores determine the total score. That would be too easy and too logical. The subscores are determined independently and do not necessarily add up to the total score in a section.
- A percentile score tells you where you rank in your state and nationwide.

So how do I know that I'm a genius? What scores mean

Look at the percentiles. Just knowing you got a 26 doesn't tell you much. You need to know whether a 26 is a 50th percentile, a 75th percentile, or a 99th percentile. If you got a 36, be prepared to be accepted at any college nationwide!

ACT versus SAT: The Battle of the Titans

What's the difference between the ACT and the SAT I? Do they test different things? Do they require different study programs? How do you know if you do better on one test than the other? Here are the primary differences between the SAT I and the ACT:

- **The ACT emphasizes English grammar; the SAT I emphasizes vocabulary.** The ACT requires that you know grammar rules such as the distinction between *lie* and *lay* or *it's* and *its.* The SAT I does not test grammar. However, the SAT I has sentence completions and analogies that feature big, hard words like *pulchritudinous* and *pusillanimous.* The ACT does not test vocabulary.
- **The ACT does not have an essay question; the SAT II does.** You may have heard that the ACT has an essay on it. Wrong! The SAT II, which used to be known as the Achievement Test or ACH (could these initials possibly get any more confusing?), has an essay question. The grammar on the ACT is all multiple-choice questions — no essays. The SAT I (the regular SAT) does not have an essay either; only the SAT II has an essay.
- **The ACT questions are all multiple choice. The SAT I math questions include quantitative comparisons and grid-ins.** All questions on the ACT have multiple-choice responses. The SAT I has ten questions that have no multiple-choice responses. You have to solve a math problem yourself and fill in the bubble for the answer. In addition, the SAT I has a bizarre type of math question called the QC (or quantitative comparison). That style of question is not on the ACT.
- **The ACT tests science reasoning; the SAT I does not.** One of the four tests on the ACT is Science Reasoning. The test features science reading passages, sometimes with charts or diagrams that you have to read and use to answer questions. You may be required to interpret an experiment or understand information in a table.

Don't worry, you are not expected to know scientific information on your own. That is, you do not have to have had physics to answer questions on a physics passage. The passage gives you all the information you need.

The SAT I has no science reasoning per se. However, one of the reading passages (called critical reading on the SAT I) usually is on a science topic.

- **The ACT does not penalize you for guessing; the SAT I does.** The ACT allows you to guess your brains out. You don't receive a penalty for missing a question. *Never* leave anything blank. On the SAT I, however, you lose either 1/3 or 1/4 point for wrong answers (depending on the question style).
- **The ACT has four long sections; the SAT I has seven short sections.** The ACT has one 60-minute section, one 45-minute section, and two 35-minute sections. The SAT has five 30-minute sections (one of these is equating, or experimental, and doesn't count) and two 15-minute sections.
- **The ACT has no experimental sections; the SAT I has one.** On the ACT, everything counts. The SAT I has a 30-minute section (either math or verbal) that doesn't count toward your score. No, you won't know which section it is, or you wouldn't take it seriously, now, would you? The test-makers are using you as a guinea pig to try out new questions.

What Do They Want from Me?: What Is Tested

English. The ACT tests English grammar. You are expected to know the fundamentals of usage, diction, and rhetorical skills. For example, you must understand sentence construction — what makes a run-on and what makes a fragment. You need to know how to distinguish between commonly confused words, like *affect* and *effect* or *principal* and *principle*. You must be able to use the proper forms of words, distinguishing between an adjective and an adverb. If you don't have a strong grammar background (you probably have been studying literature for the past few years and haven't had grammar since about the seventh grade), don't panic. This book features a gruesomely exhaustive grammar review with just about everything you'll need to know.

Surprisingly, the ACT English Test is one of the strongest portions of this exam for international students. You learned all these picky grammar points as you learned English. You may be much more comfortable with the rules than are native English speakers.

Mathematics. The ACT requires basic skills in arithmetic, geometry, and algebra. If you have had two semesters of algebra, two semesters of geometry, and a general math background, you can answer probably 90 percent of the questions. Unfortunately, the ACT also tests a little bit of trigonometry. If you have not had trigonometry, don't worry. This book gives you the few things you need to know. In addition, the test has just a few trig questions (usually just four), and they are often so close to the end that many students don't even get to them anyway. Trig should be the least of your worries.

You do not have to know calculus. The ACT has no calculus questions. Happy day!

Reading. You are expected to be able to read a passage in a relatively short amount of time and answer questions based upon it. Your reading skills are probably pretty set by now. If you are 17, you are not going to change the way you've been reading for the past 12 years. However, this fact does not mean you cannot improve your reading *score.* Chapter 10 shows you tricks that you can use to improve your speed and tells you how to recognize and avoid traps built into the questions.

Science Reasoning. You are not required to have any specific science background. The passages may test chemistry, biology, botany, physics, or any other science, but you do not have to have had those courses. The test gives all the information you need to answer the science questions in the passages or in diagrams, charts, and tables.

Practice Makes Perfect: Repeating the Test

Are you allowed to repeat the ACT? Yes. Should you repeat the ACT? Probably. Decide whether to repeat the ACT based on your answers to the following questions:

- **What errors did I make the first time around?**

  If your mistakes were from a lack of knowledge, that is, you just plain didn't know a grammar rule or a math formula, you can easily correct those mistakes with studying. However, if you made mistakes because you were careless or if you daydreamed during the exam, that may be a personality quirk that you're not going to change. Very few people who are careless test-takers change their test style overnight.

- **Why do I want to repeat the test?**

  Is your ego destroyed because your best friend got a better score than you did? That is probably not a good enough reason to retake the ACT. Do retake the exam if you are trying to get a minimum qualifying score to enable you to get into a college or into a scholarship program.

- **Can I go through this all over again?**

  How seriously did you take studying the first time around? If you gave it all you had, you may be too burned out to go through that again. On the other hand, if you just zoomed through the booklet and didn't spend much time preparing for the test, you have a second chance to show your stuff.

- **Were the mistakes caused by factors that were not my fault?**

  Maybe you were in a fender-bender on your way to the exam, or perhaps you stayed up late the night before in an argument with your parents or your boyfriend or girlfriend. If you just weren't up to par when you took the exam, definitely take it again, and be sure to get a good night's sleep the night before.

Horror stories of the ACT

So you're sitting there feeling sorry for yourself, having to study this stuff instead of being out having a good time with your friends? Things could be worse. The following are *true* stories of events that happened to my students or their friends.

- **Double Trouble:** Skip was at a stoplight on his way to take the ACT when a drunk driver in the car behind him was slow to hit his brakes and almost rear-ended Skip's car. When Skip recovered from the fright, he angrily got out of the car to confront the drunk. The drunk got of out his car, too, faced Skip, and threw up all over him.
- **Jailhouse Rock:** Ken didn't send in his registration form in time to get his first test site choice and ended up having to take the ACT on a military base. Running late as usual, he was speeding on the base when the MPs pulled him over. Ken gave them a lotta sass, and they cuffed him, put him in the back of their car, and took him to the base prison. He couldn't reach his parents right away and sat there for nearly four hours (completely missing the ACT) before someone came to help him.
- **Love Hurts:** Marcy walked into the ACT test room . . . and came face to face with her former boyfriend whom she had dumped big time only a few months ago. He said all sorts of hurtful things before the exam started and then glared at her during the entire test. Every time Marcy looked up, George was giving her dirty looks. She lost it completely and started crying. She ended up canceling her test.
- **Timing Is Everything:** Olana's parents had a huge, extremely loud fight the night before the ACT. Olana tried talking to them, telling them she had to get her sleep, but they turned on her. They said that she was being selfish and was thinking of only herself, that they had their problems, too, and that they were only trying to work them out. When Olana came down for breakfast the next morning, already nervous and anxious about the ACT, her parents chose that time to let her know they were getting a divorce and that Olana would be moving to another state with her father.
- **The Bacon Blues:** Faye's mother, reminding Faye that breakfast is the most important meal of the day, cooked a huge breakfast for Faye the morning of the ACT and insisted that she eat every bite. Faye sat in the test room with lumpy oatmeal and greasy bacon fighting in her stomach and couldn't concentrate on anything but her internal rumblings.
- **Know-It-Alls:** Don't. In the hallway during the break, Fran and Ron discussed the first part of the test. Fran asked Ron about several questions. Ron assured her that his answers were right and that hers were wrong. Fran fretted all during the rest of the test, thinking she had already blown it big time. It wasn't until she got home and talked with her parents that she realized that Ron was mistaken a few times and that she hadn't missed as many questions as she had thought.

Part II

Serving Your "Sentence": English Usage

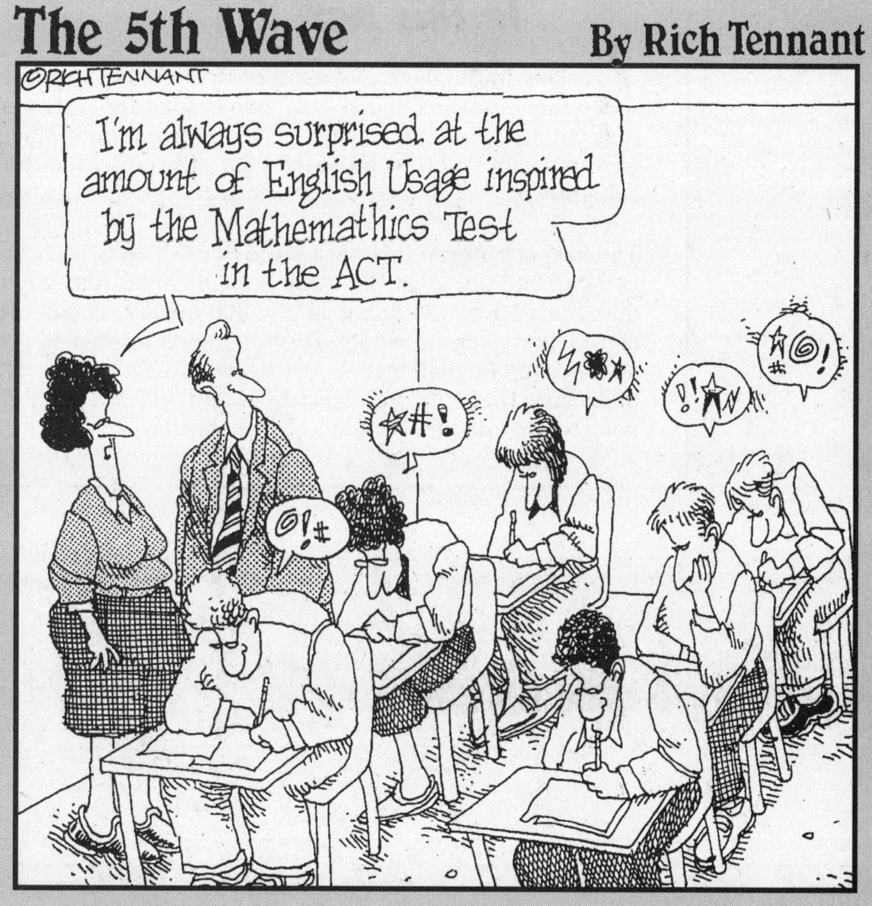

The 5th Wave
By Rich Tennant
©RICH TENNANT
I'm always surprised at the amount of English Usage inspired by the Mathemathics Test in the ACT.

In this part . . .

Lurking in the dark alleyways of the ACT is your first opponent, the English Test, one of four separate tests that you have to do battle with. The information in this part can help you to win the fight (or at least lessen the slaughter!).

The first chapter in this part is the English lecture. Here, you can find out what the exam actually looks like, which questions are worth doing, and which questions you may as well just guess at wildly. The second chapter is an abbreviated English test — just a dirty dozen questions to make sure that what you learned is forever imprinted in your brain. Life just couldn't get any better.

Chapter 2

Misspellers of the World, UNTIE! The English Test

In This Chapter

- Understanding the format of the passages with "phantom" questions
- Distinguishing the must-do easy questions from the brain-straining difficult ones
- Avoiding falling for the ACT traps . . . or creating your own

When you open your ACT booklet, the first thing you see is the English Test. Your still half-asleep brain and bleary eyes encounter 5 passages with 75 questions. Somehow, you're to read all the passages and answer all the questions within 45 minutes. This test is definitely one part of the ACT on which you have to hustle.

Seeing Is Believing: The Format of the Test

The ACT English Test passages look like standard reading comprehension passages, the kind you've seen on tests for years. The difference is that these passages have a lot of underlined portions. An underlined portion can be an entire sentence, a phrase, a word, or even just a punctuation mark. (You may want to take a quick look right now at the practice test in Chapter 3 to see what a passage looks like. I'll wait.)

Okay, you're back. Here are the details about what you get and what you're expected to do with it.

The passages

The five passages can cover a variety of topics. You may get a fun story that's a personal anecdote — someone talking about getting a car for his sixteenth birthday, for example. Or you may encounter a somewhat formal scientific passage about the way items are carbon-dated. Some passages may discuss history; some, philosophy; others, cultural differences among nations. Some passages are fiction, such as excerpts from novels, old and new. One type of passage is not necessarily more difficult than another. You don't need to use specific reading techniques for these passages (as you do with standard reading comprehension passages). Just read and enjoy. (Yeah, right.)

Although these English passages are not reading comprehension passages per se, you do need to pay at least a little bit of attention to content rather than just to the underlined portions. Why bother? Because a few of the questions at the end of the passages are reading comp–type questions, asking you about the purpose of the passage or what a possible conclusion might be. More about those in a minute.

The questions

The English Test has no questions. Well, let me rephrase that before I get your hopes up too high. You will not be faced with what you consider specific questions in the standard interrogatory form (with a few exceptions, discussed later). You will not see "Which of the following is an adjective?" or "The purpose of the subjunctive is to do which of these?" Instead, the "question" is simply an underlined portion of the exam. Your job is to determine whether that underlined portion is correct as is or whether one of the alternate answer choices is preferable.

The answer choices

The answer choices are A, B, C, and D (for the odd-numbered questions) and F, G, H, and J (for the even-numbered questions). Choices A and F are always "NO CHANGE." You select that if the original is the best of the versions offered. Occasionally, choice D or J will say "OMIT the underlined portion." Choose that answer when you want to dump the whole underlined portion and forget that you ever saw it. (And no, you can't do that with the entire test!)

The other choices are often variations on a theme. For example, if the underlined portion has the word *lay* in it, the answer choices might be

F. NO CHANGE

G. lie

H. lain

J. lying

Being Boxed In: The Box Questions

Usually at the end of a passage — but sometimes, quite annoyingly, within the passage itself — you see a small box with a number in it, like this: [49]. That box indicates what most students think of as a reading comprehension–type question. Here are a few examples:

If the purpose of this essay were to convey the author's opinion about the morality of the death penalty, did the author accomplish the purpose?

A. Yes, because the reader understands the author's philosophy of right and wrong.

B. Yes, because the author specifically refers to the church's teachings on the subject.

C. No, because the passage never addresses fundamental religious issues.

D. No, because the author never discusses life imprisonment as an alternative to the death penalty.

Notice that here you have to understand not only what the passage said but also whether it went far enough. This "Did the author accomplish his purpose?" question is pretty common. To answer it, you usually have to comprehend the passage as a whole pretty well.

Given the topic and the tone of the passage, was the author's use of the pronoun "I" proper?

F. Yes, because the only examples he cited were from his own life.

G. Yes, because he was projecting his personal feelings onto the topic.

H. No, because a formal essay should not be written in the first-person singular.

J. No, because using "I" prevents the readers from becoming involved with the topic.

In this case, you're expected to get a feel for the tone of the passage as a whole. I suggest that, as soon as you read the question, you decide whether using "I" was appropriate — *before* you even look at the answer choices. If you don't have at least some idea in your brain *before* you look at the answer choices, they all will look good. I often have students read them and say, "Choice F is true. Well, wait a minute, I agree with choice G, too. And now that I think of it, I could make a case for H. No, no, wait a minute: It's definitely choice J. I think." Don't get yourself so confused. Predict an answer of your own before you get bamboozled by the test's answers.

Here's an example of the type of box question I like least: the structure or reorganization question.

To make the passage a coherent whole, paragraph 4 should be placed

A. where it is now.

B. at the beginning of the passage.

C. after paragraph 2.

D. at the end of the passage.

Notice how much time this type of question takes up. In the passage, each paragraph is numbered. You have to go back and reread the entire passage, thinking about which order of paragraphs would make the most sense. Most of the time, you have to read the passage repeatedly, first with this order of paragraphs and then with that order. You really don't have the time to do so.

My suggestion is that you make a quick guess at this question and come back to it later if you have the time. (Never leave any question blank: Remember, the ACT does not penalize you for guessing.)

What Do They Want Outta Me? What the English Usage Questions Test

The questions fall into two basic categories. Just over half the questions cover topics of usage or mechanics. These questions include sentence structure (whether a sentence is a fragment or a run-on), grammar and usage (just about everything most people think of as English, such as adverbs, adjectives, and so on), and punctuation (don't worry; this isn't super-hard, just mostly semicolons). Just under half the questions test rhetorical skills, organization (reordering the sentences in the passage), style (which expression, slang or formal, is appropriate within the passage), and strategy ("This passage would be most appropriate in which of the following types of books . . . ?").

Some questions are much more doable than others. For example, most students would agree that a simple grammar question asking about a pronoun reference or subject-verb agreement is easier than an organization question expecting you to put the paragraphs of the entire passage in order. In the practice tests in this book, I emphasize these more doable questions, giving a slightly greater percentage of them than you might find on the real ACT. Why? Because I want you to be absolutely, positively able to get these questions correct in a heartbeat. They are the basics, the foundation of your test. If you can get the easy and medium-difficulty questions right, you'll already have a good score. Getting the harder questions correct will be the icing on the cake.

Maximize the Gain, Minimize the Pain: Questions Worth Looking For

The biggest complaint I hear from my students about the English Test is not that it's too hard but that it's too long. Five passages, 75 questions, and only 45 minutes to finish is pretty daunting. Following are a few strategies that you can use to help you to get the most bang for your buck.

Look for short, diction-type questions

A diction error is a wrong word choice. Obvious errors, such as *lie/lay, phase/faze,* and *affect/effect* are not tested as frequently as they used to be, but when they show up, they are easy questions to answer correctly. One diction error that does show up repeatedly is *its/it's.* Here's an example:

Barney told the club that it's policy of discriminating against redheads was probably illegal and certainly unethical.

A. it's policy of discrimination

B. it's discrimination policy

C. its discriminating policy

D. its discrimination

The possessive pronoun its has no apostrophe ("The cat was licking its paw.") *It's* (with an apostrophe) means it is. This example requires the possessive, *its.* Eliminate choices A and B. Choice D more directly expresses the thought of the sentence than does choice C. *Correct Answer:* D.

I put many questions like this one into the practice exams simply because they are the most doable questions. You have no excuse for missing a diction question. All you have to do is memorize the common diction twosomes (conveniently presented for your viewing pleasure in Chapter 4).

Go for pure grammar

A grammar question may test subject-verb agreement, pronoun reference, or a multitude of other concepts that you probably think of as English. Following is an example. (Keep in mind that on the real test, this question is part of a passage, not an isolated sentence.)

A full case of sodas, when opened by a horde of thirsty athletes who have been running laps, don't go very far.

F. NO CHANGE

G. do not go

H. doesn't go

J. doesn't get to go

What's the subject of the sentence? *A case.* That's singular, requiring the singular verb *doesn't.* Eliminate choices F and G immediately. Choice J is totally ridiculous, adding unnecessary words and making the sentence awkward. *Correct Answer:* H.

Did you see the trap in this sentence? Some students think that either *sodas, athletes,* or *laps* — all of which are plural — is the subject (especially *laps* because it is right next to the verb). In that case, they think that the verb has to be plural, too, and choose F. You didn't fall for that cheap trick, did you?

If English is not your first language, the diction and grammar questions are the key to your getting a good score in this section. When you studied English, you probably memorized rule after rule after rule, just the kinds of things that these questions test. In this situation, you actually have an advantage over American kids who haven't been tested on this stuff since the seventh grade. (In many American high schools, students start learning literature in the eighth or ninth grades and no longer focus on pure grammar.) Spend time studying the grammar and diction rules in Chapter 4, and head for these types of questions, especially if you're running short of time.

Ignore superfluous info

Some sentences feature redundancies, such as "red *in color*" or "the reason was *because.*" Others offer irrelevant or unnecessary information, as in the following example.

Taking a class in a foreign language can be very rewarding. You never know when you will use the knowledge. You may someday visit a country that uses that language or meet someone from that nation. Even if you never actually practice the language, you can learn more about the way languages are developed and words are created. Many students agree that they learned more English grammar by studying a foreign language than they did in English classes. <u>You could also learn both Spanish and French at the same time, for example.</u> Most teachers of a foreign language emphasize sentence structure and grammar. It is an axiom among language teachers that students who are good writers in their native languages learn foreign languages quickly.

A. NO CHANGE

B. For example, you could also learn both Spanish and French at the same time.

C. At the same time, for example, you could learn both Spanish and French.

D. OMIT the underlined portion.

Choices A, B, and C are saying basically the same thing. All they do is shuffle the words a little bit. None of them adds anything to the paragraph. The underlined sentence seems to go off on a tangent, as you can see by the fact that the next paragraph continues the previous idea, the role of grammar in foreign language classes. Dump the whole underlined sentence.

Which is better: The tortoise or the hare?

Question: Is it better to go slowly and do a good job on four passages, never getting to the fifth, or should I try to get through all five passages?

Answer: I advocate trying to get through all five passages. On average, each passage has 15 questions. I don't think you can afford to blow off that many questions. Keep reminding yourself of how different these passages are from standard reading comprehension passages. With very few exceptions, you don't have to answer "substance" questions, such as, "With which of the following would the author agree?" If you're short on time, skip the box questions (which sometimes require a lot of time, thought, and suffering) and the longer questions requiring you to rewrite an entire sentence, and zoom on to the next passage.

Let me say it yet again: *Do not* leave any answers blank. If you don't get to that last passage, at least fill in an answer for every question. The ACT has no penalty for guessing. Out of 15 questions, you're pretty sure to get at least a few right even with random guessing, and every little bit helps.

Their Pain, Your Gain: Traps That Others Have Fallen Into

I've tutored for the ACT for a couple of decades now. By this point, I think I've seen students fall for every trap the test-makers could think of — and some they probably never considered! Watch out for these most commonly tumbled-into traps:

- **Forgetting the NO CHANGE option:** Because the first answer choice (choice A for odd-numbered questions, choice F for even-numbered questions) is always NO CHANGE, students tend to gloss over it. Don't forget that you always have the option to keep things exactly the way they are.
- **Automatically choosing "OMIT the underlined portion" each time it occurs:** Although you may be tempted to shorten this section by screaming, "Dump it! Just dump the whole stupid thing!" every chance you get, don't fall into that habit. When you see the OMIT answer (either choice D or choice J), realize that it has the same one-in-four chance of being right as the other answers have. Consider it, but don't make it a no-brainer choice.
- **Automatically selecting the "other" diction or grammar choice:** When a student sees *who* in a sentence, she is often tempted to change it immediately to *whom.* Yet if that same sentence said *whom* to begin with, that same student would immediately change it to *who.* The temptation to *do* something, anything, is very strong. Don't change just for the sake of change.
- **Wasting time on the box questions:** Students sometimes ask me what I have against the box questions. Nothing, really. Some of the box questions, like the attitude ones ("Would this essay be appropriate for a group of university professors?"), can be quite simple. But others can be incredibly time-wasting and frustrating. I refer specifically to my least-favorite type of question, the "order of the sentences" or "order of the paragraphs" ("Which of the following would be the most logical sequence of sentences in paragraph 4?"). Usually, you have to read and reread and reread the paragraph, changing and rearranging the sentences over and over. And even then, students argue that the organization seems subjective: "Why does Sentence 4 go before Sentence 2? I think it sounds better the other way!" You may be able to get the question right, but at what price? How much time do you chew up? How many more of the easy questions could you have gotten right in that time?
- **Ignoring the big picture:** Some questions are style questions. A style question expects you to sense the overall picture, to know whether the tone of the passage is friendly so that you can appropriately use a slang expression (for example, *totally lame*) or whether you need to be a bit more formal (*useless* rather than *totally lame*). If you focus only on the underlined portions and do not read the passage as a whole, you can easily miss this type of question.

Even if a question doesn't seem to expect you to understand the entire passage, you should still read a few sentences ahead of the question. How you correct a run-on or a fragment, for example, may depend on how the next few sentences are structured.

To read or not to read: That is the question

Question: Should I read the passage completely first, as if it were a reading passage, before I start looking at the questions, or should I go to the questions right away?

Answer: Try both techniques as you go through the practice exams. I always tell my students not to read the entire passage first, although some students say that doing so helps them see the big picture. I think that you don't have time to make the English Test into both a reading test and an English test. If you're a fast reader and a swift worker, great; definitely read the passage first, and then go to answer the questions. That would be ideal. However, most students can't afford the time and just have to complete one question and then tackle another, plodding through the passage to find the answers.

That's a Wrap: Conclusion

Here's a quick wrap-up of what this lecture has covered.

Passages and questions

- The English Test has 5 passages with 75 questions to be answered in 45 minutes.
- A question may be an underlined portion (a sentence, phrase, or word) or a boxed, reading comprehension-type question.
- Questions testing sentence structure, grammar, usage, and punctuation may be easier than questions testing organization, style, and strategy.

The deadly don'ts

- Don't forget that you always have the NO CHANGE option.
- Don't immediately choose the OMIT option every time you see it.
- Don't automatically choose the "other" diction choice (*who* versus *whom, lie* versus *lay*); each has an equal chance of being correct.
- Don't waste too much time on the box questions.

Chapter 3

The English Practice Questions

On the real ACT, the passage is on the left side of the page, and the questions are on the right side (see the Practice Exams in this book). For this one brief test, I put the questions after the passage. That way, you can read the answer explanations with the questions.

DIRECTIONS: Below are five paragraphs containing underlined portions. Alternate ways of stating the underlined portions follow the paragraphs. Choose the best alternative. If the original is the best way of stating the underlined portion, choose NO CHANGE.

You also see questions that refer to the passage or ask you to reorder the sentences within a passage. These questions are identified by a number in a box. Choose the best answer.

Passage

[1]

[1] Marian Anderson possibly will have (1) the greatest (2) influence opening doors and gaining well-deserved opportunities for other Black singers than anyone else to date so far (3). [2] Anderson, born in Philadelphia, Pennsylvania, had an early interest in music. [3] She learns (4) to play the piano and was singing in the church at the age of six. [4] She gave her first concert at age eight, when she was still a young child (5).

[2]

[5] In 1925, Anderson won a concert hosted by the New York Philharmonic, beating out no less than (6) 300 singers. [6] It launched her career but (7), America was not quite ready for her fantastic voice, personality, or color.

[3]

[8] In 1936, asked (8) to give a performance at the White House. [8] She confessed that this occasion was the first time that she had really been nervous to sing (9). [9] She and Eleanor Roosevelt became close friends, but (10) this friendship became evident with the Daughters of the American Revolution Affair.

[4]

[11] The DAR refused to let Anderson perform in Constitution Hall in 1939. [11] The White House made arrangements for Ms. Anderson to sing on the steps of the Lincoln Memorial in D.C. instead.

[5]

[13] In 1977, First Lady Rosalynn Carter presented Marian Anderson with a Congressional Gold Medal, the first Black (11) to receive such an honor. [13] Later she was inducted into the Women's Hall of Fame in Seneca Falls, New York.

1. **A.** NO CHANGE

   B. has had

   C. has

   D. is having

To understand the tense of the passage, you have to read a few sentences ahead. Doing so makes it clear that Marian Anderson accomplished her singing several decades earlier. (The passage mentions such dates as 1936 and 1977.) Therefore, the verb needs to be in the past tense. *Correct Answer:* B.

(Alas, not all of us sing as well as Ms. Anderson. My own singing is so bad that the governor declared my last opera a disaster aria!)

2. **F.** NO CHANGE

   G. a greater

   H. one of the greatest

   J. a great

You need to read the entire sentence before deciding on an answer. If you read "the greatest influence" all by itself, it sounds correct. However, if you continue to read the sentence, you find the comparative "than." You cannot say "the greatest influence than" but rather "a greater influence than." *Correct Answer:* G.

Be very careful to read the entire sentence. You may save a few seconds by reading only the underlined portion, but you will sacrifice a lot of points.

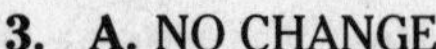

3. **A.** NO CHANGE

   B. dating so far

   C. so far dated

   D. OMIT the underlined portion

To date and *so far* are redundant; they mean the same thing. You can use one or the other, but not both. (Quick! Notify the Department of Redundancy Department!) *Correct Answer:* D.

Many students tend to choose "OMIT the underlined portion" every time they see it, reasoning that it would not be a choice unless it were correct. Not so. If you decide to omit the underlined portion, be especially careful to reread the entire sentence. Often, omitting the underlined portion makes nonsense out of the sentence.

4. **F.** NO CHANGE

   G. has been learning

   H. learned

   J. is learning

Because Marian Anderson is no longer six years old, the sentence requires the past tense, *learned*. ***Hint:*** If you aren't sure of the tense, check out the rest of the sentence. You are told that Ms. Anderson "was singing," meaning the situation occurred in the past. *Correct Answer:* H.

Notice that choices G and J both have the -ing verb *learning*. Often, -ing verbs are trap answers. They are frequently clumsy, awkward, and unnecessary. Although not *all* -ing verbs are wrong, check them carefully.

5. **A.** NO CHANGE

   B. still a young child

   C. still young

   D. OMIT the underlined portion

A person who is eight is still a young child — duh! The underlined portion is superfluous, unnecessary. Eliminate it. The period is necessary to finish the sentence. *Correct Answer:* D.

Speaking of children and sentences reminds me of a friend of mine. He got so tired of seeing cutesy bumper stickers that said things like "My child was honor citizen of the month at Sweetums Preschool" that he created his own bumper sticker. His back fender now reads, "My child was Inmate of the Month at State Prison!"

6. **F.** NO CHANGE

   G. less than

   H. fewer than

   J. no fewer than

Fewer modifies plural nouns, as in fewer brain cells, for example. *Less* modifies singular nouns, like less intelligence. Because the noun *singers* is plural, use the word *fewer. Correct Answer:* J.

If you chose H, you fell for the trap. You forgot to reread the sentence with your answer inserted. The meaning of the whole sentence changes with the phrase "fewer than 300 singers." In that case, you are denigrating, or lessening, the winner's accomplishment. The tone of the passage is one of respect. The author is impressed that Ms. Anderson beat out "no fewer than 300 singers." Keep in mind that you must make your answers fit the overall tone or attitude of the passage. If a passage is complimentary, be sure that your answers continue in that vein.

7. **A.** NO CHANGE

   B. Launching her career,

   C. Her career was launched, but

   D. Upon launching it (her career),

Be very suspicious of that two-letter rascal *it.* Always double-check *it* out because *it* is so often misused and abused. *It* must refer to one specific thing: "Where is the book? Here *it* is." In question 7, *it* doesn't refer to any one object but to Ms. Anderson's winning the contest. Dump choice A. Choices B and D sound as if America launched Ms. Anderson's career: "Upon launching it . . . America was not quite ready . . . ." Be sure to go back and reread the entire sentence with your answer inserted. *Correct Answer:* C.

Beware of *-ing* words. They often result in a misplaced modifier, changing the meaning of the sentence. Misplaced modifiers and bad grammar in general can result in some pretty funny sentences. A few of every grammar teacher's favorites, taken from newspaper headlines, are

Iraqi Head Seeks Arms

Two Convicts Escape Noose; Jury Hung

Police Discover Crack in Australia

8. **F.** NO CHANGE

   G. she was asked

   H. upon being asked

   J. asking

The original is a fragment, an incomplete sentence. The sentence has no subject. *Who* was asked? *She* was asked. *Correct Answer:* G.

Choice H has the dreaded word *being.* People often use *being* incorrectly; you should make it one of your red-flag words, words that you immediately double-check. Choices H and J both have the same problem that the original has: They lack a subject.

9. **A.** NO CHANGE

   B. about singing

   C. of singing

   D. and singing

The word *nervous* is usually followed by the word *about.* You are nervous *about* something, not nervous *to* or *by* something. (How do you feel about the ACT? You may be frightened or intimidated by it or scared of it, but if it makes you nervous, you are nervous about it.) *Correct Answer:* B.

This sentence is one of the few times when an *-ing* verb is correct, not a trap. Always double-check *-ing* verbs, but don't automatically assume that they are wrong. Watch out for an exception, like this one. (I believe it was Yogi Berra who said, "You can observe a lot by watching.")

10. **F.** NO CHANGE

    G. close friends, and

    H. close friends — which

    J. close and friendly,

The clause "but this friendship became evident . . ." makes no sense in the context. Use *but* only to indicate dissent or change; use a comma and the word *and* to indicate a short pause. *Correct Answer:* G.

11. **A.** NO CHANGE

    B. Medal, being the first Black

    C. Medal; the first Black

    D. Medal; she was the first Black

The original sounds as if the medal were the first Black to receive such an honor. The sentence obviously means to say that Ms. Anderson was the first Black to receive the honor. Note that the semicolon separates two independent sentences; each sentence could stand alone. *Correct Answer:* D.

Did the word *being* in choice B catch your eye? *Being* is a red-flag word, one that is frequently misused. You should double-check it every time you see it.

12. If the author of this passage were to add the following lines to the article, where would they be most logically placed?

    It was an era of color prejudice, a time when people were still legally excluded from jobs, housing, and even entertainment merely because of their race. Thus, the early promise of success seemed impossible until something amazing for the times happened.

    F. At the end of sentence 2

    G. At the end of sentence 6

    H. At the end of paragraph 3

    J. In the middle of paragraph 5

Because the first sentence of the addition talks about color prejudice, look in the passage for something mentioning color. That is specifically discussed only in sentence 6. *Correct Answer:* G.

Be sure to go back to the passage and reread the entire paragraph with the new lines inserted to make sure that they make sense.

This question just wastes time, requiring you to understand both the structure and the content of the passage. You have to go back and reread the passage four times, once with each answer choice inserted in the indicated position. If you didn't really understand the passage or if you just skimmed it to get the grammar points, your best bet is to make a quick guess. ***Remember:*** The ACT does not penalize you for wrong answers. Guessing at any question that has you stumped is to your advantage.

Part III

It's Not What You Say; It's How You Say It: The English Review

In this part . . .

Presented for your viewing pleasure, the only chapter in this part is a basic Grammar Review that uses enough stupid examples and silly jokes to keep you from dozing off. The part has a lot of good material — years worth of all those persnickety old grammar rules that you thought you'd left behind forever. Surprise: They're baaaaack. . . .

Chapter 4

Glamour Grammar: The Five-Star Review

The English Test portion of the ACT tests standard, written English. What's that? That's what I call Arrogant English — stuck-up, highfalutin English. In the Real World, you can use slang and casual English and communicate perfectly well with your buddies, but on the ACT you have to use the formal English that you were taught in school. When you knock on a friend's door, for example, you call out, "It's me!", right? On the ACT, you have to choose, "It is I."

About half of the ACT English Test questions test rhetorical skills — your general writing style and organization. That's the stuff you use every time you pick up a pen or turn on your word-processing program. The other half of the questions test what most people lump together in the general category they call English: punctuation, sentence structure, and basic grammar, including diction errors, subject-verb agreement, modifiers (adjectives and adverbs), and so on. That's the stuff you probably forget (or intentionally purge from your brain) ten minutes after being tested on it.

This chapter gives you a basic grammar review that brings back those thrilling days of yesteryear when you knew how to use the subjunctive and actually cared about the differences between adjectives and adverbs. The review starts off with the really easy stuff, but please don't get too bored and drop out. The harder, picky stuff comes later, and chances are that's the stuff you really need. Besides, to reward you for hanging in there and suffering through this quagmire, I've put in quite a few trivia points and a couple of jokes as bonuses.

You do not — I repeat, do not — have to fear encountering something like the pluperfect. I am very careful not to use technical terms throughout this material. Only teachers care about the technical names for things. All *you* need to know is how to use the right rules, not what to call things.

Subject-Verb Agreement

1. **A singular subject takes a singular verb.**

   Mozart's music *is* (not are) beautiful.

2. **A plural subject takes a plural verb.**

   The works of both Mozart and Brahms *are* (not is) beautiful.

   (By the way, do you know what Mozart and Brahms are doing these days? *De*composing!)

3. **A compound subject — two or more subjects often connected by the word *and* — takes a plural verb.**

   A symphony and a fugue *are* (not is) beautiful.

4. The following words are always plural and therefore require plural verbs:

- ***few:*** Few people *take* (not takes) only the ACT and not the SAT.
- ***both:*** Both the ACT and the SAT *are* (not is) entrance exams to college.
- ***several:*** Several of my friends *have* (not has) taken the ACT and the SAT.
- ***many:*** Many of my friends *wish* (not wishes) they had never heard of the ACT.

5. The following words are always singular and require singular verbs:

- ***each:*** Each question on the ACT *has* (not have) the potential to be a trick question.
- ***every:*** Every question is (not are) to be approached with trepidation and paranoia.

The *every* words — *every*one, *every*body, *every*thing, *every*where — are always singular.

6. The following words may be singular or plural, depending on what follows them: *some, any, most, all,* and *none.*

- ***some,*** plural: Some of the jokes in this book *are* (not is) beyond hope and should be given a decent burial.
- ***some,*** singular: Some of the humor in this book *is* (not are) inexcusable.

You can remember these words with the acronym S.A.M.A.N., the first letters of the words. Think of the sentence, "S.A.M.A.N. (Say, man), can you tell me which words are sometimes singular and sometimes plural?"

7. The following collective nouns look plural but are singular and require a singular verb: *group, public, club, government, union, organization,* and *collection.*

The public *is* (not are) constantly exposed to my sense of humor. My collection of jokes *is* (not are) not always fully appreciated.

8. A prepositional phrase does not affect subject-verb agreement.

When you see a prepositional phrase, draw a line through it and simply read the noun (subject) next to the verb.

That irate group of test-takers *is* (not are) bombarding the proctor with tomatoes.

(Did you remember from Rule #7 that *group* is singular even though it may look plural?)

Five words are exceptions to Rule #8: Do not ignore prepositional phrases containing the S.A.M.A.N. words.

All of the dancers *are* (not is) wearing new leotards today; all of their time *is* (not are) spent complaining about the price of workout clothes.

Trivia: Do you know who invented the leotard? It was created by and obviously named after Jules Leotard, a French trapeze artist.

9. Some nouns have irregular singular and plural forms.

Singular	*Plural*
criterion	criteria
curriculum	curricula
bacterium	bacteria
phenomenon	phenomena
medium	media
datum	data

```
Television is my favorite news medium; I get my news from several
media.
```

(I love the quote from humorist Fred Allen: "TV is called a medium because it is so rarely well done!")

When in doubt about whether a word is singular or plural, remember that, in general (but not always), the plural form of the word ends in a vowel (*data, criteria*) while the singular form of the word ends in a consonant (*datum, criterion*).

10. The second subject in an *either/or* or *neither/nor* construction determines whether the verb is singular or plural.

```
Neither Kimberly nor her parents are (not is) on the cruise.
```

```
Neither her parents nor Kimberly is (not are) able to afford cruise
tickets.
```

(Did you hear what happened when the pink cruise ship rammed into the purple one? All the passengers were marooned.)

Many people are so concerned with the subject-verb agreement of *neither/nor* that they forget that *neither* and *nor* belong together and that *either* and *or* belong together. In other words, the constructions *neither/or* and *either/nor* are wrong. Double-check whenever you see these words.

Pronouns

The next time your grammar teacher asks you to name two pronouns, you can be a smart aleck and shout out, "Who, me?"

1. A pronoun (a word that takes the place of the noun) must have the same number (singular or plural) as the noun it is replacing.

```
Everybody is on his best behavior during a college interview.
```

You would probably be wealthy if you had a dollar for each time you've heard someone say, "Yeah, everybody is trying their best." Because the construction *everybody . . . their* is so commonly used, it sounds correct. Make this expression a red-flag one. Whenever you see the word *everybody,* triple-check the pronoun to make sure that it is singular.

2. **A pronoun must have the same gender (feminine, masculine, or neuter) as the noun it is replacing.**

   ```
   The ewe is slowly making her way home from the pasture.
   ```

   Because a ewe is a female sheep, use the female pronoun *her.*

3. **A pronoun must have clarity (that is, you must be able to tell which noun the pronoun is replacing).**

   ```
   Matthew asked Franklin to pick up his laundry off the floor.
   ```

   Did Matthew want Matthew's laundry picked up, or did Matthew want Franklin's laundry picked up? This reference is unclear — and thus makes the sentence a poor one.

   An unclear pronoun reference often requires major reconstructive surgery. In this example, the entire sentence must be rewritten. Here's one possibility:

   ```
   Matthew, disgusted at seeing Franklin's laundry on the floor, picked
   it up.
   ```

   (Now you know perfectly well that the pronoun *it* is referring to Franklin's heap of clothes, not Matthew's.)

4. **A pronoun must be in the proper case: subjective (I, you, he, she, it, we, they), objective (me, you, him, her, it, us, them), or possessive (my, mine, your, yours, his, her, hers, its, our, ours, their, theirs).**

   A pronoun following any form of the verb *to be,* such as *is, are, was,* and *were,* is going to be in the subjective form. This form often sounds pretentious and bizarre (a sure clue that it's probably correct on the ACT!). Following are common constructions:

It is I.	It was she who . . .
It was he.	This is he.
It could be they.	It was they.

   ```
   I finally confessed to my family that it was I who put the dent in the
   bumper of the car.
   ```

Adjectives and Adverbs

1. **Place an adjective (which modifies a noun or pronoun) or an adverb (which modifies a verb, adjective, or adverb) as close as possible to the noun or pronoun it is modifying.**

   That rule isn't followed in this sentence:

   ```
   WRONG: Nancy and Frank left the neighborhood they had lived in for ten
   years reluctantly.
   ```

   This sentence sounds as if Nancy and Frank had been reluctant to live in the neighborhood, when in fact they were reluctant to leave. Change the sentence so that *reluctantly* comes just before *left:*

   ```
   RIGHT: Nancy and Frank reluctantly left the neighborhood they had lived
   in for ten years.
   ```

2. An adverb (which modifies a verb, adverb, or adjective) often answers the question "How?" and may end in *-ly*.

```
How do I study? I study reluctantly.
```

3. Place *not only* and *but also* in parallel positions within a sentence. People often place *not only* and *but also* incorrectly. Following is an example of a wrong way to use these expressions:

```
WRONG: Angelique not only was exasperated but also frightened when she
locked herself out of the house.
```

See the problem? In this wrong example, the phrase *not only* comes before the verb *was,* but the phrase *but also* comes before the adjective *frightened.*

```
RIGHT: Angelique was not only exasperated but also frightened when she
locked herself out of the house.
```

Not only and *but also* precede the adjectives *exasperated* and *frightened,* respectively.

Sentence Structure

1. A run-on sentence (two or more independent clauses incorrectly joined) must be changed. The following is a run-on.

```
WRONG: Jessimena was furious when she went to the party on the wrong
day, she went home and yelled at her boyfriend, who had given her the
wrong information.
```

You can choose from five ways to correct a run-on:

- **Make two separate sentences.**

  ```
  Jessimena was furious when she went to the party on the wrong day.
  She went home and yelled at her boyfriend, who had given her the
  wrong information.
  ```

- **Use a semicolon to separate independent clauses.**

  ```
  Jessimena was furious when she went to the party on the wrong day;
  she went home and yelled at her boyfriend, who had given her the
  wrong information.
  ```

- **Use a semicolon, conjunctive adverb, and comma (as in this construction: *; therefore,*) to separate the clauses.**

  ```
  Jessimena was furious when she went to the party on the wrong day;
  therefore, she went home and yelled at her boyfriend, who had given
  her the wrong information.
  ```

- **Use a subordinating conjunction (such as *because* or *since*) with one of the clauses.**

  ```
  Because Jessimena was furious when she went to the party on the
  wrong day, she went home and yelled at her boyfriend, who had given
  her the wrong information.
  ```

- **Use a comma and a coordinating conjunction (as in this construction: , *and*) between the two clauses.**

  ```
  Jessimena was furious when she went to the party on the wrong day,
  and she went home and yelled at her boyfriend, who had given her the
  wrong information.
  ```

2. A sentence fragment (an incomplete sentence) must be changed to reflect a completed thought.

```
WRONG: Wendy, singing merrily to herself as she walked to class, un-
aware that the professor was at that very moment preparing a pop quiz.
```

```
RIGHT: Wendy, singing merrily to herself as she walked to class, was
unaware that the professor was at that very moment preparing a pop
quiz.
```

Parallelism

Parallelism (also called parallel structure) means that objects in a series must be in similar form.

> WRONG: I spent my weekend *working* on a jigsaw puzzle, *doing* chores around the house, and finally *got* out on Sunday evening to play a set of tennis.

Rewrite the sentence so that the verbs are in the same form:

> RIGHT: On the weekend, I *worked* on a jigsaw puzzle, *did* chores around the house, and finally *got* out on Sunday evening to play a set of tennis.

or

> RIGHT: I spent my weekend *working* on a jigsaw puzzle and *doing* chores around the house, finally *getting* out on Sunday evening to play a set of tennis.

Items in a series may be nouns, verbs, adjectives, or entire clauses. However, nonparallel verbs are the items that most commonly have errors. When a clause contains more than one verb, watch out for this particular error.

Comparisons

1. Use the *-er* form (called the comparative form) to compare exactly two items; use the *-est* form (called the superlative form) to compare more than two items.

```
I am taller than my brother Beau, but Darren is the tallest member of
our family.
```

A particularly difficult comparison uses the words *latter* and *last.*

> My boyfriend asked whether I would like to go to Chicago, where the temperature was -5 degrees, or to Los Angeles, where the temperature was 80 degrees. I told him that I preferred the *latter* (not last).

Trivia: Did you know that the name *Chicago* is derived from an Indian term that means "place that stinks of onions"?

Comparisons may trap you when you refer to twins. Remember that *twins* indicates two people. The following is a good trick question:

> WRONG: Myron and Mayor Thibadeau are identical twins, but Myron is the *oldest* by five minutes, a fact that he never lets Mayor forget.

The error is in the comparison because there are only two twins.

> RIGHT: Myron is the *older* by five minutes.

2. **Compare only similar objects or concepts.**

> WRONG: The motor skills of a toddler are more advanced than a baby.

The problem with the preceding sentence is that it is comparing *motor skills* to a *baby.* Its intention is to compare a toddler's motor skills to a baby's motor skills. Following are two ways to correct the error:

> RIGHT: The motor skills of a toddler are more advanced than those of a baby.

or

> RIGHT: A toddler's motor skills are more advanced than a baby's.

Diction

I like to refer to diction errors as *twosomes* because they are errors that you make when you swap two (or sometimes three) commonly confused words. Following is a list of the most commonly confused words, along with short-and-sweet definitions and examples.

affect/effect

To *affect* is to influence or concern.

> A good ACT score will positively *affect* your chances of admission to college.

(It will positively *influence* your chances.)

Effect means cause or result.

> A good ACT score will have a positive *effect* on your chances for admission (a positive *result*).

> A good score will *effect* a change in which schools you consider (cause a change).

Affect has another, little-known meaning. To *affect* also means to pretend.

> When I want to get out of meeting with my friends to study for the ACT, I often *affect* a headache (pretend to have a headache).

amount/number

Amount modifies a singular noun.

```
I have a large amount of respect for the poetry of Dorothy Parker.
```

Number modifies a plural noun.

```
A number of times I have read her poem that contains the lines, "The
lads I've met in Cupid's deadlock / were, shall we say, born out of
wedlock?"
```

anxious/eager

Anxious means worried or doubtful.

```
Meg was anxious about the call from her mechanic, knowing that her
Tercel probably needed some repairs.
```

Eager means joyously anticipating.

```
The mechanic was eager to work on Meg's car, as he needed cash.
```

Tercel Trivia: They don't just make up these names for cars, you know. A tercel is a small male hawk. Maybe the carmakers wanted to give drivers the idea of being free-flying and soaring like a hawk.

assure/ensure

To *assure* means to convince.

```
Quentin talked fast, trying to assure his girlfriend that the heart-
shaped necklace in his locker was in fact a belated birthday present
for her.
```

To *ensure* is to make certain.

```
To ensure that his girlfriend believed him, Quentin called a friend,
who pretended she was the salesgirl who had sold the item to Quentin.
```

between/among

Between (note the *tw*) compares exactly two things.

```
I have difficulty choosing between cherry Jell-O and chocolate pudding.
```

Among compares more than two.

```
I go crazy when I have to choose among the desserts in a smorgasbord.
```

Trivia: Can you name five Jell-O flavors that flopped?

Apple, celery, salad, cola, and (ugh!) mixed vegetables.

The word *between* is often followed by *and:* I have difficulty choosing between this *and* that. A trap answer may have a sentence asking you to choose between this *or* that; the *or* is wrong.

complement/compliment

Complement means to complete.

> The buzz haircut *complemented* the image that Chan wanted to project as a no-nonsense guy.

Compliment means to praise.

> Chan's girlfriend was eager to *compliment* him on his new look.

eminent/immanent/imminent

Eminent means outstanding, distinguished.

> Dr. Regis Weiss is an *eminent* oncologist, well respected by his peers.

Immanent means inherent, innate.

> I think that compassion probably is an *immanent* trait in a good physician; it doesn't seem possible that someone could take a course to learn how to be caring.

Imminent means about to happen.

> When I saw Dr. Weiss shaking his head at me as I stood on the scale, I knew a lecture about weight management was *imminent*.

Think of imminent as "in-a-minute." Something imminent is about to happen in a minute.

everyday/every day

As one word, *everyday* means usual or customary.

> I wore my *everyday* clothes for a quick trip to the grocery store, little realizing that I'd run into Brad Pitt next to the kumquats.

Every day as two words means each 24-hour period.

> From now on, I'm going to go to the store *every day* to get fresh fruit.

(After all, everyone needs fruit, kumquat may. . . .)

farther/further

Farther refers to measurable distance.

> I made a mistake on the test when I said that Morocco is *farther* from Egypt than it is from New York.

Further refers to a figurative degree or quantity that can't be measured.

> Obviously, I need to study my geography *further*.

flaunt/flout

Flaunt means to show off.

> Brittany was thrilled to get her engagement ring and couldn't wait to *flaunt* it to her friends at school.

Flout means to show scorn or contempt.

> Her fiance was furious that Brittany had *flouted* their agreement to keep their engagement a secret for the next few months.

founder/flounder

To founder is to sink, fail, or collapse.

> Reports estimate that one of every two new businesses *founders* within the first three years.

To *flounder* is to thrash about.

> A new business owner, desperate for advice, will *flounder* wildly, running from government bureau to government bureau attempting to get help.

good/well

Good is an adjective that modifies a noun.

> You're doing a *good* job learning these rules.

Well is an adverb that modifies verbs, adverbs, and adjectives and usually answers the question *how*.

> How do you study? You study very *well*.

Well also refers to physical condition.

> By the time you leave the ACT, huffing, puffing, sweating, and fretting, you may not be feeling very *well*.

if/whether

If introduces a condition.

```
If the teacher allows an open-book exam, I will be ecstatic.
```

Whether compares alternatives.

```
I don't know whether I could pass a normal, closed-book exam.
```

If usually sounds correct even when it is wrong. Personally, even though I know better, I hear myself saying, "I don't know *if* I can make it tonight," when I know I should say, "I don't know *whether* I can make it tonight." Try *whether* first. If it sounds right, it probably is right.

imply/infer

To *imply* means to suggest indirectly.

```
I didn't mean to imply that your dress is ugly when I asked you whether
you bought it at an upholstery store.
```

To *infer* is to conclude or deduce, to read a meaning *in*to something.

```
Based on the evidence, the officer inferred that the man was guilty.
```

it's/its

It's (notice the apostrophe) means *it is.*

```
It's good to know the distinction between these two words.
```

Its (without an apostrophe) is possessive.

```
The ACT is ruthless in its insistence that it's important to know the
difference between these two words.
```

less/fewer

Less modifies a singular noun.

```
I have less patience with problems than I should have.
```

Fewer modifies a plural noun.

```
I would make fewer careless mistakes in math if only I had the patience
to finish each problem completely.
```

lie/lay

To *lie* is to recline.

```
I lie down in the afternoon for a nap to reduce stress.
```

To *lay* is to place.

```
I lay a cold washcloth on my head every time I get a headache from
studying for the ACT.
```

Do you often get *lie* and *lay* confused? I have an easy way to remember them. To *lie* is to recline. Listen for the long *i* sound in lie and the long *i* sound in recline. When I lie down, I recline. To *lay* is to place. Listen for the long *a* sound in lay and the long *a* sound in place. Now I lay me down to sleep. Now I place me down to sleep.

Few people know how to conjugate these words correctly. Memorize the following:

- *Lie, lay, have lain:* Today I *lie* down, yesterday I *lay* down, every day I *have lain* down.
- *Lay, laid, have laid:* Today I *lay* my keys on the table, yesterday I *laid* my keys on the table, every day this week I *have laid* my keys on the table.

Notice how confusing the past tense of *lie* is because it is the same as the present tense of *lay.* Do not use the past tense of *lie* as *lied.* The sentence "I *lied* down yesterday" is egregiously incorrect.

phase/faze

Phase means stage or time period.

```
College years are just one phase of your life.
```

Faze means to upset, bother, or disconcert.

```
Do not let the pressure of the ACT faze you.
```

Many students look at the word *faze* and immediately assume that it is misspelled. The ACT contains *no* misspelled words. If you think that a word is misspelled, you are in error.

prescribe/proscribe

Do you know the distinction between the words *prescribe* and *proscribe*? To *prescribe* is to recommend.

```
I prescribe that you learn these two words.
```

To *proscribe* is to outlaw or forbid.

```
I proscribe your believing that the ACT has typographical errors.
```

(My favorite is *judgment.* Most people misspell the word as *judgement,* but there is no *judge* in *judgment* in American English.)

principle/principal

Principle means rule.

```
The principles of justice upon which our country is founded apply
to all.
```

Principal means first in authority or importance.

```
The principal reason democracy works, in my opinion, is that it gives
everyone an equal opportunity to succeed.
```

*Princip*le means rule. Note that they both end in *-le.* If the word does not appear to mean rule, it can't be principle; choose *principal.* The English language has many uses of the word *principal,* including investment principal, the principal reason I telephoned you, and the principal of a high school.

rise/raze/raise

Rise means to ascend.

```
It is time to rise when your mother yanks the covers off the bed.
```

Raze means to tear down.

```
When she threatens to raze the bedroom around your head, you know that
she means business.
```

Raise means to lift. (It also has several other meanings.)

```
You wearily raise your body, ready to face another day.
```

stationary/stationery

Stationary means unmoving.

```
The little girl tried to remain stationary, hoping that the birds would
come up to her and eat out of her hand.
```

Stationery is writing paper.

```
The little girl used her new stationery to write a letter telling her
grandmother about the birds.
```

Stationary means something that *stays.* Note the letter *a* in stay and the letter *a* in stationary. *Stationery* is something you write a letter on. Note the letter *e* in stationery and the letter *e* in letter.

who/whom

Who is a subject and does the action.

```
Who wants to study on a weekend?
```

Whom is an object and receives the action.

```
I don't know whom to ask for help in deciding my major.
```

Miscellaneous Mistakes

Following are some of the miscellaneous grammar mistakes that many people make every day. In the real world, you can live with these mistakes; on the ACT, they are deadly.

hardly

Hardly is negative and often shows up in a trap double-negative question. Do not say, "Ms. Hawker has *hardly nothing* to do this weekend after she finishes the ACT and is looking forward to vegging out in front of the TV." The correct version is, "Ms. Hawker has *hardly anything* to do this weekend after she finishes the ACT and is looking forward to vegging out in front of the TV."

hopefully

Use *hopefully* only where you could plug in the words *full of hope.*

```
Hearing the telephone ring, Alice looked up hopefully, thinking that
Steve might be calling her to apologize for sending her flowers on his
ex-girlfriend's birthday.
```

Many people use the word *hopefully* incorrectly as a substitute for "I hope." The sentence "*Hopefully,* my ACT score will improve" is wrong. Your score won't improve unless you learn to say, "I hope that my ACT score will improve."

if . . . would

Do not place *if* and *would* in the same clause. A common error is to say, "*If* I *would* have studied more, I would have done better." The correct version is, "*If* I *had* studied more, I would have done better," or, "*Had* I studied more, I would have done better."

in regards to . . . in regard to

The English language has no such expression as *in regards to.* Dump the *s;* the proper expression is *in regard to.*

```
We need to have a heart-to-heart talk in regard to your making this
mistake.
```

where . . . that

Do not confuse *where* with *that. Where* refers only to physical location. Saying, "Did you hear *where* Principal Denges ran off to Tahiti with his secretary?" is wrong. The correct structure is, "Did you hear *that* Principal Denges ran off to Tahiti with his secretary?"

Part IV
Don't Count Yourself Out: The Mathematics Test

In this part . . .

This part features a chapter on how to approach math questions, including what to do when you don't have a clue. You can discover how to recognize and avoid built-in traps, how to use the answer choices to save yourself time and headaches in solving the problems, and which questions are time-wasters that are best to guess at quickly and leave behind in your dust. (***Remember:*** The ACT assesses NO PENALTY for guessing, so even random guessing is worthwhile.)

After that chapter is a mini-test, just 12 questions, that allows you to download some of the things you've been learning . . . and see whether you really can recognize those traps.

Chapter 5

Numb and Number: The Mathematics Test

In This Chapter

- How you're expected to perform: Amateur "mathletics"
- Grinding it out: A commonsense approach
- Time flies when you're having fun: Timing tips
- The details that make the difference: Do's, don'ts, and darns

Okay, you math whiz, here's a question for you. Quick, without your calculator, tell me:

Question: How many seconds are there in a year?

Answer: Exactly 12. January 2nd, February 2nd, March 2nd . . .

Your number's up. You cannot escape the ACT Mathematics Test, no matter how hard you try. One of the four tests of the ACT is the one-hour Mathematics Test, whose questions, alas, are not quite as much fun as the one above. This chapter tells you what the test contains.

What You See Is What You Get: The Format and Breakdown

No, the "breakdown" in the preceding heading doesn't refer to *your* (nervous) breakdown, but rather to the breakdown of the number and types of problems in the Mathematics Test. This 60-minute test features 60 questions (which makes figuring out your time per problem convenient, no?). The questions fall into pretty standard categories.

In the ACT bulletin and in many ACT study books, you have to slog through incredibly detailed analyses of the exact number of each question type on the test: 14 plane geometry questions, 4 trigonometry questions, blah blah blah. I refuse to put either of us to sleep with that sort of detail. I mean, it's not as if you have any control over the distribution of questions, right? (I can just see the letter: "Dear ACT: Please be sure that I have more geometry and fewer algebra problems — thanks . . .") The following is the short 'n' sweet version of the kinds of math questions that you will encounter in the dark alleyways of the ACT.

Pre-algebra. (Normal people refer to this as "arithmetic.") About 20 percent, or one-fifth, of the questions cover basic arithmetic, including such concepts as fractions and decimals and the dreaded word problems.

Elementary algebra. This is the type of material that you learn in your first semester or two of algebra. These questions test your ability to work with positive and negative integers, set up algebraic formulas, solve linear equations, and do the occasional FOIL problem. About 20 percent, or one-fifth, of the questions cover elementary algebra.

If you don't know what a FOIL problem is, don't despair. I discuss FOIL in excruciating detail in Chapter 8.

Intermediate algebra/coordinate geometry. About 30 percent of the questions cover more difficult quadratic problems, as well as inequalities, bases, exponents, radicals, and basic graphing (finding points on an *x, y*-coordinate graph).

Plane geometry and trigonometry. About 23 percent of the questions cover plane figures (what you think of as "just plain figures," like triangles, circles, quadrilaterals, and so on). The trig questions make up only 7 percent of the test, so if you haven't had trig yet, don't freak out. Trig questions are very basic, covering trig ratios and basic trigonometric identities.

Confused? Don't worry about the exact number of questions. Just remember two basic points:

- You have 60 minutes to do 60 questions.
- One-third of the questions are arithmetic, one-third are algebra, and one-third are geometry.

Absence Makes the Heart Grow Fonder: What Is Not on the Mathematics Test

Instead of obsessing over how awful the ACT Mathematics Test is, focus on a few of its good points.

Calculus. The ACT does not — I repeat, *does not* — test calculus. You don't even have to know how to *pronounce* "calculus" to get a good ACT Mathematics Test score. You also don't have to know trigonometry. Yes, 7 percent of the test (about four questions) covers trig concepts, but if you miss only four questions, *I'm* happy, *you're* ecstatic, and Harvard is calling.

Quantitative Comparisons, grid-ins, and so on. The bizarre math questions found in other standardized exams are also missing from the ACT. If you've taken the SAT I, for example, you've seen the Quantitative Comparison (or QC) question, which has no multiple-choice answers. (For more information about preparing for the SAT I, read *The SAT I For Dummies,* published by IDG Books Worldwide, Inc.) Some exams have a grid-in style question, in which no answer choices are given. You don't have to worry about those weird formats here. All the math questions on the ACT are in straightforward multiple-choice format.

All the math questions have *five* answer choices. The rest of the questions on the ACT have only four answer choices. Be sure to look at all the possible choices in this section. I'm always amazed at how many students, used to looking at answers A, B, C, and D in other sections, totally don't see the E answer choice in the math section.

Traps. Most math exams are full of nasty old traps. The ACT is not. It's not out to getcha, like other tests. Here, the questions really test your math knowledge, not your patience. You don't have to be quite as paranoid on the ACT as you do on other exams.

Getting into the Grind: The Approach

You've done multiple-choice math problems all your life. You don't have much more to learn about doing multiple-choice math questions. However, the following commonsense steps can help you stay focused.

1. **Identify the point of the question.**

   Yes, even the stupid word problems have a point. Each question is trying to get you to supply one specific piece of information. Does the question ask you to solve for a circumference, or for an area? Do you have to state the value of x, or of $2x$? Circle precisely what the question asks for. After you finish the problem, go back and double-check that your answer provides the circled information.

   I just said that the ACT is not out to trap you — but that doesn't mean that you can't trap yourself. Among the answer choices will be the answer you get by making a careless error. Suppose, for example, that the problem asks for the *product* of numbers, and you find the *sum*. That answer will be there. If the question asks for one-half of a quantity and you solve for twice the quantity, that answer will be there. Because these types of answer choices are available to you, it's especially important that you identify *exactly* what the problem asks for and supply only that.

2. **Budget your time and brain strain: Decide whether the problem is worth your time and effort.**

   You don't have to do every problem in order, you know. Read the question and then predict how time-consuming solving it will be. If you know that you have to take several steps to answer the question, you may want to skip the problem and go back to it later. If you're not even sure where to start the problem, don't sit there gnawing at your pencil as if it were an ear of corn (unless you're Pinocchio, wood really isn't brain food). Guess and go.

   Guess, guess, guess! The ACT has no penalty for wrong answers. (You're going to read that statement hundreds of times throughout this book. I say it every chance I get to remind you that you can guess without fear of reprisal.) Whenever you skip a problem, choose an answer, any answer, and hope that you'll get lucky. Put a big arrow in the margin of the test booklet next to the question (not on the answer grid, as it may mess up the computer grading) to remind yourself that you made a wild guess. But if you run out of time and don't get back to the question, at least you have a chance of getting the answer right.

3. **Look before you leap: Preview the answer choices.**

   I'd be a wealthy woman if I had a nickel for every student who groaned and complained as he or she looked at the answer choices, "Man, I didn't really have to work that whole problem out. I could have just estimated from the answer choices." Absolutely true.

   Look at the answer choices before you begin doing any pencil-pushing. Often, the choices are variations on a theme, like .5, 5, 50, 500, 5,000. If you see those answers, you know that you don't have to worry about the digit, only the decimal. Maybe the answers are very far apart, like 1, 38, 99, 275, and 495. You probably can make a wild estimate and get that answer correct. But if you see that the answers are close together (like 8, 9, 10, 11, and 12), you know that you have to invest a little more time and effort into being extra-careful when solving the problem.

4. **Give yourself a second chance: Use your answer to check the question.**

   Think of this as working forward and backward. First, work forward to come up with the answer to the question. Then plug the answer into the question and work backward to check it. For example, if the question asks you to solve for x, work through the equation until you get the answer. Then plug that answer back into the equation and make sure that it works out. This last step takes less time than you may think and can save you a lot of points.

Time Flies When You're Having Fun: Timing Tips

The most common complaint I hear from students about the Mathematics Test is, "There's just not enough time. If I had more time, I could probably do every single question, but I always run out of time." True enough. Although having one minute per question (60 math questions, 60-minute section) sounds good, you'd be surprised at how fast time goes by. I have a few suggestions to make the best use of your time.

Skim for your favorite questions

I think of this technique as eating dessert first (something I always do). Go for the chocolate cake first (the easy questions) to make sure that time doesn't run out before you get to the good stuff. Leave the green beans (the harder problems) for the end. If you run out of time (which happens to most test-takers), at least you will have finished those questions that you had the best chance of answering correctly.

Start in the middle when plugging in the answer choices

On many problems, you'll be able to plug in the answer choices and see which one fits. For example, suppose that the question is something like:

$x + {}^{1}/_{2}x + {}^{1}/_{3}x = 110$. What is the value of x?

A. 95

B. 90

C. 72

D. 60

E. 30

Yes, you could use a common denominator and actually work through the problem *forward* to find x directly. But it may be just as quick and easy to plug in the answer choices. Start with the middle choice, choice C. If $x = 72$, then ${}^{1}/_{2}x = 36$, and ${}^{1}/_{3}x = 24$. But $72 + 36 + 24 = 132$, not 110. Because the sum is too big, you know the number you plugged in is too big as well. Go down the list, plugging in the smaller numbers. Try choice D. Let $x = 60$. Then $x\ (60) + {}^{1}/_{2}x\ (30) + {}^{1}/_{3}x\ (20) = 110$. Voilà!

Kindly refrain from showing off everything you know

Some of the ACT problems have extraneous information. For example, a geometry problem may list all sorts of numbers, including lengths of sides and measures of interior angles. If the question asks you to find the area of a trapezoid, you need just the numbers for base and height. (Remember the formula? The area of a trapezoid is ${}^{1}/_{2}$ [base 1 + base 2] × height.) Extra red-herring info can make you waste a lot of time. I already know that you're brilliant (you bought this book, didn't you?); you don't need to prove it by doing more than you're asked during the test. If you convert every problem into two or three new problems, you'll never finish this section on time.

Put aside two minutes to fill in the remaining ovals

The ACT assesses no penalty for guessing. I'm going to say that over and over and over again until you're so exasperated that you want to cut off my air supply. It's critical to remember that you don't lose points for wrong answers; always keep in mind that wild guesses are worth making. Nothing is worse than that sinking feeling you get when the proctor calls time, and you still have ten problems you haven't even looked at. If you save a few minutes at the end, you can fill in some answers wildly for those last ten problems. You have a good chance of getting at least a few of them correct.

The proctor is *supposed* to tell you when you have only five minutes left in the test. You may want to remind your proctor to do so before the test begins.

Do's, Don'ts, and Darns: What to Do and Not Do in the Math Test

Although the math questions are pretty straightforward, a few basic do's and don'ts are worth repeating here.

Do get the lead out

Give your pencil a workout. If you have to solve a geometry problem, jot down the formula first and then just fill in the numbers. If you have the formula staring at you, you're not as likely to make a careless mistake as you would if you tried to keep everything in your head. If the geometry problem has words, words, words but no picture, draw the picture yourself. When you plug in the answer choices or make up your own numbers to substitute for variables, write down what you plugged in and tried. I see students redoing the same things over and over because they forgot what they plugged in. Doodle away. You get no scratch paper for the ACT, but the test booklet has plenty of white space.

The ACT provides very few formulas. None are given in the directions, and only rarely is a formula given in an individual problem. The test-makers actually expect you to know what you're doing and to have the formulas memorized. Heaven forbid that you disappoint them. Take the time to go through the math reviews in this book (there are three: one for geometry, one for algebra, and one for miscellaneous math) and learn every formula possible. Pay special attention to the ones you rarely use, like the formula for determining the interior angles of a figure. Based on Murphy's Law ("Whatever can go wrong will go wrong"), the exam is likely to require the use of those formulas.

Don't start working until you've read the entire problem

So you read the first part of a problem and start trying to solve for the area of the triangle or the circumference of the circle. But if you read further, you may find that the question asks for only a *ratio* of the areas of two figures, which you can figure out without actually finding the precise areas. Or you may solve a whole algebraic equation, only to realize that the question didn't ask for the variable you found, but rather for something else entirely. As I said earlier in this lecture, circle the part of the problem that specifies exactly what is needed.

Just because the answer you got is staring up at you from the test booklet does not, in the least, mean that it's the right answer. (That's as bad as thinking that someone is Mr. Right just because he's gawking at you in the lunchroom.) The answer may be an interim answer, like what x is when you're asked to find the square root of x. The answer may be a careless-mistake answer, like what you get if you don't keep your decimal point straight. Or the answer may be a write-your-own-question answer, in which you give the test-makers something they weren't asking for, like finding the perimeter when the question wants the area. (Creativity is rewarded in the Real World, but it's punished on the ACT. Much as you'd like to, you can't create your own new problems.)

Do reread the problem with your answer inserted

Very few students take this last critical step. Most test-takers are so concerned with finishing on time that they solve the problem and zoom on to the next question. Big tactical error. Rereading the question in light of your answer can show you some pretty dumb mistakes. For example, if the question asks you for the average of 5, 9, 12, 17, and 32, and your answer is 75, you can immediately realize that you found the sum but forgot to divide through by the number of terms. (And of course, 75 is one of the answer choices.) Maybe the question asks you to find one interior angle of a figure, and your answer is 190. If you look at the angle and see that it is acute (less than 90 degrees), you've made a mistake somewhere.

The ACT very carefully says that "figures are NOT necessarily drawn to scale." However, in the majority of cases, the figures are pretty darn close, and eyeballing them can help you at least eliminate wrong answers.

Don't strike out over a difficult question early on

Most standardized exams put their questions in order of difficulty, presenting the easy ones first, then the medium ones, and finally the hard ones. Things aren't as cut and dried on the ACT Mathematics Test. You may find a question that you consider really tough very early in the exam. Although "easy" and "hard" are subjective, many of my students over the years have been furious with themselves because they never looked at the last several questions — reasoning that if they couldn't get the earlier ones right, they obviously couldn't get the later ones at all. Wrong. I've seen some relatively simple questions, especially basic geometry questions, close to the end of the exam.

"Easy" and "difficult" for international students often have more to do with the language than with the math. Many students for whom English is a second language do better on the basic equations than on the word problems. I suggest that you leaf through each exam as soon as you begin it, marking which problems you want to do, and then be sure to get to them. If you have time, you can go back to the others. And don't forget to fill in an answer for every question. The ACT does not penalize you for wrong answers.

The Second Time's a Charm: A Quick Summary

Before you solve the dozen sample questions in the next chapter, remind yourself of the basic approach and tricks and traps inherent in the math questions.

Approach

1. **Identify the point of the question.**
2. **Budget your time and effort.**
3. **Preview the answer choices.**

Tips and traps

- Skim for your favorite questions.
- Start in the middle when plugging in answer choices.
- Refrain from doing extra, unnecessary work.
- Fill in something for *every* question (because there's no penalty for guessing).
- Write down formulas; draw in figures.
- Read the *entire* problem before starting to solve it.
- Double-check the problem with your answer inserted.
- Look for medium, and even easy, questions scattered throughout the test.

Chapter 6

Mathematics Practice Questions

DIRECTIONS: Each of the following questions has five answer choices. Select the best choice.

1. $\dfrac{(a^4 \times a^3)^2}{a^4} =$

A. a^{36}

B. a^{10}

C. a^9

D. a^6

E. a^4

First, do the operation inside the parentheses. When you multiply like bases, you add the exponents: $a^4 \times a^3 = a^7$. When you have a power outside the parentheses, you multiply the exponents: $(a^7)^2 = a^{14}$ Finally, when you divide by like bases, you subtract the exponents: $a^{14} \div a^4 = a^{14-4} = a^{10}$. *Correct Answer:* B.

If you chose D, you fell for a trap answer. If you said $a^4 \times a^3 = a^{12}$ and $a^{12\times2} = a^{24}$, you may have divided a^{24} by a^4 and gotten a^6.

If you chose A, you fell for another trap. You may have reasoned that $a^4 \times a^3$ is a^{12}. Because 12 squared is 144, you may have thought that $(a^{12})^2 = a^{144}$ and that $a^{144} \div a^4 = a^{36}$.

All these trap answers are intentional; the ACT-makers realize that you're likely to do simple multiplication and division rather than use the exponents correctly. If you're still confused about how to multiply and divide like bases, see the exponents section in Chapter 8.

2. The ratio of knives to forks to spoons in a silverware drawer is 3:4:5. Which of the following could be the total number of knives, forks, and spoons in the drawer?

F. 60

G. 62

H. 64

J. 65

K. 66

A total must be a multiple of the sum of the numbers of the ratios. In other words, add 3 + 4 + 5 = 12. The total must be a multiple of 12. Only one answer choice divides evenly by 12. If you're confused about ratios (supposedly one of the easiest portions of the exam), see the ratio section of Chapter 8. *Correct Answer:* F.

3. An usher passes out 60 percent of his programs before the intermission and 40 percent of the remainder after the intermission. At the end of the evening, what percent of the original number of programs does the usher have left?

A. 60

B. 40

C. 24

D. 16

E. 0

Whenever you have a percentage problem, plug in 100 for the original total. Assume that the usher begins with 100 programs. If he passes out 60 percent of them, he has passed out 60, leaving him with 40. Now comes the tricky part. After the intermission, the usher passes out 40 percent of the *remainder:* 40 percent of 40 is 16 ($.40 \times 40 = 16$) and $40 - 16 = 24$. *Correct Answer:* C.

Did you fall for the trap answer of choice E? If you thought the usher first passed out 60 programs and then the remaining 40, you believed that he had no programs left at the end of the evening. The word *remainder* is the key to this problem. The usher did not pass out 40 percent of his original total, but 40 percent of the *remainder.*

If you chose D, you made a careless mistake. The number 16 represents the percent of programs the usher passed out after the intermission. The question asks for the percent of programs the usher had left. I suggest that you circle the portion of the question that tells you what you're looking for. When you are double-checking your work, this circled portion is the first thing to review.

4. A salesman makes a commission of $1.50 per shirt sold and $2.50 per pair of pants sold. In one pay period, he sold 10 more shirts than pairs of pants. If his total commission for the pay period was $215, what was the total number of shirts and pairs of pants he sold?

A. 40

B. 50

C. 60

D. 110

E. 150

Let x be the number of pairs of pants the salesman sold. Then the number of shirts is $x + 10$ (because the problem tells you that the salesman sold 10 more shirts than pairs of pants).

Make the equation $\$1.50(x + 10) + \$2.50(x) = \$215$.

Multiply: $1.50x + 15 + 2.50x = 215$.

Combine like terms: $4.00x + 15 = 215$.

Isolate the x on one side: $4.00x = 215 - 15$.

Subtract: $4.00x = 200$.

Divide: $x = 200/4$, or $x = 50$.

If you chose answer B, you fell for the trap answer (after all that hard work)! Remember to go back and reread what the question is asking for. In this case, it wants to know the total number of pants and shirts sold. You're not done working yet. If x (50) is the number of pairs of pants, then $x + 10$ (60) is the number of shirts sold. (Note that 60 is a trap answer as well.) Combine $50 + 60$ to get the right answer, 110. *Correct Answer:* D.

5. Kim and Scott work together stuffing envelopes. Kim works twice as fast as Scott. Together they stuff 2,100 envelopes in four hours. How long would Kim working alone take to stuff 175 envelopes?

A. 20 minutes

B. 30 minutes

C. 1 hour

D. 3 hours

E. 6 hours

The ratio of Kim's work to Scott's work is 2:1. In other words, she does two out of every three envelopes. Scott does one out of every three envelopes, or 2,100 ÷ 3 = 700. Scott does 700 in four hours, and Kim does 1,400 in four hours. Divide 1,400 by 4 to find that Kim does 350 per hour. 175 is $1/2$ of 350. Therefore, in one half hour (or 30 minutes), Kim can stuff 175 envelopes. *Correct Answer:* B.

When you encounter a word problem like this, don't start thinking equations immediately. Power math will not help you on this problem as much as simply talking the problem through.

6. If DC = 6, what is the shaded area?

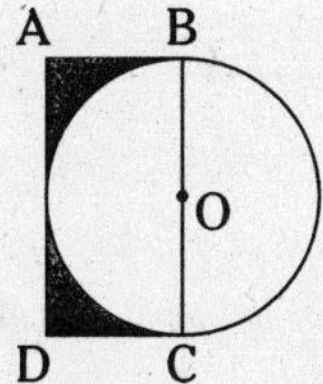

F. $72 - 18\pi$

G. $72 - 36\pi$

H. 9π

J. $36 - 18\pi$

K. $36 - 36\pi$

A shaded area is a leftover. To find a shaded area, you usually find a total, find a subtotal, and then subtract. If the side DC is 6, that is the same as the radius of the circle.

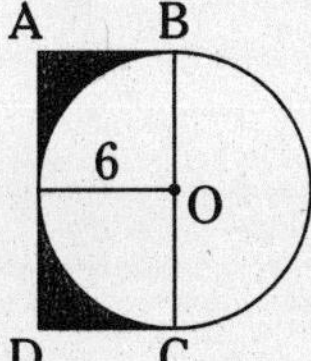

The area of a circle is πr^2; therefore, $\pi 6^2 = 36\pi$. Be careful to remember that you are working only with a semicircle. The shaded area subtracts only half the area of the circle, so you subtract 18π. That immediately narrows the answers down to F and J.

Next, find the area of the rectangle. (The area of a rectangle equals length × width.) The width of DC is 6. Because the radius of the circle is 6, the diameter of the circle is 12. BC, the diameter of the circle, is the same as the length of the rectangle. $6 \times 12 = 72$. Finally, subtract: $72 - 18\pi$. *Correct Answer:* F.

Shaded area questions should be one of the easiest types of questions to get correct. If you got confused on this problem, please go back to the shaded area portion of Chapter 7.

7. $5a^2 + (5a)^2 = 120$. Solve for a.

A. 2

B. 3

C. 4

D. 5

E. 6

$(5a)^2$ is $5a \times 5a$, which is $25a^2$.

$25a^2 + 5a^2 = 30a^2$

$30a^2 = 120$

$a^2 = 120 \div 30$

$a^2 = 4$

$a = 2$

Correct Answer: A. Choice C is the trap answer. If you divided 120 by 30 and got 4, you may have chosen C, forgetting that 4 represented a^2, not a.

Of course, you also could simply plug in each answer choice and work backwards. Here, if a = 2, then

$5(2)^2 + (5 \times 2)^2 = 120$

$(5 \times 4) + 10^2 = 120$

$20 + 100 = 120$

$120 = 120$

8. Three times as much as $^1/_3$ less than $3x$ is how much in terms of x?

F. $9x$

G. $8x$

H. $6x$

J. x

K. $^1/_3x$

It's usually easier to work backward in this type of problem. $^1/_3$ less than $3x$ is $2x$. You can calculate it this way: $3x - {^1/_3}(3x) = 3x - x = 2x$. Then $3 \times 2x$ is $6x$. *Correct Answer:* H.

If English is your second (or third or fourth) language, a problem like this can be extremely difficult to understand. The math is easy to do, but the English is hard to translate. This type of problem is a good one for you to guess at quickly and just go on.

9. The following chart shows the weights of junior high school students. What is the sum of the mode and the median weights?

Weight in Pounds	*Number of Students*
110	4
120	2
130	3
140	2

A. 230 pounds

B. 235 pounds

C. 250 pounds

D. 255 pounds

E. 258 pounds

This question tests vocabulary as much as it tests math. The *mode* is the most frequently repeated number. In this case, 110 is repeated more often than any other term. The *median* is the middle term when the numbers are arranged in order. Here you would have 110, 110, 110, 110, 120, 120, 130, 130, 130, 140, 140. Of these 11 numbers, the sixth one, 120, is the median. 110 + 120 = 230. *Correct Answer:* A.

Don't confuse *median* with *mean.* The *mean* is the average. You get the mean by adding all the terms and then dividing by the number of terms. If you chose B, you fell into a different trap. You thought that 125 was the *median,* because you added the first and last terms and divided by 2. Sorry. To find the median, you have to write out all the terms (all four 110s, both 120s, and so on) and then locate the middle term.

10. The ratio of the area of triangle EBD to triangle ABE is

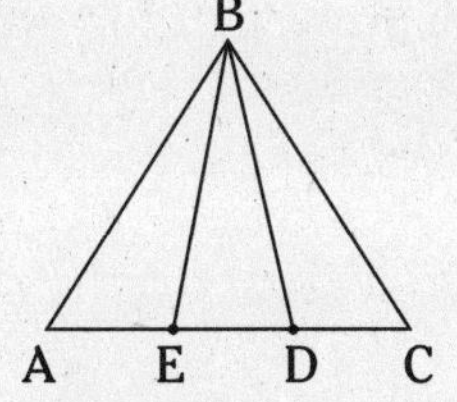

AE=ED=DC

F. 3:2

G. 3:1

H. 2:1

J. 1:1

K. 1:2

The area of a triangle is $^1/_2$ base × height. The base of EBD is ED. That is equal to AE, which is the base of triangle ABE. The bases of the two triangles are equal. The heights are equal as well. By definition, a height of a triangle is a line from the tallest point perpendicular to the base. If the triangles have the same base and the same height, the ratio of their areas is 1:1. *Correct Answer:* J.

11. $\begin{array}{r} 95c5 \\ +\ 3cbc \\ \hline ab3a2 \end{array}$

Solve for the sum of $a + b + c$.

A. 15

B. 14

C. 13

D. 12

E. 11

If you are rushed for time, this is a good problem to guess at quickly. (***Remember:*** The ACT does not assess a penalty for wrong answers. Never leave an answer blank. Even a wild guess is worthwhile.) However, if you do a few of these practice problems, you'll be surprised at how quickly you can get them right.

Don't panic. This problem is much easier than it appears. Start with the right-hand column, the ones or units column: $5 + c = 2$. You know that it must be a 12 instead of a 2, making $c = 7$. Jot $c = 7$ to the side.

Carry the 1 to the tens column: 1 + 7, which is 8, and $8 + b = a$. You don't know a yet . . . or do you? Go to the far-left column (the thousands). If the answer is $ab3a2$, the variable a must equal 1. You cannot add two four-digit numbers and get twenty-thousand something. The most you could get would be ten-thousand something (for example, 9,999 + 9,999 = 19,998). Now you know that a is 1. Jot down $a = 1$ on the side.

Go back to the tens column. 1 + 7; $8 + b = 11$ (it couldn't be 1; it must be 11). Therefore, $b = 3$. Carry the 1 to the hundreds column. 1 + 5 is 6. $6 + c$ (which is 7) = 13. Yes, this is true — a good check. Carry the 1 to the next column. 1 + 9 is 10. 10 + 3 is 13, which is what I said ab was in the first place. Therefore, $c = 7$, $b = 3$, $a = 1$ and 7 + 3 + 1 = 11. *Correct Answer:* E.

The most common mistake that students make on this type of problem is forgetting to carry the 1 to the next column. Double-check that you have done so.

12. $3 * 4 = \frac{1}{3}+\frac{1}{4}$. Solve for $\frac{2}{15} * \frac{2}{18}$.

F. 14

G. 14.5

H. 15

J. 16

K. 16.5

This problem is a symbolism one that you should think through in words instead of heading for an equation. When you have an asterisk between two numbers as in this problem, you add the reciprocals of those two numbers. For example, the reciprocal of 3 is $\frac{1}{3}$, and the reciprocal of 4 is $\frac{1}{4}$. Therefore, add the reciprocals of $\frac{2}{15}$ and $\frac{2}{18}$. Then $\frac{15}{2}+\frac{18}{2}=\frac{33}{2}=16\frac{1}{2}=16.5$. *Correct Answer:* K.

The * has this meaning *for this problem only*. The meanings of symbols vary from problem to problem; always read the directions.

Part V

More Fun Than a Root Canal: The Dreaded Math Review

In this part . . .

You knew it was coming, didn't you? There's no way to get through a test prep book without having a math review. This book gives you three for the price of one: geometry, algebra/trigonometry, and miscellaneous math. I've worked hard to make this stuff as painless as possible (you're bound to experience a little bit of sensory overload as you learn three years of math in just three chapters) by throwing in the odd joke here and there and by using some examples that are a lot more fun than any you'd actually see on the ACT.

But I don't waste your time. I don't insult you by starting too far back ("here are the multiplication tables you must know"), and I don't give you material that's not tested (like calculus) just to impress you with *my* abilities. (Hey, if I can't impress you with my jokes, forget it!) Instead, I emphasize what you're most likely to see on the test, reviewing all the formulas and even some of the math vocabulary, like prime and composite numbers.

Note: If you haven't covered some of the material in these reviews, don't worry about it. Maybe you haven't had trig yet (only four of the ACT questions cover the subject, so don't start panicking!) or even geometry. That's okay. You should still be able to follow most of the material. Just do what you can, and have fun with it.

Chapter 7

More Figures than a Beauty Pageant: Geometry Review

In This Chapter

- Angles
- Triangles
- Similar figures
- Area problems
- Quadrilaterals and other polygons
- Shaded-area problems
- Circles

Geometry is one of the areas that can mess you up on the ACT. But it's easy if you take the time to memorize some rules. This chapter provides a lightning-fast review of the major points of geometry so that you can go into the test equipped to tackle the geometry questions with ease.

You Gotta Have an Angle

Angles are a big part of the ACT geometry problems. Fortunately, understanding angles is easy after you memorize a few basic concepts. And keep in mind the best news: You don't have to do proofs. Finding an angle is usually a matter of simple addition or subtraction. These three rules generally apply to the ACT:

- There are *no negative angles.*
- There are *no zero angles.*
- It is extremely unlikely that you'll see any *fractional angles.* (For example, an angle won't measure $45\frac{1}{2}$ degrees or $32\frac{3}{4}$ degrees.)

Angles are whole numbers. If you're plugging in a number for an angle, plug in a whole number such as 30, 45, or 90.

1. **Angles greater than 0 but less than 90 degrees are called *acute*.** Think of an acute angle as being *a cute* little angle.

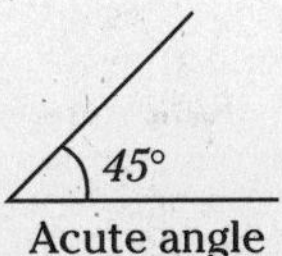

Acute angle

2. **Angles equal to 90 degrees are called *right angles.*** They are formed by perpendicular lines and are indicated by a box in the corner of the two intersecting lines.

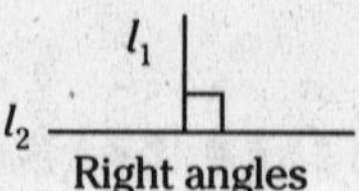

Right angles

Do not automatically assume that angles that look like right angles are right angles. Without calculating it, you know that an angle is a right angle only if (A) you're expressly told, "This is a right angle"; (B) you see the perpendicular symbol (⊥) indicating that the lines form a 90-degree angle; or (C) you see the box in the angle. Assume otherwise, and you may be headed for a trap!

a | *b*

Not necessarily right angles

3. **Angles that total 90 degrees are called *complementary angles.*** Think of *C* for corner (the lines form a 90-degree corner angle) and *C* for complementary.

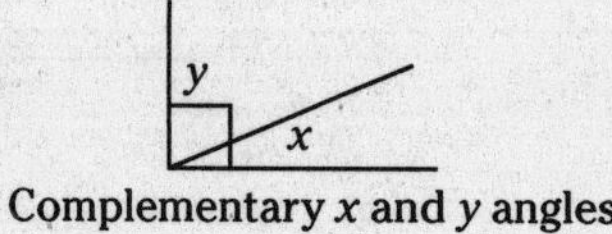

Complementary *x* and *y* angles

4. **An angle that is greater than 90 degrees but less than 180 degrees is called *obtuse.*** Think of obtuse as *obese* — an obese (or fat) angle is an obtuse angle.

110°

Obtuse angle

5. **An angle that measures exactly 180 degrees is called a *straight angle.***

180°

Straight angle

6. **Angles that total 180 degrees are called *supplementary angles.***

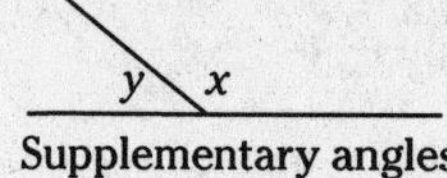

Supplementary angles

Think of *S* for *s*upplementary (or *s*traight) angles. Be careful not to confuse complementary angles (*C* for *c*omplementary or *c*orner) with supplementary angles (*S* for *s*upplementary or *s*traight). If you're likely to get these confused, just think alphabetically. *C* comes before *S* in the alphabet; 90 comes before 180 when you count.

7. **An angle that is greater than 180 degrees but less than 360 degrees is called a *reflex angle.***

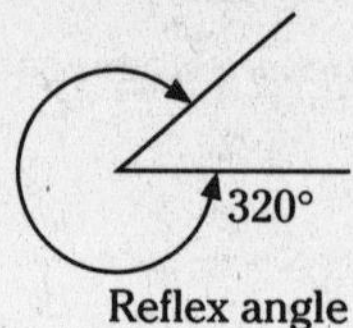

Reflex angle

Think of a reflex angle as a reflection or mirror image of an acute angle. It makes up the rest of the angle when there's an acute angle.

Reflex angles are rarely tested on the ACT.

8. **Angles around a point total 360 degrees.**

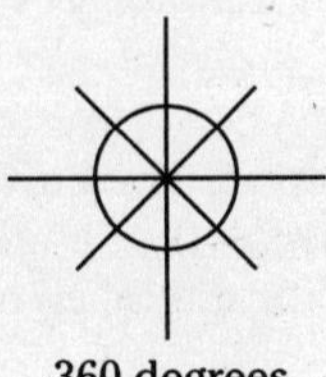

360 degrees

9. **Angles that are opposite each other have equal measures and are called *vertical angles.*** Note that vertical angles may actually be horizontal. Just remember that vertical angles are *across* from each other, whether they are up and down (vertical) or side by side (horizontal).

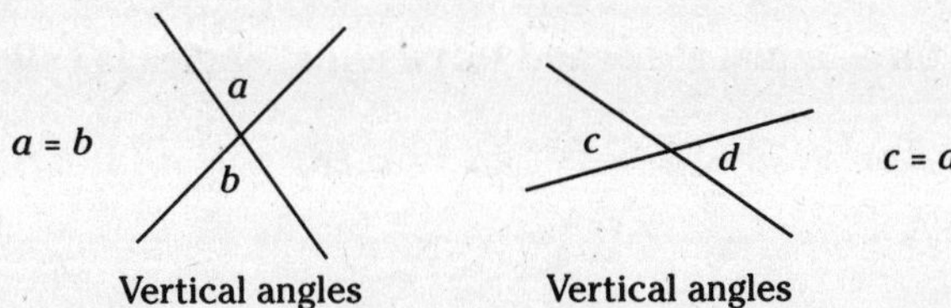

Vertical angles   Vertical angles

10. **Angles in the same position around two parallel lines and a transversal (corresponding angles) have the same measures.**

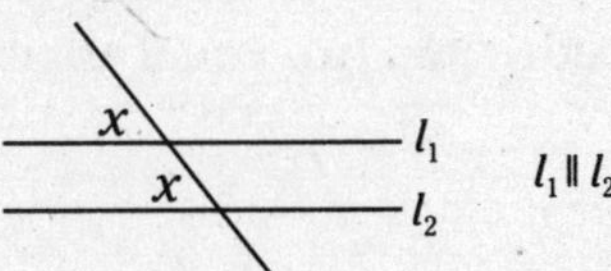

When you see two parallel lines and a transversal, number the angles. Start in the upper-right corner with 1 and go clockwise. For the second batch of angles, start in the upper-right corner with 5 and go clockwise:

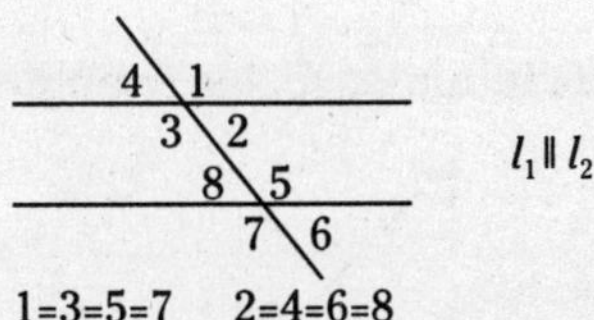

Note that all the odd-numbered angles are equal and all the even-numbered angles are equal.

Be careful not to zigzag back and forth when numbering, like this:

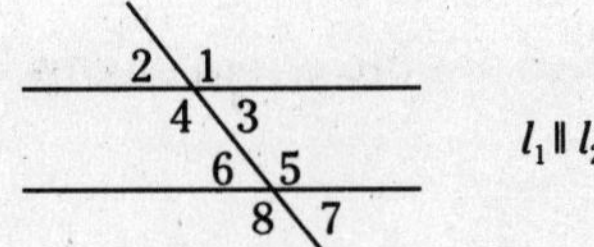

If you zig when you should have zagged, you can no longer use the tip that all even-numbered angles are equal to one another and all odd-numbered angles are equal to one another.

11. The exterior angles of any figure are supplementary to the interior angles and total 360 degrees.

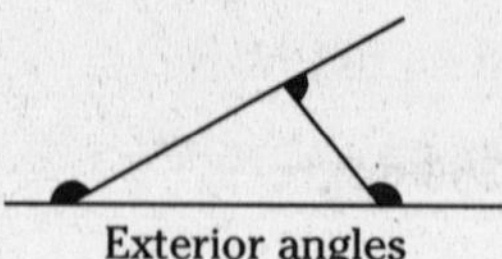

Exterior angles

Exterior angles can be very confusing. They always total 360 degrees, no matter what type of figure you have. Many people think that angles are exterior angles when they aren't. ***Remember:*** To be called an exterior angle, an angle must be supplementary to an interior angle.

Triangle Trauma

1. A triangle with three equal sides and three equal angles is called *equilateral.*

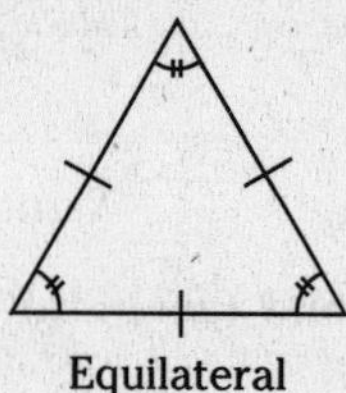

Equilateral

2. A triangle with two equal sides and two equal angles is called *isosceles.*

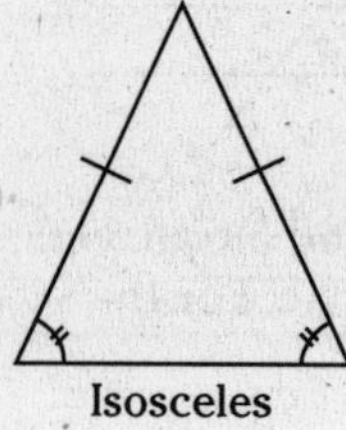

Isosceles

3. Angles opposite equal sides in an isosceles triangle are also equal.

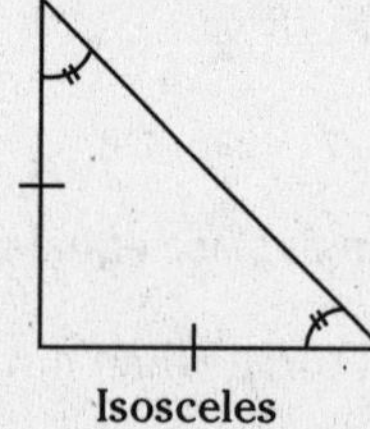

Isosceles

4. A triangle with no equal sides and no equal angles is called *scalene.*

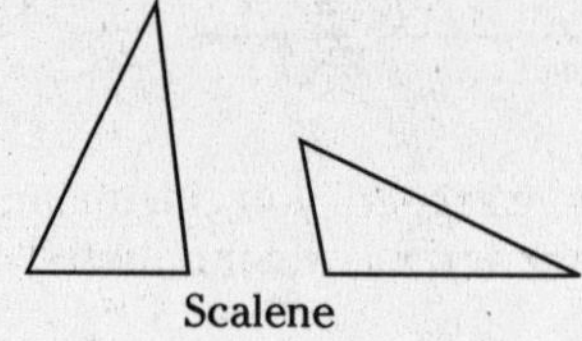

Scalene

5. **In any triangle, the largest angle is opposite the longest side.**

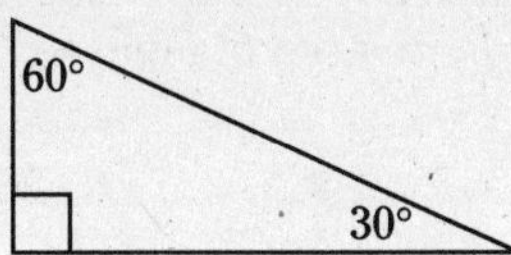

6. **In any triangle, the sum of the lengths of two sides must be greater than the length of the third side.** This statement is often written as $a + b > c$, where a, b, and c are the sides of the triangle.

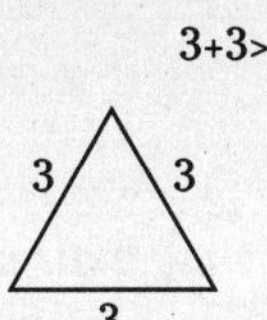

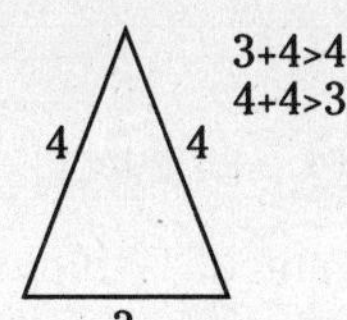

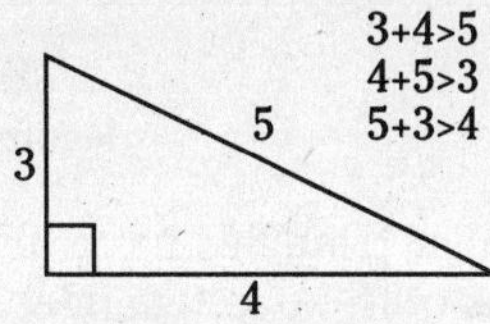

7. **In any type of plane geometry triangle, the sum of the interior angles is 180 degrees.**

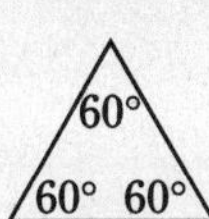

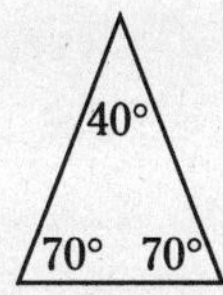

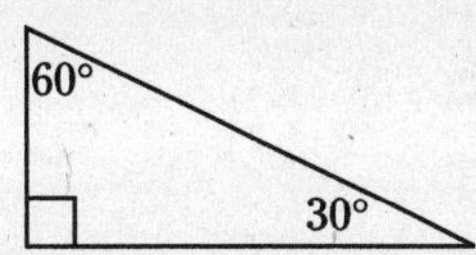

A trap question may want you to assume that different-sized triangles have different angle measures. Wrong! A triangle can be seven stories high and have 180 degrees or be microscopic and have 180 degrees. The size of the triangle is irrelevant; every triangle's internal angles add up to 180 degrees.

8. **The measure of an exterior angle of a triangle is equal to the sum of the two remote interior angles.**

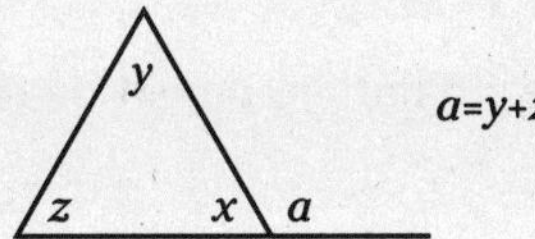

When you think about this rule logically, it makes sense. The sum of supplementary angles is 180. The sum of the angles in a triangle is 180. Therefore, angle $x = 180 - (y + z)$ or angle $x = 180 - a$. That must mean that $a = y + z$.

Similar figures

1. **The sides of similar figures are in proportion.** For example, if the heights of two similar triangles are in a ratio of 2:3, then the bases of those triangles are in a ratio of 2:3 as well.

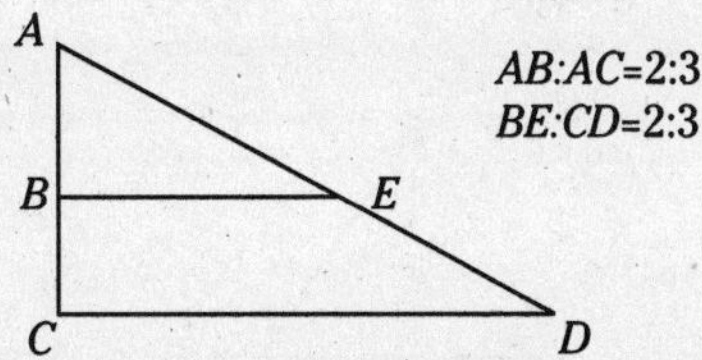

2. **The ratio of the areas of similar figures is equal to the square of the ratio of their sides.** For example, if each side of Figure A is $^1/_3$ the length of each side of similar Figure B, then the area of Figure A is $\frac{1}{9}\left[\left(\frac{1}{3}\right)^2\right]$ the area of Figure B.

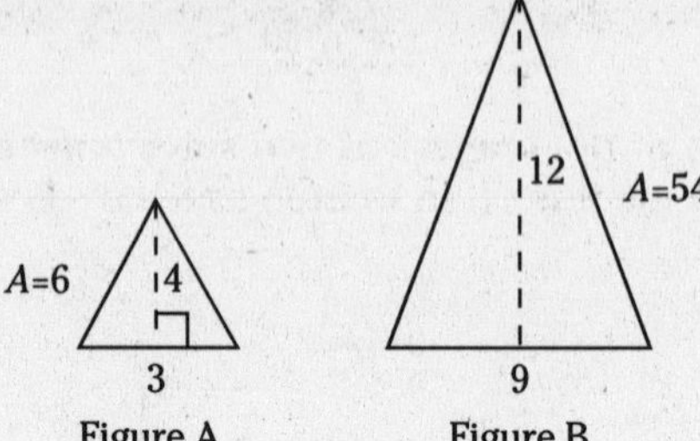

Figure A Figure B

Two similar triangles have bases of 5 and 25. Which of the following expresses the ratio of the areas of the two triangles?

A. 1:5

B. 1:15

C. 1:25

D. 1:30

E. 1:50

The ratio of the sides is $^1/_5$. The ratio of the areas is the square of the ratio of the sides: $^1/_5 \times {}^1/_5 = {}^1/_{25}$. *Correct Answer:* C.

Bonus: What do you suppose the ratio of the *volumes* of two similar figures is? Because volume is found in cubic units, **the ratio of the volumes of two similar figures is the *cube* of the ratio of their sides.** If figure A has a base of 5 and similar figure B has a base of 10, then the ratio of their volumes is 1:8 (1:2^3, which is $^1/_2 \times {}^1/_2 \times {}^1/_2 = {}^1/_8$).

Don't assume that figures are similar; you must be told that they are.

Area

1. **The area of a triangle is $^1/_2$ *base* × *height*.** The height is always a line perpendicular to the base. The height may be a side of the triangle, as in a right triangle.

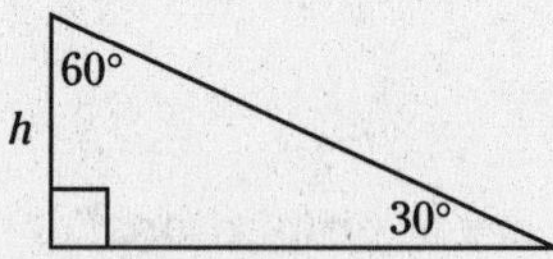

The height may be inside the triangle. It is often represented by a dashed line and a small 90-degree box.

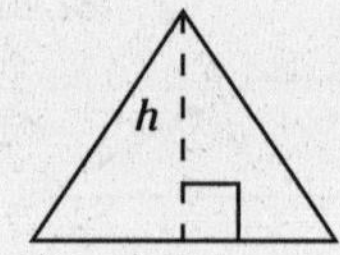

The height may be outside the triangle. This is very confusing and can be found in trick questions. ***Remember:*** You can always drop an altitude. That is, put your pencil on the tallest point of the triangle and draw a line straight from that point to where the base would be if it were extended. The line can be outside the triangle.

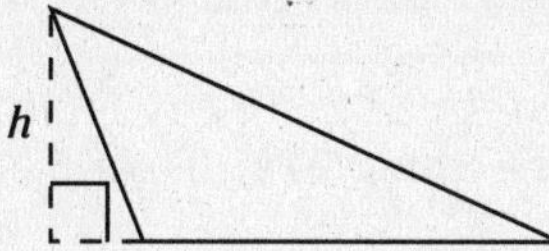

2. The perimeter of a triangle is the sum of the lengths of its sides.

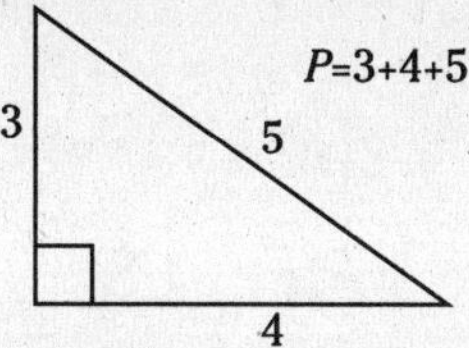

Pythagorean theorem

You have probably studied the Pythagorean theorem (known colloquially as PT). Keep in mind that it works only on *right* triangles. If a triangle doesn't have a right, or 90-degree, angle, you can't use any of the following information.

In any right triangle, you can find the lengths of the sides with the formula

$$a^2 + b^2 = c^2$$

where a and b are the sides of the triangle and c is the hypotenuse. The hypotenuse is always opposite the 90-degree angle and is always the longest side of the triangle. Why? Because if one angle in a triangle is 90 degrees, no other angle can be more than 90 degrees. All the angles must total 180 degrees, and there are no negative or zero angles. Because the longest side is opposite the largest angle, the hypotenuse is the longest side.

Pythagorean triples

Having to do the whole PT formula every time you want to find the length of a side is a pain in the posterior. You'll find five very common PT ratios in right triangles.

1. **Ratio 3:4:5** If one side of the triangle is 3 in this ratio, the other side is 4 and the hypotenuse is 5.

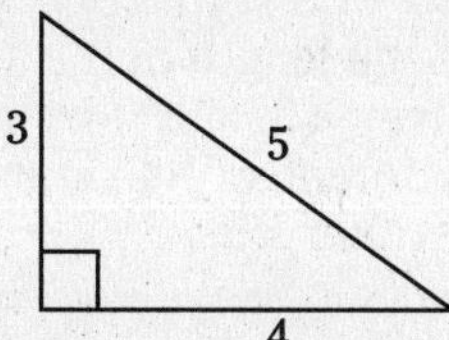

Because this is also a ratio, the sides can be in any multiple of these numbers, such as 6:8:10 (twice 3:4:5), 9:12:15 (three times 3:4:5), or 27:36:45 (nine times 3:4:5).

2. **Ratio 5:12:13** If one side of the right triangle is 5 in this ratio, the other side is 12 and the hypotenuse is 13.

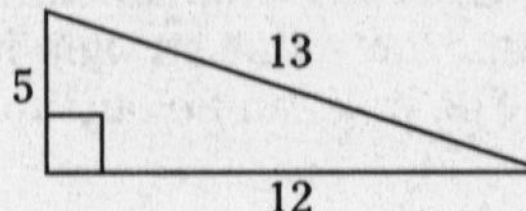

Because this is a ratio, the sides can be in any multiple of these numbers, such as 10:24:26 (twice 5:12:13), 15:36:39 (three times 5:12:13), or 50:120:130 (ten times 5:12:13).

3. **Ratio $s:s:s\sqrt{2}$, where *s* stands for the side of the figure.** Because two *s*'s are alike or two sides are the same, this formula applies to an isosceles right triangle, also known as a 45:45:90 triangle. If one side is 2, then the other side is also 2 and the hypotenuse is $2\sqrt{2}$.

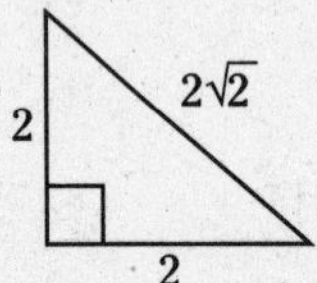

This formula is great to know for squares. If a question tells you that the side of a square is 5 and wants to know the diagonal of the square, you know immediately that it is $5\sqrt{2}$. Why? A square's diagonal cuts the square into two isosceles right triangles (*isosceles* because all sides of the square are equal; *right* because all angles in a square are right angles). What is the diagonal of a square of side 64? $64\sqrt{2}$. What is the diagonal of a square of side 12,984? $12{,}984\sqrt{2}$.

There's another way to write this ratio. Instead of $s:s:s\sqrt{2}$, you can write it as $(s/\sqrt{2}):(s/\sqrt{2}):s$, in which *s* still stands for the side of the triangle, but now you've divided everything through by $\sqrt{2}$. Why do you need this complicated formula? Suppose you're told that the diagonal of a square is 5. What is the area of the square? What is the perimeter of the square?

If you know the formula $(s/\sqrt{2}):(s/\sqrt{2}):s$, you know that *s* stands for the hypotenuse of the triangle, the same as the diagonal of the square. If $s = 5$, then the side of the square is $5/\sqrt{2}$, and you can figure out the area or the perimeter. After you know the side of a square, you can figure out just about anything.

4. **Ratio $s:s\sqrt{3}:2s$** This special formula is for the sides of a 30:60:90 triangle.

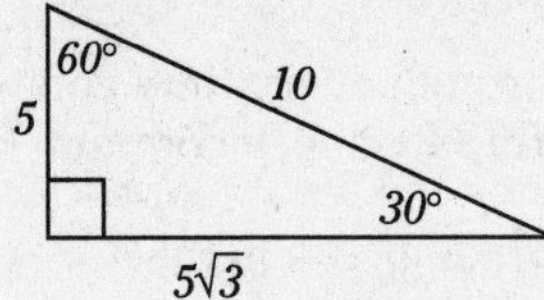

This type of triangle is a favorite of test-makers. The important thing to keep in mind here is that the hypotenuse is twice the length of the side opposite the 30-degree angle. If you get a word problem saying, "Given a 30:60:90 triangle of hypotenuse 20, find the area" or "Given a 30:60:90 triangle of hypotenuse 100, find the perimeter," you can do so because you can find the lengths of the other sides.

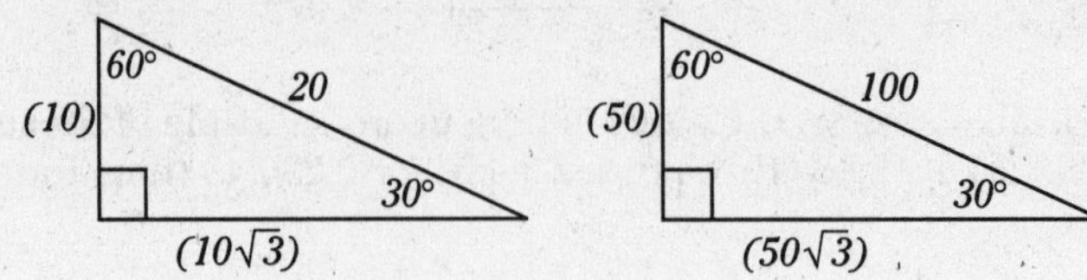

Thanks 4 Nothing: Quadrilaterals

1. **Any four-sided figure is called a *quadrilateral.***

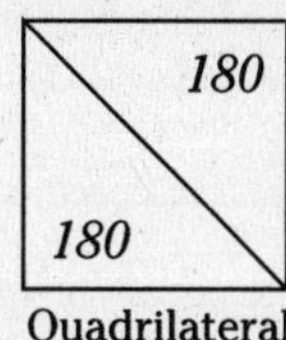

Quadrilateral

The interior angles of any quadrilateral total 360 degrees. Any quadrilateral can be cut into two 180-degree triangles.

2. **A *square* is a quadrilateral with four equal sides and four right angles.**

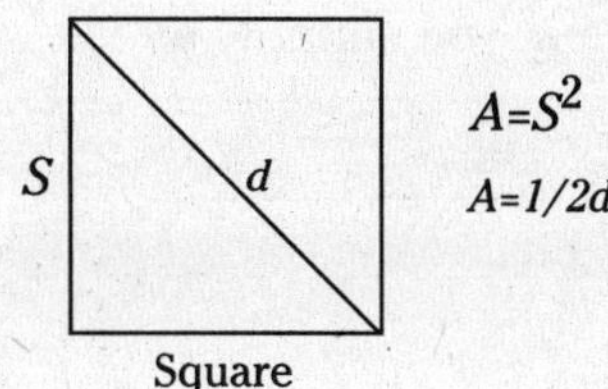

Square

The area of a square is side^2 (also called *base* × *height*), or $\frac{1}{2}d^2$, where *d* stands for *diagonal.*

3. **A *rhombus* is a quadrilateral with four equal sides and four angles that are not necessarily right angles.** A rhombus often looks like a drunken square, tipsy on its side and wobbly.

   The area of a rhombus is $\frac{1}{2}d_1d_2$ (or $\frac{1}{2}$ diagonal$_1$ × diagonal$_2$).

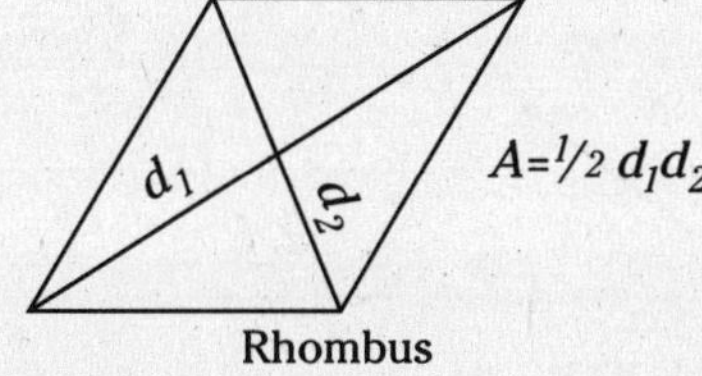

Rhombus

TRAPS & TRICKS

Any square is a rhombus, but not all rhombuses are squares.

4. **A *rectangle* is a quadrilateral with two opposite and equal pairs of sides.** That is, the top and bottom sides are equal, and the right and left sides are equal. All angles in a rectangle are right angles (*rectangle* means "right angle").

   The area of a rectangle is *length* × *width* (which is the same as *base* × *height*).

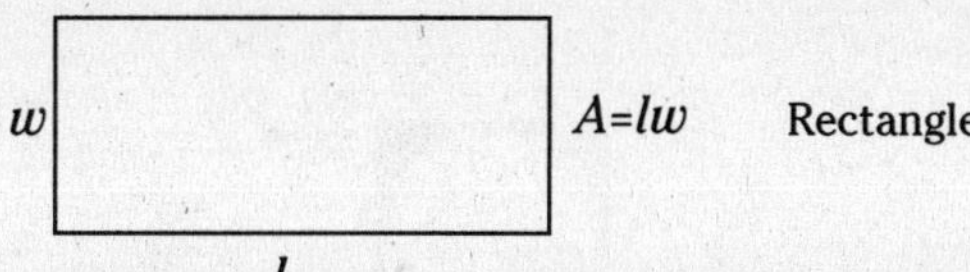

5. **A *parallelogram* is a quadrilateral with two opposite and equal pairs of sides.** The top and bottom sides are equal, and the right and left sides are equal. Opposite angles are equal but not necessarily right (or 90 degrees).

The area of a parallelogram is *base* × *height.* Remember that the height always is a perpendicular line from the tallest point of the figure down to the base. Diagonals of a parallelogram bisect each other.

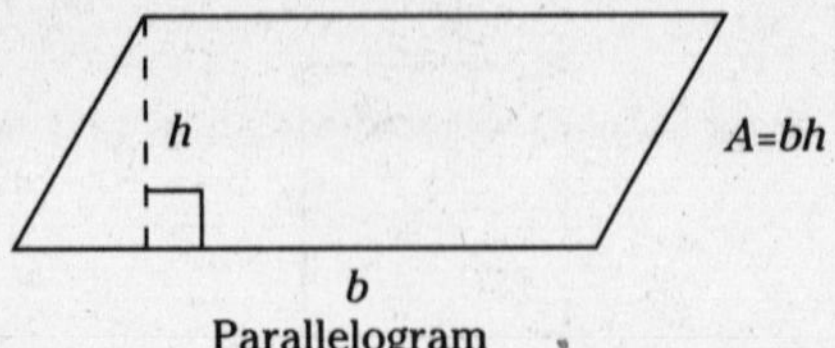

Parallelogram

All rectangles are parallelograms, but not all parallelograms are rectangles.

6. **A *trapezoid* is a quadrilateral with two parallel sides and two nonparallel sides.**

   The area of a trapezoid is $\frac{1}{2}$(*base 1* + *base 2*) × *height.* It makes no difference which base you label base 1 and which you label base 2, because you're adding them together anyway. Just be sure to add them *before* you multiply by $\frac{1}{2}$.

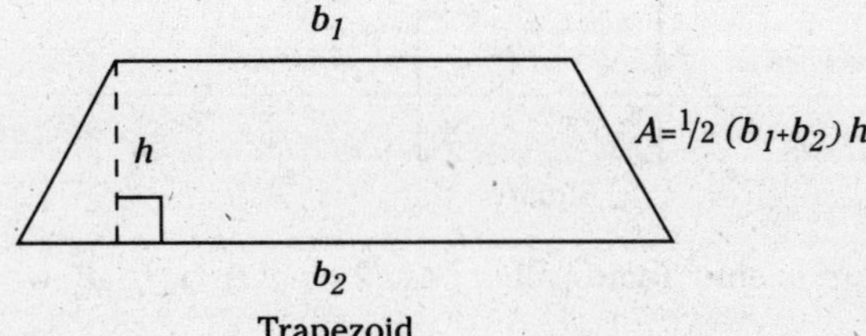

Trapezoid

Quaint quads: Bizarre quadrilaterals

Some quadrilaterals don't have nice, neat shapes or special names.

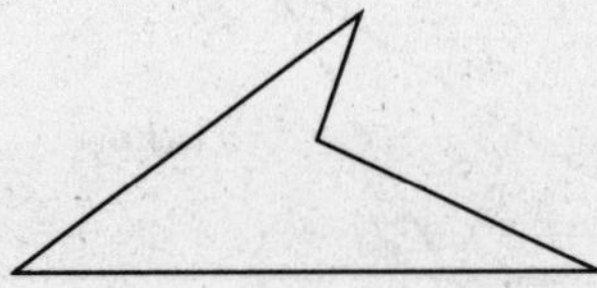

If you see a strange shape, don't immediately say that you have no way to find the area of it. You may be able to divide the quadrilateral into two triangles and find the area of each triangle. You may also see a strange quadrilateral in a shaded-area problem.

Leftovers again: Shaded-area problems

Think of a shaded area as a *leftover.* It is "left over" after you subtract the unshaded area from the total area.

Shaded areas are often very unusual shapes. Your first reaction may be that you can't possibly find the area of that shape. Generally, you're right, but you don't have to find the area directly. Instead, be sly, devious, and sneaky; in other words, think the ACT way! Find the area of the total figure, find the area of the unshaded portion, and subtract.

1. $s = 8$
Area of square = 64
2. $r = 4$
Area of circle = 16π
3. Shaded area = $64 - 16\pi$

Missing Parrots and Other Polly-Gones

Triangles and quadrilaterals are probably the most common polygons tested on this exam. Here are a few other polygons you may see:

Number of Sides	***Name***
5	Pentagon
6	Hexagon (think of *x* in *six* and *x* in *hex*)
7	Heptagon
8	Octagon
9	Nonagon
10	Decagon

1. **A polygon with all equal sides and all equal angles is called *regular*.** For example, an equilateral triangle is a regular triangle and a square is a regular quadrilateral.

   You are rarely asked to find the areas of any polygons with more than four sides.

2. **The *perimeter* of a polygon is the sum of the lengths of all the sides.**
3. **The *exterior angle measure* of any polygon is 360.**

Total interior angle measure

To find the interior angle measure, use the formula $(n - 2)\,180°$, where n stands for the number of sides.

For example, the interior angles of the following polygons are

- **Triangle:** $(3 - 2)180 = 1 \times 180 = 180°$
- **Quadrilateral:** $(4 - 2)180 = 2 \times 180 = 360°$
- **Pentagon:** $(5 - 2)180 = 3 \times 180 = 540°$
- **Hexagon:** $(6 - 2)180 = 4 \times 180 = 720°$
- **Heptagon:** $(7 - 2)180 = 5 \times 180 = 900°$
- **Octagon:** $(8 - 2)180 = 6 \times 180 = 1080°$
- **Nonagon:** $(9 - 2)180 = 7 \times 180 = 1260°$
- **Decagon:** $(10 - 2)180 = 8 \times 180 = 1440°$

Have you learned that proportional multiplication is a great time-saving trick? Numbers are in proportion, and you can fiddle with them to make multiplication easier.

For example, suppose that you're going to multiply 5×180. Most people have to write down the problem and then work through it. However, you can double one and halve the other: Double 5 to make it 10. Halve 180 to make it 90. Now your problem is 10×90, which you can multiply in your head: 900.

Try another one: $3 \times 180 = ?$ Double the first number: $3 \times 2 = 6$. Halve the second number: $180 \div 2 = 90$. $6 \times 90 = 540$. You can do this shortcut multiplication in your head very quickly and impress your friends.

One interior angle

1. To find the average measure of one angle in a figure, use the formula

$$\frac{(n-2)180}{n}$$

where *n* stands for the number of sides (which is the same as the number of angles).

Pentagon: $\frac{(5-2)\times 180}{5} = \frac{3\times 180}{5} = \frac{540}{5} = 108$

Because all angles are equal in a regular polygon, the same formula applies to one angle in a regular polygon.

2. If you are given a polygon and are *not* told that it's regular, you can't solve for just one angle.

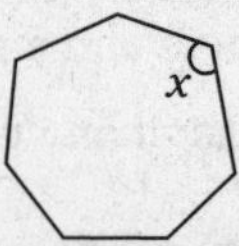

What's the measure of angle *x?* It cannot be determined. You cannot assume that it is

$$\frac{(7-2)180}{7} = \frac{900}{7} = 128.57$$

Be sure to divide through by *n,* the number of sides (angles), not by $(n - 2)$. If you divide through by $(n - 2)$, you always get

$$180\left(\frac{900}{5}\right) = 180$$

Knowing this, triple-check your work if you come up with 180 for an answer to this type of problem; you may have made this (very typical) careless error.

Volume

The volume of any polygon is *(area of the base)* × *height.* If you remember this formula, you don't have to memorize any of the following more specific formulas.

1. Volume of a cube: e^3

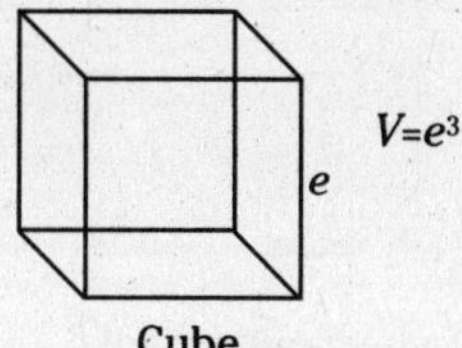

Cube

A cube is a three-dimensional square. Think of a die (one of a pair of dice). All of a cube's dimensions are the same; that is, *length* = *width* = *height*. In a cube, these dimensions are called *edges*. The volume of a cube is *edge* × *edge* × *edge* = *edge*^{3} = e^3.

2. Volume of a rectangular solid: $l \times w \times h$

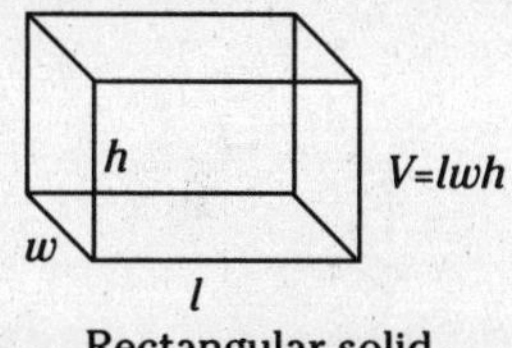

Rectangular solid

A rectangular solid is a box. The base of a box is a rectangle, which has an area of *length* × *width*. Multiply that by height to fit the original formula: Volume = *(area of base)* × *height*, or V = $l \times w \times h$.

3. Volume of a cylinder: (πr^2)*height*

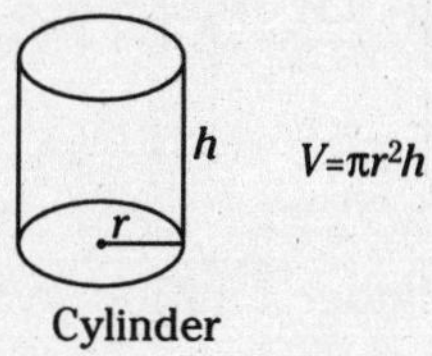

Cylinder

Think of a cylinder as a can of soup. The base of a cylinder is a circle. The area of a circle is πr^2. Multiply that by the height of the cylinder to get *(area of base)* × *height* = (πr^2) × *height*. Note that the top and bottom of a cylinder are identical circles. If you know the radius of either the top base or the bottom base, you can find the area of the circle.

Total surface area (TSA)

The total surface area, logically enough, is the sum of the areas of all the surfaces of the figure.

1. TSA of a cube: $6e^2$

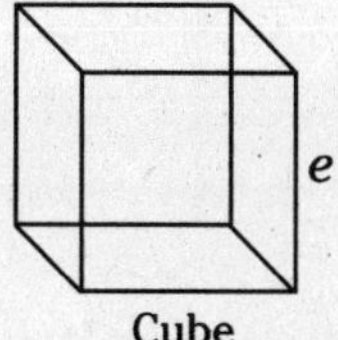

Cube

A cube has six identical faces, and each face is a square. The area of a square is *side*^{2}. Here, that is called *edge*^{2}. If one face is *edge*^{2}, then the total surface area is 6 × *edge*^{2}, or $6e^2$.

2. TSA of a rectangular solid: $2(lw) + 2(wh) + 2(hl)$

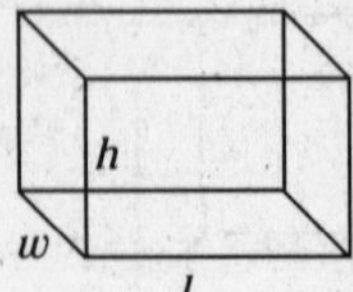

Rectangular solid

A rectangular solid is a box. You need to find the area of each of the six surfaces. The bottom and top have the area of *length* × *width*. The left side and right side have the area of *width* × *height*. The front side and the back side have the area of *height* × *length*. Together, they total $2(lw) + 2(wh) + 2(hl)$ or $2(lw + wh + hl)$.

3. TSA of a cylinder: (*circumference* × *height*) + $2(\pi r^2)$

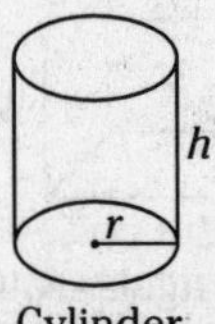

Cylinder

This is definitely the most difficult TSA to figure out. Think of it as pulling the label off the can, flattening it out, finding its area, and then adding that to the area of the top and bottom lids. The *label* is a rectangle. Its *length* is the length of the circumference of the circle.

Its *height* is the height of the cylinder. Multiply *length* × *height* to find the area of the label.

You also need to find the area of the top and bottom of the cylinder. Because each is a circle, the TSA of the top and bottom is $2(\pi r^2)$. Add everything together.

I'm Too Much of a Klutz for Coordinate Geometry

1. The horizontal axis is the *x*-axis. The vertical axis is the *y*-axis.

2. Points are labeled *(x,y)*, with the first number in the parentheses being how far to the right or left of the vertical line the point is and the second number being how far above or below the horizontal line the point is.

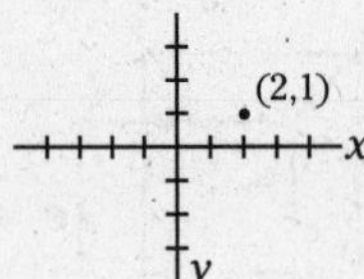

3. The intersection of the *x*- and *y*-axes is called the *point of origin,* and its coordinates are (0,0).

4. A line connecting points whose *x*- and *y*-coordinates are the same forms a 45-degree angle.

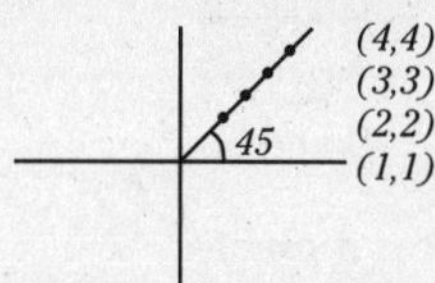

5. To find the distance between two points, you can use the distance formula:

$$\sqrt{(x_2 - x_1)^2 + (y_2 - y_1)^2}$$

Find the distance from (9,4) to (8,6).

$9 = x_1$

$8 = x_2$

$4 = y_1$

$6 = y_2$

$(8 - 9)^2 = -1^2 = 1$

$(6 - 4)^2 = 2^2 = 4$

$\sqrt{1+4} = \sqrt{5}$

The distance between the two points is $\sqrt{5}$.

Running Around in Circles

Did you hear about the rube who pulled his son out of college, claiming that the school was filling his head with nonsense? As the rube said, "Joe Bob told me that he learned πr^2. But any fool knows that pie are round; *cornbread* are square!"

Circles are among the less complicated geometry concepts. The most important things are to remember the vocabulary and to be able to distinguish an arc from a sector and an inscribed angle from a central angle. Here's a quick review of the basics.

1. A *radius* goes from the center of a circle to its circumference (perimeter).

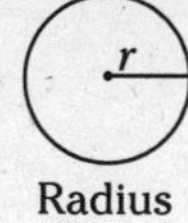

Radius

2. A circle is named by its *center* (midpoint).

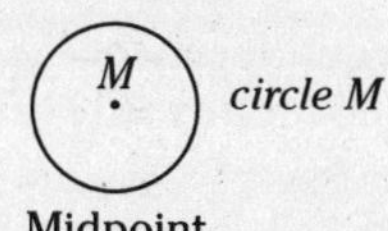

Midpoint

3. A *diameter* connects two points on the circumference of the circle, going through the center, and is equal to two radii.

Diameter

4. A *chord* connects any two points on a circle.

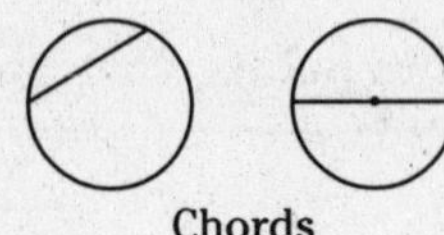
Chords

5. The longest chord in a circle is the diameter.

Here's a lovely question you may see on the test. What is the area of a circle of longest chord 12?

F. 144π

G. 72π

H. 36π

J. 12π

K. Cannot be determined from the information given

The longest chord in a circle is the diameter. The diameter of this circle is 12, which means its radius is 6, because a diameter is twice the radius. The area of a circle is πr^2. Here, $\pi 6^2 = 36\pi$. *Correct Answer:* H.

Choice K is the trap answer. If you know only that *a chord* of the circle is 12, you can't solve the problem. A circle has many different chords. You need to know the length of *the longest chord,* or the diameter.

Bonus: You may encounter a wheel question in which you're asked how much distance a wheel covers or how many times a wheel revolves. The key to solving this type of question is knowing that one rotation of a wheel equals one circumference of that wheel.

A child's wagon has a wheel of radius 6 inches. If the wagon wheel travels 100 revolutions, approximately how many feet has the wagon rolled?

A. 325

B. 314

C. 255

D. 201

E. 200

One revolution is equal to one circumference: $C = 2\pi r = 2\pi 6 = 12\pi$ = approximately 37.68 inches. Multiply that by 100 = 3,768 inches = 314 feet. *Correct Answer:* B.

6. The area of a circle is π • *radius*².

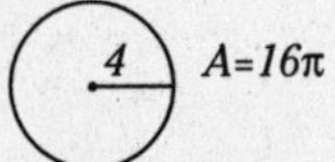

7. A *central angle* has its endpoints on the circumference of the circle and its center at the center of the circle. The degree measure of a central angle is the same as the degree measure of its intercepted arc.

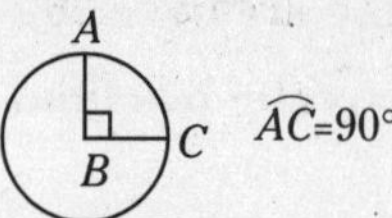

8. An *inscribed angle* has both its endpoints and its center on the circumference of the circle. The degree measure of an inscribed angle is half the degree measure of its intercepted arc.

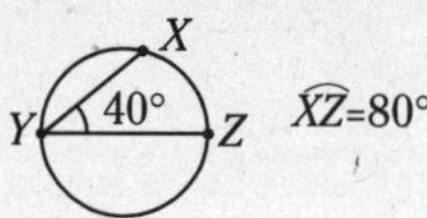

You may see a figure that looks like a string picture you made at summer camp, with all sorts of lines running every which way. Take the time to identify the endpoints of the angles and the center point. You may be surprised at how easy the question suddenly becomes. In this figure, for example, find the sum of $a + b + c + d + e$.

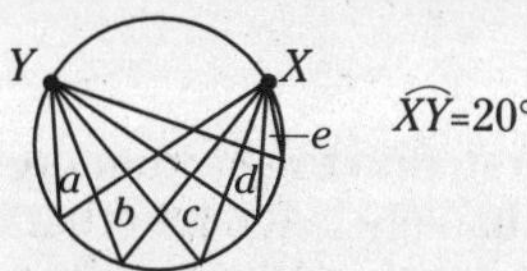

Note: Figure not drawn to scale.

F. 65°

G. 60°

H. 55°

J. 50°

K. 45°

Each angle is an inscribed angle; it has half the degree measure of the central angle, or half the degree measure of its intercepted arc. If you look carefully at the endpoints of these angles, they're all the same. They are along arc *XY,* which has a measure of 20 degrees. Therefore, each angle is 10 degrees, for a total of 50. *Correct Answer:* J.

9. When a central angle and an inscribed angle have the same endpoints, the degree measure of the central angle is twice that of the inscribed angle.

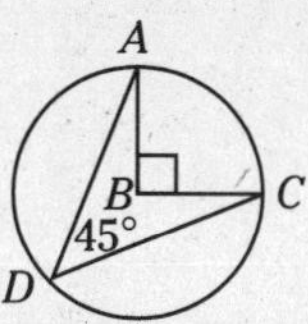

10. The degree measure of a circle is 360.

11. An *arc* is a portion of the circumference of a circle. The degree measure of an arc is the same as its central angle and twice its inscribed angle.

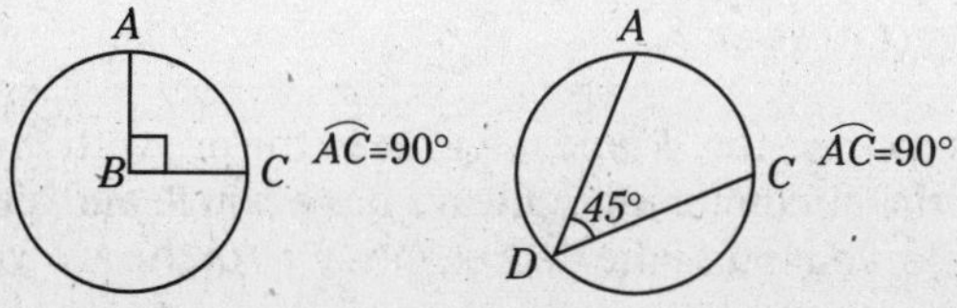

To find the length of an arc, follow these steps:

1. **Find the circumference of the entire circle.**
2. **Put the degree measure of the arc over 360 and then reduce the fraction.**
3. **Multiply the circumference by the fraction.**

Find the length of arc *AC*.

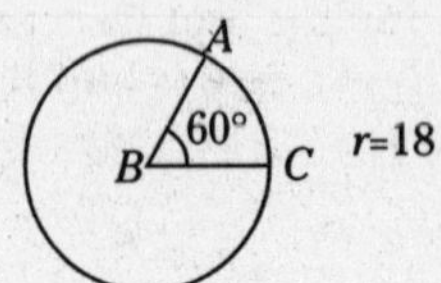

A. 36π

B. 27π

C. 18π

D. 12π

E. 6π

Take the steps one at a time. First, find the circumference of the entire circle. $C = 2\pi r = 36\pi$. Don't multiply π out; problems usually leave it in that form. Next, put the degree measure of the arc over 360. The degree measure of the arc is the same as its central angle, 60 degrees.

$$\frac{60}{360} = \frac{1}{6}$$

The arc is $^1/_6$ of the circumference of the circle. Multiply the circumference by the fraction: $36\pi \times {}^1/_6 = 6\pi$. *Correct Answer:* E.

After you get the hang of these, they're kinda fun. Try another one.

Find the length of arc *RS* in this figure.

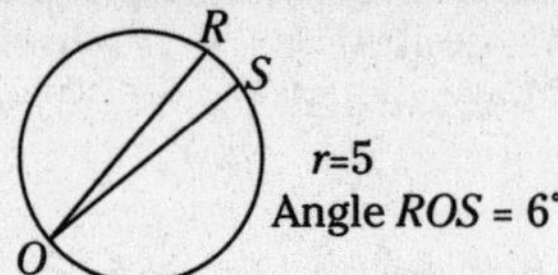

F. $^1/_3\pi$

G. π

H. 3π

J. 4π

K. 12

First, find the circumference of the entire circle. $C = 2\pi r = 10\pi$. Second, put the degree measure of the arc over 360. Here, the inscribed angle is 6°. Because an inscribed angle is $^1/_2$ of the central angle and $^1/_2$ of its intercepted arc, the arc is 12°. $^{12}/_{360} = {}^1/_{30}$. The arc is $^1/_{30}$ of the circle. Finally, multiply the circumference by the fraction: $10\pi \times {}^1/_{30} = {}^{10}/_{30}\pi = {}^1/_3\pi$. The length of the arc is $^1/_3\pi$. *Correct Answer:* F.

Be very careful not to confuse the *degree measure* of the arc with the *length* of the arc. The length is always a portion of the circumference, always has a π in it, and always is in linear units. If you chose K in this example, you found the degree measure of the arc rather than its length.

12. A *sector* is a portion of the area of a circle. The degree measure of a sector is the same as its central angle and twice its inscribed angle.

To find the area of a sector, do the following:

1. **Find the area of the entire circle.**
2. **Put the degree measure of the sector over 360 and then reduce the fraction.**
3. **Multiply the area by the fraction.**

Finding the area of a sector is very similar to finding the length of an arc. The only difference is in the first step. Whereas an arc is a part of the *circumference* of a circle, a sector is a part of the *area* of a circle. Try a few examples for sectors.

Find the area of sector *ABC*.

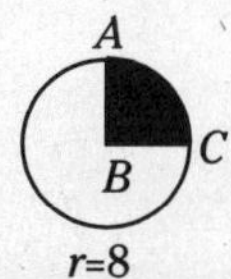

Angle *ABC* = 90°

A. 64π

B. 36π

C. 16π

D. 12π

E. 6π

First, find the area of the entire circle. $A = \pi r^2 = 64\pi$. Second, put the degree measure of the sector over 360. The sector is 90°, the same as its central angle. $^{90}/_{360} = {}^{1}/_{4}$. Third, multiply the area by the fraction: $64\pi \times {}^{1}/_{4} = 16\pi$. *Correct Answer:* C.

Find the area of sector *XYZ* in this figure.

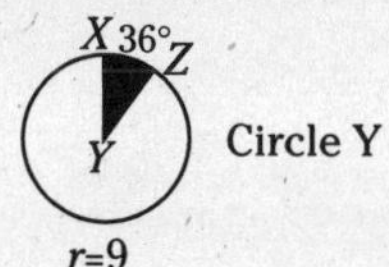

F. 9.7π

G. 8.1π

H. 7.2π

J. 6.3π

K. 6π

First, find the area of the entire circle. $A = \pi r^2 = 81\pi$. Second, put the degree measure of the sector over 360. A sector has the same degree measure as its intercepted arc, here 36°: $^{36}/_{360} = {}^{1}/_{10}$. Third, multiply the area by the fraction: $81\pi \times {}^{1}/_{10} = 8.1\pi$. *Correct Answer:* G.

Chapter 8

Catching Some (Xs, Ys, and) Zs: Algebra and Other Sleeping Aids

In This Chapter

- Bases and exponents
- Ratios
- Symbolism
- Algebra basics and the FOIL method
- Roots and radicals
- Probability
- Mean, median, and mode
- Trigonometry

Trivia Question: Where was algebra supposedly invented? *Answer:* Algebra was invented in Zabid, Yemen, by Muslim scholars. See? You can't blame the Greeks for everything!

The Powers That Be: Bases and Exponents

Many ACT questions require you to know how to work with bases and exponents. The following sections explain some of the most important concepts.

1. The *base* is the big number (or letter) on the bottom. The *exponent* is the little number (or letter) in the upper-right corner.

In x^5, x is the base and 5 is the exponent.

In 3^y, 3 is the base and y is the exponent.

2. A base to the zero power equals one.

$x^0 = 1$

$5^0 = 1$

$129^0 = 1$

There is a long, boring explanation as to why a number to the zero power equals one, but you don't really care, do you? For now, just memorize the rule.

3. A base to the second power is base × base.

This is pretty familiar stuff, right?

$x^2 = x \times x$

$5^2 = 5 \times 5$

$129^2 = 129 \times 129$

The same is true for bigger exponents. The exponent tells you how many times the number is repeated. For example, 5^6 means that you write down six fives and then multiply them all together.

$5^6 = 5 \times 5 \times 5 \times 5 \times 5 \times 5$

4. A base to a negative exponent is the reciprocal of itself.

This one is a little more confusing. A *reciprocal* is the upside-down version of something. When you have a negative exponent, just put the base and exponent under a 1 and make the exponent positive again.

$x^{-4} = 1/(x^4)$

$5^{-3} = 1/(5^3)$

$129^{-1} = 1/(129^1)$

The number is not negative. When you flip it, you get the reciprocal, and the negative just sort of fades away. *Don't* fall for the trap of saying that $5^{-3} = -(1/5)^3$, or $-1/125$.

When you take a base of ten to some power, the number of the power equals the number of zeroes in the number.

$10^1 = 10$ (one zero)

$10^4 = 10{,}000$ (four zeroes)

$10^0 = 1$ (zero zeroes)

5. To multiply like bases, add the exponents.

You can multiply two bases that are the same; just add the exponents.

$x^3 \times x^2 = x^{(3+2)} = x^5$

$5^4 \times 5^9 = 5^{(4+9)} = 5^{13}$

$129^3 \times 129^0 = 129^{(3+0)} = 129^3$

You cannot multiply *unlike* bases. Think of it as trying to make dogs and cats multiply — it doesn't work. All you end up with is a miffed meower and a damaged dog.

$x^2 \times y^3 = x^2 \times y^3$ (no shortcuts)

$5^2 \times 129^3 = 5^2 \times 129^3$ (you actually have to work it out)

6. To divide like bases, subtract the exponents.

You can divide two bases that are the same by subtracting the exponents.

$x^5 \div x^2 = x^{(5-2)} = x^3$

$5^9 \div 5^3 = 5^{(9-3)} = 5^6$

$129^4 \div 129^0 = 129^{(4-0)} = 129^4$

(Did I getcha on that last one? It should make sense. Any base to the 0 power is 1. Any number divided by 1 is itself.)

Did you look at the second example, $5^9 \div 5^3$, and think that the answer was 5^3? It's easy to fall into the trap of dividing instead of subtracting, especially when you see numbers that just beg to be divided, like 9 and 3. Keep your guard up.

7. **Multiply the exponents of a base inside and outside the parentheses.**

   That's quite a mouthful. Here's what it means:

   $(x^2)^3 = x^{(2\times3)} = x^6$

   $(5^3)^3 = 5^{(3\times3)} = 5^9$

   $(129^0)^3 = 129^{(0\times3)} = 129^0$

8. **To add or subtract like bases to like powers, add or subtract the numerical coefficient of the bases.**

   The *numerical coefficient* (a great name for a rock band, don't you think?) is simply the number *in front of* the base. Notice that it is *not* the little exponent in the right-hand corner but the full-sized number to the left of the base.

   $31x^3$: 31 is the numerical coefficient.

   $-8y^2$: -8 is the numerical coefficient.

   x^3: What is the numerical coefficient? One, because any number is itself times 1; the 1 is not always written out. Good trap.

   $37x^3 + 10x^3 = 47x^3$: Just add the numerical coefficients: $37 + 10 = 47$.

   $15y^2 - 10y^2 = 5y^2$: Just subtract the numerical coefficients: $15 - 10 = 5$.

You cannot add or subtract like bases with *different exponents.*

$13x^3 - 9x^2$ is *not* equal to $4x^3$ or $4x^2$ or $4x$. All it is equal to is $13x^3 - 9x^2$. The bases *and* exponents must be the same for you to add or subtract the terms.

9. **You cannot simply add or subtract the numerical coefficients of unlike bases.**

   Even though I'm the Queen of Shortcuts, I want to make sure that you know that not every shortcut works. Some can sabotage your efforts. For example, $16x^2 - 4y^2 = 16x^2 - 4y^2$. It is *not* $12x^2$ or $12y^2$ or $12xy^2$.

Keep It in Proportion: Ratios

After you know the tricks, ratios are some of the easiest problems to answer quickly. I call them "heartbeat" problems because you can solve them in a heartbeat. Of course, if someone drop-dead gorgeous sits next to you and makes your heart beat faster, it may take you two heartbeats to solve a ratio problem. So sue me.

1. **A *ratio* is written as $\frac{of}{to}$ or of:to.**

   The ratio *of* sunflowers *to* roses = $\frac{sunflowers}{roses}$.

   The ratio *of* umbrellas *to* heads = umbrellas:heads.

2. A *possible total* is a multiple of the sum of the numbers in the ratio.

You may be given a problem like this: At a party, the ratio of blondes to redheads is 4:5. Which of the following could be the total number of blondes and redheads at the party?

Mega-easy. Add the numbers in the ratio: 4 + 5 = 9. The total must be a multiple of 9, such as 9, 18, 27, 36, and so on. If this "multiple of" stuff is confusing, think of it another way: The sum must divide evenly into the total. That is, the total must be divisible by 9. Can the total be 54, for example? Yes, 9 goes evenly into 54. Can it be 64? No, 9 does not go evenly into 64.

After a rough hockey game, Bernie checks his body and finds that he has three bruises for every five cuts. Which of the following could be the total number of bruises and cuts on poor ol' Bernie's body?

A. 53

B. 45

C. 35

D. 33

E. 32

Add the numbers in the ratio: 3 + 5 = 8. The total must be a multiple of 8 (or, looking at it another way, the total must be evenly divisible by 8). Only choice E is a multiple of 8: 8 × 4 = 32. *Correct Answer:* E.

Did you notice the trap answers? 53 is a good trap because it features both 5 and 3, the numbers in the ratio. 45 is a trap. If you multiply 3 × 5 = 15, you may think that the total has to be a multiple of 15. No, the total is a multiple of the *sum,* not the product. *Add* the numbers in the ratio; don't multiply them. 35 again has both terms of the ratio. 33 is a multiple of 3. Only 32 is a multiple of the *sum* of the terms in the ratio.

One more, because you should always get this type of problem correct.

Trying to get Willie to turn down his stereo, his mother pounds on the ceiling and shouts up to his bedroom. If she pounds seven times for every five times she shouts, which of the following could be the total number of poundings and shouts?

F. 75

G. 57

H. 48

J. 35

K. 30

Add the numbers in the ratio: 7 + 5 = 12. The total must be a multiple of 12 (it must be evenly divisible by 12). Here, only 48 is evenly divisible by 12. Of course, the numbers 75 and 57 may trick you by using the numbers 7 and 5 from the ratio. Choice J is the product of 7 × 5. *Correct Answer:* H.

3. When given a ratio and a total and asked to find a specific term, do the following, in order:

1. **Add the numbers in the ratio.**
2. **Divide that sum into the total.**
3. **Multiply that quotient by each term in the ratio.**
4. **Add the answers to double-check that they sum to the total.**

Pretty confusing stuff. Take it one step at a time.

Yelling at the members of his team, which had just lost 21–0, the irate coach pointed his finger at each member of the squad, calling everyone either a wimp or a slacker. If there were 3 wimps for every 4 slackers, and every member of the 28-person squad was either a wimp or a slacker, how many wimps were there?

1. **Add the numbers in the ratio: 3 + 4 = 7.**
2. **Divide that sum into the total: 28 ÷ 7 = 4.**
3. **Multiply that quotient by each term in the ratio: 4 × 3 = 12; 4 × 4 = 16.**
4. **Double-check that the numbers add up to the total: 12 + 16 = 28.**

Now you have all the information you need to answer a variety of questions: How many wimps were there? Twelve. How many slackers were there? Sixteen. How many more slackers than wimps were there? Four. How many slackers would have to be kicked off the team for the number of wimps and slackers to be equal? Four. The ACT's Math Moguls can ask all sorts of things, but if you have this information, you're ready for anything they throw at you.

Be sure that you actually do Step 4, adding the terms to double-check that they add up to the total. Doing so catches any careless mistakes that you may have made. For example, suppose that you divided 7 into 28 and got 3 instead of 4. Then you said that there were 3 × 3, or 9, wimps, and 3 × 4, or 12, slackers. That means that the total was 9 + 12 = 21 — *ooooops!* You know the total has to be 28, so you can go back and try again. You'll also catch careless mistakes in your multiplication by taking this step. Suppose that you correctly divide 7 into 28 and get 4. But when you multiply 4 × 3, you get 43 instead of 12. (Hey, when the adrenaline's flowing during the exam, you'd be surprised at the kinds of mistakes you can make.) When you add the numbers, you get 43 + 16 = 59 instead of the 28 you know is the total.

Things Aren't What They Seem: Symbolism

You may encounter two basic types of symbolism problems. If so, do one of the following:

- Substitute the number given for the variable in the explanation.
- Talk through the explanation to see which constraint fits and then do the indicated operations.

1. Substitute for the variable in the explanation.

You see a problem with a strange symbol. It may be a variable inside a circle, a triangle, a star, or a tic-tac-toe sign. That symbol has no connection to the Real World at all. Don't panic, thinking that your teachers forgot to teach you something. Symbols are made up for each problem.

The symbol is included in a short explanation. It may look like this:

$$a\#b\#c=\frac{(a+b)^c}{b+c}$$

$$x*y*z=z/x+\left(\frac{y}{z}\left(\frac{y}{z}\right)^x\right)$$

$$m@n@o=mn+no-om$$

Again, the symbols don't have any meaning in the outside world; they mean only what the problem tells you they mean, and that meaning holds true only for this problem.

Below the explanation is the question itself:

3 # 2 # 1 =

4 * 6 * 8 =

2 @ 5 @ 10 =

Your job is one of substitution. Plug in a number for the variable in the equation. Which number do you plug in? The one that's in the same position as that variable. For example:

$$a\#b\#c = \frac{(a+b)^c}{b+c}$$

$$3\#2\#1 = \frac{(3+2)^1}{(2+1)}$$

Because *a* was in the first position and 3 was in the first position, substitute 3 for *a* throughout the equation. Because *b* was in the second position and 2 was in the second position, substitute 2 for *b* throughout the equation. Because *c* was in the third position and 1 was in the third position, substitute 1 for *c* throughout the equation.

Do the same for the other problems.

$$x*y*z = \left(\frac{z}{x}\right) + \left(\frac{y}{z}\right)^x$$

$$4*6*8 = (8/4) + (6/8)^4 = 2 + (6/8)^4 = 2 + .316 = 2.316$$

$$m@n@o = mn + no - om$$

$$2@5@10 = (2\times5) + (5\times10) - (10\times2) = 10 + 50 - 20 = 40$$

This is the simpler of the two types of symbolism problems. Just substitute the number for the variable and work through the equation.

2. Talk through the explanation and do the operations.

This type of symbolism problem may seem more confusing until you've done a few. Then they become so easy that you wonder why you didn't see it before. Following are two possibilities.

Ⓧ = 3*x* if *x* is odd

Ⓧ = *x*/2 if *x* is even

Solve for ⑤ + ⑧

First, talk through the explanation. You have something in a circle. If that something in the circle is odd, you multiply it by 3. If that something in the circle is even, you divide it by 2.

In the question, there's a 5 in the circle. Because 5 is odd, you multiply it by 3 to get 5 × 3 = 15. In the second half of the question, there's an 8 in a circle. Because 8 is even, you divide it by 2. 8 ÷ 2 = 4. Now add: 15 + 4 = 19.

Don't keep going. Do *not* say, "Well, 19 is odd, so I have to multiply it by 3, getting 57." You can bet that 57 is one of the trap multiple-choice answers.

You may still think of this second type of problem as a plug-in or substitution problem because you are plugging the number into the equation for x and working it through. However, you first have to figure out which equation to plug it into. That requires talking things through. You have to understand what you're doing in this type of problem. Try another.

triangle(x) $= 3x + {}^1/_3x$ if x is prime

triangle(x) $= x^2 + \sqrt{x}$ if x is composite

triangle(16) + triangle(3) =

Aha! Now you have to know some math vocabulary. Prime numbers are not the numbers that have stars next to them in your little black book. ***Prime numbers*** are numbers that cannot be divided other than by 1 and themselves, such as 2, 3, 5, 7, 11, and 13. ***Composite numbers*** are numbers that *can* be divided other than by just 1 and themselves, such as 4, 6, 8, 9, 10, and 12. The first thing you do is decide whether the term in the triangle is a composite number or a prime number.

triangle(16): Because 16 is a composite number, use the second equation. Square 16: $16 \times 16 = 256$. Take the square root of 16: $\sqrt{16} = 4$. Add them together: $256 + 4 = 260$.

triangle(3): Because 3 is a prime number, use the first equation. $3(3) + {}^1/_3(3) = 9 + 1 = 10$. Add the two solutions: $260 + 10 = 270$.

Sometimes, the solutions have symbols in them as well. Here's an example:

circle(x) $= {}^1/_2x$ if x is composite

circle(x) $= 2x$ if x is prime

Solve for circle(5) × circle(10)

A. circle(15)

B. circle(25)

C. circle(50)

D. circle(100)

E. Cannot be determined from the information given

First, you know to eliminate answer E. This is the sucker's answer, the one for people who have no idea what the cute little circle means and are clueless as to where to begin. You know by now that you *can* solve a symbolism problem — and pretty quickly, too.

Because 5 is prime, you multiply it by 2: $5 \times 2 = 10$. Because 10 is composite, you multiply it by ${}^1/_2$: $10 \times {}^1/_2 = 5$. Multiply: $10 \times 5 = 50$.

Noooo! Don't choose answer C; that's the trap answer. Choice C doesn't say 50; it says circle(50). The 50 is in a circle. That means that you have to solve the answer choice to see what *circle* 50 is. Because 50 is even, you take half of it: $50 \div 2 = 25$. That's not the answer you want. Now go through the rest of the choices:

circle(15): Because 15 is composite, multiply it by ${}^1/_2$: $15 \times {}^1/_2 = 7.5$.

circle(25): Because 25 is composite, multiply it by ${}^1/_2$: $25 \times {}^1/_2 = 12.5$.

circle(100): Because 100 is composite, multiply it by ${}^1/_2$: $100 \times {}^1/_2 = 50$. You have a winner!

Whenever you see a symbol, get to work. That symbol may be in the question or in the answer choices. You still follow the explanation. But remember the trap that I discussed earlier: *Be super careful not to keep on going.* That is, when you come up with 50 as your answer, don't say, "Well, 50 is composite, so I have to multiply it by $^1/_2$, getting 25." Stop when there are no more symbols. *Correct Answer:* D.

Have you studied functions yet? Maybe not in school, but if you read the preceding material on symbolism, you have studied functions. A function is very much like the symbolism you've just read about. You may see a problem like this:

$f(x) = (2x)^3$. Solve for f(2).

The *f* stands for function. You do the same thing you did before: Talk through the problem. You say, "I have something in parentheses. My job is to multiply that something by 2 and then cube the whole disgusting mess." In other words, just plug in the 2 where you see an *x* in the explanation.

$f(2) = (2 \times 2)^3 = 4^3 = 64$

Try another one.

$f(x) = x + x^2 + x^3$. Solve for f(10).

Just plug the 10 in for the *x*: $f(10) = 10 + 10^2 + 10^3 = 10 + 100 + 1{,}000 = 1{,}110$.

Now that you've acquired this skill, you can call yourself "fully functional."

Abracadabra: Algebra

You must be able to do three basic algebra concepts for the ACT.

Solve for x in an equation

The first concept to understand is how to solve for *x* in an equation. To solve for *x*, follow these steps:

1. **Isolate the variable, which means get all the *x*s on one side and all the non-*x*s on the other side.**
2. **Add all the *x*s on one side; add all the non-*x*s on the other side.**
3. **Divide both sides of the equation by the number in front of the *x*.**

Now you try it: $3x + 7 = 9x - 5$.

1. **Isolate the variable. Move the 3*x* to the right, *changing the sign* to make it –3*x*.**

   Forgetting to change the sign is one of the most common careless mistakes that students make. The test-makers realize that and often include trap answer choices to catch this mistake.

   Move the –5 to the left, *changing the sign* to make it +5. You now have $7 + 5 = 9x - 3x$.

2. **Add the *x*s on one side; add the non-*x*s on the other side.**

$12 = 6x$

3. Divide both sides through by what is next to the x.

$\frac{12}{6} = \frac{6x}{6}$

$2 = x$

If you're weak in algebra or know that you often make careless mistakes, plug the 2 back into the equation to make sure that it works.

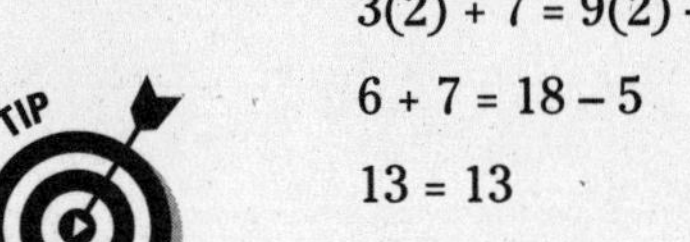

$3(2) + 7 = 9(2) - 5$

$6 + 7 = 18 - 5$

$13 = 13$

If you absolutely hate algebra, see whether you can simply plug in the answer choices. If this were a problem-solving question with multiple-choice answers, you could plug 'n' chug.

$3x + 7 = 9x - 5$. Solve for x.

A. 7

B. $5^1/_2$

C. 5

D. $3^1/_2$

E. 2

Don't ask for trouble. Keep life simple by starting with the simple answers first, and begin in the middle, with answer C, as suggested in the lecture. That is, try plugging in 5. When it doesn't work, don't bother plugging in $3^1/_2$. That's too much work. Go right down to 2. If all the easy answers don't work, then you can go back to the hard answer of $3^1/_2$, but why fuss with it unless you absolutely have to? Test-makers often put mind-boggling choices at the beginning of the answers (or at the bottom, for those of you who like to work upside down); skip them.

Curses! FOILed again

The second thing you need to know to do algebra is how to use the FOIL method. FOIL stands for *First, Outer, Inner, Last* and refers to the order in which you multiply the variables in parentheses. You can practice by using this equation: $(a + b)(a - b) =$

1. **Multiply the *First* variables: $a \times a = a^2$.**
2. **Multiply the *Outer* variables: $a \times -b = -ab$.**
3. **Multiply the *Inner* variables: $b \times a = ba$ (which is the same as ab).**
4. **Multiply the *Last* variables: $b \times -b = -b^2$.**

Add like terms: $-ab + ab = 0ab$. (Remember that you can multiply numbers forward or backward, such that $ab = ba$.) The positive and negative ab cancel each other out. You're left with only $a^2 - b^2$.

Try another one: $(3a + b)(a - 2b) =$

1. **Multiply the *First* terms: $3a \times a = 3a^2$.**
2. **Multiply the *Outer* terms: $3a \times -2b = -6ab$.**
3. **Multiply the *Inner* terms: $b \times a = ba$ (which is the same as ab).**
4. **Multiply the *Last* terms: $b \times -2b = -2b^2$.**
5. **Combine like terms: $-6ab + ab = -5ab$.**

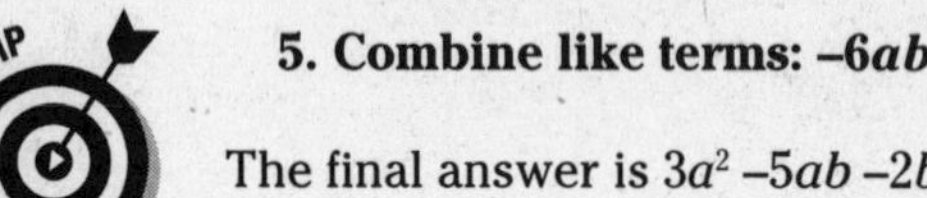

The final answer is $3a^2 -5ab -2b^2$.

You should out-and-out *memorize* the following three FOIL problems. Don't bother to work them out every time; know them by heart.

$(a + b)^2 = a^2 + 2ab + b^2$

You can prove this equation by using FOIL: $(a + b)(a + b)$

1. **Multiply the *First* terms: $a \times a = a^2$.**
2. **Multiply the *Outer* terms: $a \times b = ab$.**
3. **Multiply the *Inner* terms: $b \times a = ba$ (which is the same as ab).**
4. **Multiply the *Last* terms: $b \times b = b^2$.**
5. **Combine like terms: $ab + ab = 2ab$.**

The final solution is $a^2 + 2ab + b^2$.

$(a - b)^2 = a^2 - 2ab + b^2$

You can prove this equation by using FOIL: (a – b)(a – b)

1. **Multiply the *First* terms: $a \times a = a^2$.**
2. **Multiply the *Outer* terms: $a \times -b = -ab$.**
3. **Multiply the *Inner* terms: $-b \times a = -ba$ (which is the same as $-ab$).**
4. **Multiply the *Last* terms: $-b \times -b = +b^2$.**
5. **Combine like terms: $-ab + -ab = -2ab$.**

The final solution is $a^2 - 2ab + b^2$.

Be careful to note that the b^2 at the end is *positive,* not negative, because multiplying a negative times a negative gives a positive.

$(a - b)(a + b) = a^2 - b^2$

You can prove this equation by using FOIL: $(a - b)(a + b)$

1. **Multiply the *First* terms: $a \times a = a^2$.**
2. **Multiply the *Outer* terms: $a \times b = ab$.**
3. **Multiply the *Inner* terms: $-b \times a = -ba$ (which is the same as $-ab$).**
4. **Multiply the *Last* terms: $-b \times b = -b^2$.**
5. **Combine like terms: $ab + -ab = 0ab$.**

The final solution is $a^2 - b^2$. Note that the middle term drops out because $+ab$ cancels out $-ab$.

Again, *memorize* these three equations:

$$(a + b)^2 = a^2 + 2ab + b^2$$

$$(a - b)^2 = a^2 - 2ab + b^2$$

$$(a - b)(a + b) = a^2 - b^2$$

Doing so saves you time, careless mistakes, and acute misery on the actual exam.

Fact-or Fiction: Factoring

Now you know how to do algebra forward; are you ready to do it backward? You need to be able to factor down a ***quadratic equation*** (an equation with a variable to the second power) and take an algebraic expression from its final form back to its original form of two sets of parentheses.

Given $x^2 + 13x + 42 = 0$, solve for x. Take this problem one step at a time.

1. **Draw two sets of parentheses.**

   $(\ \ )(\ \ ) = 0$

2. **You know that to get x^2, the *First* terms have to be x and x. Fill those in.**

   $(x\ \ )(x\ \ ) = 0$

3. **Look now at the *Outer* terms.**

   You need two numbers that multiply together to be +42. Well, there are several possibilities: 42×1, 21×2, or 6×7. You can even have two negative numbers: -42×-1, -21×-2, or -6×-7. You aren't sure which numbers to choose yet. Go on to the next step.

4. **Look at the *Inner* terms.**

   You have to add two values to get +13. What's the first thing that springs to mind? 6 + 7, probably. Hey, that's one of the possibilities in the preceding step! Plug it in and try it.

   $(x + 6)(x + 7) = x^2 + 7x + 6x + 42 = x^2 + 13x + 42$

5. **Great, but you're not done yet. If the whole equation equals 0, then either $(x + 6) = 0$ or $(x + 7) = 0$.**

   That's because any number times 0 equals 0. Therefore, x can equal -6 or -7.

Again, if you have a multiple-choice problem, you can simply try the answer choices. Never start doing a lot of work until you absolutely have to.

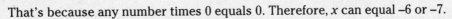

Hip to Be Square: Roots and Radicals

To simplify working with square roots (or cube roots or any roots), think of them as variables. You work the same way with $\sqrt{7}$ as you do with x, y, or z.

Addition and subtraction

1. To add or subtract *like radicals* (for the purpose of this exam, think of "radicals" as "roots"), add or subtract the number in front of the radical (your old friend, the numerical coefficient).

$2\sqrt{7}+5\sqrt{7}=7\sqrt{7}$ $2x+5x=7x$

$9\sqrt{13}-4\sqrt{13}=5\sqrt{13}$ $9x-4x=5x$

2. You *cannot* add or subtract unlike radicals (just as you cannot add or subtract unlike variables).

$6\sqrt{5}+4\sqrt{3}=6\sqrt{5}+4\sqrt{3}$. You cannot add the two and get $10\sqrt{8}$.

$6x + 4y = 6x + 4y$. You cannot add the two and get $10xy$.

Don't glance at a problem, see that the radicals are not the same, and immediately assume that you cannot add the two terms. You may be able to simplify one radical to make it match the radical in the other term.

$\sqrt{52}+\sqrt{13}=2\sqrt{13}+\sqrt{13}=3\sqrt{13}$

1. Begin by simplifying. Take out a perfect square from the term.

$\sqrt{52}=\sqrt{4}\times\sqrt{13}$

2. Because $\sqrt{4}=2$, $\sqrt{52}=2\sqrt{13}$.

Look at this one:

$\sqrt{20}+\sqrt{45}=(\sqrt{4}\times\sqrt{5})+(\sqrt{9}\times\sqrt{5})=2\sqrt{5}+3\sqrt{5}=5\sqrt{5}$

You must simplify *first.* You can't say that $\sqrt{20}+\sqrt{45}=\sqrt{65}=8.06$. When you work out the correct answer, $5\sqrt{5}$, you see that it's not 8.06 but 11.18.

Multiplication and division

Just do it. When you multiply or divide radicals, you just multiply or divide the numbers and then pop the radical sign back onto the finished product.

$\sqrt{5}\times\sqrt{6}=\sqrt{30}$

$\sqrt{15}\div\sqrt{5}=\sqrt{3}$

If you have a number in front of the radical, multiply it as well. Let everyone in on the fun.

$6\sqrt{3}\times4\sqrt{2}=$

$6\times4=24$

$\sqrt{3}\times\sqrt{2}=\sqrt{6}$

$24\sqrt{6}$

Here's a pretty typical problem: $37\sqrt{5}\times3\sqrt{6}$

F. $40\sqrt{11}$

G. $40\sqrt{30}$

H. $111\sqrt{11}$

J. $111\sqrt{30}$

K. 1,221

This problem takes straightforward multiplication: $37 \times 3 = 111$ and $\sqrt{5} \times \sqrt{6} = \sqrt{30}$, so $111\sqrt{30}$. *Correct Answer:* J.

Inside out

When there is an operation under the radical, do it first and then take the square root.

$$\sqrt{\frac{x^2}{40} + \frac{x^2}{9}}$$

First, solve for $x^2/40 + x^2/9$. You get the common denominator of 360 (40×9) and then find the numerators: $9x^2 + 40x^2 = 49x^2/360$. *Now* take the square roots: $\sqrt{49x^2} = 7x$ (because $7x \times 7x = 49x^2$). $\sqrt{360} = 18.97$. Gotcha, I bet! Did you say that $\sqrt{360} = 6$? Wrong! $\sqrt{36} = 6$, but $\sqrt{360}$ = approximately 18.97. Beware of assuming too much; you can be led down the path to temptation.

By the way, you don't really have to do square roots. The answer choices will be far enough apart for you to estimate. It's a good idea, however, to know the perfect squares of numbers from 1 to 20. If you know, for example, that $19 \times 19 = 361$, you know that the square root of 360 is just slightly less than 19.

Your final answer is $7x/18.97$. Of course, you can bet that the answer choices will include $7x/6$.

Probably Probability

Probability questions are usually word problems. They may look intimidating, with a lot of words that make you lose sight of where to begin. Two simple rules can solve nearly every probability problem that the ACT tosses at you.

Rule 1: Create a fraction

To find a probability, use this formula:

$$P = \frac{\text{Number of possible desired outcomes}}{\text{Number of total possible outcomes}}$$

Make a probability into a fraction. The denominator is the easier of the two parts to begin with. The *denominator* is the total possible number of outcomes. For example, when you're flipping a coin, there are two possible outcomes, giving you a denominator of 2. When you're tossing a die (one of a pair of dice), there are six possible outcomes, giving you a denominator of 6. When you're pulling a card out of a deck of cards, there are 52 possible outcomes (52 cards in a deck), giving you a denominator of 52. When 25 marbles are in a jar and you're going to pull out one of them, there are 25 possibilities, giving you a denominator of 25. Very simply, the denominator is the whole shebang — everything possible.

The *numerator* is the total number of the things you want. If you want a head when you toss a coin, there is exactly one head, giving you a numerator of 1. Your chances of tossing a head, therefore, are $^1/_2$, one possible head, two possible outcomes altogether. If you want to get a 5 when you toss a die, there is exactly one 5 on the die, giving you a numerator of 1. Notice that your numerator is *not* 5. The number you want happens to be a 5, but there is only *one* 5 on the die. The probability of tossing a 5 is $^1/_6$: There are one 5 and six possible outcomes altogether.

If you want to draw a jack in a deck of cards, there are four jacks: hearts, diamonds, clubs, and spades. Therefore, the numerator is 4. The probability of drawing a jack out of a deck of cards is $^4/_{52}$ (which reduces to $^1/_{13}$). If you want to draw a jack of hearts, the probability is $^1/_{52}$ because there is only one jack of hearts.

A jar of marbles has 8 yellow marbles, 6 black marbles, and 12 white marbles. What is the probability of drawing out a black marble?

Use the formula. Begin with the denominator, which is all the possible outcomes: $8 + 6 + 12 = 26$. The numerator is how many there are of what you want: six black marbles. The probability is $^6/_{26}$, which can be reduced or (as is more customary) changed to a percentage. The correct answer is $^6/_{26}$, or $^3/_{13}$, or 23 percent. What's the probability of drawing out a yellow marble? $^8/_{26}$, or $^4/_{13}$. A white marble? $^{12}/_{26}$, or $^6/_{13}$.

A drawer contains 5 pairs of white socks, 8 pairs of black socks, and 12 pairs of brown socks. In a hurry to get to school, Austin pulls out a pair at a time and tosses them on the floor if they are not the color he wants. Looking for a brown pair, Austin pulls out and discards a white pair, a black pair, a black pair, and a white pair. What is the probability that on his next reach into the drawer he will pull out a brown pair of socks?

This problem is slightly more complicated than the preceding one, although it uses the same formula. You began with 25 pairs of socks. However, Austin, that slob, has thrown four pairs on the floor. That means that there are only 21 pairs left. The probability of his pulling out a brown pair is $^{12}/_{21}$, or $^4/_7$, or about 57 percent.

A cookie jar contains chocolate, vanilla, and strawberry wafer cookies. There are 30 of each type. Bess reaches in, pulls out a chocolate and eats it, and then in quick succession pulls out and eats a vanilla, a chocolate, a strawberry, a strawberry, a chocolate, and a vanilla. Assuming that she doesn't get sick or get caught, what is the probability that the next cookie she pulls out will be a chocolate one?

Originally, there were 90 cookies. Bess has scarfed down 7 of them, leaving 83. Careful! If you're about to put $^{30}/_{83}$, you're headed for a trap. There are no longer 30 chocolate cookies; there are only 27, because Bess has eaten 3. The probability is now $^{27}/_{83}$, or about 33 percent.

Probability must always be between 0 and 1. You cannot have a negative probability, and you cannot have a probability greater than 1, or 100 percent.

Rule 2: Multiply consecutive probabilities

What is the probability that you'll get two heads when you toss a coin twice? You find each probability separately and then *multiply* the two. The chance of tossing a coin the first time and getting a head is $^1/_2$. The chance of tossing a coin the second time and getting a head is $^1/_2$. Multiply those consecutive probabilities: $^1/_2 \times {}^1/_2 = {}^1/_4$. The chances of getting two heads is 1 out of 4.

What is the probability of tossing a die twice and getting a 5 on the first toss and a 6 on the second toss? Treat each toss separately. The probability of getting a 5 is $^1/_6$. The probability of getting a 6 is $^1/_6$. Multiply consecutive probabilities: $^1/_6 \times {}^1/_6 = {}^1/_{36}$.

The Stats Don't Lie: Statistics

Don't panic; the ACT tests your skill with statistics in only the most rudimentary way. If you can master three basic concepts, you can do any statistics on this exam. Those concepts are median, mode, and range.

Median

Simply put, the ***median*** is the middle number when all the terms are arranged in order. Think of the median strip, which is the middle of the road. Median = middle. Be sure that you arrange the numbers in order (increasing or decreasing, it makes no difference) before you find the median.

Find the median of –3, 18, –4, $^1/_2$, 11.

A. –3

B. 18

C. –4

D. $^1/_2$

E. 11

Put the numbers in order: –4, –3, $^1/_2$, 11, 18. The one in the middle, $^1/_2$, is the median. It's as simple as that. *Correct Answer:* D.

Mode

The ***mode*** is the most frequent number. I suggest that you put the numbers in order again. Then look for the one that shows up the most often. It's the mode.

Find the mode of 11, 18, 29, 17, 18, –4, 0, 11, 18.

F. 11

G. 17

H. 18

J. 19

K. 29

The question has three 18s but no more than two of any other number. *Correct Answer:* H.

Range

The ***range*** is the distance from the greatest to the smallest. In other words, you subtract the smallest term from the largest term, and you have the range.

Find the range of the numbers 11, 18, 29, 17, 18, –4, 0, 11, 18.

A. 33

B. 29

C. 19

D. 0

E. –4

Ah, did this one getcha? True, 33 is not one of the numbers in the set. But to find the range, subtract the smallest from the largest number: 29 – (–4) = 29 + 4 = 33. *Correct Answer:* A.

Trig-O-Trivia: A few soothing words

Don't know a sine from a sign? Don't worry about it. The ACT has only four trigonometry questions. If you guess wildly at all four, you'll probably get at least one correct. (You should always guess, because the ACT has no penalty for wrong answers.) This means that a total lack of trig is likely to cost you only three questions, which translates to only one or two points on the mathematics scale and half a point or less on the composite score scale. In other words, you can still get a great ACT score, get into a good college, have an excellent career, win a Nobel prize or two, marry a movie star, and rear children who find the cure for cancer, all without knowing the first thing about trigonometry. Feel better now?

The only trap you are likely to see in the statistics questions is in the answer choices. The questions themselves are quite straightforward, but the answer choices may assume that some people don't know one term from another. For example, one answer choice to a median question may be the mean (the average). One answer choice to a range question may be the mode. In each question, circle the word that tells you what you're looking for to keep from falling for this trap.

Don't Soak Your Head: SOH CAH TOA

You can go a long way in trigonometry with just a few basic points. The most important thing to know is the name of the famous Native American chief and skilled mathematician, SOH CAH TOA.

SOH CAH TOA stands for

Sine = Opposite/Hypotenuse

Cosine = Adjacent/Hypotenuse

Tangent = Opposite/Adjacent

Are you scratching your head now and saying, "Opposite? Opposite *what?*" Take a look at the following right triangle:

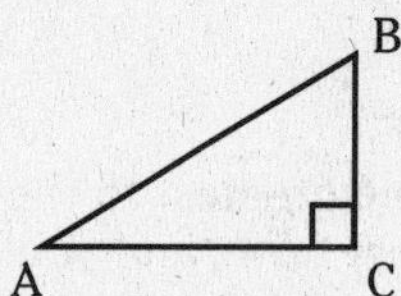

1. **Side AB is the hypotenuse.**

   It is the longest side of the right triangle, the side opposite the right angle.

2. **To find sin A (sine is usually abbreviated to *sin;* the terms mean the same thing), all you need to do is find the length of side BC and divide it by the length of the hypotenuse.**

   This is because $\sin A = \frac{\text{opposite A}}{\text{hypotenuse}}$, and side BC is opposite A. It follows that $\sin A = \frac{\text{opposite A}}{\text{hypotenuse}}$, which in turn is equal to $\frac{\text{length of BC}}{\text{length of AB}}$.

3. To find cos A (*cosine* is usually abbreviated to *cos;* the terms mean the same thing), find the length of side AC and use the CAH part of SOH CAH TOA.

$$\text{Cos A} = \frac{\text{adjacent A}}{\text{hypotenuse}} \text{ which in turn equals } \frac{\text{length of AC}}{\text{length of AB}}.$$

4. To find tan A (yes, tangent is usually abbreviated to *tan;* they mean the same thing), use the TOA part of SOH CAH TOA:

$$\text{Tan A} = \frac{\text{opposite A}}{\text{adjacent A}} \text{ which in turn is equal to } \frac{\text{length of BC}}{\text{length of AC}}.$$

Here's an example of just how far you can go when you SOH CAH TOA. What is sin A if $\tan A = \frac{9}{40}$?

F. $\frac{9}{41}$

G. $\frac{40}{41}$

H. $\frac{41}{40}$

J. $\frac{40}{9}$

K. $\frac{41}{9}$

Because $\tan A = \frac{9}{40}$, you can draw a picture with opposite A = 9 and adjacent A = 40.

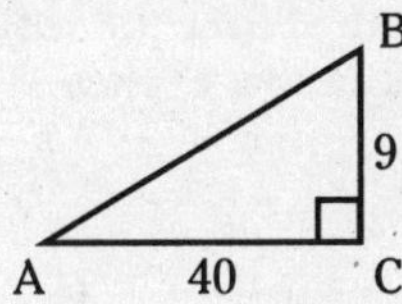

Use the Pythagorean Theorem to determine the length of hypotenuse AB:

$9^2 + 40^2 = (AB)^2$

$1681 = (AB)^2$

$41 = AB$

$\text{Sin A} = \frac{\text{opposite A}}{\text{hypotenuse}}$, so $\sin A = \frac{9}{41}$.

You could have eliminated choices H, J, and K immediately if you realized that the sin cannot be greater than 1. *Correct Answer:* F.

5. $\text{Sin} = \frac{\text{opposite}}{\text{hypotenuse}}$. No side in a triangle can be greater than the hypotenuse, so this makes it impossible to have a sin greater than 1.

6. $\text{Cos} = \frac{\text{adjacent}}{\text{hypotenuse}}$. The side adjacent cannot be greater than the hypotenuse, so cos cannot be greater than 1.

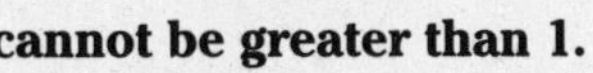

TIP

That's so important that I'm repeating it here as a tip for you to burn into your brain: **A sin and a cos cannot be greater than 1.**

Let's make things a little more interesting. What if you were asked for secant A (also called sec A), cosecant A (also called csc A), or cotangent A (known to his friends as cot A) in the preceding example? Just remember the following:

$$\sec A = \frac{1}{\cos A}$$

$$\csc A = \frac{1}{\sin A}$$

$$\cot A = \frac{1}{\tan A}$$

Therefore, because $\cos A = \frac{40}{41}$, $\sec A = \frac{41}{40}$. $\text{Sin } A = \frac{9}{41}$, so $\csc A + \frac{40}{9}$, and $\cot A = \frac{40}{9}$ because $\tan A = \frac{9}{40}$.

How to Use All This Junk: Trigonometric Ratios of Angles

You can combine SOH CAH TOA with some basic geometry knowledge to figure out the trigonometric ratios of some key angles.

What is cos 30°? (***Note:*** On the real exam, you have multiple-choice answers. Here, I'm going to let you figure this out from scratch.)

Draw a 30:60:90 triangle. (Remember that the ratio is $s{:}s\sqrt{3}{:}2s$. I discuss this ratio in detail in the triangles section of the geometry review.)

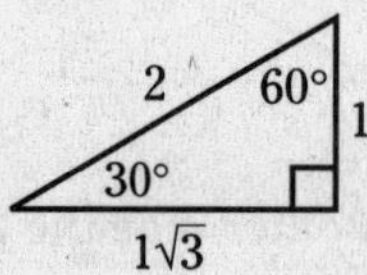

$\cos 30° = \text{adjacent } 30°/\text{hypotenuse}$, which equals $\sqrt{3}/2$.

What is tan 45°? (Again, remember the actual ACT has multiple-choice answer responses, but I want you to do this one all on your own.)

Draw a 45:45:90 triangle. Remember, the ratio of the sides of this triangle is $s{:}s{:}s\sqrt{2}$, where s stands for the length of the side. (I discuss this ratio in the triangles portion of the geometry review.)

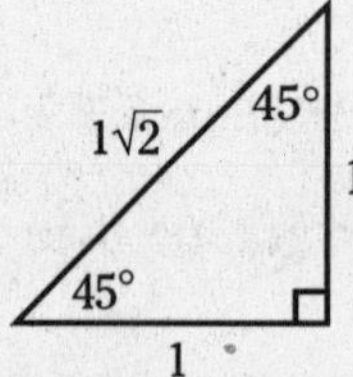

$\tan 45° = \text{opposite } 45°/\text{adjacent } 45° = 1/1 = 1$.

The Unit Circle

Knowing SOH CAH TOA will probably get you at least two of the four trig questions correct. To get you through the remaining questions, you probably need to know about the *unit circle.*

The unit circle received its catchy name because the radius is one unit. (That unit may be one inch, one foot, one whatever; you don't care. Just call it one unit.) Here it is with some key degree markers:

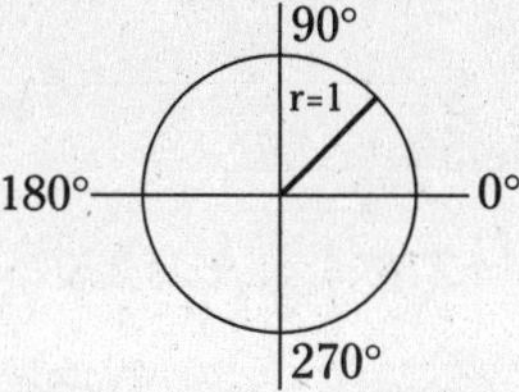

I used to have a trig teacher who would coyly say, "When is a radius not a radius? When it's a hypotenuse!" He was trying to make the point to us snoring students that a radius can serve as the hypotenuse of a right triangle. Identify the horizontal leg as *x* (as in *x*-axis) and the vertical leg as *y* (as in *y*-axis). The following illustration shows this concept, using a radius that is at a 45° angle with the 0° marker:

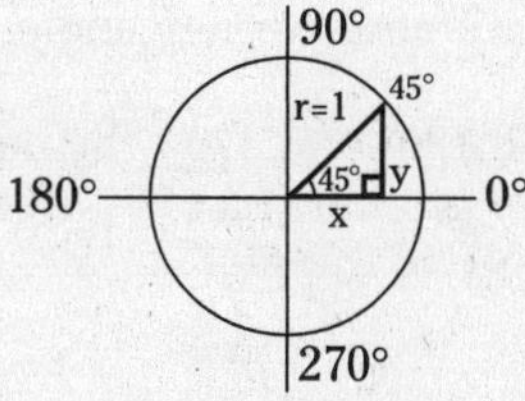

Think about SOH CAH TOA.

sin = opposite/hypotenuse = $y/1 = y$. In other words, sin = *y*, which is the vertical leg.

cos = adjacent/hypotenuse = $x/1 = x$. In other words, cos = *x*, which is the horizontal leg.

tan = opposite/adjacent = y/x.

Because this radius is 45° up from the 0° marker, the angle at the intersection of the two axes is 45°. This means that the triangle is a 45:45:90 triangle with a hypotenuse of 1. Because the ratio of sides in a 45:45:90 triangle is $s{:}s{:}s\sqrt{2}$, divide the hypotenuse by $\sqrt{2}$ to find the length of each leg. Here, that gives you $1/\sqrt{2}$.

The ACT doesn't usually accept a square root in the denominator, so you have to rationalize your answer. ("To rationalize your answer" doesn't mean to justify to the teacher how on earth you came up with that answer, but to get rid of the root in the denominator.) Do so by multiplying both top and bottom by the square root:

$$\frac{1}{\sqrt{2}} \times \frac{\sqrt{2}}{\sqrt{2}} = \frac{\sqrt{2}}{2}$$

Because this is the value for both *x* and *y* and because cos = *x* and sin = *y*, $\cos\ 45° = \sin\ 45° = \left(\sqrt{2}\right)/2$. Tan 45° = y/x = 1.

Are you still with me? This stuff isn't as complicated as it looks, although you may have to read it over several times. If you're completely lost, don't worry about it. Go back and read the reassuring words with which the trig portion starts and remind yourself how few points trig counts for. If you're still following, congratulations, and let's go on.

A look at the unit circle readily reveals the trigonometric ratios for 0°, 90°, 180°, and 270°. At 0°, x is the same as the radius, so $x = 1$, which means that cos 0° = 1. What about the sin? Well, $y = 0$ at this point, so sin 0° = 0. Because tan = y/x, tan 0° = 0/1 = 0.

At 180°, the situation is similar to that at 0°, except that $x = -1$, sin 180° = 0, and $\tan 180° = \frac{0}{-1} = 0$.

At 90°, y is the same as the radius, so $y = 1$ and sin 90° = 1.

$x = 0$ at 90°, so cos 90° = 0.

$\text{Tan } 90° = \sqrt{1/0}$, which is undefined.

At 270°, $y = -1$, and $x = 0$, so sin 270° = –1, cos 270° = 0, and tan 270° = $\frac{-1}{0}$, which is undefined.

Take another look at the triangle with the dark line as the hypotenuse. According to the Pythagorean theorem, $x^2 + y^2 = 1^2$. Because cos = x and sin = y, you can substitute and get the useful trigonometric identity of

$$\sqrt{\cos\theta + \sin 2\theta} = 1$$

In case you were wondering, θ stands for any angle.

As you have already seen with 180° and 270°, the unit circle enables you to figure out the trigonometric ratios for angles greater than 90°. Here are a few more examples of how this knowledge can be useful to you on the ACT.

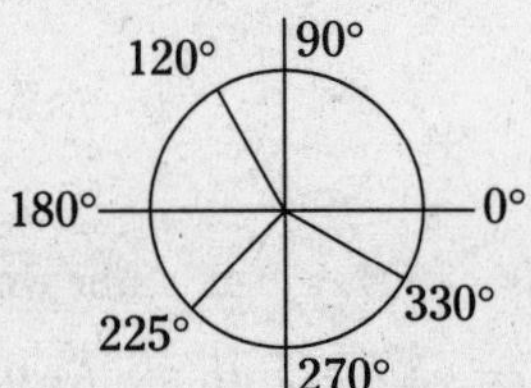

The 225° angle is 225° from the 0° marker, but it is useful to realize that it forms a 45° angle with the 180° marker. A 45° angle is something you have seen before. You just have to realize that both x and y are negative here in the third quadrant. Here is the essence of what you have:

$x = \frac{-\sqrt{2}}{2}$

45°

$y = \frac{-\sqrt{2}}{2}$

45°

r=1

From this, you can see that cos 225° (same as x) = sin 225° (same as y) = $-2/\sqrt{2}$. Tan 225° = y/x = 1.

Say that you needed to figure out cos 120°. This angle is 60° in a clockwise direction from the 180° marker. Here's basically what you have:

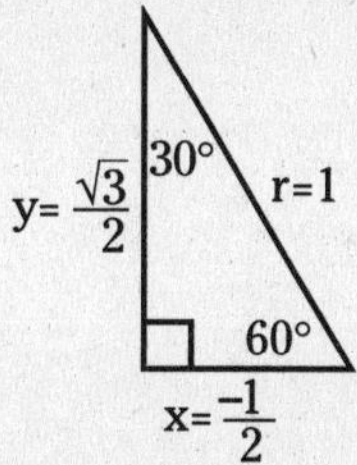

In a 30:60:90 triangle, the side opposite the 30° angle is 1/2 the hypotenuse. (You learned this in the triangles portion of the math review.) To figure the side opposite the 60° angle, simply multiply the side opposite the 30° angle by $\sqrt{3}$. Note that *x* is negative because it is to the left of the origin.

From this diagram, you can see that $\cos\ 120^{\circ} = x = \sqrt{-1/2}$.

You figure sin 330° in a similar fashion. The angle is 30° clockwise from 0°. This is what you have:

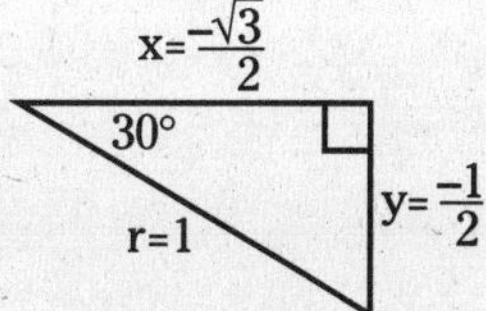

$\text{Sin}\ 330^{\circ} = y = \sqrt{-1/2}.$

No Nervous Breakdowns, Please

Let me end this section on trig the way I began it, with a few words of reassurance. With a little practice of the preceding material, you should be able to handle just about anything the test-makers throw at you on the ACT. (And remember, the answer explanations to the trig problems in the practice exams repeat all this info and take you through everything step by step.) If you're still confused after those exams or are concerned about some of the more advanced trigonometry that has only a very slight chance of appearing on the test, don't worry. Keep chanting to yourself, "Only four, no more; only four, no more." The entire ACT has only four trig problems. Trigonometry will not make or break your ACT score.

Chapter 9

Miscellaneous Math You Probably Already Know

In This Chapter

- Time, rate, and distance problems
- Averages
- Percentages
- Number sets and prime and composite numbers
- Mixture, interest, and work problems
- Order of operations
- Units of measurement
- Decimals and fractions

Even though you may already know most or all of the math discussed in this chapter, it never hurts to refresh your memory. These questions tend to be the easiest, so they offer you the best chance for a correct answer. Brush up on your miscellaneous math, and you're sure to improve your score on the math section of the ACT.

DIRTy Math: Time, Rate, and Distance

Let's dish the dirt here, shall we? D.I.R.T. Distance Is Rate × Time. $D = RT$. When you have a time, rate, and distance problem, use this formula. Make a chart with the formula across the top and fill in the spaces on the chart.

Jennifer drives 40 mph for $2^1/_2$ hours. Her friend Ashley goes the same distance but drives at $1^1/_2$ times Jennifer's speed. How many minutes longer does Jennifer drive than Ashley?

Do *not* start making big, hairy formulas with *x*s and *y*s. Make the DIRT chart.

	Distance	=	**Rate**	×	**Time**
Jennifer	100		40 mph		$2^1/_2$ hours
Ashley	100		60 mph		100 minutes

When you fill in the 40 mph and $2^1/_2$ hours for Jennifer, you can calculate that she went 100 miles. Think of it this simple way: If she goes 40 mph for one hour, that's 40 miles. For a second hour, she goes another 40 miles. In a half hour, she goes $^1/_2$ of 40, or 20 miles. (See? You don't have to write down $40 \times 2^1/_2$ and do all that pencil-pushing; use your brain, not your yellow No. 2.) Add them together: 40 + 40 + 20 = 100. Jennifer has gone 100 miles.

Because Ashley drives the same distance, fill in 100 under distance for her. She goes $1^1/_2$ times as fast. Uh-uh, put down that calculator. Use your brain! 1×40 is 40; $^1/_2 \times 40$ is 20. Add $40 + 20 = 60$. Ashley drives 60 mph. Now this gets really easy. If she drives at 60 mph, she drives one mile a minute. (60 minutes in an hour, 60 miles in an hour. You figure it out, Einstein.) Therefore, to go 100 miles takes her 100 minutes. Because the question asks for your final answer in minutes, don't bother converting this to hours; leave it the way it is.

Last step. Jennifer drives $2^1/_2$ hours. How many minutes is that? Do it the easy way, in your brain. One hour is 60 minutes. A second hour is another 60 minutes. A half hour is 30 minutes. Add them together: $60 + 60 + 30 = 150$ minutes. If Jennifer drives for 150 minutes and Ashley drives for 100 minutes, Jennifer drives 50 minutes more than Ashley. However, Ashley gets a speeding ticket, has her driving privileges taken away by an irate father, and doesn't get to go to this weekend's party. Jennifer goes and gets her pick of the hunks, ending up with Tyrone's ring and letterman's sweater. The moral of the story: Slow . . . but steady!

Be careful to note whether the people are traveling in the *same* direction or in *opposite* directions. Suppose that you're asked how far apart drivers are at the end of their trip. If you're told that Jordan travels 40 mph east for 2 hours and Connor travels 60 mph west for 3 hours, they are going in opposite directions. If they start from the same point at the same time, Jordan has gone 80 miles one way, and Connor has gone 180 miles the opposite way. They are 260 miles apart. The trap answer is 100, because careless people (not *you*!) simply subtract $180 - 80$.

It All Averages Out: Averages

You can always do averages the way Ms. Jones taught you when you were in third grade: Add all the terms and then divide by the number of terms. Or you can save wear-and-tear on the brain cells and know the following rules:

1. The average of evenly spaced terms is the middle term.

$5 + 11 + 17 + 23 + 29 = 85$

$^{85}/_5 = 17$

First, check that the terms are evenly spaced. That means that there is an equal number of units between each term. Here, the terms are six apart. Second, circle the middle term, which here is 17. Third, go home, make popcorn, and watch the late-night movie with all the time you've saved.

Try another one. Find the average of 32, 41, 50, 59, 68, 77, 86, 95, and 104.

You look and see that the terms are all nine units apart. Because they are evenly spaced, the middle term is the average: 68.

This is an easy trick to love, but don't march down the aisle with it yet. The tip works only for *evenly spaced* terms. If you have just any old batch of numbers, such as 4, 21, 97, 98, and 199, you can't look at the middle term for the average. You have to find the average of those numbers the old-fashioned way.

Find the average of these numbers: 3, 10, 17, 24, 31, 38, 45, and 52.

First, double-check that they are evenly spaced. Here, the numbers are spaced by sevens. Next you look for the middle number . . . and there isn't one. You can, of course, find the two central terms, 24 and 31, and find the middle between them. That works, but what a pain. Not only that, but suppose that you have 38 numbers. It's very easy to make a mistake as to which term is the central one. If you're off just a little bit, you miss the question. Instead, use rule number two.

2. The average of evenly spaced terms is $^{(\text{first + last})}/_2$.

Just add the first and the last terms, which are obvious at a glance, and divide that sum by 2.

$3 + 52 = 55$

$^{55}/_2 = 27.5$

Note: Double-check by using your common sense. Suppose that you made a silly mistake and got 45 for your answer. A glance at the numbers tells you that 45 is not in the middle and therefore cannot be the average.

This tip works for *all* evenly spaced terms. It doesn't matter whether there is a middle number, as in the first example, or no middle number, as in the second example. Go back to the earlier example.

32, 41, 50, 59, 68, 77, 86, 95, 104

Instead of finding the middle term, add the first and last terms and divide by 2, like this:

$32 + 104 = 136$

$^{136}/_2 = 68$

Either way works.

Missing term average problem

You are likely to find a problem like this:

Jeanette takes seven exams. Her scores on the first six are 91, 89, 85, 92, 90, and 88. If her average on all *seven* exams is 90, what did she get on the seventh exam?

This problem is called a ***missing term average problem*** because you are given an average and asked to find a missing term. Duh.

1. You can do this the basic algebraic way: Average = $^{\text{Sum}}/_{\text{Number of terms}}$

$90 = {}^{\text{Sum}}/_7$

Because you don't know the seventh term, call it x. Add the first six terms (and get 535) and x.

$90 = {}^{(535 + x)}/_7$

Cross-multiply: $90 \times 7 = 535 + x$

$630 = 535 + x$

$95 = x$

The seventh exam score was 95.

2. There is another quick way to do this problem: the Cancellation Boogie. You've probably done it this way all your life without realizing what a genius you are.

Suppose that your dad tells you that if you average a 90 for the semester in advanced physics, he'll let you buy that motorcycle the two of you have been arguing about for months. (He figures he's safe because there's no way you're going to get such a high grade in that incredibly difficult class.) You take him at his word and begin working hard.

On the first exam, you get 91, and you're +1 point. That is, you're 1 point above the ultimate score you want, a 90.

On the second exam, you get 89 and you're –1. On that test, you're 1 point below the ultimate score you want, a 90.

On the third exam, you get an 85, which is –5. You're 5 points below the ultimate score you want, a 90.

Are you getting the hang of this? Here's how it looks (using the scores from Jeanette's exams).

91 = +1

89 = –1

85 = –5

92 = +2

90 = 0

88 = –2

The +1 and –1 cancel each other out, and the +2 and –2 cancel each other out. You're left with –5; you're 5 points in the hole. You have to make up those 5 points on the last exam or get 5 points *above* what you want for your ultimate score. Because you want a 90, you need a 95 on the last test.

Try another example, using the no-brainer method. Ray takes seven exams. He gets an 88 average on all of them. His first six scores are 89, 98, 90, 82, 88, and 87. What does he get on the seventh exam?

Average = 88

89 = +1

98 = +10

90 = +2

82 = –6

88 = 0

87 = –1

The +1 and the –1 cancel. Then Ray has (10 + 2) = +12 and –6, for a total of +6. He is 6 points *above* what he needs for the ultimate outcome. He can afford to lose 6 points on the final exam, or be 6 points *below* the average. That gives him an 82.

You may be given only five out of seven scores and asked for *the average of the missing two terms.* Do the same thing and then divide by 2.

Average of seven exams: 85

Scores of the first five exams: 86, 79, 82, 85, 84

Find: The average score of each of the remaining exams

Algebraic way: $85 = \dfrac{(86+79+82+85+84)+x+x}{7}$

Cross-multiply: $595 = 416 + 2x$

$595 - 416 = 2x$

$179 = 2x$

$89.5 = x$

Cancellation Boogie way: Average = 85

86 = +1

79 = –6

82 = –3

85 = 0

84 = –1

The +1 and –1 cancel each other out. You're left with –9 for *two* exams or –4.5 per exam. If you are *down* $4^1/_2$ points, you must *gain* those $4^1/_2$ points on each of the two exams:

85 + 4.5 = 89.5

The shortcut, commonsense way is quick and easy, but don't forget to make the change at the end. That is, if you decide that you are *–8* points going into the final exam, you need to be *+8* points on that last exam to come out even. If you subtract 8 points from the average rather than add them, you'll probably come up with one of the trap answers.

Weighted averages

In a ***weighted average***, some scores count more than others.

Number of Students	Score
12	80
13	75
10	70

If you are asked to find the average score for the students in this class, you know that you cannot simply add 80, 75, and 70 and divide by 3, because the scores weren't evenly distributed among the students. Because 12 students got an 80, multiply 12 × 80 = 960. Do the same with the other scores:

13 × 75 = 975

10 × 70 = 700

960 + 975 + 700 = 2635

Divide *not by 3* but by the total number of students: 35 (12 + 13 + 10)

$^{2635}/_{35}$ = 75.29

Percentage Panic

The mere mention of the word *percentage* may strike terror in your heart. There's no reason to panic over percentages; there are ways of getting around them.

1. **The first way is to ignore their very existence. You can express a percentage as a decimal, which is a lot less intimidating. You do so by putting a decimal point two places to the left of the percentage and dropping the percent sign.**

- 35% = .35
- 83% = .83
- 50% = .50
- 33.3% = .333
- 66.6% = .666

If you have a choice of working with percentages or decimals, it's better to choose decimals (in my humble opinion).

2. **Another way to ignore a percentage is to convert it to a fraction. The word *percent* means *per cent,* or *per hundred.* Every percentage is that number over 100.**

   - 50% = $^{50}/_{100}$
   - 33% = $^{33}/_{100}$
   - 75% = $^{75}/_{100}$

If you can't ignore the percentage, remember that a percent is $^{\text{part}}/_{\text{whole}} \times 100$, or $^{\text{is}}/_{\text{of}} \times 100$.

What percent *is* 45 *of* 90? Put the part, 45, over the whole, 90. Or put the *is,* 45, over the *of,* 90:

$$^{45}/_{90} = {}^{1}/_{2} \times 100 = {}^{100}/_{2} = 50\%$$

42 *is* what percent *of* 126? Put the part, 42, over the whole, 126. Or put the *is,* 42, over the *of,* 126.

$$^{42}/_{126} = {}^{1}/_{3} \times 100 = {}^{100}/_{3} = 33^{1}/_{3}\%$$

Here's a slightly harder one: What is 40% of 80? You may be tempted to put the *is,* 40, over the *of,* 80, and get $^{40}/_{80} = {}^{1}/_{2} \times 100 = {}^{100}/_{2} = 50\%$. However, when the problem is worded this way ("what is x% of y?" rather than "what % is x of y?"), you don't know the *is.* Your equation must be: $^{x}/_{80} = {}^{40}/_{100}$. Cross-multiply: $3200 = 100x$. $x = 32$. There's an easier way to do it: *of* means times, or multiply. Because 40% = .40, multiply that by 80 to get 32.

Life has its ups and downs: Percent increase/decrease

You may see a problem asking you what percent increase or decrease occurred in the number of games a team won or the amount of commission a person earned. To find a percent increase or decrease, use this formula:

$$\text{percent increase or decrease} = \frac{\text{number increase or decrease}}{\text{original whole}}$$

In basic English, to find the percent by which something has increased or decreased, you take two simple steps:

1. **Find the *number* (amount) by which the thing has increased or decreased.**

   For example, if a team won 25 games last year and 30 games this year, the number increase was 5. If a salesperson earned $10,000 last year and $8,000 this year, the number decrease was 2,000. Make that the numerator of the fraction.

2. **Find the *original whole*.**

   This figure is what you started out with before you increased or decreased. If a team won 25 games last year and won 30 games this year, the original number was 25. If the salesperson earned $10,000 last year and $8,000 this year, the original number was 10,000. Make that the denominator.

3. **You now have a fraction. Make it a decimal and multiply by 100 to make it a percentage.**

In 1992, Coach Denges won 30 prizes at the county fair by tossing a basketball into a bushel basket. In 1993, he won 35 prizes. What was his percent increase?

A. 100

B. 30

C. $16^2/_3$

D. 14.28

E. $.1\overline{66}$

The number by which his prizes increased, from 30 to 35, is 5. That is the numerator. The original whole, or what he began with, is 30. That is the denominator. $^5/_{30} = ^1/_6 = 16^2/_3\%$. *Correct Answer:* C.

If you chose E, I fooled you. The question asks what *percent* increase there was. If you say E, you're saying that the increase was .166%. Not so. The .166 increase *as a percentage* is $16^2/_3\%$. If you chose D, you fell for another trap. You put the 5 increase over the 35 instead of over the 30.

Two years ago, Haylie scored 22 goals at soccer. This year, she scored 16 goals. What was her approximate percentage decrease?

F. 72

G. 37.5

H. 27

J. 16

K. .27

Find the number of the decrease: 22 – 16 = 6. That is the numerator. Find the original whole from which she is decreasing: 22. That is the denominator. $^6/_{22} = .27$, or approximately 27 percent. *Correct Answer:* H.

If you chose F, you put 16 over 22 instead of putting the decrease over the original whole. If you chose K, you forgot the difference between .27 and .27 *percent.* If you chose G, you put the decrease of 6 over the new amount, 16, rather than over the original whole. Note how easy these traps are to fall for. My suggestion: Write down the actual formula and then plug in the numbers. Writing down the formula may be boring, but doing so takes only a few seconds and may save you points.

Here's a tricky question that many people do in their heads (instead of writing down the formula and plugging in numbers) and blow big-time. Carissa has three quarters. Her father gives her three more. Carissa's wealth has increased by what percent?

A. 50

B. 100

C. 200

D. 300

E. 500

Did you fall for the trap answer, C? Her wealth has doubled, to be sure, but the *percent* increase is only 100. You can prove that with the formula: The number increase is 75 (she has three more quarters, or 75 cents). Her original whole was 75. $^{75}/_{75}$ = 1 = 100%. *Correct Answer:* B.

Do not fall into the trap of assuming that a 200 percent increase means that something doubled. When you double something, you increase it by 100 percent because you have to subtract the original "one" you began with. When you triple something, you increase by 200 percent because you have to subtract the original you began with. If you had three dollars and you now have nine dollars, for example, you have tripled your money but increased it by only 200 percent. Do the formula:

number increase = 6 dollars

original whole = 3 dollars

$^{6}/_{3}$ = 2 = 200 percent

Take a wild guess at what percent you increase when you quadruple your money? That's right, 300 percent. Just subtract the original 100 percent.

Ready, Sets, Go: Number Sets

How can you solve a problem that asks you to "state your answer in integral values only" if you don't know what integral values are? Here are the number sets with which you'll be working. (I once got a call from a *very* irate parent, who misunderstood her child to say that I was teaching "number sex." Life as an ACT tutor is never dull.)

- **Counting numbers:** 1, 2, 3 . . . Note that 0 is *not* a counting number.
- **Whole numbers:** 0, 1, 2, 3 . . . Note that 0 *is* a whole number.
- **Integers:** . . . –3, –2, –1, 0, 1, 2, 3 . . . When a question asks for integral values, make sure that the answer is in integers only. For example, you can't give an answer like 4.3 because that's not an integer. You need to round down to 4.
- **Rational numbers:** Rational numbers can be expressed as $^{a}/_{b}$, where a and b are integers.

  Examples: 1 (because 1 = $^{1}/_{1}$ and 1 is an integer), $^{1}/_{2}$ (because 1 and 2 are integers), $^{9}/_{2}$ (because 9 and 2 are integers), and $–^{4}/_{2}$ (because –4 and 2 are integers).

  Notice that every number set so far has included the previous number sets. Whole numbers include counting numbers, integers include counting numbers and whole numbers, and rational numbers include counting numbers, whole numbers, and integers.

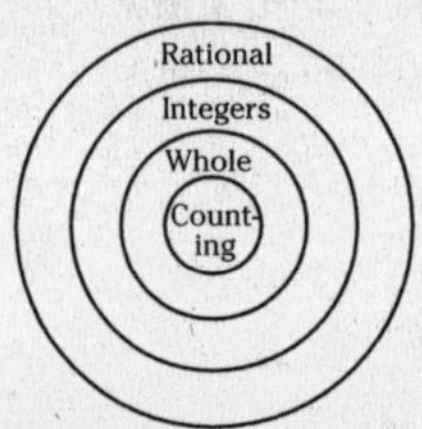

- **Irrational numbers:** The highly technical definition here is "anything not rational." That is, an irrational number cannot be written as a/b, where a and b are integers. Numbers that do not terminate and do not repeat cannot be written as fractions and therefore are irrational.

  Examples: π cannot be written exactly as 3.14; it is nonterminating and nonrepeating. $\sqrt{2}$ is approximately 1.4142 but is nonterminating and nonrepeating.

  Irrational numbers do not include the previous numbers sets. That is, irrational numbers *don't* include counting numbers, whole numbers, integers, and rational numbers.

- **Real numbers:** Briefly put, all of the above. Real numbers include counting numbers, whole numbers, integers, rationals, and irrationals. For all practical purposes, real numbers are everything you think of as numbers. When a question tells you to "express your answer in real numbers," don't sweat it. That's almost no constraint at all, because nearly every number you see is a real number.

Prime and Composite Numbers

1. ***Prime numbers*** **have exactly two factors; they cannot be divided by numbers other than 1 and themselves. Examples include 2, 3, 5, 7, and 11.**

   There are a few lovely tricks to prime numbers:

   - Zero is *not* a prime number. Why? Because it is divisible by more than two factors. Zero can be divided by 1, 2, 3, and on to infinity. Although division *by* zero is undefined (and isn't tested on the ACT), you *can* divide zero by other numbers; the answer, of course, is always zero. $0 \div 1 = 0$; $0 \div 2 = 0$; $0 \div 412 = 0$.
   - One is *not* a prime number. There are not two factors of 1. It cannot be divided only by 1 *and* itself. Confused? Don't worry about it. Just memorize that 1 is not a prime number.
   - Two is the *only* even prime. People tend to think that all prime numbers are odd. Well, almost. Two is prime because it has only two factors; it can be divided only by 1 and itself.
   - Not all odd numbers are prime. Think of 9 or 15; those numbers are odd but not prime, because they have more than two factors and can be divided by more than just 1 and themselves. $9 = (1 \times 9)$ and (3×3). $15 = (1 \times 15)$ and (3×5).

2. ***Composite numbers*** **have more than two factors and can be divided by more than just 1 and themselves. Examples include 4, 6, 8, 9, 12, 14, and 15.**

   Note that composite numbers (called that because they are *composed* of more than two factors) can be even or odd.

Don't confuse *even* and *odd* with *prime* and *composite*. That's an easy mistake to make in the confusion of the exam. If a problem that you know should be easy is flustering you, stop and ask yourself whether you're making this common mistake.

I said that 0 and 1 are not prime. They are also not composite. What are they? Neither. You express this as, "0 and 1 are neither prime nor composite."

I'm All Mixed Up: Mixture Problems

A mixture problem is a word problem that looks much more confusing than it actually is. There are two types of mixtures: those in which the items remain separate (when you mix peanuts and raisins, you still have peanuts and raisins, not pearains or raispeans) and those in which the two elements blend (these are usually chemicals, like water and alcohol). Check out the separate mixture type first.

> Marshall wants to mix 40 pounds of beads selling for 30 cents a pound with a quantity of sequins selling for 80 cents a pound. He wants to pay 40 cents per pound for the final mix. How many pounds of sequins should he use?

The hardest part for most students is knowing where to begin. Make a chart.

	Pounds	*Price*	*Total*
Beads	40	.30	$12.00
Sequins	x	.80	$.80x$
Mixture	$40 + x$	.40	$.40\,(40 + x)$

Reason it out. The cost of the beads (1200) plus the cost of the sequins ($80x$) must equal the cost of the mixture ($1600 + 40x$). Note that you dump the decimal point (officially, you multiply by 100 to get rid of the decimal point, but really you dump it). Now you have a workable equation:

$$1200 + 80x = 1600 + 40x$$

$$80x - 40x = 1600 - 1200$$

$$40x = 400$$

$$x = 10$$

Careful! Keep in mind what x stands for. It represents the number of pounds of sequins, what the question asks for.

Go back and double-check by plugging this value into the equation. You already know that Marshall spent $12 on beads. If he buys 10 pounds of sequins for 80 cents, he spends $8, for a total of $20. He spends that $20 on 50 pounds: $2000 \div 50 = 40$. How about that? It works!

With a multiple-choice question, it may be easier to plug in the answer choices and work backward through the problem. Don't forget that you have that option.

Greed Is Great: Interest Problems

A problem usually asks you how much interest someone earned on an investment. This is a pretty problem: PRTI, to be exact.

- P = Principal, the amount of money you begin with, or the amount you invest
- R = Rate, the interest rate you're earning on the money
- T = Time, the amount of time you leave the money in the interest-bearing account
- I = Interest, the amount of interest you earn on the investment

The formula is *PRT = I,* or *Principal* × *Rate* × *Time = Interest*

> Janet invested $1,000 at 5 percent annual interest for one year. How much interest did she earn?

This is the simplest type of problem. Plug the numbers into the formula.

> PRT = I
>
> 1000 × .05 × 1 = 50. She earned $50 interest.

The answer choices may try to trap you with variations on a decimal place, making the answers 5, 50, 500, and so on. You know that 5% = $^5/_{100}$ = .05; be careful how you multiply.

These problems are not intentionally vicious. You won't see something that gets crazy on interest rates, like "5 percent annual interest compounded quarterly for 3 months and 6 percent quarterly interest compounded daily," blah, blah, blah.

(Useless but fascinating trivia I learned on a trip a few years ago: In Bulgarian, the word for *thank you* is pronounced *blah-go-dah-ree-uh.* But a shortened form, like *thanks,* is simply *blah.* If your mother takes you to task for being a smart aleck and going "blah, blah, blah" when she talks, you can innocently claim that you're practicing your Bulgarian and are just thanking her for her wisdom.)

All Work and No Play: Work Problems

The formula most commonly used in a work problem is

$$\frac{\text{Time put in}}{\text{Capacity (or time to do the whole job)}}$$

Find each person's contribution. The denominator is the easy part; it represents how many hours (minutes, days, weeks, and so on) it would take the person to do the whole job, working alone. The numerator is how long the person has already worked. For example, if Janie can paint a house in six days and has been working for one day, she has done $^1/_6$ of the work. If Evelyn can paint a house in eight days and has been working for five, she has done $^5/_8$ of the project.

So far, so good. The problem comes when more than one person works at a task. What happens when Janie and Evelyn work together? Janie working alone can paint a house in six days. Evelyn working alone can paint it in eight days. Working together, how long will it take them to paint the house?

Find Janie's capacity: $^x/_6$. Find Evelyn's capacity: $^x/_8$. Together, the two fractions must add up to 1, the entire job.

> $^x/_6 + {}^x/_8 = 1$

Multiply by the common denominator, 48, to eliminate the fractions:

> $^{48x}/_6 + {}^{48x}/_8 = 48$
>
> $8x + 6x = 48$
>
> $14x = 48$

x = approximately 3.43. It would take the two women working together about 3.43 days to paint the house.

Double-check by using your common sense. If you get an answer of 10, for example, you know that you must have made a mistake, because the two women working together should be able to do the job *more quickly* than either one working alone.

Smooth Operator: Order of Operations

When you have several operations (addition, subtraction, multiplication, division, squaring, and so on) in one problem, you must perform the operations in a definite order:

1. **Parentheses.** Do what's inside the parentheses first.
2. **Power.** Do the squaring or the cubing, whatever the exponent is.
3. **Multiply or divide.** Do multiplication and division left to right. If multiplication is to the left of division, multiply first. If division is to the left of multiplication, divide first.
4. **Add or subtract.** Do addition and subtraction left to right. If addition is to the left of subtraction, add first. If subtraction is to the left of addition, subtract first.

An easy mnemonic (memory device) for remembering these is *Please Praise My Daughter And Son* (PPMDAS): Parentheses, Power, Multiply, Divide, Add, Subtract.

$$10(3-5)^2 + (^{30}/_5)^0 =$$

First, do what's inside the parentheses: $3 - 5 = -2$. $^{30}/_5 = 6$. Next, do the power: $-2^2 = 4$ and $6^0 = 1$. (Did you remember that any number to the 0 power equals 1?) Next, multiply: $10 \times 4 = 40$. Finally, add: $40 + 1 = 41$. *Correct Answer:* 41.

Try another:

$$3 + (9-6)^2 - 5(^8/_2)^{-2} =$$

First, do what's inside the parentheses: $9 - 6 = 3$ and $^8/_2 = 4$. Second, do the powers: $3^2 = 9$ and $4^{-2} = {^1/_{(4^2)}} = {^1/_{16}}$. Multiply: $5 \times {^1/_{16}} = {^5/_{16}}$. Finally, add and subtract left to right. $3 + 9 = 12$. $12 - {^5/_{16}} = 11^{11}/_{16}$. *Correct Answer:* $11^{11}/_{16}$.

Bonus: Speaking of mnemonics, here's my favorite. Can you tell me what it stands for?

My Very Educated Mother Just Served Us Nine Pickles.

Give up? It's the mnemonic of the planets in our solar system: Mercury, Venus, Earth, Mars, Jupiter, Saturn, Uranus, Neptune, Pluto.

Measuring Up: Units of Measurement

Occasionally, you may be expected to know a unit of measurement that the test-makers deem obvious but that you have forgotten. Take a few minutes to review this brief list.

Because the units of measurement in your native land may be different from these (especially pints and quarts and gallons), it's especially important that you memorize these units. I'd really hate to see you work through an entire question beautifully and then miss it because of an unfamiliarity with the units of measurement.

1. Time

- **60 seconds = 1 minute**
- **60 minutes = 1 hour**
- **24 hours = 1 day**
- **7 days = 1 week**
- **52 weeks = 1 year**
- **365 days = 1 year**
- **366 days = 1 leap year**

Leap year is an interesting concept in terms of math problems. It comes around every four years. The extra day, February 29, makes 366 days in the year. Why do you need to know this? Suppose that you see this problem:

> Mr. Pellaton's neon sign flashes four hours a day, every day all year, for four years. If it costs him three cents a day for electricity, how much will he owe for electricity at the end of the fourth year?

You may be tempted to say that this problem is super-easy — multiply 365 × 4 to find the number of days and then multiply that number by .03. Wrong-o! You forgot that extra day for leap year, and your answer is off by three cents. You *know* that the test-makers will have that wrong answer lurking among the answer choices just to trap you. Whenever there is a four-year period, look out for the leap year with an extra day.

2. Quantities

- **16 ounces = 1 pound**
- **2,000 pounds = 1 standard ton**
- **2 cups = 1 pint**
- **2 pints = 1 quart**
- **4 quarts = 1 gallon**

You can calculate that a gallon has 16 cups, or 8 pints. To help you remember, think of borrowing a cup of sugar, sugar is sweet, and you have a Sweet 16 birthday party: 16 sweet cups of sugar in a gallon. It may be silly, but the best memory aids usually are.

3. Length

- **12 inches = 1 foot**
- **3 feet (36 inches) = 1 yard**
- **5,280 feet (1,760 yards) = 1 mile**

Everyone knows that there are 12 inches in a foot. How many square inches are there in a square foot? If you say 12, you've fallen for the trap. 12 × 12 = 144 square inches in a square foot.

Bonus: How many cubic inches are there in a cubic foot? Not 12, and not even 144. A cubic foot is 12 × 12 × 12 = 1,728 cubic inches.

Broken Hearts, Broken Numbers: Fractions

Did you hear about the town so small it had a fraction as a zip code?

Adding or subtracting fractions

1. **You can add or subtract fractions only if they have the same denominator.**

   $^1/_3 + {}^4/_3 = {}^5/_3$

   $^3/_8 - {}^2/_8 = {}^1/_8$

2. **When fractions have the same denominator, add or subtract the numerators only.**
3. **When fractions don't have the same denominator, you have to find a common denominator.**

   You can, of course, multiply all the denominators, but that often doesn't give you the *lowest* common denominator. You end up with some humongous, overwhelming number that you'd rather not work with.

4. **To find the lowest (least) common denominator, identify the highest denominator and count by it.**

   Here's an example: Find the lowest common denominator of 15 and 6. Sure, you can multiply 15 × 6 = 90, but that's not the *lowest* common denominator. Instead, count by fifteens, because it's the larger of the two. 15? No, 6 doesn't go into that. 30? Yes, both 15 and 6 go into 30. That's the *lowest* common denominator.

   Try another problem. Find the lowest common denominator for 2, 4, and 5. Count by fives: 5? No, 2 and 4 don't go into it. 10? No, 2 and 4 don't go into it. 15? No, 2 and 4 don't go into it. 20? Yes, all the numbers divide evenly into 20.

   In many problems, you don't even have to find the lowest common denominator. You can find any common denominator by multiplying the denominators.

   $^4/_{15} + {}^1/_6 =$

   The common denominator is 15 × 6 = 90. Cross-multiply: 4 × 6 = 24. The first fraction becomes $^{24}/_{90}$. Cross-multiply: 1 × 15 = 15. The second fraction becomes $^{15}/_{90}$. Now add the numerators: 24 + 15 = 39. Put the sum over the common denominator: $^{39}/_{90}$. Can you reduce? Yes, by 3: $^{13}/_{30}$.

   Do the same thing when working with variables instead of numbers.

   $^a/_b - {}^c/_d =$

   Find the common denominator by multiplying the two denominators: $b \times d = bd$. Cross-multiply: $a \times d = ad$. Cross-multiply: $c \times b = cb$. Put the difference of the results of the cross-multiplication over the common denominator: $^{(ad - cb)}/_{bd}$.

Multiplying fractions

This is the easy one. Just do it. Multiply horizontally: Multiply the numerators and then multiply the denominators.

$$\frac{3}{4} \times \frac{2}{5} = \frac{(3 \times 2)}{(4 \times 5)} = \frac{6}{20} = \frac{3}{10}$$

Always check whether you can cancel before you begin working to avoid having to deal with big, awkward numbers and having to reduce at the end. In the preceding example, you can cancel the 4 and the 2, leaving you with

$$\frac{3}{\cancelto{2}{4}} \times \frac{\cancelto{1}{2}}{5} = \frac{(3 \times 1)}{(2 \times 5)} = \frac{3}{10}$$

You get to the right solution either way; canceling in advance just makes the numbers smaller and easier to work with.

Dividing fractions

To divide by a fraction, invert it (turn it upside down) and multiply.

$$\frac{1}{3} \div \frac{2}{5} = \frac{1}{3} \times \frac{5}{2} = \frac{5}{6}$$

Working with mixed numbers

A ***mixed number*** is a whole number with a fraction tagging along behind it, such as $2^1/_3$, $4^2/_5$, or $9^1/_2$. Multiply the whole number by the denominator and add that to the numerator. Put the sum over the denominator.

$2^1/_3 = (2 \times 3) + 1 = 7 \rightarrow {}^7/_3$

$4^2/_5 = (4 \times 5) + 2 = 22 \rightarrow {}^{22}/_5$

$9^1/_2 = (9 \times 2) + 1 = 19 \rightarrow {}^{19}/_2$

Part VI
Time to Read the Riot ACT: The Reading Test

The 5th Wave
By Rich Tennant
THEY'RE MOVING ON TO THE READING QUESTIONS. THAT SHOULD DAZE AND CONFUSE THEM ENOUGH FOR US TO FINISH CHANGING THE TIRE AND GET THE HECK OUT OF HERE.
ACT TEST BOOK PUBLISHERS

In this part . . .

How long have you been reading now: 10 years? 12 years? The purpose of this part is not to teach you how to read. I assume that you can sound out the words and make at least a little sense of the passages (although with some of *these* passages . . .). Instead, most of the material in this part discusses the types of questions you're going to encounter on the test and the traps built into them. After you learn the techniques of handling each question type, you get to put the techniques into action with a mini-reading test based on two abbreviated passages and eight questions.

Kids, don't try this at home! In other words, the reading passages in the ACT have little connection to the reading passages in the Real World, so don't try to use the information I give you here on your reading assignments at school. Learn the techniques, use them on the ACT, and then file them away under "Been there, done that."

Chapter 10

This Too Shall Pass(age): The Reading Test

In This Chapter

- 3,000 words of wisdom: The reading comprehension passages
- Questioning your sanity: The reading comprehension questions
- Illusion, delusion, and confusion: Tips and traps

Facing Forty (Questions): The Reading Test

I once had a student tell me, "If I'd known it would end up like this, I never would have let my first-grade teacher show me how to read!" Ah, we never know what consequences our actions will have someday. The first day with your ABCs led you straight to today's RC questions. (*RC* stands for reading comprehension.)

The Reading Test consists of four passages. Each passage is supposed to be similar in difficulty to materials you will encounter in your freshman year of college. The test contains one passage on each of the following topics:

- **Humanities.** This can be about music, dance, theater, art, architecture, language, ethics, literary criticism, and even philosophy. Most students tend to like these passages because they are actually (believe it or not) interesting.
- **Social Studies.** The social studies passage covers sociology, anthropology, history, geography, psychology, political science, and economics. That's an incredibly wide range of topics when you think about it. The history passages are usually pretty good; some of the psychology ones can be intense.
- **Natural Sciences.** This is what most of us think about when we say "science." The natural science passage can cover chemistry, biology, physics, and other physical sciences.

  Are you panicking right now, screaming, "I haven't taken physics! No fair!" Not to worry. The questions don't require you to know any particular subjects. Everything you need to answer the questions is right there in the passages, and you can go back to the passages as often as you like.
- **Prose Fiction.** The fiction passage can be taken from a novel or can be a short story. Some of these are very fun to read. But don't expect that you'll have read them before. In all the years I've been teaching, I've had only one student tell me she remembers having read the passage before in a novel. The ACT test-makers obviously don't want to test you on what you are familiar with (and maybe have even discussed in class), but on how well you evaluate a passage that is new to you.

Each passage has 10 questions, for a grand total of 40 questions.

Timing

The Reading Test is 35 minutes long. Assuming you live to an average age of 72, the Reading Test, therefore, is only about 1/1,081,975th of your life. Now that doesn't seem so bad, does it?

Scoring

You get three reading scores. One is the total score, based on all 40 questions. Then you get two subscores: one in Natural Sciences/Social Studies (based, obviously on those two passages) and one on Arts/Literature (based on those two passages).

Reading strategies

You've been reading since you were about 5 years old. It's a little late for me to teach you the basics. What I *can* do, however, is teach you how to make the best use of your time in this test. (After all, 35 minutes for four passages and 40 questions means you have only about 8 or 9 minutes per passage. That's not a great deal of time for most of us.)

1. **Preview.** You are naturally going to like one type of passage more than the others. Look for it and do it first, being *extremely* careful to shade in the correct bubbles on your answer grid. (When you skip around, it's easy to mess up the grid.)

   What happens if your brain takes a little vacation and you suddenly find you've filled in the bubbles all wrong? Maybe you started off by reading passage 2, with questions 11–20, but you filled in the bubbles for questions 1–10? Hey, you laugh now, but that's easy to do. The first reaction is usually panic; first you erase all your answers, and then you try to remember what they were. Bad move. Here's how to handle this problem: As you answer a question, first circle the correct response in your booklet, and then fill in the bubble for that response on the answer grid. This way, if you mess up and have to erase your answer grid, you can just glance at your answer booklet and find the right answers again.

2. **Decide on a strategy.** Some students do well under time pressures and can finish all four passages and the questions. These are students who don't have to read slowly and carefully, getting every little morsel the passages have to offer, but can get the overall idea. Other students get totally nervous if they have to rush and will mess up completely. For these students, it may be better to concentrate on reading three of the passages carefully and answering all the questions correctly on them.

   If you do decide to do only three passages, be sure to fill in answers for the last passage. Remember, the ACT has no penalty for wrong answers, meaning that you should guess your brains out. *Never, ever leave an answer blank.*

3. **Pay special attention to the first and last paragraphs and to the first and last lines of each paragraph.** Most writers (except writers of literature) pay attention to the maxim, "Tell 'em what you're gonna tell 'em; tell 'em; and tell 'em what you told 'em." That means that the first sentence of a paragraph or the first paragraph of a passage usually gives the main idea and sets up the paragraph or the passage. The last sentence or paragraph summarizes what's been said. If you are absolutely short on time, you can often get away with focusing on these parts of the passage. Even if you are reading carefully and have plenty of time, think about these parts carefully.

   This tip works best if the passage is a complete essay or short story. It doesn't work as well if the passage is an excerpt from a longer work. Occasionally, an excerpt seems to begin in the middle and end just as abruptly. However, most passages have some coherent format that you can concentrate on.

4. ***DON'T MEMORIZE!*** I see some students stop reading, gaze out into the distance, and mutter to themselves, counting off on their fingers. It's apparent that these students are trying to memorize facts from the passage: "Let's see, the three basic elements that make up Kleinschwab's Elixir are. . . ." You do not have to memorize anything; in fact, doing so can be counterproductive. Although you naturally want to remember *some* of what you've read, you can always go back to the passage as often as you'd like.

5. **Summarize.** As you're reading, think about what you've learned, and maybe summarize it in your own words. Don't make things complicated. A simple "This passage is about the differences in the way the Greeks looked at nature and the way the Romans looked at nature" helps to focus your thoughts.

   Question: Should I underline or outline as I go?

   Answer: If doing so is your normal method of reading, yes. If you rarely outline or underline, doing so now may tend to confuse you. I see students who have been told to underline or outline spending more time worrying about what to underline than thinking about what's in the passage. I personally like to circle key words (especially unusual vocabulary that I think may be important) and occasionally jot a note in the margin, summarizing a paragraph. For example, next to paragraph 1, I may write, "Need for elixir." Next to paragraph 2, I write, "Failed experiments." By paragraph 3, I write, "Success; uses of elixir." You get the idea. You are allowed to refer to the passages as often as you want; having an idea of what is where in the passage can save you precious seconds.

6. **Look for relationships and connections.** Maybe the concepts are given in a contrasting form: what makes one idea different from another. Perhaps you are given thoughts in sequence, like what came first, next, last. Some passages talk about the cause and effect, how one thing impacts another.

   Question: Should I read the questions before the passages?

   Answer: Probably not. I would not suggest starting off by reading the questions before even glancing at the passages, as the questions make no sense out of context. You'll just confuse yourself. Some students use a worthwhile technique of looking at the first few sentences of the passage to get an overview, then reading the questions, and then going back and reading the passage, keeping the ideas in the back of their brains. And of course, some of us just read the passage and then go back and forth looking at the questions. There's no one right or wrong way. When you're doing the passages in the practice exams, try each technique and see which one works best for you individually.

I've Been Meaning to Ask You Something: The Questions

Although you may encounter many different types of questions on the ACT, the following are some that have shown up frequently in the past. Make like a Boy Scout and Be Prepared.

Main idea

A question may ask, "Which of the following is the main idea of the passage?" or "The theme of paragraph 3 is which of these?" You've done "main-idea" questions on other exams before. Keep in mind three things:

- *A main idea is broad and general.* It covers the entire passage (or, if the question is asking about a paragraph, the entire paragraph). Be sure not to choose a "little" answer. The mere fact that a statement is true does not mean it is the *main* idea. Suppose that you have a passage about high school education, and a question asks for the main idea. One answer choice says, "The ACT gives students the heebie-jeebies." No one can argue with that statement, but it's not the main idea of the passage.
- *The right answer often repeats the topic sentence or key words.* If the passage is about Asian philosophy, the correct answer will most likely have the words *Asian philosophy* in it. Don't immediately choose any answer *just* because it has those words, but if you're debating between two answers, the one with the key words may be a better choice.
- *Keep in mind the tone of the passage and the attitude of the author.* If the passage is positive, if the author is impressed by the philosophy, then the main idea will be positive, not negative or neutral. If the author is criticizing something, the main idea will be negative. The main idea should always reflect the attitude of the author or the tone of the passage.

Details

The detail question is the opposite of the main idea. It covers one particular point, not the passage as a whole. This is one of the easiest questions to get correct; you need only go back to the passage and find the specific answer. Some examples include, "According to the passage, James confronted Gary about the business when which of the following occurred?" or "The results of the experiments were considered unacceptable because. . . ."

If you're running short of time or your brain cells are about ready to surrender, look for this type of question and answer it first. You can often answer this detail question correctly even if you haven't read the entire passage. Find the key word in the question (such as "elixir") and then skim for that word in the passage.

Tone, attitude, inference

This question is more of a read-between-the-lines question. You can't go back to one specific line of the passage to find the answer. Nowhere in the passage will it say, for example, "My belief is that physical violence rarely solves problems." You have to infer from the passage as a whole that the author prefers negotiation to confrontation. You have to infer that the author is contemptuous of violence and those who practice it, that his or her attitude throughout the passage is negative. Examples of this sort of question include, "The author implies that he believes violence is. . . ." and "The fact that the product line included a new model that James insisted upon carrying despite Gary's objections indicates that. . . ."

Vocabulary in context

You may have to determine the meaning of a word by its use in context.

Sometimes, the words are common words but are used in an uncommon way. For example, the author may mention that, "Lawrence was unable to cow Michael, despite his frequent threats." Although "cow" usually refers to a four-footed bovine, in this case, the word is used as a verb, meaning to intimidate or frighten (don't let the ACT cow you).

A question may ask you to interpret what the author means by a short phrase, not just a word. Here's an example.

When the author states, "He had done nothing but suffer in silence, which in itself is a type of strength," the author means that

A. only strong people are able to go without complaining.

B. the strength required for suffering is greater than that required for inflicting suffering.

C. the person who can suffer the longest is the strongest.

D. criticism is a sign of weakness.

Negative or reverse questions

Although this type of question is rare, a question may be phrased in the negative, such as "Which of the following is NOT indicative of dissatisfaction in a relationship?" or "With which one of the following statements would the author disagree?" You may also have a question that is phrased positively but expects you to find an inconsistency or a logical fallacy. You're really pointing out what is wrong, given the reasoning of the passage. For example, if the passage states that all strong people are able to handle adversity, you can't also state that all people who can handle adversity can also handle tragedy. That's going too far in the reasoning.

The ACT features many different types of reading questions. Don't panic if you see some question styles beyond the basic ones covered in this chapter. You may also encounter comparison questions, cause-and-effect questions, and generalization questions, just to mention a few. The ACT is always coming up with new ways to test your reading skills.

Tips and Traps

The ACT is not an exam that is especially tricky (unlike, say, the SAT, for those of you who are taking it). However, some basic tips can prevent you from falling for the few traps that do exist . . . or from creating traps of your own.

1. **Be willing to move around.** I'm often asked, "Should I do the questions in order or skip around?" My answer is that, for the most part, it's best to go in order. However, if you are running short of time, look for the "easier" types of questions. For most people, these are the detail questions, in which you may just go back and skim for a specific fact. A main idea/primary purpose question is also a pretty good candidate for doing quickly, because you can answer it from your overall impression of the passage, or by looking at just the first paragraph.

   Negative questions ("Which of the following is NOT true?" or "The author would reject which of the following conclusions?") can often take a long time to answer because you have to find four statements that are true and then, by process of elimination, choose the one that is not. Roman numeral questions ("Solana Beach is renowned for its athletes because: I. it has an Olympic training center. II. the junior training program is excellent. III. world-class coaches have moved there to retire.") can also take a great deal of time because you have to go through the passage looking for each point.

2. **Look for key connecting or changing words.** A simple word such as *but* or *however* or *whereas* can indicate that things are about to change. There you are, reading a passage about how an economic theory has failed to prove valid, when you encounter a *however*. That may indicate an entire switch, such that the author is now going to tell you that he or she believes that the policy will be effective in the future. I make a habit of circling "indicator" words like these. Here's a short list of words I look for:

but	although	despite
however	whereas	in spite of
nonetheless	on the other hand	

3. **Keep an eye on the time.** As I've said before, you have to make a decision about whether to do all the passages pretty quickly or three of the passages more slowly. Whichever you choose (and you should have your strategy firmly in mind before you get into the test room), divide your time appropriately and stick to that schedule. If you get bogged down on one question, fill in something, anything (there's no penalty for wrong answers on the ACT), and go on to the next question. You can always come back to it if you have time left at the end of the section.

4. **Don't read more into the passage than is there.** Many questions are based on information that is specifically stated in the passage. Other questions are based on information that is implied by the passage. Don't take matters to extremes or bring in background information that you happen to have. Suppose that the passage talks about the fall of communism in the Soviet Union and its satellite countries. You cannot automatically assume the author also believes that communism will fail in China. Don't take the reasoning that one step too far (and of course, nestled snugly among the answer choices, will be one that does just that).

One final word: Try to enjoy the passages. Yeah, I know that's easy for me to say. But believe it or not, some of this reading material is very interesting. If you approach it with a negative attitude, your mind is already closed to it, making the material much more difficult to comprehend and remember. If you at least *pretend* that you're going to have a good time getting through it, you're much more likely to put things in perspective and get a better handle on the material.

Short 'n' Sweet: A Summary

In this chapter, you were privileged to make the acquaintance of perhaps the most forthright and straightforward of the ACT tests, the Reading Test. Here's a quick review of what you've learned.

Format

- The test features four passages with ten questions each.
- Topics include humanities, social studies, natural science, and prose fiction.
- Question styles include main idea, details, tone-attitude-inference, vocabulary in context, and negative/reverse questions.

Tips and traps

- Preview the passages; move around to maximize your time.
- Look for key connecting or changing words.
- Decide on a strategy ahead of time (do all passages quickly; do fewer passages more thoroughly) and stick to it.
- Don't read too much into the passages.
- GUESS, GUESS, GUESS! The ACT has no penalty for guessing; leave nothing blank.

Chapter 11

The Reading Practice Questions

On the actual ACT, you have four full-length (about 750 words each) passages. Each passage is followed by ten questions. You have only 35 minutes to do that whole test. This abbreviated practice exam (I want to ease you into this stuff slowly) has two shorter passages and a total of eight questions. Don't worry about timing now. Think about what type of passage each portion is (humanities, prose fiction, science, or social studies) and identify each of the question types.

DIRECTIONS: Read each passage and then complete the questions that follow.

Passage 1

Social Science

Multinational corporations frequently have difficulty explaining to politicians, human rights groups, and (perhaps most important) their consumer base why they do business with, and even seek closer business ties to, countries whose human rights records are considered very bad by United States standards. The CEOs say that in the business trenches, the issue of human rights must effectively be detached from the wider spectrum of free trade.

Discussion of the uneasy alliance between trade and human rights has trickled down from the boardrooms of large multinational corporations to the consumer on the street who, given the wide variety of products available to him, is eager to show support for human rights by boycotting the products of a company he feels does not do enough to help its overseas workers.

International human rights organizations also are pressuring the multinationals to push for more humane working conditions in other countries and to, in effect, develop a code of business conduct that must be adhered to if the American company is to continue working with the overseas partner.

The President, in drawing up a plan for what he calls the "economic architecture of our times," wants economists, business leaders, and human rights groups to work together to develop a set of principles that the foreign partners of United States corporations will voluntarily embrace. Human rights activists, angry at the unclear and indefinite plans for implementing such rules, charge that their agenda is being given low priority by the State Department. The President strongly denies their charges, arguing that each situation is approached on its merits without prejudice, and hopes that all the groups can work together to develop principles based on empirical research rather than political fiat, emphasizing that the businesses with experience in the field must initiate the process of developing such guidelines. Business leaders, while paying lip service to the concept of these principles, secretly fight against their formal endorsement as they fear such "voluntary" concepts may someday be given the force of law. Few business leaders have forgotten the Sullivan Principles, in which a set of voluntary rules regarding business conduct with South Africa (giving benefits to workers and banning apartheid in the companies that worked with U.S. partners) became legislation.

1. Which of the following best states the central idea of the passage?

   A. Politicians are quixotic in their assessment of the priorities of the State Department.

   B. Multinational corporations have little if any influence on the domestic policies of their overseas partners.

   C. Disagreement exists between the desires of human rights activists to improve the working conditions of overseas workers and the practical approach taken by the corporations.

   D. It is inappropriate to expect foreign corporations to adhere to American standards.

The main idea of the passage is usually stated in the first sentence or two. The first sentence of this passage discusses the difficulties that corporations have in explaining their business ties to certain countries to politicians, human rights groups, and consumers. From this statement, you may infer that those groups disagree with the policies of the corporations. *Correct Answer:* C.

Did you choose A just because of the hard word, *quixotic*? It's human nature (we're all so insecure) to think that the hard word we don't know must be the right answer, but it's not always so. Never choose a word you can't define unless you're sure that all the words you *can* define are wrong. ***Quixotic*** means idealistic, impractical (think of the fictional character Don Quixote tilting at windmills). The President's belief is not the main idea of the passage.

Just because a statement is (or may be) true does not necessarily mean that it is the correct answer to a question. The answer choices to a main-idea question in particular often are true or at least look plausible.

To answer a main-idea question, I like to pretend that a friend of mine just came up behind me and said, "Hey, what'cha reading there?" My first response is the main idea: "Oh, I read this passage about how corporations are getting grief from politicians and other groups because they do business with certain countries." *Before* you look at the answer choices, predict in your own words what the main idea is. You'll be pleasantly surprised how close your prediction is to the correct answer (and you won't be confused by all the other plausible-looking answer choices).

Choice D is a moral value, a judgment call. Who is to say what's appropriate and what's inappropriate? An answer that passes judgment, one that says something is morally right or morally wrong, is almost never the correct answer.

2. The author of the passage would most likely agree with which of the following statements?

   F. Business leaders, human rights groups, and economists will create the guidelines or principles; business leaders will initiate the processes.

   G. Workers will not accept principles drawn up by politicians whom they distrust but may agree to principles created by the corporations that pay them.

   H. Political activist groups have concerns that are too dramatically different from those of the corporations for the groups to be able to work together.

   J. Foreign nations are distrustful of U.S. political intervention and are more likely to accept suggestions from multinational corporations.

The passage gives you the answer quite specifically. In line 20, you are told that ". . . businesses with experience in the field must initiate the process of developing such guidelines." *Correct Answer:* F.

Choices G, H, and J are all judgment calls. You are assuming facts not in evidence, as the lawyers say. Although you personally may believe the statements in these answer choices to be true, they don't answer the specific question. The concerns in G and J aren't even mentioned in the passage, a tip-off that they probably will not be the correct answer to an "according-to-the-passage" question.

3. Which of the following best describes the reason the author mentions the boycott of a corporation's products by its customers?

   A. to ridicule the consumers for believing that their small boycott would significantly affect the sales of a multinational corporation

   B. to predict the inevitability of failure of any plan that does not involve customer input

   C. to disagree with the President's contention that big business is best qualified to draw up the voluntary principles of workplace conduct

   D. to indicate the pressures that are on the multinational corporations

This question is one of those mind-reading questions I warned you about. You are expected to get into the author's mind and understand why he or she said what he or she did. The concept of the consumer boycott follows closely the main idea of the passage, which is that the corporations have difficulty trying to explain themselves and their actions to all sorts of groups, including their customers. From this, you may infer that the point of the statement is to indicate the pressures placed on the corporations.

The first line in paragraph 3 states that human rights organizations *also* are pressuring multinational corporations, allowing you to infer that the consumers are applying pressure. Remember that one of your tips was to expand your horizons. Read until you find what you think is the right answer . . . and then read a little further. *Correct Answer:* D.

Choices A and C begin with negative words, "ridicule" and "disagree." Negative answer choices are rarely correct. Be careful, however, not to take this tip as a hard-and-fast rule. If you go back to the correct answer to question number one, you can see that you might interpret that answer as negative.

Choice B seems logical; common sense tells you that a company that ignores its customers will probably fail. However, a strong, dramatic word like *inevitably* is rarely correct. Few things in life are inevitable: just death, taxes, and the ACT.

4. Which of the following statements about the Sullivan Principles can best be inferred from the passage?

   F. They had a detrimental effect on the profits of those corporations doing business with South Africa.

   G. They represented an improper alliance between political and business groups.

   H. They placed the needs of the foreign workers over those of the domestic workers whose jobs would therefore be in jeopardy.

   J. They will have a chilling effect on future adoption of voluntary guidelines.

Choice F is the major trap here. Perhaps you assumed that because the companies seem to dislike the Sullivan Principles, they hurt company profits. However, nothing was said in the passage about profits. Maybe the companies still made good profits but objected to the Sullivan Principles, well, on principle. The companies just may not have wanted such governmental intervention even if profits weren't decreased. If you chose F, you read too much into the question and probably didn't read the rest of the answer choices.

In choice J, the words "chilling effect" mean negative effect, discouraging effect. Think of something with a chilling effect as leaving you cold. Because few corporations have forgotten the Sullivan Principles, you may infer that these principles will discourage the companies from agreeing to voluntary principles in the future. *Correct Answer:* J.

In order to get this question correct, you really need to understand the whole passage. If you didn't know what was going on here, you would be better off to just guess and go. An inference question usually means you have to read between the lines; you can't just go back to one specific portion of the passage and get the answer quickly.

Passage 2

Prose Fiction. This passage is from the Robert Louis Stevenson novel *Kidnapped,* 1886.

Meanwhile such of the wounded as could move came clambering out of the fore-scuttle and began to help; while the rest that lay helpless in their bunks harrowed me with screaming and begging to be saved.

The captain took no part. It seemed he was struck stupid. He stood holding by the shrouds, talking to himself and groaning out aloud whenever the ship hammered on the rock. His brig was like wife and child to him; he had looked on, day by day, at the mishandling of poor Ransome; but when it came to the brig, he seemed to suffer along with her.

All the time of our working at the boat, I remember only one other thing; that I asked Alan, looking across at the shore, what country it was; and he answered, it was the worst possible for him, for it was a land of the Campbells.

We had one of the wounded men told off to keep a watch upon the seas and cry us warning. Well, we had the boat about ready to be launched, when this man sang out pretty shrill: "For God's sake, hold on!" We knew by his tone that it was something more than ordinary; and sure enough; there followed a sea so huge that it lifted the brig right up and canted her over on her beam. Whether the cry came too late or my hold was too weak, I know not; but at the sudden tilting of the ship I was cast clean over the bulwarks into the sea.

I went down, and drank my fill; and then came up, and got a blink of the moon; and then down again. They say a man sinks the third time for good. I cannot be made like other folk, then; for I would not like to write how often I went down or how often I came up again. All the while, I was being hurled along, and beaten upon and choked, and then swallowed whole, and the thing was so distracting to my wits, that I was neither sorry nor afraid.

Presently, I found I was holding to a spar, which helped me somewhat. And then all of a sudden I was in quiet water, and began to come to myself.

It was the spare yard I had got hold of, and I was amazed to see how far I had traveled from the brig. I hailed her indeed; but it was plain she was already out of cry. She was still holding together; but whether or not they had yet launched the boat, I was too far off and too low down to see.

While I was hailing the brig, I spied a tract of water lying between us, where no great waves came, but which yet boiled white all over, and bristled in the moon with rings and bubbles. Sometimes the whole tract swung to one side, like the tail of a live serpent; sometimes, for a glimpse, it all would disappear and then boil up again. What it was I had no guess, which for the time increased my fear of it; but I now know it must have been the roost or tide race, which carried me away so fast and tumbled me about so cruelly, and at last, as if tired of that play, had flung me and spare yard upon its landward margin.

5. The narrator compares the ship to the captain's wife and child to

A. lament the captain's long separation from his family.

B. demonstrate the difficulty the captain has keeping focused on his job.

C. predict the captain's future madness.

D. show the depth of the connection the captain has to his ship.

The focus of the second paragraph is on how the captain is very upset by the condition of his ship. To compare his ship to his wife and child is to show how much he loves the ship and thus to emphasize the deep attachment he has to the vessel. *Correct Answer:* D.

6. Which of the following may you infer from the passage?

F. Alan and the Campbells are enemies.

G. The ship had been attacked by another ship.

H. The narrator was on his first sea voyage.

J. Alan and the author are brothers.

This is a pretty simple question. In lines 8 and 9, you read that Alan felt the land was the worst possible for him because it was a land of the Campbells. From this, you may readily infer that he and the Campbells weren't about to sit down to soup together — that they were enemies. *Correct Answer:* F.

7. By saying that he "got a blink at the moon," in line 16, the narrator means that

A. he foresaw his own demise.

B. he saw the sky as he came up out of the water to get air.

C. he was hallucinating as he was drowning.

D. he saw the captain with his pants down.

The fifth paragraph, in which this statement is found, describes the narrator's dunking and near drowning. He was bobbing up and down in the water, going under the sea and then coming up for air, at which point he saw the moon. Make sure that you answer the question in the context in which you find the statement; don't use your own common sense. And if you chose D (which of course would never be on the actual exam) — man, you're having altogether too much fun for the ACT! *Correct Answer:* B.

8. The purpose of the passage is

F. to portray a mood of terror.

G. to urge others not to go to sea.

H. to describe an event.

J. to contrast lifestyles of sailors from different countries.

The passage merely tells of something that happened to the author. (Choices using the words *describe, discuss,* and *explain* are often excellent answers to a "What is the purpose?" question.) Choice F is tempting, but surprisingly, the passage is not all that terrifying. You read in lines 19 and 20 that the narrator was so distracted that he was "neither sorry nor afraid" to describe an event. *Correct Answer:* H.

Part VII

Proven to Cause Brain Defects in Laboratory Students: The Science Reasoning Test

The 5th Wave
By Rich Tennant
Igor prepares for the Science Reasoning portion of the ACT.
©RICH TENNANT
OK, CAREFUL NOW. THIS IS WHERE IT GETS TRICKY. YOU'VE DROPPED THE NORMAL BRAIN. BUT THE ABNORMAL BRAIN REMAINS INTACT IN THE JAR. YOU SHOULD Ⓐ SCOOP THE NORMAL BRAIN UP IN A HANKY AND RETURN TO THE CASTLE WITH IT IN YOUR POCKET; Ⓑ RETURN TO THE CASTLE WITH THE ABNORMAL BRAIN AND HOPE FOR THE BEST; Ⓒ TAKE NEITHER BRAIN AND RETURN TO THE CASTLE EXPLAINING YOU GOT LOST IN THE STORM.
ABNORMAL BRAIN

In this part . . .

I've had students complain that the ACT Science Reasoning Test made them feel as confused as rats in a maze, but things aren't quite that bad. This part introduces you to the three types of ACT Science Reasoning passages; you can see what they look like, how to approach them, and when to run like heck and leave them alone. You'll also see several of the most common questions that follow the passages and discover what traps are built into them.

The material in this part does not — I repeat, does not — lecture on science per se. That is, I'm not about to give you chemistry formulas or physics principles or biology maxims. That's not laziness or stupidity on my part (although you probably do know more about chemistry, physics, and biology than I do), but rather a matter of focus. The ACT Science Reasoning Test doesn't expect you to know those sorts of things. All the information that you need to answer the questions is given to you in the passages themselves.

Chapter 12

Frankenstein to Einstein: Science Reasoning

In This Chapter

- Science fiction: What you *don't* need to know
- The three you'll see: Data Representation, Research Summaries, Conflicting Viewpoints
- Questionable behavior: Questions and the traps built into them

Return your brain to the full upright and locked position. You're not going to need to use it as much as you may fear for this section.

I'm Mad, but I'm No Scientist: What Do I Need to Know?

Relax. Unclench your hands. Take a few deep breaths. You are not, repeat, *not* expected to be able to remember the entire periodic table or to know the difference between the substantia nigra and a Lorentz transformation. This section of the test is called science *reasoning*, which means that you are generally not required to know a lot of science facts. After all, your grades in science classes are there on the transcript for the admissions officers to read if they really want to assess your science knowledge. That's not the point here. The point is to demonstrate that you have an important collegiate skill: the ability to approach novel information, sort it out, and draw conclusions from it. The ACT actually includes bizarre and weird information to give science "dummies" (that's me!) a break. In other words, you don't have to know what a scientist knows, but you should be able to think as a scientist thinks. (Question: Did ya ever stop to think — and forget to start again?)

Too Graphic for Words: The Format

The Science Reasoning Test consists of 40 questions that are based on seven passages (five to seven questions per passage). You have 35 minutes to answer these questions, about an average of 5 minutes per passage.

Each passage should take you about 2 minutes to read and — at least partially — understand. As you go through the following material, and especially as you are held spellbound by the excruciatingly detailed answer explanations to the practice exam questions, you'll learn which types of passages require a lot of up-front work and which you should straight-arm on your way to the questions.

Plan on allotting yourself approximately 30 seconds per question. You may not think that that sounds like a lot, but some of the questions will be so easy that you'll answer them in a heartbeat and build up a reservoir of time for the harder questions. But of course, some of the questions will be so impossible that you'll want to sue your brain for nonsupport. If you can't answer a question within a half minute, put down something, anything, and go on.

Remember: The ACT has *no* penalty for wrong answers. Never leave any bubble blank. Fill in something and hope you get lucky.

Chalk Talk: Developing a Game Plan

The ACT features three basic types of science passages. One of the best things you can do for yourself is to have a game plan: Recognize which type of passage the material is, have a strategy for reading or evaluating it, and know which types of questions are likely to follow it. The following is a brief overview of what to expect and how to approach each type of passage.

The Android's Favorite: Data Representation

Not only Mr. Data's favorite, this passage should be your favorite as well. Most of my students tell me that this is the easiest type of passage . . . not coincidentally because it usually has the least text to read. The ACT has 3 Data Representation passages, 5 questions each, for a total of 15 questions. This is the only passage in the science section with only 5 questions; all the other sections have at least 6 questions per passage.

The Data Rep questions are based on one or more tables, graphs, or diagrams chock-full of information, preceded or followed by text. Read the text so that you can get an idea about what point the table, graph, or diagram is trying to make, but don't get hung up on any complicated terms or sentences. Here's an example.

Scientists studied the effect that variations in paraloxin had on the rate of samanity in the species *Braisia idioticus*. The results are summarized in Table 1 (an example of a Data Rep table).

Table 1

Paraloxin (microshels)	*Samanity Rate (rics/sec)*
0	14
1	18
2	23
3	27
4	31
5	89
6	90
7	34
8	29
9	24

What? You don't know what paraloxin, samanity, rics, and microshels are? That's not surprising, considering that I've just made them up. I'm babbling here to make the point that you can get an idea of what the passage is discussing *without* having a clue about what all the terms mean. Say to yourself, "When this thing called paraloxin is changed, samanity rate, whatever it is, may also change. I'll take a look at the table and see if this happens. The weird units simply measure paraloxin and samanity rate."

No, no, alas, the actual ACT will not be as much fun as this book is. On the real test, all the science is dull, boring . . . real. But my point is that if you don't know the big hairy terms, they may as well be made up as far as you're concerned. As I mentioned earlier in this chapter, the ACT gives everyone, science geniuses and science morons alike, an equal chance by using unfamiliar science.

International students, this unfamiliar science is a boon for you. Yes, the passages can be difficult to read, but they are just as hard for someone who is a native English speaker as they are for you. The terminology is unfamiliar to everyone, giving you all an equal opportunity . . . and an equal headache.

After the game plan: Executing the play

When you encounter a Data Representation passage, here's a suggested approach.

1. **Read the introductory text.** Remember, don't get psyched out over unfamiliar terms. And don't try to understand every little thing. Just get an overview of what the passage is about.
2. **Look at the table, diagram, or graph.** Identify what is being displayed (for example, drug dosages, reaction times, kinetic energy, astronomical distances).
3. **Look at what the columns, rows, axes, and so on represent and determine how they are related to one another.**

An *independent,* or *controlled, variable* is the factor that the experimenter can change to a specific value, such as the amount of water added. The *dependent* variable is the factor that is not under the experimenter's direct control, such as the amount of energy released.

Here's another way to remember which variable does what: The terms *dependent variable* and *independent variable* mean almost the opposite of what you may think. The independent variable is not really independent; it is the one that the experimenter is changing. The dependent variable is dependent on the independent variable. The most typical relationship is one in which one column, row, axis, and so on, presents values for the independent, or controlled, variable and another shows what happens to the dependent variable.

The following graph presents a classic relationship.

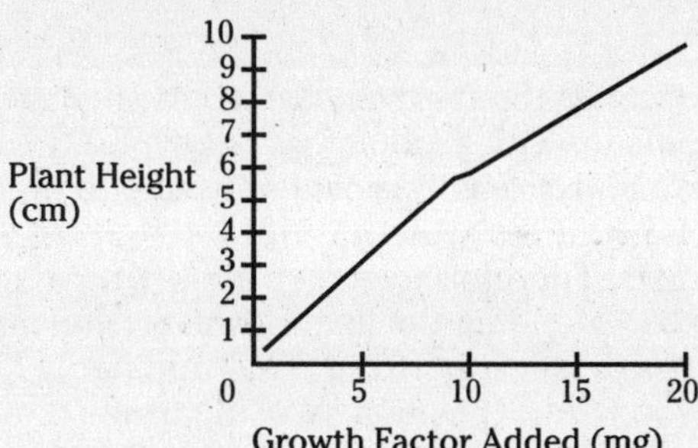

Here, the amount of growth factor added is the *independent* variable, and the plant height is the *dependent* variable. The experimenter can't directly manipulate plant height. He or she can add a certain amount of growth factor but then has no choice but to wait and see what happens to the plant.

The ability to distinguish the independent from the dependent variable is essential for understanding many passages. You may even get a question directly asking about this distinction.

4. **Note the units of measurement.** I mentioned earlier that you should not freak out if the units are unfamiliar to you. Units of measurement (even the bizarre ones) are presented very clearly. The axes on graphs are usually labeled, legends typically accompany diagrams, and graphs and column and row headings usually include the units.

5. **Look for trends in the data, noting any significant shifts.** Take another look at the first example. In the paraloxin-samanity table, you see that samanity increases at regular intervals as paraloxin is gradually increased up through 4 microshels. Samanity rate hits a sharp peak when paraloxin rises to 5 and 6 microshels and then falls to levels comparable to those obtained when paraloxin was lower. In the plant growth graph, note that for the range of values shown on the graph, plant height steadily increases with increases in growth factor.

Don't waste time trying to memorize the numbers! If a question requires specific details, you can always go back and look at the table for them. Why destroy any more brain cells than you absolutely have to?

Going for pay dirt: The "data-analysis" question

The most common type of question you will get on Data Representation passages is one that requires some sort of data analysis. This type of question simply tests your ability to read the table or figure and extract information from it.

Use the graph on plant growth shown earlier in this chapter to answer the following question:

What is the plant height when 5 mg of plant growth factor is used?

Find 5 mg along the horizontal axis, go up to the plotted line, and then go left to the vertical axis to read the value, which is 3 cm. Notice that you don't have to know anything about plants. You only have to look at what's in front of you.

What if a point is not actually plotted (or a value specifically given) on the table? You can still answer the question. You interpolate by looking at the two closest values (translated into plain English, that means insert an intermediate term by estimating). For example, you may be asked (from Table 1, shown earlier in this chapter) for the samanity rate when paraloxin is 1.5. Because the samanity rate is 18 when paraloxin is 1, and 23 when paraloxin is 2, the samanity rate when paraloxin is 1.5 is probably between 18 and 23. Given that the values are going up in a regular fashion in this region of the table, it is reasonable to say that the samanity rate is close to 20.5 when paraloxin is 1.5.

Along with *interpolation,* you have to worry about *extrapolation*. As the "extra" in its name implies, extrapolation asks you to come up with a value that is beyond the range depicted in the table or figure. In the plant growth passage, it is probably safe to predict that the straight upward line will continue for a while as growth factor moves past 20 mg, the last number presented in the horizontal axis. Therefore, you can make predictions about plant growth when growth factor is 21 mg by extending the line. However, you are *not* justified in predicting what will happen when growth factor is 50 mg. That number is far greater than what is shown on the graph. For all you know, the plants will die from an overdose of growth factor if 50 mg is administered.

That's It in a Nutshell: Research Summaries

The ACT has three Research Summary passages, with six questions each. The Research Summary questions make up 18 of the 40 questions — almost half — that you will encounter on the ACT Science Reasoning. Like Data Representation passages, Research Summaries usually include one or more tables or diagrams. Research Summaries, however, are a little more sophisticated than Data Representation. Here, you must pay attention to what is being tested in the experiments and how the researchers go about performing the studies.

Fortunately, Research Summary passages are predictable. You can expect each passage to tell you three things that you should always note:

- **The purpose of the study** (You may be very familiar with identifying the goal of the project or the purpose of the study, as you have probably done so on every lab write-up you've turned in since kindergarten. Sometimes the ACT is kind enough to do your work for you by stating or implying the purpose in the introductory paragraph.)
- **The experimental design**
- **The results** (which are usually presented in the same table, chart, or graph format that I discuss in the Data Representation section)

Here's more detail on these three concepts.

Purpose

Identifying the purpose of the experiment takes only a few seconds. Usually, the purpose is to examine what effect *x* has on *y*. The ACT expects you to understand some key principles of why the researchers created the experiment in the first place. After you pick up on the purpose, you must analyze how the researchers set up experiments to investigate these possible cause-and-effect relationships.

Experimental design

A proper experiment systematically varies the factor that is the possible cause and holds all other factors constant. For example, if scientists are interested in investigating what effect having the flu has on one's ability to perform multiplication problems, a proper experiment will compare people who have the flu with those who do not, while keeping the groups equal in terms of such factors as age, mathematical ability, and the presence of psychological disorders. If the groups differ on one or more of these other factors, it cannot be certain that any observed difference in multiplication performance was a *result* of the flu. What would you think if the nonflu group did better on multiplication but that nonflu group consisted of 12-year-olds while the flu group children were all 8 years old? You could not be certain whether age or the flu virus accounted for the difference.

Defective designs produce limited results. The experimenters don't always include proper controls. Some studies, by their very nature, cannot adhere to ideal experimental design. For example, if a scientist suspected that 2-year-olds who had been vaccinated for measles got more colds than 2-year-olds who had not been vaccinated, a proper design would be to give one group the vaccine and to withhold it from another group. However, it's not fair to keep one group of kids unvaccinated (mothers tend to get cranky when you make their kids sick "in the best interests of science"). What the experimenters would try to do is collect data on how frequently the children came down with colds before they were immunized (children are not immunized against measles until they are at least 1 year old) and perhaps collect data about the children's parents when the parents themselves were 2 years old. (The measles vaccine was not developed then.)

When an experiment lacks certain controls, take note of how the experiment is limited. You may be asked to come up with a good control. If you have noted the limitation, you can quickly say what "shoulda been done." If you are asked about what conclusions can be made, be very cautious. It's hard to come up with definitive conclusions when the experiments don't have proper controls.

The different studies presented in a Research Summary passage may differ in terms of what factor is being manipulated. For example, a study could look at how flu affects multiplication ability or how multiplication ability varies according to the child's age. Another study may examine what dependent variable is being measured (multiplication drills in one study, word problems involving multiplication in another). Be sure to follow the key way in which the studies differ. You may want to write some very brief notes in the margin to help you keep everything straight: "having the flu" or "kids' ages," for example.

Although the studies may differ somewhat, they are all designed to answer a key question stated in the purpose. Read each study with an eye toward how it fills in the big picture.

Just tell me what you want: Question styles

Some of the Research Summaries' questions are similar to the Data Analysis questions already discussed in Data Representation. Here are a couple of other question styles that are more typical of the Research Summaries.

1. **Experiment design.** This question tests your ability to follow the logic of the design itself. Why or how was the experiment designed? What was the purpose of choosing one variable or one control?

2. **Conclusions that can be drawn from one or more of the studies.** Be sure to pay attention to the question stem. If a question asks you about what can be concluded in Experiment 1 about the effects of one factor on the dependent variable, you don't want to spend a lot of time searching through the information for Experiments 2 and 3.

   To answer result/conclusion-type questions, you must be careful not to go overboard. Suppose that the study about the flu and multiplication showed that the flu group made substantially more errors on a multiplication drill than did the nonflu group. (And let's assume that this study *did* control for other factors.)

   Here is an example of a *correct* way of thinking about this question.

   Question: Which of the following statements is consistent with the study?

   Answer: The flu impaired the ability of the students studied to perform multiplication drills.

   Notice that this question asked for something probable, not a big, sweeping conclusion. You are not going out on a limb by saying that the flu seemed to have an effect. The study didn't prove that the flu was the definite cause of the multiplication difficulties, but the statement certainly follows from the data presented.

   Now for an example of going too far (remember that this answer is *wrong!*):

   Question: What can be concluded about the effects of the flu?

   Answer: The flu impairs mathematical functioning by interfering with connections in the brain.

   Did the study investigate how the flu changed brain functioning? The study investigated multiplication drills. "Mathematical functioning" is much too broad a topic.

3. New or additional results.

The results of one study may have an effect on another study. Your job is to determine how these new results fit into what you already learned. Do the new results confirm what the studies showed, or are they in conflict? If they don't invalidate what you concluded earlier, do they limit what you can say? Perhaps the results of the flu and multiplication study investigated only children of elementary-school age. If a question gives you the additional information that there was no difference between the flu and nonflu groups when high school students were studied, you have to limit your conclusion about the flu's impairing-multiplication ability to a group of *younger* children. If the results with high school students were similar to what was found with elementary school children, *then* you may generalize your conclusions to include a wider range of students.

Warring Factions: Conflicting Viewpoints

The ACT has one Conflicting Viewpoints passage, with seven questions. You can recognize the Conflicting Viewpoints passage because it has two major portions of text with headings similar to "Scientist 1" and "Scientist 2" or titles of theories, such as "extinction by meteorites" and "extinction by natural selection." (Research Summaries have headings, too, but the headings on those passages are almost always "Experiment 1, 2, 3" or "Study 1, 2, 3.")

The Conflicting Viewpoints passage, as the title indicates, presents two different explanations about the same scientific situation. The following approach can help you to get started:

1. **Read the introduction.** Find out what phenomenon is being debated. Maybe the scientists disagree on whether objects can travel faster than the speed of light or whether other planets in the solar system could support life. (Know why there are no restaurants on the moon? Great food, but no atmosphere. . . .)

2. **Read the first viewpoint and make some kind of brief notation (using your own words) about the author's main idea.** This main idea will express the scientist's position on the situation discussed in the passage's introduction. It is important to note this main idea because you want to be able to identify, for example, that Scientist 1 says "pro" while Scientist 2 says "con." You don't want to become engrossed in a question that asks you to support Scientist 1 and forget that he or she took the "pro" side. (And yes, sometimes your notes to yourself *should* be as succinct as "pro" and "con" or "yes" and "no.")

3. **Identify the evidence that the first scientist uses to support his or her main idea.** Does the evidence support the main idea, or is the scientist making a leap of faith? This "leap of faith" is called an *assumption.* Questionable assumptions open up the door for the other scientist to dispute the first scientist and come up with an explanation of his (or her) own.

   Assumptions are usually pretty sneaky and can be well disguised. Suppose, for example, that the scientist claims that pandas are carnivores. He or she backs this up by showing that bears are carnivores. Do you see a gap between the main idea and the evidence? There is evidence that *bears* are carnivores, but is this enough to say that *pandas* are carnivores? You can do so only if you assume that pandas are bears, which may or may not be true.

4. **Identify and analyze the second scientist's point of view.** After you finish with the first viewpoint, follow the same procedure to identify and analyze the second viewpoint. Usually the second viewpoint is easier to follow because it is so predictable. The main idea of the second scientist is a statement that is basically directly opposed to the main idea of the first scientist.

The evidence used *may* be different, but it may also be the same as that which was used by the first scientist. The key difference lies in how the second scientist interprets the evidence. Don't look exclusively for differences between the two viewpoints. The ACT may throw in some similarities.

Your job is to follow the logic of each viewpoint. Do not try to decide which viewpoint is correct. No one cares — not the ACT, not the college admissions office, and certainly not you. In fact, the ACT sometimes presents a viewpoint that is clearly false. For example, one scientist may claim that evolution takes place as a result of inheritance of *acquired* characteristics. You know that this does not happen. Think about it. If you gnaw your fingernails down to the bone worrying about the ACT, it does not follow that someday your children will be born with no fingernails! Again, worry only about the logic of the viewpoint, not whether it is correct or wrong.

Bonus: Are you in fact an onychophagist? Nah, it's not as serious as it sounds. Onychophagia is merely nail biting. The next time that you want to get out of going to school, tell your mom that you are suffering from onychophagia. She may be too embarrassed to ask what it is, and let you stay home.

Asking for Trouble: Question Styles

Some questions in Conflicting Viewpoints passages ask you to support or weaken a scientist's viewpoint. To do so, you first have to identify any *assumption* that the scientist made in creating his or her theory. The best way to strengthen a viewpoint is to come up with evidence that confirms that the assumption is valid. The best way to weaken a viewpoint is to present evidence that casts doubt on the assumption. For example, the previous conclusion that pandas are carnivores is strengthened if pandas are bears. The conclusion is weakened if pandas are not bears.

Be careful to keep in mind all the time just which of the two viewpoints you are addressing. Some of the wrong (trap!) answer choices deal with the other viewpoint and, as a consequence, do not answer the question.

The answer choices for a strengthening/supporting question usually follow a predictable pattern. One choice, the correct answer, supports the correct viewpoint. One incorrect choice deals with the correct viewpoint but weakens it rather than strengthens it. Another incorrect choice deals with the other viewpoint. Usually this choice strengthens the other viewpoint, so it is testing your ability to keep the viewpoints straight. Occasionally, this incorrect choice weakens the other viewpoint. Such a choice is tough to eliminate, but you must remember that weakening one viewpoint does not automatically strengthen the other. The third incorrect choice will likely present irrelevant evidence.

Suppose that you have a passage about whether smoking cigarettes causes cancer. Scientist 1 says that it does, citing the fact that smokers have a higher incidence of cancer than do nonsmokers. Scientist 2 says that smoking cigarettes does not cause cancer, claiming that there is no proof that smoking causes the uncontrolled growth seen in cancer. Scientist 2 (yes, the ACT does use catchy names like "Scientist 1" and "Scientist 2") explains the association between smoking and cancer as a result of the fact that some people have a certain body chemistry that leads to both a smoking habit and cancer.

The first question asks you to identify evidence to support Scientist 1. Here are some very typical answer choices.

A. Nicotine, a major cigarette ingredient, has been shown to cause cancer in laboratory rats. (This statement supports Scientist 1's theory and is the right answer.)

B. Smokers invariably eat a lot of fatty foods, which have been shown to cause cancer. (This statement weakens Scientist 1's point of view by suggesting that another cause is at work.)

C. Injecting rats with Chemical ABC caused them to seek out tobacco and also produced cancer cells. (This statement goes right along with Scientist 2's suggestion.)

D. Lack of exercise causes heart disease. (This statement is irrelevant. It discusses neither cigarettes nor cancer.)

Remember: You don't care whether the statement is actually true in the Real World or false in the Real World. For example, statement D, claiming that lack of exercise causes heart disease, may very well be true. So what? It has nothing to do with supporting Scientist 1's statement that smoking cigarettes causes cancer.

Parting Is Such Sweet Sorrow: The Conclusion

The ACT follows a pretty dependable format. Therefore, you can develop and stick to a plan of attack.

- **Identify the type of passage** (three are Data Representation, three are Research Summaries, and one is Conflicting Viewpoints).
- **For Data Representation, read the intro, look at the table/graph** (paying special attention to the units of measurement), **note the relationship between the units, and identify any trends or patterns.**
- **For Research Summaries, note the purpose of the study, the experimental design, and the results.**
- **For Conflicting Viewpoints, jot down the viewpoint of each scientist and the evidence used to support his or her main idea.**

Chapter 13

The Science Practice Questions

Question: What happened to the band director when he stuck his finger into an electrical outlet?

Answer: Nothing. He was a bad conductor!

If your store of science knowledge is so low that you don't even understand my joke, don't worry. You don't need any specific science knowledge to do well in the science section. Everything that you need is stated or implied in the passages or experiments. (If you get the joke but don't laugh, maybe your standards are higher than my comedic ability!)

The following is a Research Summary with twice the usual number of questions. On the actual ACT, a Research Summary has only 6 questions, not 12, as in this practice test. I give you double the usual number so that you can get an idea of the various ways in which the same basic points are tested. For now, don't worry about the format or the timing. Review the material that you learned in the preceding and then apply that material to these questions.

DIRECTIONS: Read the science reasoning passage and the analysis that follows it. Then complete the 12 questions that follow and study the answer explanations.

Passage

By using electrical recording devices, scientists have shown that many cells in the part of the brain involved with processing visual information respond only to lines of a certain orientation. For example, some brain cells fire when vertical lines are present but do not respond to horizontal lines. Animals that rely on vision must have an entire set of cells so that at least some part of their brains responds when lines of a given orientation are present in their environment.

A major question is, how much is brain organization affected by the animal's environment? The following series of studies investigates this possible environmental role in the development of cat vision.

Study 1

Scientists presented lines of various orientations to newborn kittens while recording electrical activity from the visual part of the brain. No matter what the orientation, some cells fired while others did not.

These kittens were able to walk around both vertical and horizontal obstacles without bumping into them.

Study 2

Scientists conducted the same test used in Study 1 on 6-month-old kittens that were raised in a normal environment. Results matched those of Study 1.

Study 3

Scientists raised newborn kittens for six months in a completely dark environment. The scientists recorded very little brain cell activity when the kittens were presented with a wide variety of stimuli.

These kittens had great difficulty navigating around various mazes. They bumped into both vertical and horizontal obstacles.

Study 4

Scientists placed newborn kittens in an environment in which all they saw were vertical lines. At 6 months, none of their brain cells responded to horizontal lines, but their brain cells had more activity than what was found in Studies 1 and 2 when vertical lines were present.

These 6-month-old kittens easily walked around a maze of vertical obstacles but bumped into and could not walk around horizontal obstacles placed in their paths.

Study 5

This study was identical to Study 4 except that the scientists exposed the kittens to only horizontal lines. At 6 months, their brain cells showed no activity in response to vertical lines and, when presented with horizontal lines, showed increased activity as compared to the kittens in Studies 1 and 2.

These kittens negotiated a maze of horizontal obstacles but could not navigate around vertical obstacles.

Study 6

Scientists placed 1-year-old cats that were raised in a normal environment and had normal vision in a dark environment for six months. At the end of this time, these cats displayed a brain-cell firing pattern similar to that of the cats used in Studies 1 and 2.

Study 7

For six months, scientists exposed 1-year-old cats with normal vision and a prior normal environment to only vertical lines. Results were identical to those of Study 6.

Study 8

For six months, scientists exposed 1-year-old cats with normal vision and a prior normal environment to only horizontal lines. No difference was found between these cats and those of Study 7.

Initial Analysis

Are you complaining that you're not "feline" too well after that, uh, *cat*astrophic passage? Actually, the passage isn't that bad. The language is a bit technical but understandable. First, try to understand the introductory material, the point of the passage. Then determine what each study tells you.

The first paragraph basically says that brain cells controlling vision are specialized. Each cell does a particular job. To cover all possible jobs, a brain needs many different specialized cells.

You can grasp a concept easily if you relate it to something in your own life. Think about how physicians, for example, specialize in their fields. An ophthalmologist treats your eyes. A dermatologist cures your zits. If you have a zit, the ophthalmologist doesn't treat you, just as a vertical-responding cell doesn't fire in response to a horizontal line.

The question in the second paragraph is one you have probably heard applied to many aspects of development: How much of a characteristic is caused by your genes and how much by environment? For example, do you have a Tom Cruise smile because you inherited good teeth from your parents or because you eat the right foods and brush after meals? Can you outrun the Road Runner because your parents are athletic or because you train very hard?

In Study 1, don't sweat the details regarding how the scientists measured the electrical activity. All you have to get from this study is that the scientists came up with a way to determine which cells respond to a certain type of line. The results of Study 1 were entirely expected. Because the visual part of the brain has the whole spectrum of specialized cells, the fact that some, but not all, cells respond makes sense. If no cells respond, the animal has a tough time seeing certain kinds of objects in the world. If all cells respond, the brain cells aren't specialized.

The most significant result of Study 1 is that the cells responded the way they did soon after the kittens were born. This result seems to indicate that the cat brain is wired the way it should be at birth and suggests that genes play a major, if not the only, role in determining how vision is handled by a cat brain.

On to Study 2. Its results make complete sense. If a newborn kitten is well equipped to handle its visual world, six months of normal development does not change that ability.

So far, no evidence implicates an environmental role in the development of cat vision. Ah, but so far, the experiments have been conducted in normal environments. What about abnormal environments?

Study 3 shows that after six months of no stimulation from the environment, the cells in the visual part of the brain do not function properly. Do not, I repeat, *do not* immediately go overboard and say that a normal environment is necessary for normal responses. Remember, newborn kittens had normal responses. Instead, play it safe (think like a scientist and don't jump to conclusions too rapidly) and say that a normal environment *seems* to be necessary to maintain normal response from the visual part of the brain.

In Study 4, the kittens were denied exposure to horizontal lines. You probably shouldn't be too surprised, then, to learn that their brain cells did not respond to horizontal lines or that the brain cells, at least functionally, did not see the horizontal obstacles.

Study 3 shows that, when the cells in the visual part of the brain are not given proper stimulation, they lose their ability to respond. The cells that normally respond to horizontal lines were not stimulated, so they lost their ability to respond to horizontal lines.

Study 4 also indicates that at least some of these horizontal-responding cells convert to vertical-responding cells. This result provides strong support for the argument that favors environment over genetics. Under certain circumstances, the environment can change what the genes set up. (Using our earlier analogy, you can inherit your parents' gorgeous teeth, but if you live on nothing but soda pop and candy bars, those gorgeous teeth are going to turn brown and fall out.)

You can breeze through Study 5. *Vertical* and *horizontal* switch roles and results perfectly. Everything is as expected; zoom on to the next study.

The results of Study 6 may surprise you. As in Study 3, the scientists deprived the cats of visual stimulation for six months. This time, however, everything was normal when the cats were tested. At the very least, you can deduce that being a year old makes a difference. A good scientist would reason that the visual part of the brain is flexible for at least some part of the first year of a cat's life, but thereafter the wiring becomes somewhat permanent.

Study 7 follows from Study 6. The wiring of the visual part of a cat's brain becomes somewhat fixed at about 1 year of age. You can't teach an old cat new tricks.

And finally, Study 8 also follows from Study 6. The environment loses much of its ability to influence the organization of the visual part of a cat's brain when the cat is about 1 year of age.

In general, you want to summarize briefly to yourself, and maybe even write a note in the margin, what each study tested and what the conclusions were. Be sure to note the variables tested, such as the age of the cats and the horizontal or vertical lines.

1. On the basis of Study 1, can newborn kittens see vertical lines?

A. No, because newborn kittens have brain cells that respond to horizontal lines.

B. No, because newborn kittens can move around horizontal obstacles.

C. Yes, because newborn kittens have been exposed to many vertical lines in their environment.

D. Yes, because newborn kittens have brain cells that respond to vertical lines.

The newborn kittens' brains responded the way that you would expect if the cats were to get around in their environment, so the Yes answers, choices C and D, are the most probable. Besides, choices A and B give pretty weak reasons for the lack of responses. The ability to respond to horizontal lines does not make it impossible to respond to vertical lines.

Choice C is illogical; you can dump that choice by using your common sense alone. If the kittens are newborns, how much exposure could they have had?

Choice D provides a good explanation. The kittens had brain cells that responded to vertical lines; you can logically make the conclusion that the vertical-lines information gets to the kittens' brains. This conclusion in turn makes it likely that the kittens can see the lines. *Correct Answer:* D.

2. Scientists place a 3-month-old kitten that was raised in a normal environment in a maze of vertical and horizontal obstacles. Which of the following is the most likely result?

F. The kitten bumps into horizontal obstacles but gets around vertical obstacles.

G. The kitten bumps into vertical obstacles but gets around horizontal obstacles.

H. The kitten bumps into both vertical and horizontal obstacles.

J. The kitten negotiates around both vertical and horizontal obstacles.

If a newborn kitten can get around the maze and a kitten raised in a normal environment for six months can get around the maze, then you logically can conclude that a kitten raised in a normal environment for three months would be able to do so also. Only choice J has a kitten that doesn't need a crash helmet. *Correct Answer:* J.

Did you have Smart Students' Disease on this question and read more into the question? If you said, "Yeah, but what if . . . " and started imagining all sorts of horrible and unlikely possibilities ("Maybe the kitty OD'd on catnip and staggered around . . . "), you made this problem much harder than it really was. Keep it simple, okay?

3. Scientists place a 1-year-old cat that was raised in a normal environment in a maze of vertical and horizontal obstacles. Which of the following is the most likely result?

   A. The cat makes no attempt to get around the obstacles.

   B. The cat negotiates around both vertical and horizontal obstacles.

   C. The cat bumps into horizontal obstacles but gets around vertical obstacles.

   D. The cat bumps into vertical obstacles but gets around horizontal obstacles.

Did you try to answer this question based on Studies 1 and 2? Doing so worked for the previous question because it spoke of an age, 3 months, that was between newborn (Study 1) and 6 months (Study 2). In this question, the cat is twice as old as the oldest kitten in Studies 1 and 2, meaning that you can't be sure that the present trend continues. (Common sense tells you that the trend probably will continue, but you must be able to distinguish between what will probably happen and what will necessarily happen.)

A more definitive answer comes from looking at Studies 6, 7, and 8. In these studies, scientists gave normal cats that had a normal environment for one year an abnormal environment for six months. The cat in this question still responded normally, the same way that the cats in Studies 6, 7, and 8 responded, but didn't have to endure an abnormal experience. If the vision of the cats exposed to the abnormal environments turned out okay, then the cat that was not placed in such an environment should also be okay. *Correct Answer:* B.

If you were really lost on this problem, eliminate choice A as much too extreme. You'll do better when you hedge by using words such as *rarely* or *infrequently* than when you use dramatic terms like *no* or *never*. Because nothing indicates a favoring of vertical over horizontal lines or vice versa, you can eliminate choices C and D as well.

4. Which of the following was not under the direct control of the experimenters?

   F. The length of time that the cat spent in an abnormal environment

   G. The number of brain cells that responded to horizontal lines

   H. The age at which the cat was tested for visual response

   J. The types of obstacles placed in a maze

When an experimental factor, or *variable,* is under the direct control of the experimenters, the experimenters are able to decide exactly how much (or what type) of that factor to use without having to depend on any intervening process. Choice F is clearly under the control of the experimenters. The experimenters can let the cat out of the bag (the environment) any time they want. Choice J is just as clear. The experimenters can throw in more vertical or horizontal obstacles at will.

Choice H is a little tougher to eliminate. You may think that the cat's age is up to the cat (or at least up to its parents), but the experimenters can decide exactly how old the cats have to be in order to be used in a certain part of the experiment.

By process of elimination, choice G is correct. The experimenters can try to change this factor by changing the environment, but exactly how many cells are going to respond depends on the way the cat's brain is set up and on how the cat's brain interacts with the environment. *Correct Answer:* G.

You can use this basic science info in many different passages: *Independent variables* (choices F, H, and J, in this case) are those that can be manipulated independently of any other factor. For example, the experimenter can change the time spent in the dark environment from six months to five months without changing the type of obstacles in the maze. A *dependent variable* (choice G in this case) depends on what else was done in the experiment.

5. Why is Study 6 so important in relation to Study 3?

A. Study 6 shows that the effects of six months in darkness may depend on the cat's age when scientists place it in such an environment.

B. Older cats have more reliable brain-cell responses than younger cats.

C. Study 6 extends the findings of Study 3 by showing that longer periods of darkness also change brain-cell responses.

D. Study 6 contradicts the findings of Study 3 by showing that, when cats are placed in darkness for a longer period of time, the effect found in Study 3 disappears.

Dump choices C and D immediately. Study 6 used older cats (ones that have been alive for a longer period of time), but these cats, as well as those of Study 3, were in darkness for only six months.

The ACT tests no expert knowledge. You can answer all questions based on what is stated or implied in the passages. In other words, you are not required to be an expert on cat brain physiology. Because only such experts (and maybe Garfield) know whether choice B is true, you can reject it. Six months in darkness does not have such a devastating effect when the cats are older. *Correct Answer:* A.

6. Some humans who have suffered brain injuries have been able to recover a lost brain function by having the brain reorganize itself. On the basis of all the cat-vision studies, which of the following humans would be most likely to recover a lost function through brain reorganization?

F. A 50-year-old man who suffers a stroke (lack of oxygen to a certain region of the brain)

G. An 80-year-old woman who suffers a stroke

H. A 30-year-old combat soldier who suffers a bullet wound in the brain

J. A baby who has had part of the left side of his brain surgically removed along with a tumor

Calm down, calm down — no one expects you to know exactly how each of these brain traumas affects brain functioning. Everything you need to answer this question is given in the passage. The key is to pick up on the ages. Which cats showed a change from the ordinary response pattern when the environment changed? The young cats. Similarly, a young human's brain is likely to be more flexible than that of an older human (haven't you always yelled at your parents not to be so narrow-minded and set in their ways?). Choice J, which features the youngest human, is the correct answer. *Correct Answer:* J.

If you're almost stroking out yourself right now arguing with me, you probably didn't notice how carefully the question was worded: "Which of the following humans would be *most likely* to. . . ." True, you don't know for sure that the baby would have some lost brain function, but all you are asked is which of the answer choices (no, "a student studying for the ACT" was not among them) is the most likely.

7. Scientists exposed a 2-year-old cat that was raised in a normal environment and had normal vision to only horizontal lines. Which of the following is the most reasonable prediction?

A. After three months, the cells in the visual part of the cat's brain fail to respond to vertical lines.

B. After six months, the cells in the visual part of the cat's brain fail to respond to vertical lines.

C. After six months, the cells in the visual part of the cat's brain respond to vertical lines.

D. After 12 months, the cells in the visual part of the cat's brain respond to vertical lines.

Study 8 shows that 1-year-old cats exposed to only horizontal lines for six months still have brain cells capable of responding to vertical lines. This info knocks out choices A and B. After one year, the wiring in the cat's visual part of the brain seems to be fixed, so you can assume that the 2-year-old cat's brain has fixed wiring.

Be careful of choice D. You cannot say for sure what effects an exposure longer than six months will have. Choice C is a much safer choice and is the correct answer. *Correct Answer:* C.

Have you been noticing throughout these answer explanations how often you can narrow the answers down to two choices very quickly? If you're in a hurry or if you're confused, make a quick guess. Remember that the ACT does not penalize you for wrong answers.

8. In considering all the studies, which of the following is true regarding the brain-cell electrical measurements and the maze results?

F. The measurements and results are consistent with each other.

G. The measurements and results are consistent with each other only for newborn kittens.

H. The measurements and results are consistent with each other only for cats more than 1 year old.

J. The measurements and results are inconsistent with each other.

When the electrical measurements showed reduced response to vertical lines, the cats could negotiate around vertical obstacles. Reduced response to horizontal lines corresponds to failure to negotiate around horizontal obstacles. The electrical measurements and the maze results always provided the same information regarding what type of lines the cats could handle. *Correct Answer:* F.

9. Which of the following studies shows that environmental stimulation can lead to a change in the way the cells in the visual part of a cat's brain respond?

I. Study 1

II. Study 4

III. Study 5

IV. Study 8

A. II only

B. II and III only

C. III and IV only

D. I, III, and IV only

Study 1 was performed with newborn kittens. With such minimal environmental stimulation, this study can't be used to show that the environment has an effect. This eliminates option I; put a big X through it. You can now dump choice D.

Study 4 looks good. Exposure to only vertical lines caused a loss of cells able to respond to horizontal lines and a gain of those able to respond to vertical lines. Option II is correct. Put a circle around it. Because the correct answer must have II in it, eliminate choice C.

Study 5 is very similar to Study 4, except that the roles of the vertical and horizontal lines are reversed. Study 5 shows a loss of cells able to respond to vertical lines and a gain of those able to respond to horizontal lines. Circle option III. *Correct Answer:* B.

To check your work, verify that option IV doesn't work. Study 8 shows that the environment has no effect on 1-year-old cats. This study, taken by itself, lends no support to an environmental contribution.

10. If Study 4 is conducted but Studies 3 and 5 are not, can the scientists conclude that all cells in the visual part of a kitten's brain require stimulation in order to function?

F. Yes, because some brain cells stop responding to horizontal lines.

G. Yes, because some brain cells respond to vertical lines.

H. No, because some brain cells respond to vertical lines.

J. No, because Study 4 does not test whether vertical-responding cells require stimulation.

This question tests whether you understand that experimental results are limited when only certain conditions are tested. The results of Study 4 indicate only that horizontal-responding cells require stimulation early in a kitten's life in order to function. Study 4 does not establish whether vertical-responding cells require such stimulation because the study does not examine what happens to the cells when they are deprived of vertical-line input. A conclusion regarding *all* cells is not justified. Eliminate choices F and G. For all you know, horizontal lines and the cells that respond to them can be special.

Choice H is out because all this study establishes in regard to vertical lines is that the cells continue to respond when given vertical-line input. Perhaps the cells could have responded in the absence of such input.

Choice J pinpoints the limitations of the study and is the correct answer. Studies 3 and 5 did test this factor and allow for a more general conclusion regarding brain cells and environmental input. *Correct Answer:* J.

11. On the basis of all the studies, which of the following best summarizes the role of the environment in the development of a cat's visual brain-cell responses?

A. The environment has no effect.

B. Environmental input early in a cat's life contributes to the continuation of normal responding.

C. Environmental input can change the pattern of responses throughout a cat's life.

D. The environment is the only factor that influences the responses.

If choice A is true, the kittens in Studies 3, 4, and 5 would have normal visual responses. Eliminate choice A. If choice C were true, the cats in Studies 6, 7, and 8 would show a change in response patterns. Choice D is at odds with Study 1. If the environment is the only factor, why do newborn cats show responses to all types of stimuli? This reasoning leaves only choice B. *Correct Answer:* B.

Are you noticing and using the wording to help you choose and eliminate answers? The conservative language ("contributes to the continuation" rather than "directly determines") reinforces choice B as the answer. It is tough to argue with a choice that doesn't say something so extreme that one example would be enough to contradict it. Notice how easily you can contradict choice A, which has the word "no," choice C, which says "throughout," and choice D, which contains "only."

12. Which of the following studies would probably add the most new information to the work done in this set of experiments?

 F. A study identical to Study 3, except that the kittens are in the dark environment for seven months

 G. A study identical to Study 6, except that the cats are in the dark environment for five months

 H. A study identical to Study 6, except that the study uses 2-year-old cats

 J. A study identical to Studies 4 and 5, except that the cats are exposed only to diagonal lines

Study 3 shows that six months of darkness almost entirely wipes out the cells' ability to respond. Perhaps seven months would cause a complete cessation of responding, but the point made from Study 3 (namely, that lack of visual stimulation leads to impaired brain-cell responding) is already established. Therefore, the study mentioned in choice F will not add much.

Study 6 strongly suggests that the response patterns in the visual part of a cat's brain are fixed enough at 1 year so that six months of an abnormal environment has no noticeable effect. If six months has no noticeable effect, why would five months be any different? Eliminate choice G. If the brain-cell responses are fixed by the time that a cat is 1 year old, it seems reasonable to expect that a 2-year-old cat would show the same responses. Eliminate choice H.

The study mentioned in choice J would help because it would show what happens to cells that respond to lines that are in between vertical and horizontal. This study would add some information regarding how precise the brain cells are in regard to lines in the environment. For example, is a diagonal line close enough to a vertical line that the exposure only to diagonal lines still allows the cat to respond to vertical lines? The answer to this question would increase understanding of how the environment interacts with the visual part of a cat's brain. *Correct Answer:* J.

Part VIII

I'd Rather Wait for the Movie: Full-Length Practice ACTs

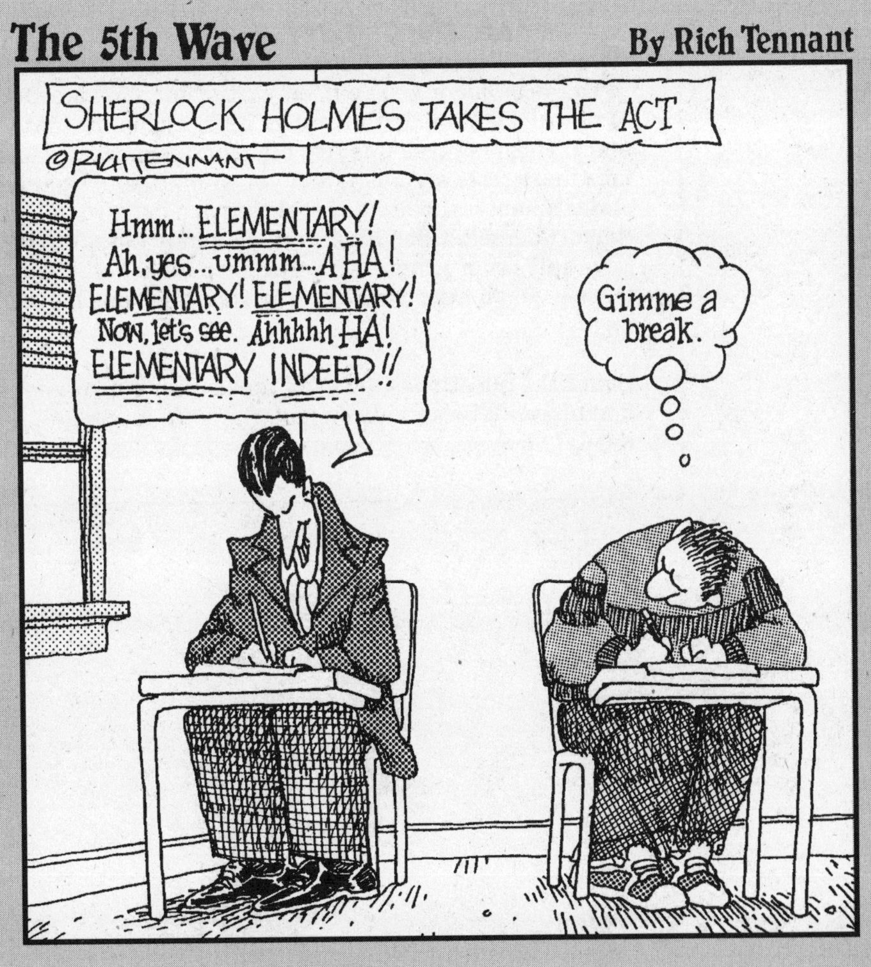

In this part . . .

It's the moment you've been waiting for: a chance to download all that stuff you've been cramming into your brain. This part contains two full-length practice exams. I take these tests seriously, and you should, too. Do them under actual test conditions, sitting in a quiet room and timing yourself. Open books are definitely out. (Sorry!) I have spies everywhere. I'll know if you cheat on these tests — you'll hear a knocking at your door one foggy night. . . .

Unlike the questions, however, the answer explanations don't have to be serious; in fact, they're a lot of fun. Ready? Show me what you can do.

Chapter 14

Practice Exam 1: Questions

You are now ready to take a sample ACT. The following exam consists of four tests: a 45-minute English Test, a 60-minute Mathematics Test, a 35-minute Reading Test, and a 35-minute Science Reasoning Test. You probably are familiar with the format of each test by now.

Please take this test under normal exam conditions. (This is serious stuff!)

1. **Sit where you won't be interrupted (even though you'd probably welcome any distractions).**
2. **Use the answer grid provided.**
3. **Set your alarm clock for the intervals indicated at the beginning of each test.**
4. **Do not go on to the next test until the time allotted for the test you are taking is up.**
5. **Check your work for that test only.**
6. **Do not take a break during any test.**
7. **Give yourself one ten-minute break between tests two and three.**

When you've completed the entire test, check your answers with the answer key at the end of this chapter. A section explaining your score precedes the answer key.

Chapter 15 gives detailed explanations of the answers. Go through the answer explanations to *all* the questions, not just the ones you missed. You will find a plethora of worthwhile information, material that provides a good review of everything you've learned in the other chapters of the book. I even toss in a few good (?) jokes to keep you somewhat sane.

Answer Sheet

Begin with Number 1 for each new section.

English Test

1. Ⓐ Ⓑ Ⓒ Ⓓ
2. Ⓕ Ⓖ Ⓗ Ⓙ
3. Ⓐ Ⓑ Ⓒ Ⓓ
4. Ⓕ Ⓖ Ⓗ Ⓙ
5. Ⓐ Ⓑ Ⓒ Ⓓ
6. Ⓕ Ⓖ Ⓗ Ⓙ
7. Ⓐ Ⓑ Ⓒ Ⓓ
8. Ⓕ Ⓖ Ⓗ Ⓙ
9. Ⓐ Ⓑ Ⓒ Ⓓ
10. Ⓕ Ⓖ Ⓗ Ⓙ
11. Ⓐ Ⓑ Ⓒ Ⓓ
12. Ⓕ Ⓖ Ⓗ Ⓙ
13. Ⓐ Ⓑ Ⓒ Ⓓ
14. Ⓕ Ⓖ Ⓗ Ⓙ
15. Ⓐ Ⓑ Ⓒ Ⓓ
16. Ⓕ Ⓖ Ⓗ Ⓙ
17. Ⓐ Ⓑ Ⓒ Ⓓ
18. Ⓕ Ⓖ Ⓗ Ⓙ
19. Ⓐ Ⓑ Ⓒ Ⓓ
20. Ⓕ Ⓖ Ⓗ Ⓙ
21. Ⓐ Ⓑ Ⓒ Ⓓ
22. Ⓕ Ⓖ Ⓗ Ⓙ
23. Ⓐ Ⓑ Ⓒ Ⓓ
24. Ⓕ Ⓖ Ⓗ Ⓙ
25. Ⓐ Ⓑ Ⓒ Ⓓ
26. Ⓕ Ⓖ Ⓗ Ⓙ
27. Ⓐ Ⓑ Ⓒ Ⓓ
28. Ⓕ Ⓖ Ⓗ Ⓙ
29. Ⓐ Ⓑ Ⓒ Ⓓ
30. Ⓕ Ⓖ Ⓗ Ⓙ
31. Ⓐ Ⓑ Ⓒ Ⓓ
32. Ⓕ Ⓖ Ⓗ Ⓙ
33. Ⓐ Ⓑ Ⓒ Ⓓ
34. Ⓕ Ⓖ Ⓗ Ⓙ
35. Ⓐ Ⓑ Ⓒ Ⓓ
36. Ⓕ Ⓖ Ⓗ Ⓙ
37. Ⓐ Ⓑ Ⓒ Ⓓ
38. Ⓕ Ⓖ Ⓗ Ⓙ
39. Ⓐ Ⓑ Ⓒ Ⓓ
40. Ⓕ Ⓖ Ⓗ Ⓙ
41. Ⓐ Ⓑ Ⓒ Ⓓ
42. Ⓕ Ⓖ Ⓗ Ⓙ
43. Ⓐ Ⓑ Ⓒ Ⓓ
44. Ⓕ Ⓖ Ⓗ Ⓙ
45. Ⓐ Ⓑ Ⓒ Ⓓ
46. Ⓕ Ⓖ Ⓗ Ⓙ
47. Ⓐ Ⓑ Ⓒ Ⓓ
48. Ⓕ Ⓖ Ⓗ Ⓙ
49. Ⓐ Ⓑ Ⓒ Ⓓ
50. Ⓕ Ⓖ Ⓗ Ⓙ
51. Ⓐ Ⓑ Ⓒ Ⓓ
52. Ⓕ Ⓖ Ⓗ Ⓙ
53. Ⓐ Ⓑ Ⓒ Ⓓ
54. Ⓕ Ⓖ Ⓗ Ⓙ
55. Ⓐ Ⓑ Ⓒ Ⓓ
56. Ⓕ Ⓖ Ⓗ Ⓙ
57. Ⓐ Ⓑ Ⓒ Ⓓ
58. Ⓕ Ⓖ Ⓗ Ⓙ
59. Ⓐ Ⓑ Ⓒ Ⓓ
60. Ⓕ Ⓖ Ⓗ Ⓙ
61. Ⓐ Ⓑ Ⓒ Ⓓ
62. Ⓕ Ⓖ Ⓗ Ⓙ
63. Ⓐ Ⓑ Ⓒ Ⓓ
64. Ⓕ Ⓖ Ⓗ Ⓙ
65. Ⓐ Ⓑ Ⓒ Ⓓ
66. Ⓕ Ⓖ Ⓗ Ⓙ
67. Ⓐ Ⓑ Ⓒ Ⓓ
68. Ⓕ Ⓖ Ⓗ Ⓙ
69. Ⓐ Ⓑ Ⓒ Ⓓ
70. Ⓕ Ⓖ Ⓗ Ⓙ
71. Ⓐ Ⓑ Ⓒ Ⓓ
72. Ⓕ Ⓖ Ⓗ Ⓙ
73. Ⓐ Ⓑ Ⓒ Ⓓ
74. Ⓕ Ⓖ Ⓗ Ⓙ
75. Ⓐ Ⓑ Ⓒ Ⓓ

Mathematics Test

1. Ⓐ Ⓑ Ⓒ Ⓓ Ⓔ
2. Ⓕ Ⓖ Ⓗ Ⓙ Ⓚ
3. Ⓐ Ⓑ Ⓒ Ⓓ Ⓔ
4. Ⓕ Ⓖ Ⓗ Ⓙ Ⓚ
5. Ⓐ Ⓑ Ⓒ Ⓓ Ⓔ
6. Ⓕ Ⓖ Ⓗ Ⓙ Ⓚ
7. Ⓐ Ⓑ Ⓒ Ⓓ Ⓔ
8. Ⓕ Ⓖ Ⓗ Ⓙ Ⓚ
9. Ⓐ Ⓑ Ⓒ Ⓓ Ⓔ
10. Ⓕ Ⓖ Ⓗ Ⓙ Ⓚ
11. Ⓐ Ⓑ Ⓒ Ⓓ Ⓔ
12. Ⓕ Ⓖ Ⓗ Ⓙ Ⓚ
13. Ⓐ Ⓑ Ⓒ Ⓓ Ⓔ
14. Ⓕ Ⓖ Ⓗ Ⓙ Ⓚ
15. Ⓐ Ⓑ Ⓒ Ⓓ Ⓔ
16. Ⓕ Ⓖ Ⓗ Ⓙ Ⓚ
17. Ⓐ Ⓑ Ⓒ Ⓓ Ⓔ
18. Ⓕ Ⓖ Ⓗ Ⓙ Ⓚ
19. Ⓐ Ⓑ Ⓒ Ⓓ Ⓔ
20. Ⓕ Ⓖ Ⓗ Ⓙ Ⓚ
21. Ⓐ Ⓑ Ⓒ Ⓓ Ⓔ
22. Ⓕ Ⓖ Ⓗ Ⓙ Ⓚ
23. Ⓐ Ⓑ Ⓒ Ⓓ Ⓔ
24. Ⓕ Ⓖ Ⓗ Ⓙ Ⓚ
25. Ⓐ Ⓑ Ⓒ Ⓓ Ⓔ
26. Ⓕ Ⓖ Ⓗ Ⓙ Ⓚ
27. Ⓐ Ⓑ Ⓒ Ⓓ Ⓔ
28. Ⓕ Ⓖ Ⓗ Ⓙ Ⓚ
29. Ⓐ Ⓑ Ⓒ Ⓓ Ⓔ
30. Ⓕ Ⓖ Ⓗ Ⓙ Ⓚ
31. Ⓐ Ⓑ Ⓒ Ⓓ Ⓔ
32. Ⓕ Ⓖ Ⓗ Ⓙ Ⓚ
33. Ⓐ Ⓑ Ⓒ Ⓓ Ⓔ
34. Ⓕ Ⓖ Ⓗ Ⓙ Ⓚ
35. Ⓐ Ⓑ Ⓒ Ⓓ Ⓔ
36. Ⓕ Ⓖ Ⓗ Ⓙ Ⓚ
37. Ⓐ Ⓑ Ⓒ Ⓓ Ⓔ
38. Ⓕ Ⓖ Ⓗ Ⓙ Ⓚ
39. Ⓐ Ⓑ Ⓒ Ⓓ Ⓔ
40. Ⓕ Ⓖ Ⓗ Ⓙ Ⓚ
41. Ⓐ Ⓑ Ⓒ Ⓓ Ⓔ
42. Ⓕ Ⓖ Ⓗ Ⓙ Ⓚ
43. Ⓐ Ⓑ Ⓒ Ⓓ Ⓔ
44. Ⓕ Ⓖ Ⓗ Ⓙ Ⓚ
45. Ⓐ Ⓑ Ⓒ Ⓓ Ⓔ
46. Ⓕ Ⓖ Ⓗ Ⓙ Ⓚ
47. Ⓐ Ⓑ Ⓒ Ⓓ Ⓔ
48. Ⓕ Ⓖ Ⓗ Ⓙ Ⓚ
49. Ⓐ Ⓑ Ⓒ Ⓓ Ⓔ
50. Ⓕ Ⓖ Ⓗ Ⓙ Ⓚ
51. Ⓐ Ⓑ Ⓒ Ⓓ Ⓔ
52. Ⓕ Ⓖ Ⓗ Ⓙ Ⓚ
53. Ⓐ Ⓑ Ⓒ Ⓓ Ⓔ
54. Ⓕ Ⓖ Ⓗ Ⓙ Ⓚ
55. Ⓐ Ⓑ Ⓒ Ⓓ Ⓔ
56. Ⓕ Ⓖ Ⓗ Ⓙ Ⓚ
57. Ⓐ Ⓑ Ⓒ Ⓓ Ⓔ
58. Ⓕ Ⓖ Ⓗ Ⓙ Ⓚ
59. Ⓐ Ⓑ Ⓒ Ⓓ Ⓔ
60. Ⓕ Ⓖ Ⓗ Ⓙ Ⓚ

Reading Test	Science Test
1. Ⓐ Ⓑ Ⓒ Ⓓ	1. Ⓐ Ⓑ Ⓒ Ⓓ
2. Ⓕ Ⓖ Ⓗ Ⓙ	2. Ⓕ Ⓖ Ⓗ Ⓙ
3. Ⓐ Ⓑ Ⓒ Ⓓ	3. Ⓐ Ⓑ Ⓒ Ⓓ
4. Ⓕ Ⓖ Ⓗ Ⓙ	4. Ⓕ Ⓖ Ⓗ Ⓙ
5. Ⓐ Ⓑ Ⓒ Ⓓ	5. Ⓐ Ⓑ Ⓒ Ⓓ
6. Ⓕ Ⓖ Ⓗ Ⓙ	6. Ⓕ Ⓖ Ⓗ Ⓙ
7. Ⓐ Ⓑ Ⓒ Ⓓ	7. Ⓐ Ⓑ Ⓒ Ⓓ
8. Ⓕ Ⓖ Ⓗ Ⓙ	8. Ⓕ Ⓖ Ⓗ Ⓙ
9. Ⓐ Ⓑ Ⓒ Ⓓ	9. Ⓐ Ⓑ Ⓒ Ⓓ
10. Ⓕ Ⓖ Ⓗ Ⓙ	10. Ⓕ Ⓖ Ⓗ Ⓙ
11. Ⓐ Ⓑ Ⓒ Ⓓ	11. Ⓐ Ⓑ Ⓒ Ⓓ
12. Ⓕ Ⓖ Ⓗ Ⓙ	12. Ⓕ Ⓖ Ⓗ Ⓙ
13. Ⓐ Ⓑ Ⓒ Ⓓ	13. Ⓐ Ⓑ Ⓒ Ⓓ
14. Ⓕ Ⓖ Ⓗ Ⓙ	14. Ⓕ Ⓖ Ⓗ Ⓙ
15. Ⓐ Ⓑ Ⓒ Ⓓ	15. Ⓐ Ⓑ Ⓒ Ⓓ
16. Ⓕ Ⓖ Ⓗ Ⓙ	16. Ⓕ Ⓖ Ⓗ Ⓙ
17. Ⓐ Ⓑ Ⓒ Ⓓ	17. Ⓐ Ⓑ Ⓒ Ⓓ
18. Ⓕ Ⓖ Ⓗ Ⓙ	18. Ⓕ Ⓖ Ⓗ Ⓙ
19. Ⓐ Ⓑ Ⓒ Ⓓ	19. Ⓐ Ⓑ Ⓒ Ⓓ
20. Ⓕ Ⓖ Ⓗ Ⓙ	20. Ⓕ Ⓖ Ⓗ Ⓙ
21. Ⓐ Ⓑ Ⓒ Ⓓ	21. Ⓐ Ⓑ Ⓒ Ⓓ
22. Ⓕ Ⓖ Ⓗ Ⓙ	22. Ⓕ Ⓖ Ⓗ Ⓙ
23. Ⓐ Ⓑ Ⓒ Ⓓ	23. Ⓐ Ⓑ Ⓒ Ⓓ
24. Ⓕ Ⓖ Ⓗ Ⓙ	24. Ⓕ Ⓖ Ⓗ Ⓙ
25. Ⓐ Ⓑ Ⓒ Ⓓ	25. Ⓐ Ⓑ Ⓒ Ⓓ
26. Ⓕ Ⓖ Ⓗ Ⓙ	26. Ⓕ Ⓖ Ⓗ Ⓙ
27. Ⓐ Ⓑ Ⓒ Ⓓ	27. Ⓐ Ⓑ Ⓒ Ⓓ
28. Ⓕ Ⓖ Ⓗ Ⓙ	28. Ⓕ Ⓖ Ⓗ Ⓙ
29. Ⓐ Ⓑ Ⓒ Ⓓ	29. Ⓐ Ⓑ Ⓒ Ⓓ
30. Ⓕ Ⓖ Ⓗ Ⓙ	30. Ⓕ Ⓖ Ⓗ Ⓙ
31. Ⓐ Ⓑ Ⓒ Ⓓ	31. Ⓐ Ⓑ Ⓒ Ⓓ
32. Ⓕ Ⓖ Ⓗ Ⓙ	32. Ⓕ Ⓖ Ⓗ Ⓙ
33. Ⓐ Ⓑ Ⓒ Ⓓ	33. Ⓐ Ⓑ Ⓒ Ⓓ
34. Ⓕ Ⓖ Ⓗ Ⓙ	34. Ⓕ Ⓖ Ⓗ Ⓙ
35. Ⓐ Ⓑ Ⓒ Ⓓ	35. Ⓐ Ⓑ Ⓒ Ⓓ
36. Ⓕ Ⓖ Ⓗ Ⓙ	36. Ⓕ Ⓖ Ⓗ Ⓙ
37. Ⓐ Ⓑ Ⓒ Ⓓ	37. Ⓐ Ⓑ Ⓒ Ⓓ
38. Ⓕ Ⓖ Ⓗ Ⓙ	38. Ⓕ Ⓖ Ⓗ Ⓙ
39. Ⓐ Ⓑ Ⓒ Ⓓ	39. Ⓐ Ⓑ Ⓒ Ⓓ
40. Ⓕ Ⓖ Ⓗ Ⓙ	40. Ⓕ Ⓖ Ⓗ Ⓙ

English Test

45 Minutes — 75 Questions

DIRECTIONS: Following are five passages with underlined portions. Alternate ways of stating the underlined portions are to the right of the passages. Choose the best alternative; if the original is the best way of stating the underlined portion, choose NO CHANGE.

The test also has questions that refer to the passage or ask you to reorder the sentences within the passages. These questions are identified by a number in a box. Choose the best answer and blacken in the corresponding oval on your answer grid.

Passage 1

My Favorite Zoo Animal

Last weekend my mother took my younger brother and I (1) to the zoo. The zoo, it is not far from our house, (2) is my favorite place to visit. My brother, too. (3) My brother asked me which animal I liked best. I told him I had trouble choosing among the giraffe and the zebra, (4) but I finally decided on the latter (5). We stood and watched the giraffe for an hour. The keeper, noticing our interest, and coming over to us to tell us about the animal. (6) I learned a lot I didn't know before.

1. **A.** NO CHANGE
   B. my younger brother and me
   C. I and my younger brother
   D. me and my younger brother

2. **F.** NO CHANGE
   G. The zoo is not far from our house, it
   H. It is not far from our house (the zoo) and it
   J. The zoo, which is not far from our house,

3. **A.** NO CHANGE
   B. It is my brother's favorite place to visit, too.
   C. The zoo being my brother's favorite place also to visit.
   D. My brother, his favorite place is the zoo, too.

4. **F.** NO CHANGE
   G. trouble to choose among the giraffe and the zebra,
   H. trouble choosing between the giraffe and the zebra,
   J. trouble, to choose between the giraffe and the zebra,

5. **A.** NO CHANGE
   B. last
   C. better
   D. best

6. **F.** NO CHANGE
   G. noticed our interest, and coming over to tell us about the animal.
   H. noticing our interest by coming over to tell us about the animal.
   J. noticed our interest, and came over to tell us about the animal.

Go on to next page

For example, I learned that the word giraffe is thought to be derived from the Arabic word *zirafah*, which means "tallest of all." The name is not inappropriate. [7] Giraffes are the tallest animals on earth, and may reach a height of more than 15 feet. The more detailed scientific name also interesting. [8] Scientists officially call this animal *Giraffa camelopardalis* because it considers [9] the animal to look like a camel with the markings of a leopard.

It appears that no two sets of markings are alike. While most visitors to the zoo consider all giraffes to have the same markings, a trained eye can distinguish subtle differences. The patterns vary from subspecies to subspecies, [10] as does the location of the patterns. Some giraffes, for example, have spots running down their legs, and others do not. The colors can also vary, from a blackish hue to a light yellow. The colors serve the purpose of camouflaging the giraffe, being that it [11] blends in well [12] with the leaves of the trees in which it hides. The long neck of the giraffe is mistaken for a tree branch. [13] The theory that the markings on a giraffe are comparable to the fingerprints of a human has [14] gained ground. [15]

7. **A.** NO CHANGE
   B. not appropriate
   C. not appropriately
   D. not inappropriately

8. **F.** NO CHANGE
   G. name is also interesting.
   H. name also is interested.
   J. name, also interesting

9. **A.** NO CHANGE
   B. they consider
   C. they are considering
   D. it is considered

10. **F.** NO CHANGE
    G. from subspecies and subspecies
    H. between subspecies to subspecies
    J. subspecies and subspecies

11. **A.** NO CHANGE
    B. which
    C. to
    D. OMIT the underlined portion.

12. **F.** NO CHANGE
    G. good
    H. best
    J. and does well

13. Which of the following would be the best placement of the last sentence of the passage?
    A. At the beginning of the first paragraph
    B. At the beginning of the second paragraph
    C. At the end of the second paragraph
    D. At the beginning of the third paragraph

14. **F.** NO CHANGE
    G. have
    H. have been
    J. are starting to

15. Which of the following additions would be the best conclusion to this paragraph?
    A. Giraffes may be just as unique as human beings.
    B. Giraffes are evolving and changing their color patterns to meet their environments.
    C. Giraffes are the most colorful creatures in the animal kingdom.
    D. Giraffes are my favorite animal.

Go on to next page

Passage 2

Alex Haley, *Roots* Author

[1]

[1]*Roots* author Alex Haley turned his African ancestors [16] into a book who's [17] emotional impact on Black Americans cannot be overestimated. [2]Born in 1921 in Ithaca, New York, his early years were spent [18] with his grandmother in Henning, Tennessee. [3]The oldest of [19] three sons in his family. [20]

[2]

As a child, Alex wasn't desirous of becoming a writer. [21] As an adult, Alex took a variety of jobs, eventually joining the Coast Guard and becoming a cook. Unchallenged by his daily routine in the U.S. Coast Guard, Haley wrote articles [22] which he sent to many different magazines, hoping to catch an editor's attention. Eventually [23] his submissions were accepted, and occasionally he received payment for his work. Haley's literary abilities afforded him an opportunity [24] to change his career. It is not every cook who can become a military journalist. By 1959 when Haley retired from military service, he held the title of Chief Journalist.

16. **F.** NO CHANGE
    G. stories about his African ancestors
    H. his (African) ancestors
    J. African, his ancestors' stories

17. **A.** NO CHANGE
    B. whos'
    C. who is
    D. whose

18. **F.** NO CHANGE
    G. Alex's early years were spent
    H. Alex spent his early years
    J. the years that Alex was early, he was spending

19. **A.** NO CHANGE
    B. Tennessee — the oldest of
    C. Tennessee because he was the oldest of
    D. Tennessee. Alex was the oldest of

20. Which of the following is true about sentence 3 of paragraph 1?
    F. It should be the first sentence of the passage.
    G. It should be deleted because it adds little to the narrative and doesn't forward the passage.
    H. It disagrees with information presented earlier in the passage.
    J. It repeats information given elsewhere in the passage.

21. **A.** NO CHANGE
    B. Alex's desires to become a writer were unstated when he was a child.
    C. Alex didn't write much as a child.
    D. OMIT the underlined portion.

22. **F.** NO CHANGE
    G. articles written by Haley
    H. Haley, writing articles
    J. and writing articles

23. **A.** NO CHANGE
    B. Although
    C. Because
    D. Nonetheless

24. **F.** NO CHANGE
    G. allow him an opportunity
    H. enabled him an opportunity
    J. give him an opportunity

Go on to next page

[3]

Alex Haley wrote many articles on a variety of topics, both domestic and international. Eventually, he did family history research in the National Archives in Washington, D.C. Haley took more than a dozen years to do <u>the research and he traveled</u> [25] more than a half a million miles to work in huge archives and small libraries ranging over three continents. Researching his ancestors <u>took them</u> [26] to Juffure, a small village in The Gambia. The Gambia's historian spoke about Kunta Kinte, who was sent to the United States on a British slave ship. <u>After Haley completed his research, then he knew</u> [27] he had to tell everyone the story of Kunta Kinte. The author emphasized that this <u>was the saga of not only</u> [28] the Haley family but also the story of Black Americans. That Black Americans agreed was amply demonstrated by the fascination surrounding the miniseries developed from the book. The miniseries *Roots* has been repeated and continues to earn high ratings every time it shows on television. [29]

25. **A.** NO CHANGE
B. research; but he traveled
C. research which traveled
D. the research, during which he traveled

26. **F.** NO CHANGE
G. takes him
H. took him
J. takes us

27. **A.** NO CHANGE
B. After Haley completed his research, he knew
C. When Haley, after completing his research, knew
D. Then, after having completed his research, Haley knew

28. **F.** NO CHANGE
G. was not only the saga of
H. was of not only his saga but
J. saga was not only of

Question 29 refers to the passage as a whole.

29. This passage was written as a homework assignment to "Discuss the literary abilities of Alex Haley." Did the passage fulfill the assignment?

A. Yes, because the derivation of *Roots* is discussed.
B. Yes, because the reader learns the sources of Haley's ideas.
C. No, because the emphasis is on Haley's life, not his skill as a writer.
D. No, because the focus is more on Haley's family than on Haley.

Go on to next page

Passage 3

Understanding the Elderly

[1]

And important[30], it is essential to have better knowledge of older persons' capabilities so that they will be better encouraged to participate and contribute in a meaningful way. As the birth rate declines and the aging segment of our population increase[31], our work force will depend more and more on older workers for reinforcements. With our unemployment statistics as high as they are today, its[32] hard to imagine the time when our society will be depending[33] more on older workers, but it will. For this reason alone, we should be knowing[34] more about the capabilities of older workers and how their skills can best be utilized so that we can identify ways the job force can be altered to match the skills of older workers. [35]

[2]

I have thought a lot about the elderly lately and have had more than a few misconceptions corrected. Recently, due to the fact that[36] my aunt lives there, I went to talk to a senior citizens' home in Columbus, Ohio. It was their annual founders' day[37]. In discussing beforehand what I was going to talk with them about, I learned that they didn't want to talk about old folks or Social Security; but about[38]

30. **F.** NO CHANGE
G. More importantly,
H. It's more important, even
J. So important in fact it is,

31. **A.** NO CHANGE
B. our population's increase
C. our population increases
D. our increasing population increase

32. **F.** NO CHANGE
G. its'
H. it's
J. it was

33. **A.** NO CHANGE
B. have depended
C. will depend
D. , having depended

34. **F.** NO CHANGE
G. we need to know
H. knowing
J. we have to know (because it's important)

35. Which of the following best describes the tone and purpose of the paragraph?
A. The tone is argumentative; the purpose is to continue a debate.
B. The tone is derogatory; the purpose is to ridicule the elderly.
C. The tone is persuasive; the purpose is to urge readers to learn more.
D. The tone is lighthearted; the purpose is to amuse the readers.

36. **F.** NO CHANGE
G. since then
H. owing to the fact that
J. because

37. **A.** NO CHANGE
B. on the home's annual founders day
C. and it was on their founders day
D. , being that it was the annual founders day, celebrated annually

38. **F.** NO CHANGE
G. , but about
H. : but about
J. OMIT the underlined portion.

Go on to next page

what is going on in Bosnia and the Middle East. I spent about 45 minutes talking to them on those subjects, and you could have heard a pin drop. They were vitally interested. They don't want to be treated as though they [39] are no longer capable. [40]

[3]

Capabilities change but don't necessarily diminish or disappear as people age. Studies show that the ability to handle new verbal tasks, such as pairing up a word with a particular stimulus, changes much smaller than [41] the age differences. (Something like learning vocabulary in a foreign language [42]; you learn [43] to pair up the unfamiliar word with a corresponding word in your language.) When you study the individual, you often find that performance on new verbal tasks diminishes much less than what you might have predicted from looking at the group of elderly persons as a whole.

39. A. NO CHANGE
B. like they
C. as being
D. because they

40. Which of the following best summarizes the idea of this paragraph?
F. Foreign affairs don't involve the elderly.
G. Elderly people can remain interested in current topics.
H. Old people don't want to be reminded of their age.
J. Wars are a universal topic of conversation.

41. A. NO CHANGE
B. have lesser changes
C. changes much less then
D. changes much less than

42. F. NO CHANGE
G. This learning, something like learning a foreign language
H. Like learning vocabulary in a foreign language, this is learning too
J. You use this method to learn vocabulary in a foreign language

43. A. NO CHANGE
B. would learn
C. learning
D. had learned

Go on to next page

Passage 4

The Findings of the Paleontologists

[1]

Paleontologists have called (44) the preserved burrows "devil's corkscrews" (or *Daemonelix*) when (45) the time they were first found. At that time there were then (46), scientists thought the corkscrews might be holes (47) left by the giant tap roots of some unknown plant. But when, however, (48) *Palaeocastor* skeletons were found in the bottoms of the spirals, almost everyone had to concede that they were truly beaver burrows. Admittedly, the skeleton of a *Nothocyon* been (49) found in one burrow; but this (50) predator probably followed a beaver home for supper and just stayed. Three other kinds of beavers lived around Agate in the early Miocene epoch, but their bones have never been found in the burrows, in fact, no one (51) knows what they did for homes. Perhaps there burrows (52) were much shallower or were in the river banks where running water soon destroyed them.

44. F. NO CHANGE
G. calling
H. have been called by
J. used to be called

45. A. NO CHANGE
B. then
C. since
D. while

46. F. NO CHANGE
G. There were at that time
H. Then at that time
J. At that time

47. A. NO CHANGE
B. the bottoms of
C. the roots
D. it

48. F. NO CHANGE
G. knowing
H. there were
J. OMIT the underlined portion.

49. A. NO CHANGE
B. was
C. his
D. is being

50. F. NO CHANGE
G. burrow — however, this
H. burrow. But the
J. burrow, but this

51. A. NO CHANGE
B. burrows. In fact, no one
C. burrows, no one, in fact,
D. burrows, because in fact no one

52. F. NO CHANGE
G. there, burrows
H. their burrow's
J. their burrows

Go on to next page

[2]

[1]The paleontologists' findings seem incompatible with the divisions of epochs, periods, and eras until one considers that the divisions were based on breaks in the European sedimentary record reflecting local events that did not necessarily show up in North America's sediments. [2]Paleontologists can tell that no dramatic change layed (53) in store for the fauna at the beginning of the Miocene epoch and that many Oligocene genera carried over into the new epoch. [3]Most of the primitive animals that had survived in the extensive forests become extant (54) when the forests began to retreat: but for the most part, the (55) record continued undisturbed. [4]This is to be expected where the accumulation of sediments continued nonstop (56) without interruption. [57] [58] [59]

53. A. NO CHANGE
B. lay
C. lies
D. was laying

54. F. NO CHANGE
G. extensive forests, became extant
H. extensive forests became extinct
J. OMIT the underlined portion.

55. A. NO CHANGE
B. retreat. However, for the most part, the
C. retreat. Moreover, for the most part, the
D. retreat. But most of the part of the

56. F. NO CHANGE
G. nonstopping
H. nonstop but
J. OMIT the underlined portion.

57. Is the word *reflecting* in sentence 1 of paragraph 2 used appropriately in this passage?
A. Yes, because it means "indicating" or "corresponding."
B. Yes, because it refers to the smooth, mirrorlike lake in which the fossils were found.
C. No, because *reflecting* means "thinking back on, examining."
D. No, because it means the same as *record,* making the sentence redundant.

Question 58 refers to the passage as a whole.

58. The passage as a whole is best expressed by which of the following titles?
F. Tracking Ancient Rodents
G. What Fossils Reveal
H. A Paleontologist's Duties
J. The Extinction of Species

59. Which of the following represents the best order of the sentences in the second paragraph?
A. 2—3—4—1
B. 3—2—1—4
C. 3—4—1—2
D. 2—4—3—1

Go on to next page

Passage 5

Vietnam

In 111 B.C., ancestors of the present-day Vietnamese, inhabiting part of what is now southern China and northern Vietnam, were conquered, there being the warlike [60] forces of China's Han dynasty. Chinese rule lasted more than 1,000 years, since [61] A.D. 939, when the Vietnamese ousted their conquerors and began a southward expansion, that, by the mid-eighteenth century, reached [62] the Gulf of Siam.

The Vietnamese were rent by internal political divisions, however, and [63] for nearly two centuries contending families in the north and south struggled to control the powerless kings of the Le dynasty. During this period, Vietnam affectively [64] was divided near the 17th parallel. Just a [65] few kilometers above the demarcation line established at the 1954 Geneva Conference.

Vietnam having been [66] reunited following a devastating civil war in the eighteenth century but soon fell prey to the expansion of European colonialism. While the [67] French conquest of Vietnam began in 1858 with an attack on what is now the city of Da Nang. France imposed control gradually, to meet [68] heavy resistance, and only in 1884 was Vietnam officially incorporated into the French empire.

60. **F.** NO CHANGE
G. due to the warlike
H. by the warlike
J. OMIT the underlined portion.

61. **A.** NO CHANGE
B. when
C. from
D. until

62. **F.** NO CHANGE
G. expansion that is reaching, by the mid-eighteenth century,
H. expansion, by the mid-eighteenth century, reaching,
J. expansion, by mid-eighteenth century having been reached

63. **A.** NO CHANGE
B. divisions; however, and
C. divisions. And however,
D. divisions, although

64. **F.** NO CHANGE
G. in affect
H. in effect
J. ineffective

65. **A.** NO CHANGE
B. parallel, just a
C. parallel, that is just a
D. parallel; just a

66. **F.** NO CHANGE
G. being
H. was
J. OMIT the underlined portion.

67. **A.** NO CHANGE
B. When the
C. Whenever the
D. The

68. **F.** NO CHANGE
G. meeting
H. and meeting
J. about to have met

Go on to next page

Vietnam's resistance was the precursor of nationalist activity directed against foreign rule. By 1930, the Vietnam Nationalist Party had staged the first significant armed uprising against the French, but its [69] virtual destruction in the ensuing French repression left the leadership of the anticolonial movement to those more adapt at [70] underground organization and survival — the Communists. In that same year, the recently formed Indochinese Communist Party (ICP) took the led in setting up [71] short-lived "soviets" in Nghe An and Ha Tinh provinces, an action that identified the ICP with peasant unrest.

The Vietnamese communist movement began in Paris in 1920 when Ho Chi Minh became a charter member of the French Communist Party. Two years later, Ho went to Moscow to study Marxist doctrine, then he went [72] to China. While in China, he formed the Vietnamese Revolutionary Youth League, setting the stage for the formation of the ICP in 1930. French repression of nationalists and Communists forced some of the insurgents underground. Other dissidents were imprisoned, [73] some emerging later to play an important role in the anticolonial movement. [74] [75]

69. **A.** NO CHANGE
B. but it's
C. but, it's
D. so its

70. **F.** NO CHANGE
G. adept at
H. adopted from
J. adept with

71. **A.** NO CHANGE
B. took the lead in setting up
C. taking the led in setting up
D. taking the lead in setting up

72. **F.** NO CHANGE
G. doctrine; then went
H. doctrine, and then going
J. doctrine, then went

73. **A.** NO CHANGE
B. Other dissidents was imprisoned,
C. Other dissidents imprisoned
D. Other dissidents, imprisoned,

Questions 74 and 75 refer to the passage as a whole.

74. This passage may have been written for which of the following purposes?
F. to ridicule the futility of fighting Communism
G. to provide an historical overview of the government of Vietnam
H. to criticize foreign powers that attempt to control Vietnam
J. to show Ho Chi Minh's role in the development of modern communism

75. Which of the following topics would be most appropriate for the next paragraph in this passage?
A. the Vietnamese war for independence
B. the Vietnamese development of nuclear weapons
C. the change of Vietnam from an agrarian to an industrialized society
D. the role of the United States in developing a stronger human-rights program in Vietnam

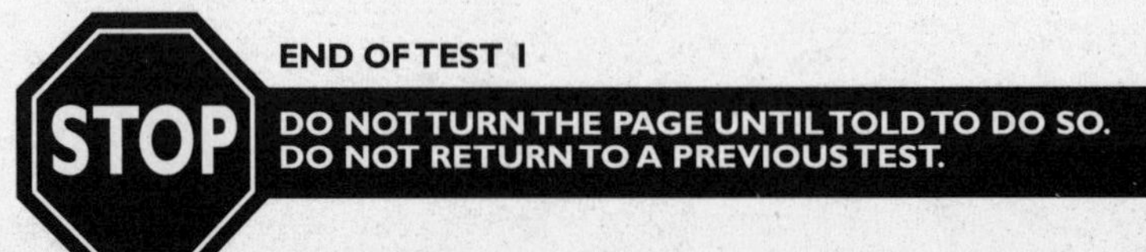

STOP
END OF TEST 1
DO NOT TURN THE PAGE UNTIL TOLD TO DO SO.
DO NOT RETURN TO A PREVIOUS TEST.

Mathematics Test

60 Minutes — 60 Questions

DIRECTIONS: Each question has five answer choices. Choose the best answer for each question and shade the corresponding oval on your answer grid.

---

1. Putty has picked x pecks of peppers per hour for y hours. How many pecks of peppers has Putty picked?

A. xy
B. $x + y$
C. $\frac{x}{y}$
D. $\frac{y}{x}$
E. $\frac{x + y}{2}$

2. 20% of $x = 50$. What is x?

F. 5
G. 10
H. 25
J. 250
K. 500

3. Three friends, Mike, Ken, and Debi, earned an average of $50,000 each on a project. Their total earnings were exactly 40% of the total earnings of everyone in their company. How much were the total earnings of the entire company?

A. $600,000
B. $450,000
C. $375,000
D. $340,000
E. $40,000

4. $10^{-1} + 10^{0} + 10^{1} = ?$

F. 101.10
G. 101.01
H. 11.1
J. 1
K. 0

5. An office receives 80 calls a day for 6 days. In order to average 100 calls per day for 12 days, how many calls must the company get in the next 6 days?

A. 1,200
B. 1,100
C. 1,020
D. 720
E. 120

6. What is the fifth term in the series: 2, 4, 16, 256 . . . ?

F. 70,100
G. 65,536
H. 43,004
J. 41,022
K. 2,566

7. If one of the angles in a triangle is obtuse, which of the following is a true statement regarding the other two angles in the triangle?

A. They are in a ratio of 2:1.
B. They total 90 degrees.
C. One must be a right angle.
D. Both angles must be acute.
E. Both angles must be obtuse.

8. 5% of $(a + b)$ = 10% of b. Which of the following must be a true statement?

F. $a > b$
G. $a < b$
H. $a = b$
J. $a + b = 0$
K. $a, b < 0$

9. The areas of Figures I and II are equal. x =

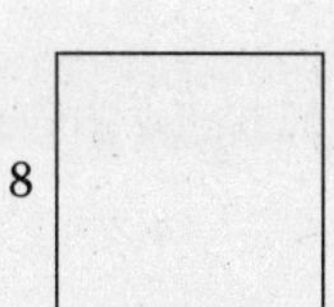

Figure 1

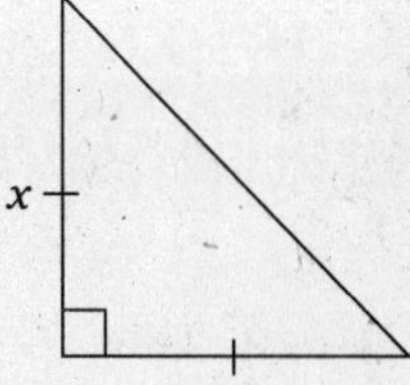

Figure 2

A. $4\sqrt{2}$
B. $8\sqrt{2}$
C. $4\sqrt{3}$
D. $8\sqrt{3}$
E. $12\sqrt{3}$

Go on to next page

10. $x! = x(x-1)(x-2)(x-3)\ldots 1$

Solve for 6!

F. 1,296
G. 600
H. 720
J. 60
K. 1

11. The cost of a textbook increased by 25% from 1998 to 1999. In 2000, the cost of the textbook was 1/4 below its 1998 cost. By what percentage did the cost of the textbook decrease from 1999 to 2000?

A. 0
B. 20
C. 25
D. 40
E. 75

12. A wheel of circumference 10π has a diameter of ?

F. 2
G. 5
H. 2π
J. 10
K. 5π

13. What is the measure of angle *x*?

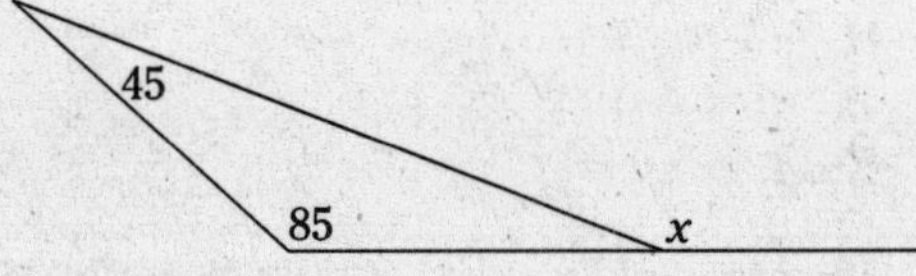

A. 130°
B. 110°
C. 50°
D. 40°
E. 35°

14. $(5x^2y^5)^2(3x^3y^4)^3 = ?$

F. $675x^{13}y^{22}$
G. $675x^{36}y^{120}$
H. $15x^{36}y^{120}$
J. $15x^{13}y^{22}$
K. $15x^7y^{14}$

15. A circle with a radius of 4 inches has 1/4 the area of a circle with a radius of how many inches?

A. 1
B. 2
C. 8
D. 16
E. 64

16. A hiker walks nonstop for 2 hours and 20 minutes and travels 7 miles. At what rate did he walk?

F. 2 mph
G. $2\frac{1}{10}$ mph
H. $2\frac{1}{2}$ mph
J. 3 mph
K. $3\frac{1}{2}$ mph

17. A dollhouse is to be an exact replica of a collector's own home on a reduced scale. If the main bedroom of the dollhouse is 18 inches long by 24 inches wide, the real bedroom of 12 feet long will be how many feet wide?

A. 24
B. 18
C. 16
D. 10
E. 8

18. Triangles I and II (not shown) are similar figures. The angles of triangle I are in the ratio 1:2:3. If the perimeter of triangle I is $15+5\sqrt{3}$, and the shortest side of triangle II is 15, then what is the perimeter of triangle II?

F. $150+20\sqrt{3}$
G. $60+15\sqrt{3}$
H. $60+5\sqrt{3}$
J. $45+15\sqrt{3}$
K. 45

19. When asked her age, Lael responded, "Take the square root of 625, add it to the square of 5, and take 40 percent of the resulting sum." Which of the following expresses Lael's age?

A. $L=\sqrt{(625+5)40}$
B. $L=.40\cdot\sqrt{625+5^2}$
C. $L=.40\cdot\sqrt{625}\cdot 5^2$
D. $L=.40+\sqrt{625}+5^2$
E. $L=.40(\sqrt{625}+5^2)$

20. In a classroom of children, every child has either blond, brown, or red hair. The probability of randomly selecting a child with red hair is 1/6. The probability of randomly selecting a child with brown hair is 1/3. If 30 children have blond hair, how many children are in the classroom?

F. 30
G. 45
H. 60
J. 90
K. 120

Go on to next page

21. $\dfrac{3^2 - 4^0}{4^0 - 3^2} = ?$

A. $-\dfrac{5}{4}$
B. $-\dfrac{4}{5}$
C. –1
D. 1
E. $\dfrac{5}{4}$

22. What is the interior degree measure of figure ABCDE?

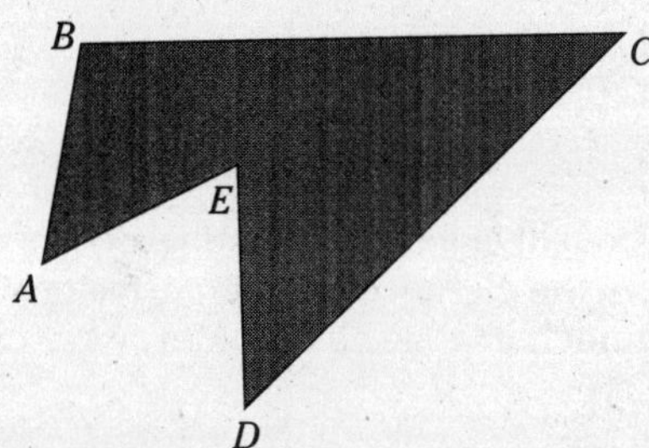

F. 900
G. 720
H. 540
J. 360
K. 300

23. A city is visited one month by 200 German, 320 American, 140 Moroccan, 180 French, and 240 Japanese tourists. If a circle graph were made representing the various categories, the angle made by the segment representing the French would be how many degrees?

A. 360
B. 270
C. 60
D. 1
E. $1/6$

24. $\sqrt{12} + \sqrt{75} = ?$

F. $\sqrt{900}$
G. $\sqrt[3]{900}$
H. $9\sqrt{3}$
J. $7\sqrt{3}$
K. $\sqrt{2}$

25. For all x and y, $(3x^2y + xy^2) - (2x^2y - 2xy^2) = ?$

A. $x^2 - x$
B. $x^2y - xy^2$
C. $x^2y + 3xy^2$
D. $5x^2 - xy^2$
E. $xy^2 + 3x^2y^2$

26. Two similar triangles have sides in the ratio 3:4. What is the ratio of the areas of the triangles?

F. 16:9
G. 4:4
H. 3:4
J. 9:16
K. 9:64

27. The ratio of looseleaf notebooks to spiral-bound notebooks is 4:7. If there are 60 more spiral-bound notebooks than looseleaf notebooks, how many looseleaf and spiral-bound notebooks are there altogether?

A. 280
B. 240
C. 220
D. 200
E. 140

28. Given that x is an integer, for what value of x is $x + {}^2/_3x > 15$ and $x + 4 < 15$?

A. 8
B. 9
C. 10
D. 11
E. 12

29. A third of the product of 6 and 4 is the same as 3 less than $2x$. What is x?

A. 8
B. 7
C. 6
D. $11/2$
E. $5/2$

Go on to next page

30. A gambler's lucky number is 12. On any roll of two dice, what is the probability that he will roll his lucky number?

F. $\frac{1}{2}$
G. $\frac{1}{3}$
H. $\frac{1}{6}$
J. $\frac{1}{12}$
K. $\frac{1}{36}$

31. What is the base of a triangle of area 25 and altitude (height) 10?

A. 2
B. 2.5
C. 4
D. 4.5
E. 5

32. Paul wants to buy a new aquarium with the same volume as the old. His old aquarium measures 6×4 units on the base and is 10 units tall. If his new aquarium has a base in which each side is 50 percent longer than the corresponding side in the old aquarium, approximately how many units tall will the new aquarium be?

F. 4.4
G. 4.5
H. 4.9
J. 5.0
K. 5.1

33. Triangles ABC and DEF are similar figures. What is the perimeter of triangle DEF?

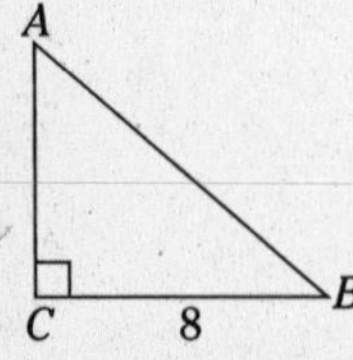

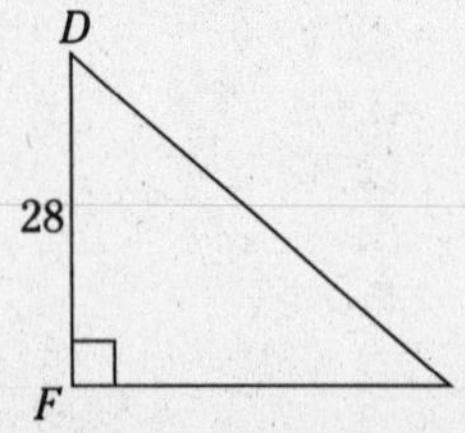

Area of ABC = 32

A. $56+28\sqrt{2}$
B. 84
C. $84\sqrt{2}$
D. $84+28\sqrt{2}$
E. $90\sqrt{2}$

34. Given that $-|3-3a|=-12$, which of the following could be a?

F. 5
G. 4
H. 3
J. 2
K. 1

35. Triangle ABC is an equilateral triangle with an area of 32. Triangle DEF is an isosceles right triangle of area 64. Which of the following represents the ratio of the sum of the interior angles in triangle ABC to the sum of the interior angles in DEF?

A. 4:1
B. 3:1
C. 2:1
D. 1:1
E. 1:2

36. Marcy bought eight items costing x cents each. She gave the clerk y dimes. In terms of x and y, how much change should Marcy get back?

F. $y-8x$
G. $10y+8x$
H. $10y-8x$
J. $8x-y$
K. $8x-10y$

37. Arc AB = 3 units. What is the circumference of Circle O in units?

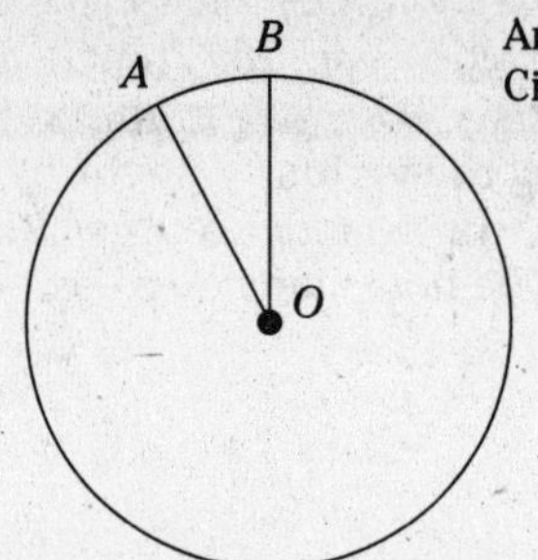

A. $108/\pi$
B. 36
C. 36π
D. 108
E. 108π

Go on to next page

38. Kim starts at point X and walks 50 yards straight north. Scott starts at the same point X and walks due east. The shortest distance between Kim and Scott is 120 yards. How many yards did Scott walk?

F. 13,000
G. 11,900
H. $\sqrt{13,000}$
J. $\sqrt{11,900}$
K. 50

39. What point on the graph of $x^2 - y = 4$ has an x-coordinate of 3?

A. (3, –5)
B. $(3, \sqrt{5})$
C. (3, 4)
D. (3, 5)
E. (3, 13)

40. $(\sqrt{5}+\sqrt{6})(\sqrt{3}+\sqrt{6}) =$

F. $6+\sqrt{30}+\sqrt{15}+3\sqrt{2}$
G. $6+4\sqrt{2}+2\sqrt{15}$
H. $6+6\sqrt{30}$
J. $6+\sqrt{63}$
K. $3\sqrt{11}$

41. An automatic water system fills an empty pool half full in one hour. Each hour thereafter the system fills one-half of the capacity that is still empty. After how many hours is the pool $^1/_{64}$ empty?

A. 12
B. 10
C. 7
D. 6
E. 5

42. If m pencils cost n cents, which of the following expresses the cost of p pencils?

F. mnp cents
G. $\frac{mp}{n}$ cents
H. $m+\frac{p}{n}$ cents
J. $n+\frac{p}{m}$ cents
K. $\frac{np}{m}$ cents

43. Hal can assemble 600 widgets in $2^1/_2$ hours. Faye can pack 200 widgets in 45 minutes. If Faye wants to work for exactly $4^1/_2$ hours and finish the same number of widgets as Hal, how many hours will Hal have to work?

A. 5
B. $4^2/_3$
C. $4^1/_4$
D. 4
E. $3^3/_5$

44. The cost of a swimsuit goes up 50 percent in June, down 20 percent in July, and down another 30 percent in August. The cost of the swimsuit in August is what percent of the cost of the swimsuit before June?

F. 110
G. 100
H. 90
J. 84
K. 61

45. A wheel covers a distance of 300π meters in 15 revolutions. What is the radius of the wheel?

A. 30π
B. 25
C. 20
D. 10π
E. 10

46. A prime number times a composite number must be

F. prime
G. composite
H. zero
J. a fraction
K. even

47. Sector AOC has an area of 120π square units. What is the circumference of the circle?

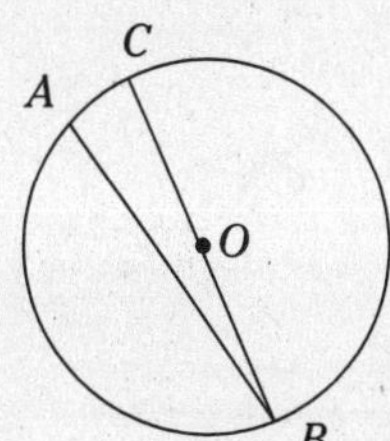

Angle ABC = 6°
O is the midpoint of the circle

A. 34,600π
B. 1,200π
C. 120π
D. 120/π
E. $\sqrt{120}/\pi$

Go on to next page

48. On a circle with the equation $x^2 + y^2 = 25$, if the x-coordinate is -3, the y-coordinate could be

F. -3
G. 0
H. 4
J. 9
K. 16

49. $(a + 3)^2 + (a - 4)^2 =$

A. $2a^2 - 2a + 25$
B. $2a^2 + 14a + 25$
C. $a^2 + 2a + 25$
D. $a^2 - 2a - 25$
E. $2a^2 - 2a - 4$

50. Helen drove from Roger's house to the store in a friend's car. From the store, she bicycled six miles to Brian's office. From Brian's office, Helen took the subway 18 miles to the university. If Helen drove only one-fourth of the distance, how long was her entire trip (one way only)?

A. 16 miles
B. 24 miles
C. 32 miles
D. 96 miles
E. 100 miles

51. In the right triangle XYZ below, what is the value of tan Z?

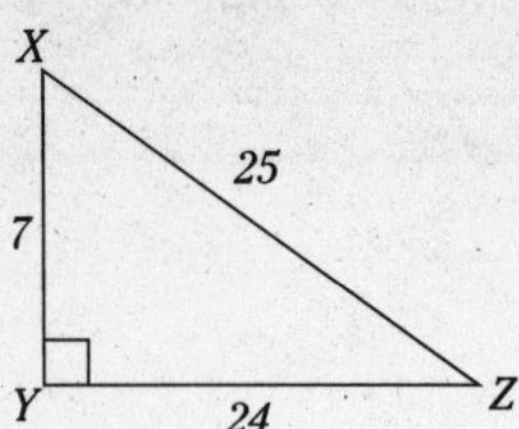

A. 7/25
B. 7/24
C. 24/25
D. 25/24
E. 24/7

52. Which of the following is best expressed by the figure below?

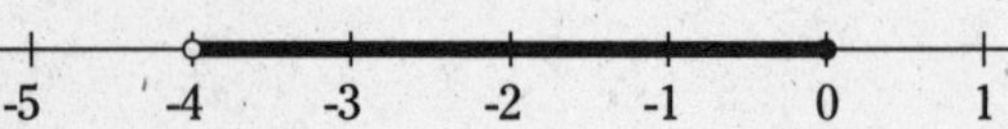

A. $x > -4$
B. $x < -4$
C. $-4 \leq x < 0$
D. $-4 < x \leq 0$
E. $-5 < x \leq 1$

53. If $4cx - \frac{3d}{e} = 4cy$, then $x - y = ?$

A. $-\frac{3d}{4ce}$
B. $-\frac{3d}{e} + \frac{1}{4c}$
C. $\frac{3d}{4e} - c$
D. $\frac{3d}{4ce}$
E. $\frac{3d}{e} + 4c$

54. For all $a \neq 0$, what is the slope of the line passing through (a,b) and $(-a,-b)$?

F. 0
G. 1
H. a/b
J. b/a
K. $-b/a$

55. From a lookout point on a cliff, the angle of depression to a boat on the water is 14 degrees, and the distance from the boat to the shore just below the cliff is 2 km. How far is the lookout from the water surface?

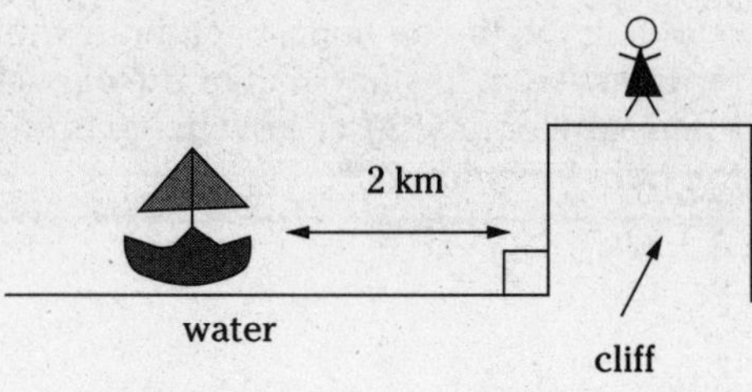

A. $\frac{2}{\sin 14°}$
B. $\frac{2}{\tan 14°}$
C. $\frac{2}{\cos 14°}$
D. $2 \sin 14°$
E. $2 \tan 14°$

Go on to next page

56. A computer is printing a novel. It prints 60 pages in the first hour, after which it breaks. Two hours later, the computer is fixed and resumes printing at the rate of 60 pages per hour. To finish the job on time, another computer that prints at the same rate is brought in and begins printing when the first computer is repaired. The two computers finish printing one hour later. The graphs of the number of pages printed (*p*) as a function of time (*t*) would most resemble which of the following?

F. 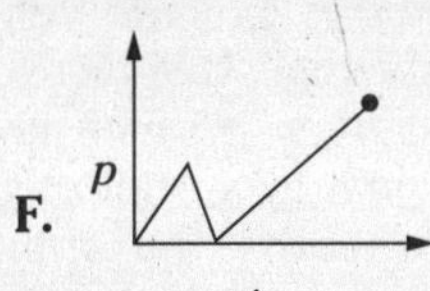

G. 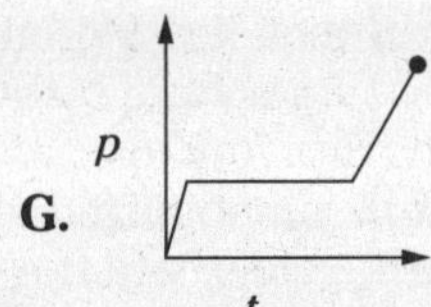

H. 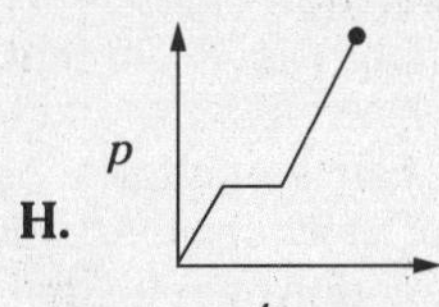

J. p
t

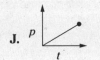

K. p
t

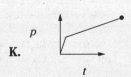

57. Which of the following is equivalent to

$$\frac{\sin^2\theta + \cos^2\theta}{\sec^2\theta}?$$

A. $\cos^2\theta$
B. $\sin^2\theta$
C. $\tan^2\theta$
D. $\dfrac{1}{\cos^2\theta}$
E. $\sin^2\theta + 1$

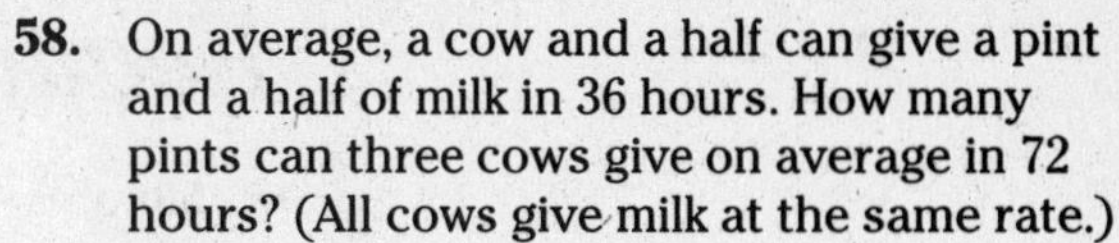
58. On average, a cow and a half can give a pint and a half of milk in 36 hours. How many pints can three cows give on average in 72 hours? (All cows give milk at the same rate.)

F. 3
G. 4
H. 5
J. 6
K. 7

59. From an observer on the ground, the angle of elevation to a hot-air balloon is 21 degrees and the distance from the observer to a point on the ground directly underneath the balloon is 1,500 meters. How many meters high is the balloon?

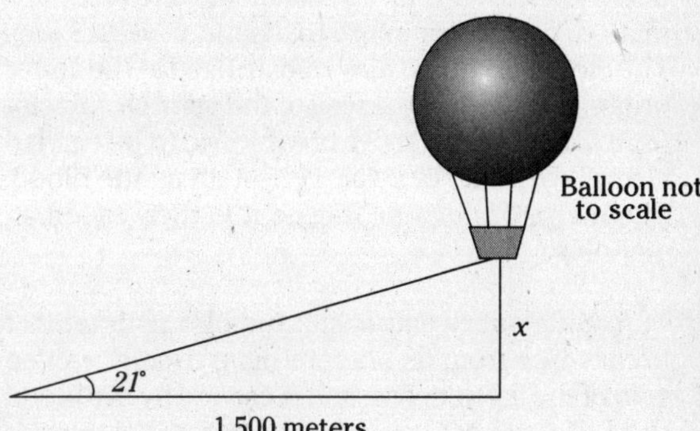

F. 1,500/cos 21°
G. 1,500/tan 21°
H. 1,500 sin 21°
J. 1,500 cos 21°
K. 1,500 tan 21°

60. If A measures between 0° and 180° and tan A = 4/3, what are the possible values of cos A?

F. –3/5 only
G. –3/5 and 3/5
H. –4/5 and 4/5
J. 3/5 only
K. 4/5 only

END OF TEST 2

STOP DO NOT TURN THE PAGE UNTIL TOLD TO DO SO.
DO NOT RETURN TO A PREVIOUS TEST.

Reading Test

35 Minutes — 40 Questions

DIRECTIONS: Each of the four passages in this section is followed by ten questions. Answer each question based on what is stated or implied in the passage and shade the corresponding oval on your answer grid.

Passage 1

Natural Science

Thrombosis refers to abnormal clotting that causes the blood flow in a blood vessel to become obstructed. Venous thrombosis refers to such an obstruction in a vein, often at some site of inflammation, disease, or injury to the blood vessel wall. The clot (thrombus) may remain fixed at the site of origin, adhering to the wall of the vein. Or the clot (or a fragment of it) may break loose to be carried elsewhere in the circulatory system by the blood. The migratory clot or fragment is then called an embolus.

In pulmonary embolism, the clot or fragment breaks free from its site of origin, usually a deep vein of the leg or pelvis, and is carried by the blood through progressively larger veins into the inferior vena cava, a very large abdominal vein that empties into the right side of the heart. The embolus is pumped through the right side of the heart and into the pulmonary artery, whose branches supply blood to the lungs. Depending on its size, the embolus may pass through the larger pulmonary branches, but may eventually enter a branch too narrow to allow it to pass. Here it lodges, obstructing blood flow to the lung tissues supplied by that vessel and its finer divisions "downstream" from the embolus.

The clinical consequences of pulmonary embolism vary with the size of the embolus and the extent to which it reduces total blood flow to the lungs. Very small emboli cause so little circulatory impairment that they may produce no clinical signs or symptoms at all. In fact, among the estimated 300,000 patients who experience pulmonary embolism each year, the great majority suffer no serious symptoms or complications, and the disorder clears up without significant aftereffects.

However, in a significant percentage of patients, the pulmonary embolism is massive, sometimes reducing total pulmonary blood flow by 50 percent or more; and the consequences may be grave: seriously strained circulation, shock, or acute respiratory failure. Massive pulmonary embolism causes some 50,000 deaths each year in the U.S.

Certain classes of patients are more likely than others to develop venous thrombosis with its attendant risk of pulmonary embolism. Disorders that increase susceptibility include venous inflammation (phlebitis), congestive heart failure, and certain forms of cancer. Women are more susceptible during pregnancy and during recovery from childbirth than at other times, and those taking birth control pills appear to be at slightly higher risk than are women who do not. Postoperative patients constitute a high risk group, particularly following pelvic surgery and orthopedic procedures involving the hip. Any operations requiring that the patient be immobilized for prolonged periods afterward exacerbate the risk of this problem. Among patients recovering from hip fractures, for example, the incidence of venous thrombosis may run as high as 50 percent.

Venous thrombosis can sometimes be diagnosed by the presence of a swollen extremity with some evidence of inflammation or a clot that can be felt when the affected vein is examined. But sometimes venous thrombosis produces no clear-cut clinical signs so that other tests may be needed to confirm the diagnosis.

One such test entails injecting fibrinogen tagged with a radioactive isotope of iodine into the blood. Fibrinogen has a strong affinity for blood clots and is incorporated into them, carrying its radioactive label with it. The clot can then be located with a radiation-sensing device.

Another diagnostic technique, called venography, involves injecting a dye (one that shows clearly on x-rays) into the vein where obstruction is suspected. The x-ray venogram provides very detailed information on the extent and location of the obstruction.

A third technique uses sensitive instruments that measure blood flow in vessels of the extremities to detect any circulatory impairment that may result from thrombosis.

Go on to next page

Signs of nonfatal pulmonary embolism may include sudden shortness of breath, chest pain, increased heart rate, restlessness and anxiety, a fall in blood pressure, and loss of consciousness. But clinical symptoms may vary by their presence or absence and in their intensity, and their similarity to symptoms that may result from other disorders can make the diagnosis of pulmonary embolism difficult on this basis alone.

Pulmonary angiography (x-ray visualization of the pulmonary artery and its branches after injection of a radiopaque dye) is the most reliable diagnostic technique, but it is a complex test that cannot be done routinely in all patients. A somewhat simpler test involves injecting extremely fine particles of a radioactively labeled material such as albumin into a vein and then scanning the lungs with a radiation detector while the particles traverse the pulmonary blood vessels.

1. The purpose of the first paragraph is
   - **A.** to analyze the causes of blood clots.
   - **B.** to describe types of blood clots.
   - **C.** to predict who is most likely to get a blood clot.
   - **D.** to inform the readers of steps to take for the prevention of blood clots.

2. Which of the following best describes the difference between a thrombosis and an embolus?
   - **F.** A thrombosis is in the lung; an embolism may be anywhere.
   - **G.** A thrombosis is usually fatal; an embolism is rarely fatal.
   - **H.** A thrombosis remains stationary; an embolism moves within the circulatory system.
   - **J.** A thrombosis is larger than an embolism.

3. Which of the following may you infer about pulmonary embolism?
   - **A.** It may cure itself.
   - **B.** It is invariably fatal.
   - **C.** It is more severe in children than in adults.
   - **D.** It is directly related to diet.

4. According to the passage, a common origin for a pulmonary thrombosis is in the
   - **F.** heart.
   - **G.** brain.
   - **H.** leg.
   - **J.** arm.

5. In line 46, the phrase "attendant risk" means
   - **A.** risks faced by those who aid others.
   - **B.** risks that accompany something else.
   - **C.** minimal, almost nonexistent risks.
   - **D.** risks for women only, not for men.

6. In line 58, *exacerbate* means
   - **F.** reduce.
   - **G.** cure.
   - **H.** heal.
   - **J.** make worse.

7. Which of the following may you substitute for "clinical signs" (line 67)?
   - **A.** Hospitals
   - **B.** Deaths
   - **C.** Diseases
   - **D.** Symptoms

8. Which of the following may be the best title for the passage?
   - **F.** How to Cure Embolisms
   - **G.** How Blood Clots Develop
   - **H.** Means of Preventing Blood Clots and Embolisms
   - **J.** Description and Diagnosis of Blood Clots

9. The three tests discussed in lines 69–84 are introduced for which of the following purposes?
   - **A.** to lament the high cost of diagnosis
   - **B.** to prove that any blood clot can eventually be diagnosed
   - **C.** to describe the means of confirming a suspected diagnosis
   - **D.** to reject the premise that all blood clots are fatal

10. According to the author, using clinical symptoms to diagnose pulmonary embolisms
    - **F.** is cheaper and more time-effective than using high-tech machinery.
    - **G.** should be done cautiously and in conjunction with other tests.
    - **H.** may be done only in the least-acute cases.
    - **J.** cannot be done routinely on all patients.

Go on to next page

Passage 2

Prose Fiction
(From *Nicholas Nickleby* by Charles Dickens)

This was a young lady who could be scarcely eighteen, of very slight and delicate figure, but exquisitely shaped, who, walking timidly up to the desk, made an inquiry, in a very low tone of voice, relative to some situation as governess, or companion to a lady. She raised her veil, for an instant, while she preferred the inquiry, and disclosed a countenance of most uncommon beauty, though shaded by a cloud of sadness, which, in one so young, was doubly remarkable. Having received a card of reference to some person on the books, she made the usual acknowledgment, and glided away.

She was neatly, but very quietly attired; so much so, indeed, that it seemed as though her dress, if it had been worn by one who imparted fewer graces of her own to it, might have looked poor and shabby. Her attendant — for she had one — was a red-faced, round-eyed slovenly girl, who, from a certain roughness about the bare arms that peeped from under her draggled shawl, and the half-washed-out-traces of smut and blacklead which tattooed her countenance, was clearly of a kin with the servant-of-all-work on the farm: between whom and herself there had passed various grins and glances, indicative of the freemasonry of the craft.

The girl followed her mistress; and before Nicholas had recovered from the first effect of his surprise and admiration, the young lady was gone. It is not a matter of such utter improbability as some sober people may think, that he would have followed them out, had he not been restrained by what passed between the fat lady and her bookkeeper.

"When is she coming again, Tom?" asked the fat lady.

"Tomorrow morning," replied Tom, mending his pen.

"Where have you sent her to?" asked the fat lady.

"Mrs. Clark's," replied Tom.

"She'll have a nice life of it, if she goes there," observed the fat lady, taking a pinch of snuff from a tin box.

Tom made no other reply than thrusting his tongue into his cheek, and pointing the feather of his pen towards Nicholas — reminders which elicited from the fat lady an inquiry of, "Now, sir, what can we do for *you*?"

Nicholas briefly replied, that he wanted to know whether there was any such post to be had, as secretary or amanuensis to a gentleman.

"Any such!" rejoined the mistress; "a dozen such. An't there, Tom?"

"I should think so," answered that young gentleman; and as he said it, he winked towards Nicholas with a degree of familiarity which he, no doubt, intended for a rather flattering compliment, but with which Nicholas was most ungratefully disgusted.

Upon reference to the book, it appeared that the dozen secretaryships had dwindled down to one. Mr. Gregsbury, of Manchester Buildings, Westminster, wanted a young man, to keep his papers and correspondence in order; and Nicholas was exactly the sort of young man that Mr. Gregsbury wanted.

"I don't know what the terms are, as he said he'd settle them himself with the party," observed the fat lady; "but they must be pretty good ones, because he's a member of Parliament."

Inexperienced as he was, Nicholas did not feel quite assured in the face of this reasoning, or the justice of this conclusion; but without troubling himself to question it, he took down the address, and resolved to wait upon Mr. Gregsbury without delay.

"I don't know what the number is, "said Tom, "but Manchester Buildings isn't a large place; and if the worst comes to worst, it won't take you very long to knock at all the doors on both sides of the way till you find him out. I say, what a good-looking girl that was, wasn't she?"

"What girl?" demanded Nicholas sternly.

"Oh yes. I know — what gal, eh?" whispered Tom, shutting one eye, and cocking his chin in the air. "You didn't see her, you didn't — I say, don't you wish you was me, when she comes tomorrow morning?"

Nicholas looked at the ugly clerk, as if he had a mind to reward his admiration of the young lady by beating the ledger about his ears, but he refrained and strode haughtily out of the office; setting at defiance, in his indignation, those ancient laws of chivalry, which not only made it proper and lawful for all good knights to hear the praise of the ladies

Go on to next page

to whom they were devoted, but rendered it incumbent upon them to roam about the world, and knock on the head all such matter-of-fact and unpoetical characters, as declined to exalt, above all the earth, damsels whom they had never chanced to look upon or hear of—as if that were any excuse!

11. Which of the following is the best way of rewriting the expression "preferred the inquiry" (line 7) without changing the author's original meaning?

    A. liked one question better than another
    B. asked the question
    C. recommended one specific question
    D. answered a question

12. The author probably chose the word "glided" in line 12 to

    F. create a feeling of subterfuge and cunning on the part of the young woman.
    G. show how unusual the young woman's conduct was in a person so young.
    H. make the reader feel the young woman's shyness and quietness, or grace.
    J. indicate the speed with which the entire transaction took place.

13. The first sentence in the second paragraph

    A. demonstrates a bias towards brighter clothing.
    B. expresses contempt and scorn at the girl's unfashionable attire.
    C. contrasts the quality of the clothing with the shabbiness of the surroundings.
    D. indicates that the author believes that "the woman makes the clothes," rather than "the clothes make the woman."

14. Which of the following is another way to express the author's statement, ". . . was clearly of a kin with the servant-of-all-work on the farm. . ." (lines 22 and 23)?

    F. held the same status as the farm servant
    G. was obviously a relative of the farm servant
    H. had previously worked as a laborer on a farm
    J. was trying to better her position in life

15. The statement that "It is not a matter of such utter improbability as some sober people may think . . . " (lines 28–30) means that

    A. the narrator was intoxicated at the time this event occurred.
    B. the event was obviously inevitable.
    C. it would not be as surprising or as unexpected as some people might think
    D. it is completely impossible.

16. The conversation between Tom and the fat lady about the young woman's coming again tomorrow (lines 34–43) indicates that

    F. the girl comes to the office every day as part of her routine.
    G. the girl will probably not enjoy the post to which she was sent.
    H. the girl will begin working for Tom and the fat lady the next day.
    J. the girl wants to see the narrator again.

17. "'I should think so,' answered that young gentleman, and as he said it, he winked towards Nicholas with a degree of familiarity which he, no doubt, intended for a rather flattering compliment. . ." (lines 54–57). The author implies by this statement

    A. that Tom and Nicholas are friends.
    B. that Tom recognized and approved of Nicholas's interest in the young woman who had just left.
    C. that Tom meant to imply that Nicholas was such a man that his services would be greatly valued.
    D. that the young gentleman knew that the fat lady was going to cheat Nicholas.

18. The fat lady's comments about Mr. Gregsbury's being a member of Parliament

    F. are meant to reassure Nicholas as to the superiority of the position offered.
    G. are untrue.
    H. are intended to demonstrate the high-class clientele of which the fat lady boasts.
    J. are given as an excuse for her having but the one listing.

19. In the context of the passage, "to wait upon" (line 75) means

    A. to be delayed by.
    B. to visit.
    C. to serve.
    D. to doubt.

Go on to next page

20. Which of the following most closely captures the meaning of the last paragraph of the passage?

- **F.** Nicholas and the clerk both chivalrously agreed that the young woman was beautiful and were determined to fight each other for her affections.
- **G.** Nicholas was insulted that the clerk would think that he, Nicholas, would be interested in a woman as obviously low class as the young lady.
- **H.** Nicholas had a duty to defend the young woman against what he perceived as slurs upon her character made by the clerk.
- **J.** The clerk had motivated Nicholas to forget the job and go seek the young woman in order to tell her of his feelings toward her.

Passage 3

Natural Science

Tales abound of the large snake of Trinidad, Surinam, and Bolivia known as the bushmaster. The bushmaster, found primarily in South and Central America, is the largest venomous (poisonous) snake in the New World. The names of this snake tell much about it. The Latin name of the bushmaster is Lachesis muta. The Lachesis comes from Greek mythology, and refers to one of the three Fates. The Greeks believed that the Fates were women who determined how long the "string" of a person's life would be. When the Fates cut the string, the person's life would cease. The bite of the Lachesis muta, the bushmaster snake, can indeed kill. It has been known to kill even humans (although the actual death or injury may come from the bacteria on the snake's fangs, rather than from the venom itself). The muta part of the name is similar to our common word mute, and derives from the fact that although the snake shakes its tail — as does the rattlesnake, to which it is related — when it senses danger, because there are no rattles on the bushmaster's tail, no noise is made.

A second name for the bushmaster is concha pita, meaning pineapple tail. This name reflects the fact that the snake is covered in raised scales. The bushmaster can vary in color (most frequently in shades of brown), but is often tan with dark brown markings in the shape of diamonds. The snake's coloring serves as an excellent camouflage in the forests where it lies. Bushmasters are usually solitary animals, coming together only during breeding. After breeding, the bushmaster female lays up to 12 eggs in a group called a clutch. While the eggs are in the clutch, the bushmaster exhibits a strong maternal instinct, coiling around and protecting the eggs. This maternal instinct is quite rare among reptiles. When the eggs hatch — usually in two to three months — the young are immediately capable of survival on their own.

The bushmaster is a type of pit viper. The "pit" in the snake's name comes from the fact that it has a hollow pit close to the eye. The pit is covered by skin to protect it. The purpose of the pit is to sense heat. The heat is given off by the bushmaster's prey, which consists of warm-blooded animals. The most common prey of the pit viper is a rodent. Usually, a viper will bite its prey, then retreat, letting the venom do the actual killing of the smaller animal. Should the animal wander away during its death throes, the bushmaster can follow the animal's scent to find it later. Some bushmasters, however, bite their prey, then hold their fangs in the animal, often lifting it off the ground. Bushmasters can patiently stalk their prey, hiding under the leaves or trees of the forest and waiting for the prey to pass. For this reason, some scientists refer to bushmasters as ambush predators.

The bushmaster itself has few enemies. Some larger species of snakes that are not susceptible to the pit viper's venom, such as certain constrictors, can feed on the bushmaster. And like all snakes, the bushmaster may be attacked by the large birds of prey. However, in the final analysis, the greatest foe of the snake is encroaching civilization. More and more of the animal's habitat — forests that until recently were considered remote and uninhabitable by humans — is being cleared. The bushmaster, while not an endangered species, is undergoing an alarming decline in numbers.

Go on to next page

Some think that the bushmaster's reputation for ferocity is misplaced. True, the animal is daunting by its sheer size. Some can reach lengths of 12 feet. However, except when hunting or attempting to breed, bushmasters are relatively placid, unaggressive creatures. Most of the injuries reported from bushmasters occurred when hikers accidentally stepped on drowsing snakes (whose coloration and silent warning system rarely alert humans to the snake's presence). They are nocturnal, and thus more aggressive at night than in the daytime.

21. The primary purpose of the passage is to

A. explain why bushmaster snakes are the most poisonous snakes in the world
B. distinguish between the truths and myths regarding the bushmaster snake
C. suggest ways to use the bushmaster snakes to benefit mankind
D. explain the origins of the bushmaster's name

22. Which of the following best describes the question that remains unanswered in the passage?

F. Why is the snake colored the way it is?
G. What is the purpose of the pits in the viper's head?
H. What does the bushmaster eat?
J. How does a bushmaster attract its mate?

23. According to the passage, which of the following characteristics of a bushmaster is rare among reptiles?

A. the pits around its head
B. the number of eggs it lays in one clutch
C. its maternal instincts
D. the lack of rattles on its tail

24. It can be inferred from the passage that

F. the bushmaster is not the world's largest venomous snake
G. the bushmasters have more brightly colored skins in the tropics
H. a bushmaster attacks only when threatened
J. because the central American rainforests are being threatened, the bushmaster is an endangered species

25. Which of the following is the reason the bushmaster is called an ambush predator?

A. It lives primarily in bushes in the Amazon.
B. It hides from its prey and then attacks it secretly.
C. It attacks only smaller animals.
D. It feeds off only live flesh, not carrion.

26. Which of the following does the author mean in line 70–71 by stating that "the bushmaster's reputation for ferocity is misplaced" ?

F. The bushmaster is fierce only when outside of its normal habitat.
G. The bushmaster is becoming more and more fierce because it is endangered.
H. People are wrong in considering the bushmaster fierce.
J. People fear the bushmaster.

27. Which of the following is most reasonable to infer from the second to last paragraph?

A. Bushmasters may become endangered soon.
B. Bushmasters' venom is not deadly to any birds.
C. Bushmasters' venom is not deadly to humans.
D. Bushmasters cannot survive.

28. The passage suggests that the reason hikers are more frequently attacked by bushmasters is

F. hikers disturb the snakes at sleep
G. hikers enter the territories most fiercely defended by the snakes
H. hikers disturb the snake's breeding grounds
J. snakes are out more in the night than in the daytime

29. The main point of the last paragraph is that

A. bushmasters sleep during the day
B. bushmasters will attack to protect their young and their food
C. bushmasters are quiet and hard to detect
D. bushmasters are not as aggressive as some people believe

30. Which of the following questions is NOT answered in the passage?

F. Who are the primary enemies of the bushmaster?
G. How does a bushmaster locate its prey?
H. Why is the bushmaster considered aggressive?
J. Why is a bushmaster's maternal instinct stronger than that of other snakes?

Go on to next page

Passage 4

Social Studies

Little is known of the history of Tanganyika's interior during the early centuries of the Christian era. The area is believed to have been inhabited originally by ethnic groups using a click-tongue language similar to that of southern Africa's Bushmen and Hottentots. Although remnants of these unnamed early tribes still exist, most of the people were gradually displaced by Bantu farmers migrating from the west and south and by Nilotes and related northern peoples. Some of these groups had well-organized societies and controlled extensive areas by the time that slavers, explorers, and missionaries penetrated the interior in the first half of the nineteenth century.

The coastal area, in contrast, first felt the impact of foreign influence as early as the eighth century, when monsoon winds brought the ships of Arab traders. By the twelfth century, traders and immigrants came from as far away as Persia (now Iran) and India. They built a series of highly developed cities and trading sites along the coast, the principal one being Kilwa, a settlement of Persian origin that held ascendancy until the Portuguese destroyed it in the early 1500s.

The Portuguese navigator Vasco da Gama touched the East African coast in 1498 on his voyage to India. By 1506, the Portuguese claimed control over the entire coast. This control was nominal, however, because the Portuguese did not attempt to colonize the area or explore the interior. By the early eighteenth century, Arabs from Oman had assisted the indigenous coastal dwellers in driving out the Portuguese from the area north of the Ruvuma River. The Omanis established their own garrisons and carried on a lucrative trade in slaves and ivory.

European exploration of Tanganyika's interior began in the mid-nineteenth century. Two German missionaries reached Mt. Kilimanjaro in the 1840s. In 1857, David Livingstone, the Scottish missionary-explorer who crusaded against the slave trade, established his last mission, where he was "found" by Henry Morton Stanley, an Anglo-American journalist-explorer who had been commissioned by the New York *Herald* to interview him.

German colonial interests were first advanced in 1884. Karl Peters concluded a series of treaties by which tribal chiefs in the interior accepted German protection. Although the German colonial administration brought cash crops, railroads, and roads to Tanganyika, its harsh actions provoked African resistance, culminating in the Maji Maji rebellion of 1905–07. The rebellion, which temporarily united a number of southern tribes and ended only after an estimated 120,000 Africans had died fighting or from starvation, is considered by Tanzanians today to have been one of the first stirrings of nationalism.

German colonial domination of Tanganyika ended with World War I. Control of most of the territory passed to the United Kingdom under a League of Nations mandate. After World War II, Tanganyika became a UN trust territory (also administered by the United Kingdom). In the following years, Tanganyika moved gradually toward self-government and independence.

In May 1961, Tanganyika became autonomous under Prime Minister Julius K. Nyerere. Full independence was achieved in December, and Mr. Nyerere was elected president when Tanganyika became a republic one year later. In 1964, Tanganyika united with Zanzibar to form the United Republic of Tanganyika and Zanzibar, later renamed the United Republic of Tanzania.

Tanzania is a de jure single-party state with a strong central executive. It has a five-level judiciary, combining the jurisdictions of tribal, Islamic, and British common law. All magistrates and judges, including the chief justice and eight associate judges of the high courts, are appointed by the president. For administrative purposes, Tanzania is divided into 25 regions. Since 1972, a decentralization program on the mainland has worked to increase the authority of the regions.

Tanzania bases its foreign policy on the concept of nonalignment with any major power bloc. In recent years, Tanzania has joined with many other developing countries to support a new international economic order. Tanzania supports measures to stabilize international commodity prices and provide balance-of-payments support for countries facing unfavorable terms of trade. Tanzania acknowledges the need for structural adjustment in developing economies but also stresses the importance of developed countries' cooperation in the transfer of resources and technology, the settlement of debt, and the increase of access to primary commodity markets.

The United States enjoys friendly relations with the United Republic of Tanzania. The U.S. seeks to assist Tanzania's economic and social development through bilateral and regional programs administered by the Agency for International Development (AID).

Go on to next page

31. The best title for the passage might be

A. The Flora and Fauna of Tanganyika.
B. Tracking in Africa.
C. The Origins of Humanity.
D. An Overview of Tanganyikan History.

32. Which of the following is *not* true of the ethnic groups that originally inhabited the interior of Tanganyika?

F. They are extinct.
G. They were displaced by the Bantu.
H. They used a language similar to that of the Hottentots.
J. They had organized societies.

33. In line 29, the author uses the word "nominal" to mean

A. illegal.
B. incompetent.
C. in name only.
D. vicious.

34. The main topic of lines 1–36 is

F. Persian control over and legacies to Tanganyika.
G. the history of trade in Tanganyika.
H. the initial foreign influences in Tanganyika.
J. the slave trade in Tanganyika.

35. The author implies that Mr. Stanley

A. disagreed with Dr. Livingstone's opinions on the slave trade.
B. was not the first journalist to interview Dr. Livingstone in Tanganyika.
C. exaggerated the difficulties of locating a man who was not intentionally hiding.
D. destroyed Dr. Livingstone's work among the natives.

36. The author cites which of the following as the cause of the Maji Maji rebellion?

F. the fines levied by the government on the farmers
G. the behavior of the German administration
H. the excessive zeal of the missionaries who forced Christianity on the natives
J. the fighting among the various African tribes

37. According to the passage, Tanganyika today

A. is ruled by the British.
B. is at war with Germany.
C. is seeking independence.
D. has merged with another country and expanded.

38. The author answers which of the following questions?

F. Why did the Portuguese destroy Kilwa?
G. Which African tribes fought in the Maji Maji rebellion?
H. Why did Tanganyika unite with Zanzibar?
J. What is Tanzania's judicial structure?

39. The overall tone of this passage is

A. despairing.
B. derogatory.
C. objective.
D. effervescent.

40. If the last paragraph were to continue, it would probably discuss

F. agricultural exports of Tanzania.
G. tribal warfare in Tanzania.
H. the U.S.'s role in Tanzania.
J. the UN's restrictions of aid to Tanzania.

STOP

END OF TEST 3

DO NOT TURN THE PAGE UNTIL TOLD TO DO SO.
DO NOT RETURN TO A PREVIOUS TEST.

Science Reasoning Test

35 Minutes — 40 Questions

DIRECTIONS: Following are seven passages and then questions that refer to each passage. Choose the best answer and blacken in the corresponding oval on your answer grid.

Passage 1

Clouds are classified primarily on the basis of their altitude and appearance. Table 1 lists the major cloud types.

Table 1 **Major Cloud Types**

Cloud	*Avg. Altitude (Meters)*	*Appearance*	*Composition*
Cirrus	12,000	Delicate white filaments	Ice crystals
Cirrocumulus	10,000	Thin white rippled layers	Ice crystals
Cirrostratus	8,000	Shapeless white veil	Ice crystals
Altocumulus	5,000	Rows of "blobs" forming a sheet	Water droplets
Altostratus	5,000	Uniform, striated, or fibrous sheet	Water droplets
Nimbostratus	2,000	Ragged gray layer	Water droplets
Stratocumulus	2,000	Layers of clumps or rolls in file	Water droplets
Stratus	500	Uniform gray ceiling	Water droplets
Cumulus	500	White puffy balls	Ice crystals, water droplets
Cumulonimbus	500	Tall, anvil at top	Ice crystals, water droplets

Note: The altitude stated is for the bottom of the cloud. The tops of certain clouds can be several thousand meters higher.

1. On the basis of the table, thin clouds are most commonly associated with

I. high altitudes.
II. cumulus clouds.
III. ice crystals.

A. I only
B. II only
C. I and III only
D. I, II, and III

2. On the basis of the table, which of the following is the most reasonable statement?

F. Water droplets can predominate in clouds at any altitude.
G. Water droplets are found exclusively in middle-altitude clouds.
H. Water droplets are never found in cumulus clouds.
J. Water droplets are most likely to appear in low- and middle-altitude clouds.

3. Which of the following clouds is most likely to extend to the highest altitude?

A. Nimbostratus
B. Stratocumulus
C. Stratus
D. Cumulonimbus

4. The table suggests that the primary factor that determines whether a cloud is composed of ice crystals or water droplets is

F. evaporation rate.
G. condensation rate.
H. altitude.
J. appearance.

5. Which of the following is the most likely definition of the word root *stratus?*

A. Layer
B. Heap
C. Curl
D. High

Go on to next page

Passage 2

A pharmaceutical company has developed a new drug for treating hay fever. It claims that the new drug causes less drowsiness than the current best-selling brand. To test this claim, the company ran the following three studies.

Study 1

Subjects were asked to perform a motor coordination task that requires a high degree of alertness. Subjects who made fewer errors were judged to be less drowsy. Eight subjects were given a standard dosage of the new drug, and eight other subjects were given a standard dosage of the old drug. Four persons of each group of eight were tested one hour after ingesting the drug while the other four persons were tested eight hours after ingesting the drug. Realizing that drug effects often depend on a subject's weight, the researchers weighed each subject who participated in the study. The number of errors and weights for each subject are presented in Table 1.

Table 1 Number of Errors on Coordination Task After Ingesting Drug

Old Drug					
One hour after ingestion			***Eight hours after ingestion***		
Subject	***Errors***	***Weight (kg)***	***Subject***	***Errors***	***Weight (kg)***
1	38	75	5	37	71
2	52	55	6	33	73
3	44	70	7	52	53
4	57	54	8	45	55
Average 47.75			Average 41.75		
New Drug					
One hour after ingestion			***Eight hours after ingestion***		
Subject	***Errors***	***Weight (kg)***	***Subject***	***Errors***	***Weight (kg)***
9	30	73	13	32	70
10	49	53	14	52	50
11	42	55	15	46	51
12	34	70	16	35	71
Average 38.75			Average 41.25		

Study 2

After observing a wide range in the number of errors made by the subjects, the researchers repeated Study 1 but restricted the study to males who weighed 72 kilograms (kg). The results of this study appear in Table 2.

Table 2 Coordination Task Errors for 72-kg Males

Old Drug			
One hour after ingestion		***Eight hours after ingestion***	
Subject	***Errors***	***Subject***	***Errors***
1	39	5	33
2	44	6	36
3	42	7	34
4	40	8	36
Average 41.25		Average 34.75	
New Drug			
One hour after ingestion		***Eight hours after ingestion***	
Subject	***Errors***	***Subject***	***Errors***
9	30	13	31
10	31	14	31
11	34	15	29
12	34	16	32
Average 32.25		Average 30.75	

Go on to next page

Study 3

This study was identical to Study 2 except that 54-kg females were used. The results of this study are shown in Table 3.

Table 3 Coordination Task Errors for 54-kg Females

Old Drug			
One hour after ingestion		Eight hours after ingestion	
Subject	Errors	Subject	Errors
1	54	5	49
2	56	6	49
3	53	7	51
4	54	8	50
Average 54.25		Average 49.75	
New Drug			
One hour after ingestion		Eight hours after ingestion	
Subject	Errors	Subject	Errors
9	44	13	47
10	48	14	48
11	44	15	46
12	46	16	48
Average 45.5		Average 47.25	

6. Which of the following is the most reasonable conclusion that can be made on the basis of Study 1?
   - **F.** The new drug is more effective than the old drug one hour after ingestion but not eight hours after ingestion.
   - **G.** Performance on the motor coordination task deteriorates as time after ingestion of the old drug increases.
   - **H.** As compared to the old drug, the new drug improved the ability of experimental subjects to perform the motor coordination task.
   - **J.** The new drug causes less drowsiness than the old drug one hour after ingestion but not eight hours after ingestion.

7. Which of the following best summarizes why the researchers conducted Studies 2 and 3?
   - **A.** They wished to examine the effects of weight on drowsiness produced by the drug.
   - **B.** They were interested in whether the drug would affect men and women differently.
   - **C.** They wanted to eliminate a factor that caused variability in the results.
   - **D.** Most people who suffer from hay fever weigh approximately what the subjects in those studies weighed.

8. In comparison to Study 1, what is a primary limitation of Study 2?
   - **F.** Study 2 does not measure the effects of the drugs on females.
   - **G.** Study 1 suggests that the new drug may be more effective for a variety of subjects.
   - **H.** Study 1 shows that the new drug caused less drowsiness in a wider range of subjects.
   - **J.** Study 2 produced results that were more difficult to interpret.

9. If Study 3 included a group that was tested two hours after ingesting the old drug, which of the following predictions for the average number of errors made by this group would be reasonable?

   I. 44
   II. 51
   III. 52
   IV. 56

   - **A.** II only
   - **B.** I and II only
   - **C.** II, III, and IV only
   - **D.** I, II, III, and IV

Go on to next page

10. Suppose that further study revealed that the group of subjects given the old drug and tested at eight hours in Study 1 was, under normal conditions, particularly proficient at performing the motor coordination task. How would this finding affect the overall results of the study?

   F. It would add evidence that the new drug causes less drowsiness than the old drug at eight hours after ingestion.
   G. It would suggest that side effects associated with the old drug are more common eight hours after ingesting the drug than at only one hour after ingestion.
   H. It would suggest that the new drug is more effective than the old drug at any time after ingestion.
   J. It would require that the entire experiment be repeated with the same subjects being tested at both one hour and eight hours.

11. If later studies show that the new drug is at least as effective as the old drug in relieving hay fever and that the new drug produces no side effects other than drowsiness, would it be reasonable to recommend the new drug over the old drug to lightweight individuals suffering from hay fever?

   A. Yes, but only if such individuals are given a lower dose than what was used in the current three studies.
   B. Yes, because the evidence supports the claim that the new drug is at least as effective and produces less drowsiness.
   C. No, because the individuals may operate dangerous machinery within eight hours after ingesting the drug.
   D. No, because the new drug differs from the old system with regard to how it affects the immune system, which is responsible for hay fever.

Passage 3

A wide beach protects bluffs by spreading out the energy of waves and keeping them from eroding the soil and rocks that comprise the bluff (see Figure 1).

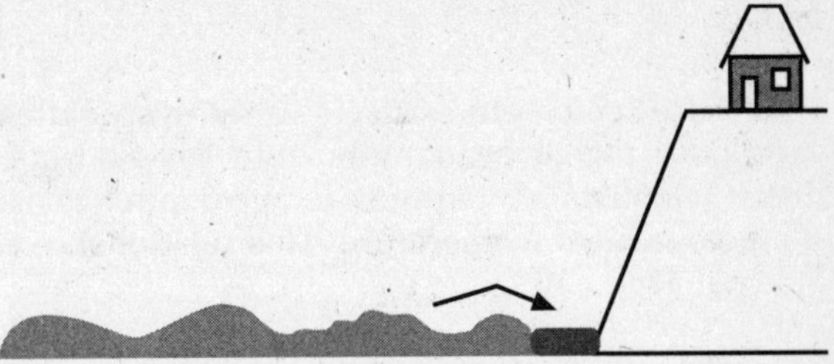

Figure 1: Simiplified illustration of waves hitting a wide beach.

When water levels rise, bluffs are vulnerable to erosion because much of the beach is now underwater, and the bluffs now bear the brunt of the waves' force (see Figure 2).

Figure 2: Simiplified illustration of waves hitting a bluff when water level rises above beach.

To gain a better understanding of how natural forces can affect future water levels and bluff erosion, scientists studied the relationship between some key meteorological factors and water depth (deeper water means a higher water level) near the shore of an inland lake.

Study 1

Scientists measured precipitation and lake depth over a 30-year period and plotted the average depth against annual precipitation, as shown in Figure 3.

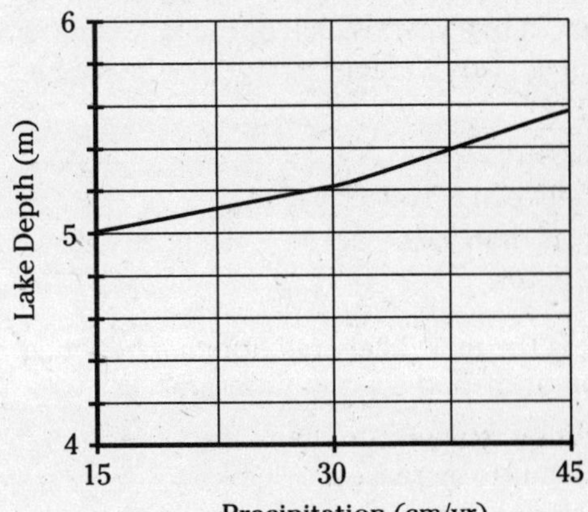

Figure 3: The average depth against annual precipitation.

Go on to next page

Study 2

Because temperature affects water evaporation rate and a higher evaporation rate lowers water levels, scientists plotted the average depth against the mean annual temperature. This relationship is shown in Figure 4.

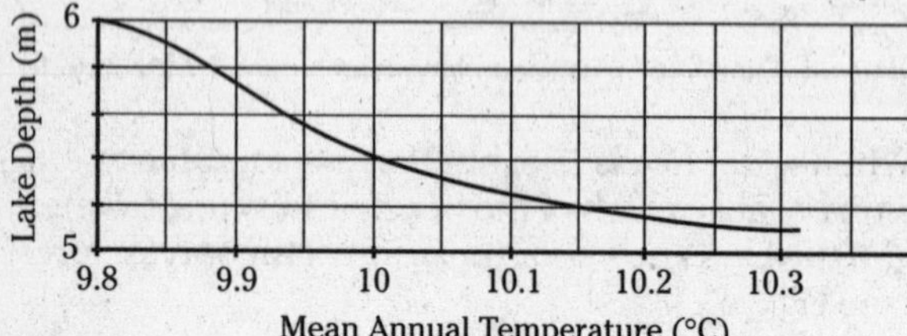

Figure 4: The average depth versus the mean annual temperature.

Study 3

Wind is another factor that affects water evaporation rate, so scientists plotted the average depth against wind speed, as shown in Figure 5.

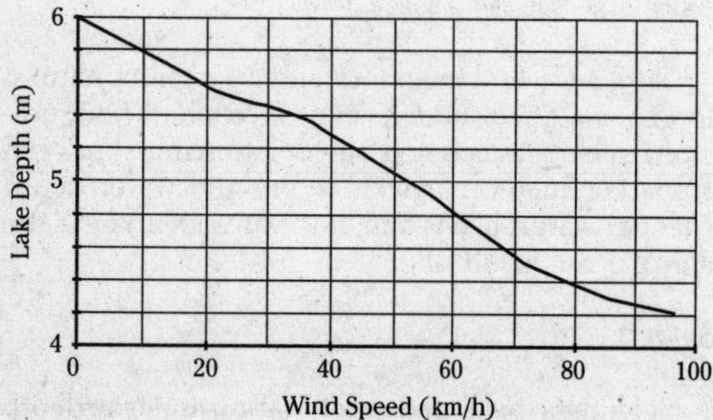

Figure 5: The average depth versus wind speed.

12. Suppose that only 10 cm of precipitation occurs in one year. Which of the following is the most reasonable lake depth estimate for that year?

    F. 5.5 m
    G. between 5.0 m and 5.5 m
    H. less than 5.0 m
    J. 2.5 m

13. What is the most likely relationship between temperature and evaporation rate?

    A. When temperature increases, evaporation rate increases.
    B. When temperature increases, evaporation rate decreases.
    C. When temperature increases, evaporation rate is unaffected.
    D. When temperature decreases, evaporation rate increases.

14. After a year of low precipitation, high temperatures, and strong winds, the lake depth would probably be

    F. low.
    G. average.
    H. high.
    J. extremely high.

15. Are strong winds definitely good for the bluff?

    A. Yes, because strong winds tend to lower water levels and help stimulate plant growth.
    B. Yes, because strong winds deposit soil on the bluff and reduce soil fertility.
    C. No, because strong winds raise temperatures.
    D. No, because strong winds produce more powerful waves, which can crash into the bluff.

16. Which of the following is the dependent variable of the investigation?

    F. precipitation
    G. lake depth
    H. mean annual temperature
    J. wind speed

17. Without any additional information, which of the following would further knowledge of how weather affects the bluff?

    I. counting the number of homes built on the bluff
    II. investigating the feasibility of constructing a protective seawall
    III. measuring erosion as a result of precipitation, temperature, and wind speed
    IV. measuring the tides over the course of several years

    A. III only
    B. I and III only
    C. II and IV only
    D. II, III, and IV only

Passage 4

The use of gasoline is directly related to the number of pollutants, such as hydrocarbons, nitrous oxide, and carbon monoxide, present in the air. As a result, drivers should take steps to minimize their gasoline consumption. One way to reduce this consumption is to drive at slower speeds. Figure 1 shows how gasoline mileage is affected by freeway driving speeds.

Go on to next page

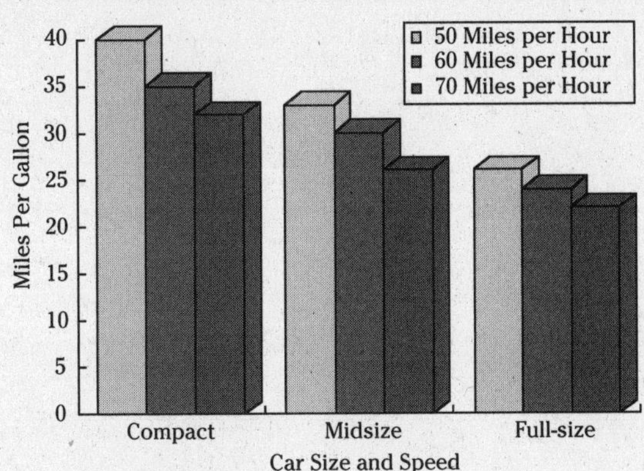

Figure 1: Gas mileage as a function of speed.

18. Which of the following will produce the most pollutants on a 100-mile trip?

F. a compact car driven at 50 mph
G. a midsize car driven at 60 mph
H. a full-size car driven at 50 mph
J. a full-size car driven at 60 mph

19. You are in the desert with no gas in sight, and your gas gauge shows that you have very little gas left. Should you speed up to get to your destination?

A. No, because you use more gas at a higher speed.
B. No, because you need more time to find a gas station.
C. Yes, because the desert has very little pollution.
D. Yes, because your car operates for less time and, as a consequence, burns less gas.

20. A full-size car driven at 55 mph will get approximately how many miles per gallon?

F. 23
G. 25
H. 32
J. 37

21. On the basis of the graph, which of the following statements is the most reasonable regarding compact gas mileage at 25 mph?

A. Gas mileage is about 40 miles per gallon.
B. Gas mileage is about 50 miles per gallon because gas mileage increases eight miles per gallon for every 10 mph increase in speed.
C. Gas mileage is about 80 miles per gallon because gas mileage doubles when speed is cut in half.
D. Gas mileage can't be determined with any reasonable certainty because 25 mph is outside the range of numbers presented in the graph.

22. Which of the following graphs best represents the relationship between freeway speed and pollutants emitted?

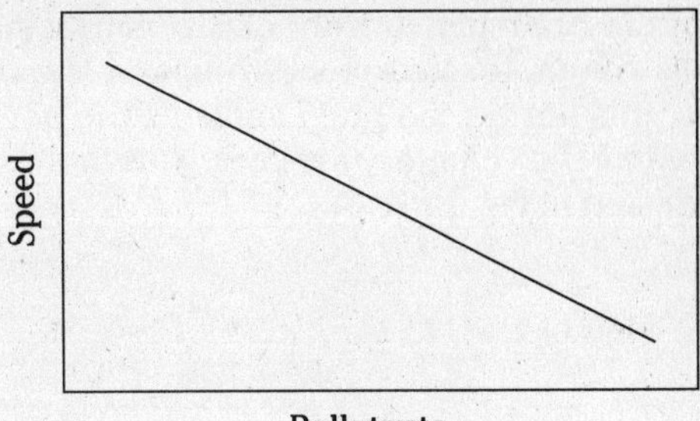

F.

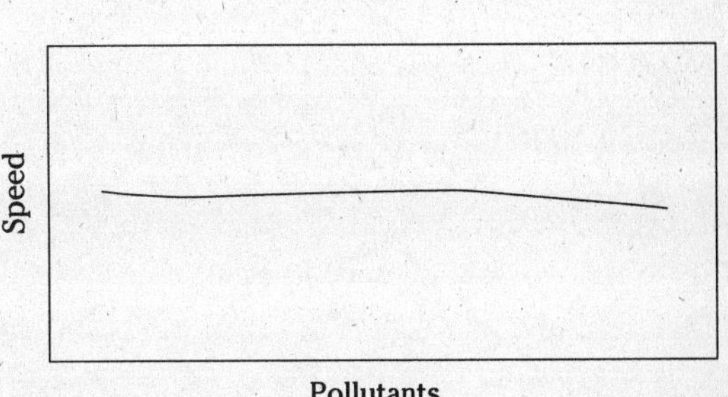

G.

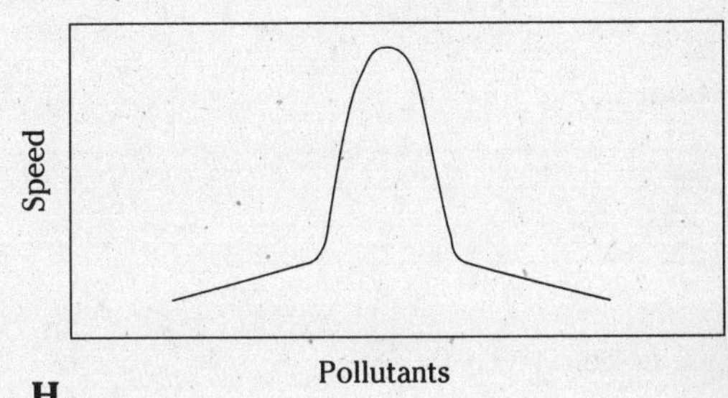

H.

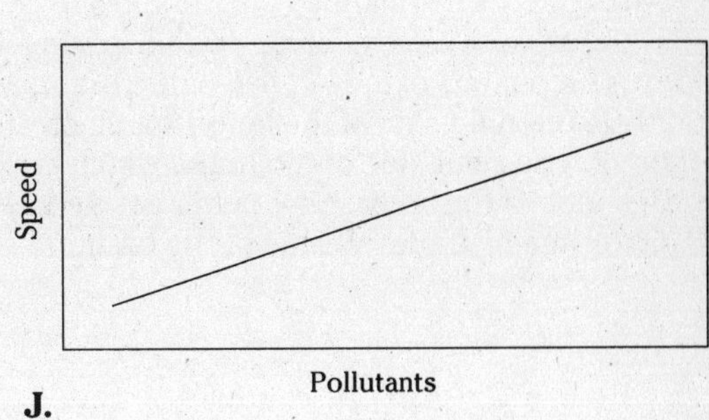

J.

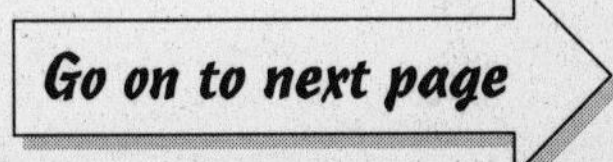

Passage 5

From stimulating the brains of patients undergoing neurosurgery, scientists have determined that a strip of the brain just in front of the central sulcus controls the motor neurons throughout the body. That is, this part of the brain controls the neurons that control the voluntary muscles. This motor area is illustrated in Figure 1.

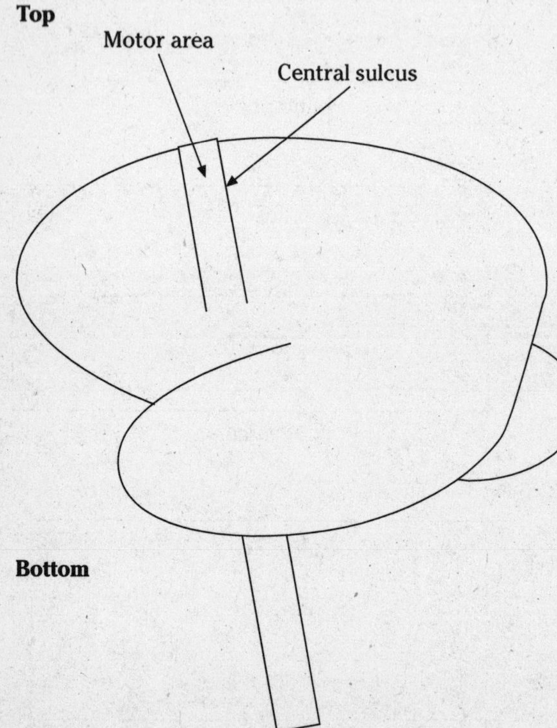

Figure 1: Slide view of the brain.

Further work has mapped out the specific parts of this motor area that control certain parts of the body. The regions of the left half of the brain, which controls the right side of the body, are illustrated in Figure 2. The right side of the brain, which controls the left side of the body and is not illustrated, shows a mirror image of the left side of the brain.

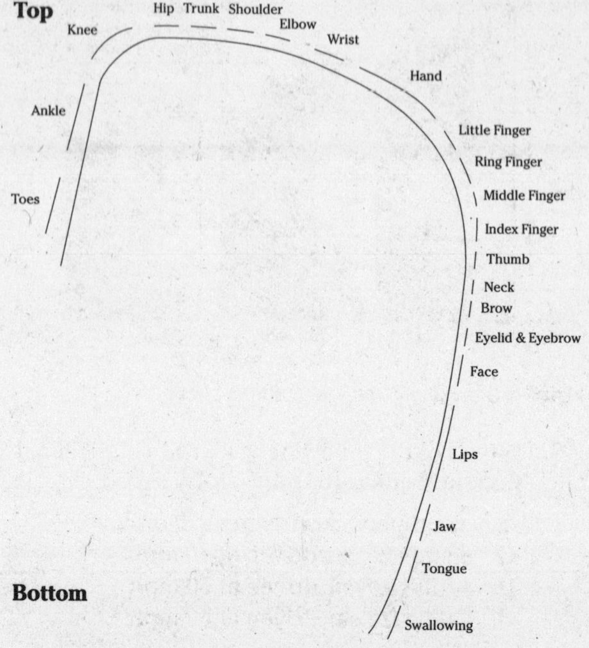

Figure 2: Simplified front view of left brain through motor area. Bands indicate region of brain that control stated part of body.

23. Which of the following is/are true regarding the organization of the motor area, shown in Figure 2?

I. No systematic relationship exists between how the motor area is organized and how the body is organized.
II. The sequence of controlling regions in the motor area is similar to the sequence of body parts.
III. Some parts of the body are controlled by larger regions of the motor area than others.

A. II only
B. III only
C. I and II only
D. II and III only

24. From an inspection of Figure 2, which of the following areas involves the most complex coordination of muscles?

F. Hip
G. Shoulder
H. Hand
J. Brow

Go on to next page

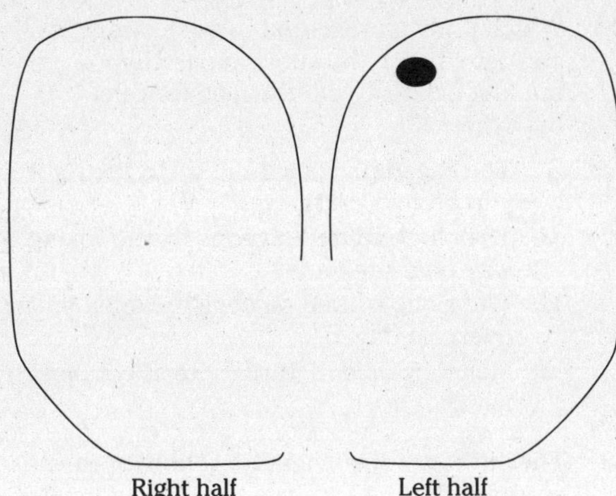

Figure 3: Slides are in reference to patient's right and left, not yours.

25. Damage to the part of the motor area marked in the above figure would most likely affect movement in which of the following areas of the body?

A. Right lips
B. Right knee
C. Left knee
D. Left jaw

26. The brain is organized so that related functions are under control of areas that are close to one another in the brain. Which of the following is the most likely location for the part of the brain that controls speech production?

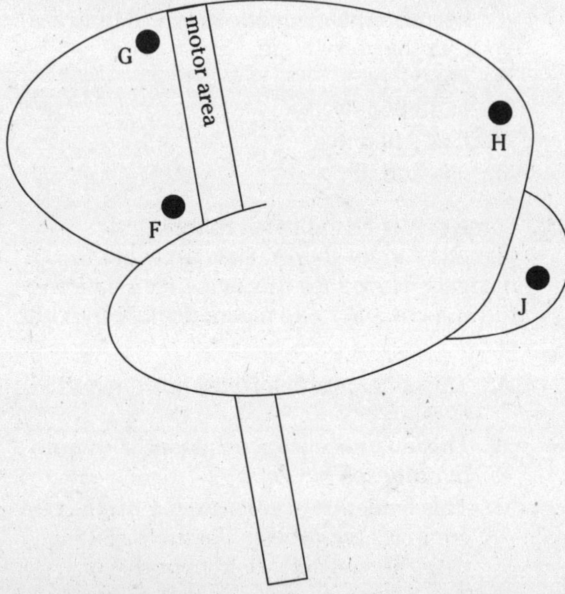

F. location F
G. location G
H. location H
J. location J

27. Damage to the part of the motor area marked in the figure below will most likely affect

A. vision.
B. hearing.
C. the ability to feel touching on the face.
D. the ability to move facial muscles.

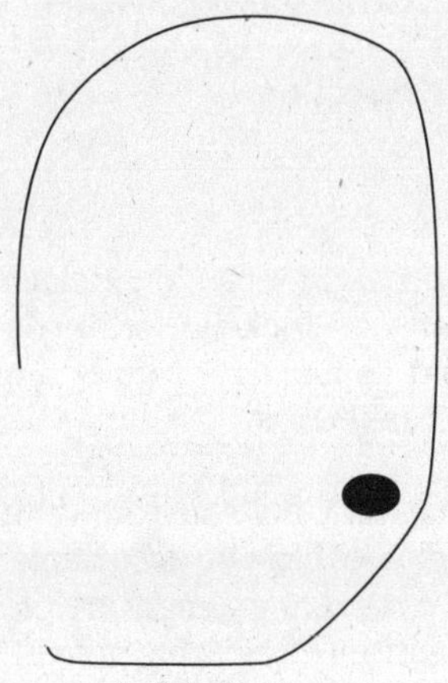

Figure 4: Left half of the brain.

Passage 6

Homing pigeons received their name because of their ability to find their way home even when they are hundreds of kilometers away. Scientists know that pigeons do not use visible landmarks to navigate, because the birds can find their way home even after they have been transported in a covered box and released in an unfamiliar area. Scientists have offered several explanations for this acute navigational ability. Following are two of these hypotheses.

Sun Compass

Pigeons use the sun as a compass to orient themselves. Evidence for this theory comes from an experiment in which pigeons were placed in a circular cage with identical food cups evenly spaced just outside the cage. After being trained to go to the cup due east of the cage's center, pigeons were observed to go to the same cup even after the cage was rotated and the background scenery was changed. Pigeons failed to go to the east cup when the skies were overcast or when the experimenters used mirrors to alter the apparent position of the sun.

The pigeons use their internal clocks in conjunction with the sun to find their way home. For example, if the internal clock of a pigeon indicates noon while the bird observes the sun about to set, the pigeon knows that it is far east of its home and flies west to get

Go on to next page

there. A northern hemisphere bird that is due south of home at noon sees that the sun is in the correct position as far as east and west are concerned but observes that the sun is higher in the sky than normal and therefore flies north to get home. Support for this mechanism comes from observing birds whose internal clocks have been experimentally shifted. Their orientation, with respect to the sun, is consistent with their internal clock, but because the clock is off, the pigeons fly in the wrong direction.

Magnetic Field

Pigeons do not rely on a sun-internal clock calculation to orient themselves. Clock-shifted birds are just as accurate and fast as normal birds at finding their way home on overcast days.

Disruptions in the magnetic field surrounding the birds, on the other hand, affect the birds' orientation under such conditions. When bar magnets are placed on pigeons, they fly in random directions on overcast days. Similar results were obtained when scientists used electrical wires to induce an electrical field in a particular direction. When the wires induced a magnetic field that pointed up through the birds' heads, the pigeons flew away from home. When the field pointed in the opposite direction, the birds flew toward home. These findings, along with the discovery that pigeons are capable of responding to a magnetic field much weaker than that of earth, indicate that pigeons use the earth's magnetic field for orientation.

28. According to the sun-compass hypothesis, how would the pigeons with the disrupted magnetic fields orient on a sunny day?

F. They would fly in random directions.
G. They would fly toward home.
H. They would fly in a direction that is a compromise between the information provided by the magnetic field and the information provided by the sun.
J. They would fly straight but in a direction away from home.

29. Scientists have found that large disturbances in the earth's magnetic field affect the pigeons' flight direction on sunny days. Which of the following is the most reasonable statement that can be made on the basis of this finding?

A. The sun-compass hypothesis is false.
B. Pigeons don't use the sun for orientation.
C. The Earth's magnetic field is the only factor that affects pigeon navigation.
D. The finding supports the magnetic-field hypothesis.

30. Which finding presented in the passage is consistent with the sun-compass hypothesis but inconsistent with the magnetic-field hypothesis?

F. The caged pigeons don't fly to the right cup on overcast days.
G. The clock-shifted pigeons fly the wrong way on a sunny day.
H. The clock-shifted pigeons fly home on an overcast day.
J. Magnetic-field disturbances affect pigeon navigation.

31. The author of the magnetic-field hypothesis assumes that

A. pigeons with magnets are not affected by the mere presence of metal.
B. magnets have absolutely no effect on pigeons on sunny days.
C. no birds use internal clocks to navigate.
D. pigeons do not use the sun to navigate.

32. According to the entire passage, which of the following statements are most reasonable to make regarding clock-shifted pigeons that are placed at their home?

I. They will fly away from their home on a sunny day because the clock-sun calculation will indicate that they are away from home.
II. They will stay home on a sunny day because they will recognize familiar landmarks.
III. They will stay home on an overcast day because the magnetic field will indicate that they are home.

F. I and II only
G. I and III only
H. II and III only
J. I, II, and III

33. Some evidence indicates that homing pigeons can use barometric pressure to navigate. How does this evidence relate to the sun-compass and magnetic-field hypotheses?

A. This evidence disproves both hypotheses.
B. This evidence is inconsistent with both hypotheses.
C. This evidence is consistent with the sun-compass hypothesis but inconsistent with the magnetic-field hypothesis.
D. This evidence may be consistent with both hypotheses.

Go on to next page

34. Research shows that pigeons can orient to light that mimics conditions present on a partially overcast day in which blue sky is present but the sun's disk is blocked. If clock-shifted pigeons navigate home on such a day, which hypothesis is supported?

F. Sun-compass, because the pigeons responded correctly to the light.
G. Sun-compass, because the sun was blocked.
H. Magnetic-field, because the pigeons responded correctly to the light.
J. Magnetic-field, because the internal clock shift did not throw the birds off.

Passage 7

A typical chemical reaction can be represented A + B → AB. A and B are reactants that react to form product AB.

Chemists have measured the rate at which various products of reactions are formed and have found that the rate varies with the concentration of the reactants. For example, when the concentration of reactant A is doubled, the rate of formation of product AB may change, depending on the nature of the chemical reaction. The rate can remain the same, double, quadruple, or change in other ways. The concentration of reactant B affects the rate of product formation, but reactant B's effect can be different from that of reactant A. For example, you can have a reaction in which doubling the concentration of A doubles the rate of product formation, while doubling B's concentration quadruples the rate.

To learn more about the chemical reaction $H_3AsO_4+3I^-+2H^+ \rightarrow H_3AsO_3+I^{3-}+H_20$, scientists ran a series of experiments to determine how the concentration of each reactant affects the rate of formation of the product H_3AsO_3.

Experiment 1

Scientists combined 0.01 moles of H_3AsO_4, 0.20 moles of I^-, and 0.10 moles of H^+ in a liter of solution. H_3AsO_3 was formed at the rate of 2.8 units. Scientists repeated the reaction three times, using different amounts of H_3AsO_4 each time. The results are summarized in Table 1.

Table 1 Results of Combining Chemicals

Concentration (moles/liter)			
H_3AsO_4	I^-	H^+	Formation rate (rate units)
0.01	0.20	0.10	2.8
0.02	0.20	0.10	5.6
0.03	0.20	0.10	8.4
0.04	0.20	0.10	11.2

Experiment 2

This experiment was identical to Experiment 1 except that the scientists varied the concentration of I^- while holding the concentration of the other reactants constant. The results of these experimental trials are presented in Table 2.

Table 2 Results of Holding the Concentration of Other Reactants Constant

Concentration (moles/liter)			
H_3AsO_4	I^-	H^+	Formation rate (rate units)
0.01	0.20	0.10	2.8
0.01	0.40	0.10	5.6
0.01	0.60	0.10	8.4
0.01	0.80	0.10	11.2

Experiment 3

This experiment was identical to the other two, except that the concentration of H+ was the one that varied. The results are presented in Table 3.

Table 3 Results of Varying H^+ Concentration

Concentration (moles/liter)			
H_3AsO_4	I^-	H^+	Formation rate (rate units)
0.01	0.20	0.10	2.8
0.01	0.20	0.20	11.2
0.01	0.20	0.30	25.2
0.01	0.20	0.40	44.8

Go on to next page

35. A chemist must make as much H_3AsO_4 as possible in a minute. If she can change the concentration of only one reactant, which reactant should she choose?

A. H_3AsO_4
B. I^-
C. H^+
D. Any reactant

36. Why did the chemists vary the concentration of only one reactant at a time?

F. Varying the concentration of more than one reactant causes a violent explosion.
G. When the concentration of more than one reactant varies and the formation rate changes, how each reactant affects the formation rate is unclear.
H. Measuring the concentration of more than one reactant at the same time is difficult.
J. When the concentration of more than one reactant is varied, the amount of product formed is too great to make an accurate determination of the formation rate.

37. If the concentrations of H_3AsO_4,, I^-, and H^+ are 0.02 moles/liter, 0.40 moles/liter, and 0.10- moles/liter, respectively, what is the formation rate?

A. 2.8 rate units
B. 5.6 rate units
C. 8.4 rate units
D. 11.2 rate units

38. If scientists combine 0.01 moles H_3AsO_4, 0.20 moles of I^-, and 0.10 moles of H^+ in two liters of solution instead of the one liter that was used in the first trial of each experiment, what happens to the formation rate?

F. The formation rate decreases.
G. The formation rate remains the same.
H. The formation rate increases for a few seconds and then decreases.
J. The formation rate increases.

39. If a fifth trial is performed in Experiment 3 at which 0.80 moles/liter of H^+ are used and all other concentrations remain unchanged, what is the likely formation rate?

A. 22.4 rate units
B. 44.8 rate units
C. 89.6 rate units
D. 179.2 rate units

40. What happens to the formation rate of H_2O when the concentration of one or more reactant is increased?

F. The formation rate decreases.
G. The formation rate is zero.
H. The formation rate remains the same.
J. The formation rate increases.

STOP

END OF TEST 4

DO NOT TURN THE PAGE UNTIL TOLD TO DO SO.
DO NOT RETURN TO A PREVIOUS TEST.

Getting Down to the Nitty-Gritty: Subscores

Three of the tests of the ACT feature subscores as an added bonus (think of these as a "gift with purchase"). In 20-plus years of tutoring for the ACT (I started when I was a mere child, you see), I have had very few students care about the subscores. By the time you get through with this book, you should know very well which sections are your best and which are your weakest. However, you'll see subscores on your score report, so a few words about them are necessary.

English Test

The English Test has 40 questions in the Usage/ Mechanics subscore area, and 35 questions in the Rhetorical Skills subscore area — a total of 75 questions. (See Chapter 2 for more info on the types of questions on the English Test.) Because I wrote these practice exams to give you more practice with the types of questions my experience shows students have the best chance of getting correct with practice, this breakdown is not really applicable to the practice exams in this book. Besides, students get headaches trying to understand the fine distinctions between what is rhetorical and what is not. Don't worry about it.

Mathematics Test

The actual ACT Mathematics Test usually has 24 prealgebra/elementary algebra problems, 18 intermediate algebra/coordinate geometry problems, and 18 plane geometry/trig problems — a total of 60 questions. Good news! The ACT has only four trig questions, so if you haven't had the subject yet, don't panic!

However, because this book is a *teaching* book and not the actual ACT (hey, you can get a free copy of an actual ACT just by walking into your guidance counselor's office and picking one up; you don't need that, but instruction on *how* to take the ACT), I'm not going to put you through the trauma of subscores. Besides, there are a lot of "gray" areas, in which one person is convinced that a problem is elementary algebra, while another will argue it is intermediate algebra, or worse. Here's the simple solution: Be able to do all the problems (easy for *me* to say!), and don't worry about typecasting and labeling them.

Reading Test

The Reading Test subscores couldn't possibly be any easier. You get a subscore for questions in social studies/sciences (20 questions, based on two passages) and arts/literature (20 questions, based on two passages).

Science Reasoning Test

The Science Reasoning test has no subscores.

Score One for Our Side: The Scoring Key

The ACT scoring may be weird (Why a 36? Why not a 21 or a 49 or a 73?), but it is very straightforward. Follow the simple directions below to score your practice exam.

1. **Count the number of correct responses in each of the practice tests: English, Mathematics, Reading, and Science Reasoning (see the Answer Key at the end of this chapter). Do NOT subtract any points for questions you missed or questions you didn't answer. Your score is based only on the number of questions you answered correctly. That number is called your *raw score*.**

2. **Locate your raw score on the following table. Move to the left or right and find the *scaled score* that corresponds to your raw score. (For example, a raw score of 50 on the English Test gives you a scaled score of 21.)**

3. **Add your four scaled scores. Divide that sum by 4. The resulting number is your *composite score*. (For example, say that your scaled scores were 23, 31, 12, and 19; your composite score would be 85 ÷ 4 = 21.25 or 21.**

	Raw Scores				
Scale Score	*English*	*Mathematics*	*Reading*	*Science Reasoning*	*Scale Score*
1	0-1	0	0	0	1
2	2	-	1	-	2
3	3	1	2	1	3
4	4-5	-	3	-	4
5	6-7	-	4	-	5
6	8-9	2	5	2	6
7	10-11	3	6	3	7
8	12-13	-	7	4	8
9	14-16	4	8	5	9
10	17-19	5	9	6	10
11	20-22	6-7	10	7	11
12	23-25	8	11-12	8-9	12
13	26-28	9-10	13	10	13
14	29-31	11-12	14	11-12	14
15	32-35	13-14	15	13-14	15
16	36-37	15-17	16	15	16
17	38-40	18-19	17	16-17	17
18	41-43	20-22	18-19	18-19	18
19	44-45	23-24	20	20-21	19
20	46-48	25-26	21	22	20
21	49-50	27-29	22	23-24	21
22	51-53	30-32	23	25	22
23	54-55	33-34	24	26-27	23
24	56-57	35-37	25	28	24
25	58-59	38-40	26-27	29	25
26	60-62	41-42	28	30	26
27	63-64	43-45	29	31	27
28	65-66	46-48	30	32	28
29	67	49-50	31	33	29
30	68-69	51-53	-	34	30
31	70	54-55	32	35	31
32	71-72	56	33	36	32
33	73	57	34	37	33
34	-	58	35	38	34
35	74	59	36	39	35
36	75	60	37-40	40	36

Answer Key

English Test

1. B	39. A
2. J	40. G
3. B	41. D
4. H	42. J
5. A	43. A
6. J	44. F
7. A	45. C
8. G	46. J
9. B	47. A
10. F	48. J
11. B	49. B
12. F	50. J
13. D	51. B
14. F	52. J
15. A	53. B
16. G	54. H
17. D	55. B
18. H	56. J
19. D	57. A
20. G	58. G
21. D	59. A
22. F	60. H
23. A	61. D
24. F	62. F
25. D	63. A
26. H	64. H
27. B	65. B
28. G	66. H
29. C	67. D
30. G	68. G
31. C	69. A
32. H	70. G
33. C	71. B
34. G	72. J
35. C	73. A
36. J	74. G
37. B	75. A
38. G	

Mathematics Test

1. A	31. E
2. J	32. F
3. C	33. A
4. H	34. F
5. D	35. D
6. G	36. H
7. D	37. D
8. H	38. J
9. B	39. D
10. H	40. F
11. D	41. D
12. J	42. K
13. A	43. A
14. F	44. J
15. C	45. E
16. J	46. G
17. C	47. C
18. H	48. H
19. E	49. A
20. H	50. C
21. C	51. B
22. H	52. D
23. C	53. D
24. J	54. J
25. C	55. E
26. J	56. G
27. C	57. A
28. C	58. J
29. D	59. K
30. K	60. J

Reading Test

1. B	21. D
2. H	22. J
3. A	23. C
4. H	24. F
5. B	25. B
6. J	26. H
7. D	27. A
8. J	28. F
9. C	29. D
10. G	30. J
11. B	31. D
12. H	32. F
13. D	33. C
14. F	34. H
15. C	35. C
16. G	36. G
17. C	37. D
18. F	38. J
19. B	39. C
20. H	40. H

Science Reasoning Test

1. C	21. D
2. J	22. J
3. D	23. D
4. H	24. H
5. A	25. B
6. J	26. F
7. C	27. D
8. H	28. G
9. C	29. D
10. F	30. F
11. B	31. A
12. H	32. G
13. A	33. D
14. F	34. J
15. D	35. C
16. G	36. G
17. A	37. D
18. J	38. F
19. A	39. D
20. G	40. J

Chapter 15

Practice Exam 1: Answers and Explanations

Now you've done it. You've completed the practice exam, checked your answers against the key, and found your score on the Raw Score chart.

Hang on! Invest another hour or so to go through this chapter, reading why one answer was correct and the others weren't. Along the way, you find zillions of tips and traps, valuable information that you can use when you face the Big One.

English Test

If you want highly technical explanations discussing the future pluperfect and subordinate subjunctive, you're in the wrong place. I've written these explanations for real people, not for grammarians. The explanations put things in terms of everyday speech, not textbook rules and regulations.

Passage 1

1. **B.** The easy way to choose between "me" and "I" is to ignore the other person. That is, read the sentence as, "My mother took I to the zoo." You would never say that; you would say, "My mother took me to the zoo." Choice D is incorrect because the other person needs to come before the "me."

2. **J.** The original has two subjects, the zoo and the it. Use only one. The pronoun *which* changes the second part of the sentence to a subordinate clause (one that can't stand on its own) and eliminates the run-on problem of choice G.

3. **B.** The original sentence is a fragment, an incomplete sentence. Use choice B to express a complete thought.

Did you notice the dreaded word *being* in choice C? *Being* often indicates sloppy English; you should be especially careful when you see this word, as it usually (not always) indicates a wrong answer.

4. **H.** *Among* compares more than two items; *between* compares exactly two. (Note the *tw* in between and the *tw* in two.) Here, the sentence compares the giraffe and the zebra, two animals, requiring the word *between.*

If you chose J, you got careless and didn't reread the sentence with your answer inserted. This final step can catch awkward sentences and save you a lot of points.

5. **A.** This was a pretty hard question; pat yourself on the back if you got it right. *Latter* is an *-er* form, and compares two items. Here, the sentence compares just two animals, the giraffe and the zebra. The word *last* is an *-st* form and compares three or more items. (If you missed this question, go back and look at the comparisons section of the grammar review.)

6. **J.** The original sentence is a fragment, an incomplete sentence. It just hangs in the air, not expressing a completed thought. (You find yourself asking, "Well, what about the keeper?")

Did you double-check the -ing verbs, *coming* and *noticing,* in choices F, G, and H? While not all -ing words are wrong, they are wrong often enough on this exam to make you very, very nervous. Always look suspiciously at *-ing* verbs.

7. **A.** A double negative is a positive in English, just as it is in math. "Not inappropriate" means "appropriate." From the rest of the passage, you learn that a name meaning "tallest of all" is appropriate, given that the giraffe is the tallest animal.

In some other languages, such as Spanish, a double negative does not make a positive and may not change the meaning of the sentence (as the double negative above does) Those of you who speak languages other than English need to be especially careful not to make a mistake with double negatives.

8. **G.** If you chose F, you probably have what I call Smart Students Disease: You automatically, instinctively corrected the error in the sentence. Go back and look at the original and you'll notice that it's missing the verb.

If you find that you have a lot of NO CHANGE answers, you're probably suffering from this insidious disease (too many brain cells can be as big of a problem as too few!) If you have a few minutes left at the end of the section, go back and check all your NO CHANGE answers to be sure that you didn't correct the errors without thinking.

9. B. Always, always, always check what *it* refers to. In this case, *it* (singular) refers to the scientists (plural). You need to use a plural pronoun to refer to a plural noun: *they.* Choice C doesn't fit when reinserted into the sentence.

10. F. The correct formation is *from . . . to,* not *from . . . and* or *between . . . to.* Choice J changes the meaning of the sentence.

11. B. The word *being* is often wrong on this exam. The expression "being that" is very sloppy grammar. Use *which* to express the same thought. Choice D is the trap answer. Don't fall into the habit of choosing OMIT every time you see it. (Subconsciously, you may want to omit the whole darn exam, but that doesn't count!) Take a minute to reread how the sentence would work without the underlined portion.

12. F. *Well* is an adverb and answers the question "how?" How does the giraffe blend in? It blends in well. If you chose G, go back and reread the grammar review section on *good* versus *well.* If you chose H or J, you changed the meaning of the sentence. A good general rule is to correct the error, and then get outta there. In other words, don't do any more work, or make any more changes, than absolutely necessary.

13. D. The sentence talks about how different the markings of giraffes are, which is the topic of the third paragraph.

This type of question is considered by many students to be more like Reading Comprehension than English Usage. It requires you to go back and reread most of the passage. If you are rushed for time (and most of us are in this section), my suggestion is that you "guess and go," making a quick guess and hoping you can come back to think more about the problem later. (Be sure not to leave the answer entirely blank. ***Remember:*** The ACT has no penalty for wrong answers. Even a wild guess might be correct.)

14. F. The subject of the verb is "the theory," which is singular, requiring the singular verb *has.* If you thought that "markings" or "fingerprints" was the subject of the sentence, you missed the point.

15. A. The last paragraph talks about how unique the giraffes are, how their markings distinguish them from each other. Choices B and C are tricky. Yes, the last paragraph talks about how giraffes have different colors and blend in well with their surroundings, but it doesn't say anything about their evolving. Don't read too much into the paragraph. And choice D may be true, but just because a statement is true does not mean that it is the answer to that specific question.

Passage 2

16. G. The original sounds as if Mr. Haley were a magician who changed a person into a book! The sentence means to say that stories about people were put into a book. Choice H has the same problem as the original, converting people into books. Choice J makes absolutely no sense when inserted into the sentence.

17. D. This should have been a very simple question. *Who's* means who is, as in, "Who's going to miss a question this easy?" The correct word is *whose,* which is the possessive of *who.* I want to know *whose* grammar skills are so weak he missed this question.

There is no such word as "whos'." The only place I can imagine that word is in the Dr. Seuss book, *Horton Hears a Who.* The plural of one Who, I suppose, would be two Whos, and they could own something. But if you find yourself thinking of Dr. Seuss stories in the middle of this exam, you're someone whose score is going to be a lot lower than that of someone who's concentrating on what he's doing.

18. H. The original sounds as if the early years were born in New York, when obviously it was Alex who was born there. When a sentence begins with a subordinate clause (a clause that can't stand by itself), the first noun or pronoun after the comma usually has to do the action of that clause. In this case, start the underlined portion with Alex, eliminating choices F and J. Choice G is tricky. It starts with Alex . . . , or does it? It actually starts with Alex's years, again sounding as if the years were born in New York. Also, choice G is passive voice — rarely preferable to the active voice.

19. **D.** The original is a sentence fragment, an incomplete sentence: The oldest of three sons. . . . Who was the oldest of three sons? The sentence is missing a subject. Predict that you need the second sentence to start with Alex, and you have the right answer quickly.

    Choices B and (especially) C look good on their own, but when you plug them back into the sentence, they don't correct the error.

20. **G.** To many students, this question seems to be more like a reading comprehension question than strictly a grammar question. The fact that Alex was the oldest of three sons doesn't mean much in the context of the passage. His brothers are never again mentioned, nor is it mentioned whether his family situation influenced him or his writing. In short, the line just dies. It goes nowhere. It can safely be eliminated because it doesn't do anything to spur on the writing in the passage.

21. **D.** The underlined portion does not fit with the rest of the paragraph, which discusses Alex's military career. Although the route Alex took to become a writer is discussed, his motivation is not.

22. **F.** The sentence is correct as written. Did you double-check that the first noun after the subordinate clause did the action of the clause? "Unchallenged by his daily routine in the U.S. Coast Guard, Haley. . . ." Haley is the one who was unchallenged. Often the first noun after the subordinate clause is wrong, making a nonsense sentence, such as, "When she was two, the fortune-teller predicted Ms. Ferraro would be president." Chances are, it was Ms. Ferraro who was two at the time of the prediction, not the fortune-teller. Rearrange the sentence to read, "When she was two, Ms. Ferraro was told . . . ."

23. **A.** "Eventually his articles were published" makes sense. The other answers change the meaning of the sentence. Did you note the correct spelling of "nonetheless" in choice D? Nonetheless is all one word. (Do you care? My best friend is so rabidly anti-spelling that she has a sign on her desk that says, "Misspellers of the world, untie!")

24. **F.** "Afforded him an opportunity" is a correct expression. Note that choice G would have been correct had it said "allowed" rather than "allow." Choices H and J would have been correct had they said "enabled him to gain an opportunity" or "gave him an opportunity." Be careful not to rewrite the answer choices, unconsciously supplying words that are not actually printed on the paper.

25. **D.** The traveling and the research were done at the same time, eliminating choice B. Choice C sounds as if the research did the traveling, whereas it was Mr. Haley who actually traveled. The original version is a run-on sentence, two sentences incorrectly joined. If you're confused by run-ons, go back to Chapter 4 to learn the four ways to correct them.

26. **H.** The original sounds as if the ancestors went to a small village, whereas Mr. Haley went to the village. Choice G and choice J are incorrect because they are present tense. The research occurred in the past, requiring the past tense: took.

Verb mistakes are among the most common errors in the English portion of the ACT. Verbs may be in the wrong number (singular versus plural) or the wrong tense. Always double-check the verb.

27. **B.** If you chose A, you read this too quickly. "After Haley . . . then he knew. . . ." You do not need both the word "after" and the word "then." Choice B eliminates the unnecessary "then."

If two answer choices appear to be identical, one probably adds or deletes the critical word and is the correct answer choice. If you are confused, choose one of those two. (Always keep in mind: The ACT has no penalty for wrong answers. Feel free to guess anytime you're not sure of the correct answer.)

28. G. Do you remember the point tested with the formation *not only . . . but also?* The rule (covered in Chapter 4, in case you've forgotten) is that *not only* and *but also* must be in parallel positions in the sentence. In other words, if *not only* is in front of a noun, *but also* must be in front of a noun. This question is even a little trickier than that. "Not only" is in front of "the Haley family" which is the object, but "but also" is in front of "the story" which is the subject. Change this sentence to read as follows: was not only the saga . . . but also the story.

You should have buzzers and alarms going off in your brain whenever you encounter one of the terrible twosomes. Diction questions, although not automatically wrong, should be checked carefully. As I often say, "Sure, I'm paranoid . . . but am I paranoid enough?"

29. C. The passage gives an overview of Haley's history and how he came to write *Roots*. However, it doesn't analyze, or even mention, any other work. The reader gains no insight into Haley's ability, just into his background.

Passage 3

30. G. The original should have sounded strange as you read the sentence to yourself. (You *are* verbalizing these sentences, aren't you?) Your ear will catch what your eye skims right over. The correct expression is "more importantly." Choices H and G do not fit when reinserted into the sentence. Choice H, in particular, looks good on its own; but when Choice H is reinserted, it says, "It's more important, even, it is essential . . . ."

31. C. This is such a beautiful question that you'd think that it was faxed from heaven. The grammar error is very straightforward. *Segment* is a singular noun. Even if you thought that the verb needed to agree with the noun *population,* that noun is also singular, requiring the verb *increases* and requires a singular verb: *increases* (not "increase").

32. H. A question like this is a freebie for you if you have memorized the terrible twosomes given in the grammar review. When *its* means *it is,* the correct structure is *it's*. There is no such word as choice G, "its'." Choice J changes the meaning by changing the tense unnecessarily.

This is the type of question that an international student for whom English is not the primary language can get correct quickly and easily. These diction mistakes (two or more words that are commonly confused) can be memorized. Look for this quick-and-dirty type of question on the exam, and do it first if you are running out of time.

33. C. Although choice A, "will be depending," is grammatically correct, it is not as sharp and succinct as "will depend." Choices B and D change the tense.

34. G. "Should be knowing" is an awkward construction. Remember that *-ing* words are often used incorrectly on this exam. The correct expression is "need to know." Choice H, when reinserted into the sentence, makes the sentence a fragment. Don't forget to take a few seconds to reinsert your answer choice. Choice J is unnecessarily long and wordy.

35. C. Words like "It is essential" tell you that the writer is recommending a course of action.

Few ACT passages are negative, allowing you to eliminate answers similar to choice A, which is argumentative, and choice B, which is derogatory. A passage may be lighthearted or amusing or entertaining (especially the fiction ones), but that is not the case here.

36. J. "Due to the fact that" is a ***prolix,*** a verbose, unnecessarily wordy expression. The correct way to say "due to the fact that" is simply the word *because.* Choice G may have trapped you. Many of us say *since* when we mean to say *because,* as in the following example: "Since I didn't study this jazz, I didn't do well." However, even if you make that common mistake, choice G actually says "Since then" and would not be correct. Choice H is too wordy.

37. B. Choice A has the plural pronoun *their.* The antecedent of *their* in this sentence actually is "home" in the previous sentence. Because a singular noun (home) cannot take a plural pronoun (their), choice A is wrong. Choice C turns the sentence into a run-on and also uses *their.* Choice D uses the *Beware!* word, *being.* As you recall from the grammar review, *being* is a frequently misused word. It makes the sentence unnecessarily long and wordy.

38. G. A comma indicates a pause. Usually your ear will catch where a comma should be placed. As you read the sentence, you pause or take a breath at the place appropriate for a comma. The semicolon is incorrect; a semicolon connects independent clauses. "But about what is going on in Bosnia" is not an independent sentence because it cannot stand on its own. Omitting the underlined portion makes nonsense of the sentence.

39. A. The original is the best way to state this phrase. *As* indicates situations. *Like* compares people or things. Choice C has the dreaded word *being,* which is rarely used correctly and doesn't fit with the "are" later in the sentence. Choice D changes the meaning of the sentence entirely, indicating that the seniors are no longer capable when it means to say the seniors are capable.

40. G. The paragraph indicates that the author learned that the elderly are interested in today's topics. Choice F is the opposite of the main idea. Choice H may be true, but it isn't the topic of the paragraph. Choice J is a truism, but it is not necessarily relevant to this paragraph.

Don't choose an answer simply because it is a fact. If that were the case, "The boiling point of water is 100° C" or "Taking the ACT destroys brain cells" would be the right answer. Check to be sure that the choice actually answers what is asked.

41. D. The correct expression is "changes less than," not "changes smaller than." If you chose C, you fell right for the trap. Choice C says "changes much less then" rather than "changes much less than." When two answer choices appear to be identical, examine them carefully, word for word, letter for letter. Chances are that one of the two is a slight variation on the other and is the correct answer.

42. J. Normally, you would not use the familiar pronoun *you* but would use the more formal pronoun *one*. However, if you read ahead, you find out that the nonunderlined, next part of the sentence also has "you" in it, meaning it's okay to use "you" in this sentence. Choice G is a fragment. Choice H is grammatically correct but is long and awkward and doesn't flow smoothly.

Are you confused between which answers "flow smoothly" and which answers do not? Hearing the correct flow of a sentence can be extremely difficult if English is not your native tongue. In a situation like this in which all answers appear to be grammatically correct, you may be able to get away with choosing the shortest answer simply because longer choices are often unnecessarily wordy. (The ACT has no penalty for wrong answers; guess as often as you need to.)

43. A. Choices B, C, and D change the verb unnecessarily. Although the informal pronoun *you* is often incorrect (the formal pronoun *one* is preferred), the nonunderlined portions of the passage use the word "you," indicating that it is correct in this case. Remember that you are not allowed to change the nonunderlined portions but have to bring the underlined portions into synch with the rest of the passage.

Passage 4

44. F. The past tense, "have called," is correct in this sentence because the burrows were found previously. Choice G has an *-ing* word. As you probably remember, *-ing* words are often misused and abused in this portion of the exam. Choices J and H change the meaning of the sentence; they sound as if the scientists themselves were called "dirt corkscrews."

45. **C.** The correct expression is "since the time they were found," meaning from that time on. The other answers make no sense when reinserted into the sentence.

If you're running out of time (a definite possibility by this point in the exam), search for a one-word question like this. You can answer such a question very quickly. All questions count the same; it's logical to head for the short ones first.

46. **J.** Choices F and H are redundant: They both have "at that time" and "then." Choice G creates a clause without a noun: "There were at that time scientists thought. . . ." A *who* is missing.

Have you noticed how often the shortest answer is the correct answer? Although you can't automatically assume that the shortest answer is always correct, check it out carefully.

47. **A.** This question tests a little reading comprehension rather than pure grammar. The previous and the subsequent sentences make it clear that the passage is talking about corkscrew spirals or holes in the ground. Choices B and C make no sense when reinserted in the sentence. Choice D has no ***antecedent*** (the noun which the pronoun is replacing). What is "it"? Remember, *it* is one of the *Beware!* words that you were cautioned to examine carefully.

48. **J.** "But" and "however" serve the same function in this sentence. Both words are not needed; eliminate the underlined one. Choices G and H do not fit when reinserted into the sentence.

Are you remembering to reinsert your answer choices and reread the entire sentence? If not, you are probably falling for some very cheesy tricks.

49. **B.** The "been" is a form of *being,* one of the *Beware!* words, words that should immediately capture your attention. On this exam, *being* is frequently used incorrectly, as it is here. Usually, you can't substitute *been* for *is, are, was,* or *were*.

50. **J.** A simple comma suffices. A semicolon connects two independent clauses, clauses that can stand on their own. You would not say as a complete sentence, "But this predator probably followed a beaver home for supper and just stayed." The *but* usually indicates a subordinate clause that is preceded by a comma.

TIP

Are you about ready to enter a Clinic for the Terminally Confused? Don't worry about the terminology. Just know that a semicolon is much stronger than a comma. If you come to a dead stop when reading, use a semicolon. If you merely pause, use a comma.

51. **B.** The comma in this case is not strong enough to connect two independent sentences. Insert a period and a capital letter to make these separate sentences. Choice D is tempting, but it is unnecessarily verbose ("because in fact").

52. **J.** *Their* is the possessive. *There* is a place. (*Their* books are over *there*.) Because "their" is already possessive, you don't also need the possessive "burrow's." Choice G looks good alone, and it fits when inserted into the sentence; but it does not make sense with the rest of the passage.

Always be sure that your answer fits into the entire passage by checking everything, not just the new sentence; always check a few sentences before and after it.

HEADS UP

53. **B.** The correct conjugation of *lie* is: *lie, lay, lay.* (Doesn't this make it easy? Any past tense of *lie* is *lay*.) The verbs *to lie* and *to lay* are often tested. Be absolutely certain that you know the distinction between them (*lie* has no object; *lay* requires an object) and their conjugation. I discuss these verbs in more detail in Chapter 4.

54. **H.** ***Extinct*** means no longer in existence (you may feel about now that your brain is extinct). ***Extant*** means in existence, able to be seen. (No matter how many times you wish that the ACT would be extinct, it remains extant.) The sentence implies that the animals no longer exist. Eliminate choices F and G. Omitting the underlined portion (choice J) makes nonsense of the sentence.

Don't fall into the bad habit of choosing the OMIT answer every time that you see it. Be sure to reread the sentence that results when you omit the underlined words. Often, the resulting sentence will make no sense at all.

55. B. A colon usually introduces a list of items. (Rochelle told her boyfriend, "If you want us to stay together, you're going to have to get a few things straight: (1) I am not to be referred to as your 'hot momma'; (2) any jewelry you give me cannot come from the gumball machine; and (3) your mother is never again to call me by your former girlfriend's name.") Colons rarely connect separate sentences. Choices C and D change the meaning of the sentence.

Did you fall for the trap in Choice D? The meaning of "but most of the part" is very different from "however, for the most part." The expression ***for the most part*** simply means *primarily* or *mostly*. You might say, "I'm avoiding the traps for the most part, only missing one or two." *For the most part* is an idiomatic expression.

56. J. Did this question trap you? If so, you probably read only the underlined portion, not the context of the entire sentence. The original is redundant; it says the same thing twice — "nonstop, without interruption." ***Nonstop*** means *without interruption*. Use one or the other, not both.

57. A. The local events correspond to, or are indicated by, what is shown in the sedimentary record. *Reflect* has several meanings. Although the other answers discuss those alternate meanings, the original is one of the correct uses.

58. G. The passage was primarily about identifying animals based on their fossils. Choice F summarizes the first paragraph only, not the second. Choice H is much too broad; the passage was primarily about the fossils, not what the paleontologists did with them. Choice J is too specific. Extinction was only briefly mentioned in the second paragraph.

If you are running out of time and know that you won't get to the grammar, try a "reading comp" question at the end. To answer this question, for example, you merely had to skim what is actually a pretty short passage. (Careful! This advice does not mean that all "box" questions are short and easy to do. Distinguish this "content" question, which is easy to answer, from a "structure" question, such as number 59, which is both difficult and time-consuming.)

59. A. An "ordering-the-sentences" question is an excellent type of question to make a wild guess on. (Don't just skip it entirely. The ACT has no penalty for wrong answers, so guessing when you don't know the answer is always worthwhile.) "Ordering-the-sentences" questions take much more time than most other question types and are somewhat subjective. I have had students pound their fists on my table and scream at me, arguing that their construction of the paragraph was preferable to mine. You can argue 'til you're blue in the face, but the test-makers' interpretation is final.

If you decide to invest some time answering this type of question, start by identifying the topic or main sentence. It usually has an introductory tone, setting up the rest of the paragraph. Here, sentence 2, talking about changes in store, is a typical *beginning* or *topic* sentence. Knowing that sentence 2 is first allows you to eliminate choices B and C. You may be even more willing to guess, now that your odds are down to 50-50.

When you do an "ordering" question, try to identify the topic sentence and, if necessary, the last sentence. Doing so is usually much easier than arranging the more generic "filler" sentences in middle of the passage.

Passage 5

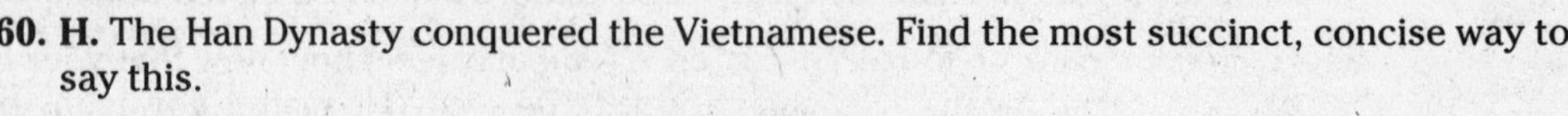

60. H. The Han Dynasty conquered the Vietnamese. Find the most succinct, concise way to say this.

Did you notice the *Beware!* word *being?* Whenever you see that word, get very nervous. It is often used incorrectly throughout this exam.

If you chose J, you didn't read the sentence as a whole without the underlined portion. If you eliminate it, you see that the sentence makes no sense as written ". . . were conquered, forces of China's Han Dynasty." The Vietnamese themselves were not Chinese forces, but they were conquered by Chinese forces. Anytime you choose to omit an underlined portion, go back and reread the new sentence to be sure that you haven't changed the meaning.

61. **D.** The Dynasty, or rule, lasted from 111 B.C. until A.D. 939. This is almost a reading comprehension question. Had you read the phrase "since A.D. 939" by itself, it would seem logical. You have to read the entire sentence (and often a few sentences above or below it) to choose the correct grammar.

62. **F.** If you look at the underlined portion by itself, it looks bizarre because it has two commas, before and after "that." However, the purpose of a comma is to express a pause or hesitation. Read this aloud, and you will see that the commas are correctly placed. Choices G and H have an *-ing* word, "reaching." Double-check all *-ing* words because they often introduce errors or unnecessarily clumsy sentences. Choice J has the wrong tense.

63. **A.** If you got this question correct, kudos to you! Normally, the word *however* is part of the construction that separates independent sentences. For example, "I was careful; however, I still missed the question." In this case, however, the commas do not separate independent sentences (if they did, they would be wrong), but simply pause, or make a parenthetical aside. Choice D changes the meaning of the sentence. Choice C is tempting, but it would turn the second sentence into a fragment: "And however for nearly two centuries contending families in the north and south struggled to control the powerless kings of the Le Dynasty." You may remember, from junior-high grammar, that you should not begin a sentence with the conjunction *and*. Although that is a good idea in general, it is not a hard-and-fast rule. There may be a few times in which *and* can correctly begin a sentence. ("You told me you loved me!" she sobbed. "And I meant it when I said it!" he assured her.)

64. **H.** ***Affect*** with an *a* means touch or concern. "How does having your boyfriend flirt with another girl affect your relationship?" The idiomatic expression ***in effect*** means primarily or generally. The *effect* is the result of something. *In effect* means a situation, basically, has that result. "When I saw him flirting with his former girlfriend, I gave Leon his ring back, in effect ending our relationship." Choice J changes the meaning of the entire sentence. ***Ineffective*** means not skillful, not efficient. "Leon's efforts to win his girlfriend back were ineffective, even pathetic."

65. **B.** The original has a fragment, "Just a few kilometers above the demarcation line established at the 1954 Geneva Conference." This clause cannot stand on its own. Change the second "sentence" into a subordinate clause, tagging on the end of the previous sentence.

    Choice D may have trapped you. A semicolon functions the same way that a period functions (by connecting two independent sentences). Choice C turns the sentence into a run-on — two sentences incorrectly joined.

66. **H.** If the word "but" weren't there, the original form would work: "Vietnam, having been reunited, soon fell prey . . . ." However, the word *but* (which is not underlined and therefore cannot be changed) requires the simple past tense, *was*.

    If you missed this question, you probably fell for the common trap of reading only the underlined portion and a small portion around it. Reading the entire sentence is critical.

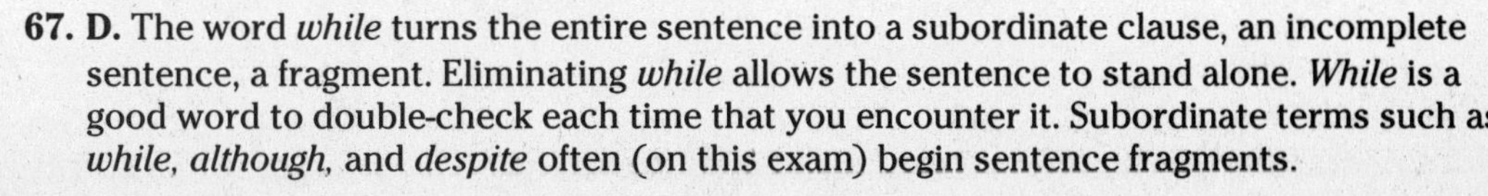

67. **D.** The word *while* turns the entire sentence into a subordinate clause, an incomplete sentence, a fragment. Eliminating *while* allows the sentence to stand alone. *While* is a good word to double-check each time that you encounter it. Subordinate terms such as *while, although,* and *despite* often (on this exam) begin sentence fragments.

68. G. Notice that this is an exception to the tip that *-ing* words are usually wrong. The original sounds as if France's purpose in imposing control gradually was in order to meet heavy resistance. The sense of the sentence indicates something entirely different. Choice H has an unnecessary *and.* (I live by the motto, "When in doubt, leave it out." It's a good thing I'm a grammar teacher, not a surgeon!) Choice J has the wrong verb tense.

69. A. This question tests *its* (possessive) versus *it's* (it is). Here, "its" refers to the uprising, making the possessive correct. That narrows the answers down to A and D. "So" indicates a corresponding thought; "but" correctly indicates here a contrary thought.

70. G. ***Adept*** means skillful and is usually followed by *at.* (You're skillful or adept at taking the ACT.) ***Adopt*** means to take as one's own; ***adopted from*** means taken from. ***Adapt*** means to fit or adjust. You have to adapt to a new schedule in order to find time to study for the ACT.

71. B. Led is the past tense of *lead.* I led you right into a trap. The required word here is the noun, ***lead,*** meaning the front position. (Rudolph takes the lead when pulling Santa's sleigh.) Choice D has the wrong verb tense, turning the sentence into a fragment.

72. J. The original is a run-on. A mere comma is not strong enough to join independent clauses.

If you chose G, you fell for the trap. A semicolon does join independent clauses, but "then went to China" (note that *he* is missing) is not an independent clause. Choice H is awkward (a common failing of *-ing* words) and isn't parallel. Choice J, by eliminating the "he," makes the second clause subordinate, correcting the run-on.

73. A. Choice B has the singular verb *was* with the plural subject *dissidents.* Choice C sounds as if the dissidents were doing the imprisoning, rather than being imprisoned. Choice D turns the sentence into a fragment.

74. G. ACT passages are rarely negative; they don't ridicule or criticize. Eliminate choices F and H. Choice J is too specific. Ho Chi Minh was mentioned only in the last paragraph.

The purpose of a passage is usually very broad and general: to introduce a topic, to give an overview, or to discuss or explain an idea. When in doubt (remember that the ACT has no penalty for guessing), choose the most generic answer.

75. A. The passage is about the various governments that Vietnam has had and the wars that put those governments in power. The next paragraph would continue the thought of the last paragraph, the paragraph that discussed the burgeoning anticolonial movement.

Nothing in the passage even hints at nuclear weapons (choice B) or human rights (choice D). And even if Vietnam were industrialized (it's still primarily agrarian, although you don't have to know that to get this question correct), the passage does not discuss that topic.

Mathematics Test

1. **A.** The easy way to do this problem is to plug in numbers for the variables. Say that Putty picks 10 pecks per hour for 5 hours. You can easily see now that she has picked 50 pecks. How did you get that number? You multiplied 10 by 5, or in the case of the variables, $x \bullet y$.

Many students think that the word *per* signals division. For example, if you were asked how many students there were per class, you would probably divide the total number of students by the number of classes. If your first instinct is to choose C, D, or E, check your answer by plugging in numbers.

2. **J.** You can approach this problem in three ways. For those of you who aren't allergic to percentages, use these steps: First, $^{20}/_{100}x = 50$. Then cross-multiply (or multiply each side by 100): $20x = 5{,}000$ and $x = {}^{5{,}000}/_{20}$. Therefore, $x = 250$.

   Maybe you prefer to work with decimals: $.20x = 50$. Move the decimal point two places to the right (in other words, multiply by 100): $20x = 5{,}000$. Then $x = {}^{5{,}000}/_{20}$. Finally, $x = 250$.

   If fractions turn you on, think that 20% = $^1/_5$ (for example, 20 cents is $^1/_5$ of a dollar). $^1/_5x = 50$. Multiply both sides through by 5 to get rid of the fraction: $x = 50 \times 5$. Then $x = 250$.

3. **C.** The three friends averaged \$50,000 each. That means their total was \$150,000 ($3 \times 50{,}000 = 150{,}000$). Make the equation: 150,000 = 40% Total, or 150,000 = .4T. Divide both sides through by what's next to the variable. 150,000/.4 = T. T = 375,000.

Were you looking for an answer like, "It cannot be determined" among the choices? If so, you were probably confused because you don't know exactly how much money each individual made. Maybe Debi made \$100,000 and both Mike and Ken together made \$50,000. It's irrelevant. The only important point is that three people together made \$150,000.

4. **H.** A number to the negative first power is the same as 1 over that number to the first power: $10^{-1} = {}^1/_{10}$. A number to the zero power is 1. A number to the first power is that number ($10^1 = 10$). Here, the terms are $.1 + 1 + 10 = 11.1$.

If you chose J or K, you fell for the trap. If you were to *multiply* like bases, then you would add the exponents: $-1 + 0 + 1 = 0$. However, when you *add* like bases, you can't take that shortcut. You have to determine the value of each term and then add the values together.

5. **D.** If the office wants 100 calls a day for 12 days, it wants 1,200 calls ($100 \times 12 = 1{,}200$). It has 480 calls ($80 \times 6 = 480$). Subtract: $1{,}200 - 480 = 720$.

If you chose E, you fell for the trap! The question does not ask how many calls per day the office receives, but how many calls altogether. Sure, if the office needs to have 720 calls in 6 days, that's 120 calls per day ($720/6 = 120$), but that's not what the question wants to know. Remember: The mere fact that the answer you got is staring you in the face does not mean that's the correct answer to the problem.

6. **G.** Of course, this question has to have a shortcut here, right? No one would make you grind out all that awful multiplication without giving you some reason to go on living. You probably see that the terms keep squaring: $2^2 = 4$ and $4^2 = 16$ and $16^2 = 256$. The fifth term, therefore, is 256^2.

7. **D.** The key here is math vocabulary (which is covered in Chapter 7). An ***obtuse angle*** is more than 90 degrees. (I always think of obtuse angles as obese angles, "fatter" than a 90-degree angle.) The interior angles of a triangle total 180 degrees. If one angle is greater than 90 degrees, the sum of the other two angles must be less than 90 degrees. An ***acute angle*** is greater than 0, but less than 90 degrees (think of it as "a cute" little angle). Each of the remaining two angles, therefore, must be acute.

8. **H.** An easy way to deal with percentages is to use the number 100. In this case, say that $(a + b) = 100$.Then 5% of 100 = 5. That means that 10% of b = 5. Solve for b: .10b = 5. Divide both sides through by what's next to the variable: $b = 5/.10b = 50$. If $a + b = 100$, then $a = 50$ and $a = b$.

   Are you saying, "Yeah, but what if I plug in something besides 100? How do I know it works with other numbers? Okay, I'll prove it to you. Try plugging in another number. (If you want to make life harder, go ahead!) Choose something truly bizarre, like –37. Let $(a + b) = -37$. Then 5% of –37 = –1.85. If –1.85 = 10% of b, solve for b. $-1.85 = .1b$. Divide both sides through by what's next to the variable: $-1.85/.1 = -18.5$. $b = -18.5$. If $(a + b) = -37$, and $b = -18.5$, then $a = -18.5$ as well. Son of a gun, it works! (But the moral of the story is: Plug in 100 when dealing with percentages. Life is so much easier.)

9. **B.** The area of a square is side squared. In this case, that's 8^2, or 64. That means the area of the triangle is also 64. The area of a triangle is $^1/_2$ base times height. In this case, that's $^1/_2x$ times x, or $^1/_2x^2$. Make the equation: $^1/_2x^2 = 64$. Multiply through by 2 to get rid of the fraction: $x^2 = 128$. Take the square root by simplifying: $\sqrt{128} = \sqrt{64} \times \sqrt{2}$. The square root of 64 = 8, giving you a final answer of $8\sqrt{2}$.

10. **H.** The "explanation" (the line that begins "x!=") tells you that when you have an exclamation point after the number, you start at that number and then multiply your way down to 1. So 6! = $6 \times 5 \times 4 \times 3 \times 2 \times 1$, which is 720.

   If you chose F, you found 6^4, doing entirely too much work. If you catch yourself doing that much multiplication, you've probably fallen for a trap.

11. **D.** If you chose answer A or answer E, you fell for a trap. Answer A caught careless students who thought, "The price rises 25% then falls $^1/_4$, or 25%, for a 0% change." Wrong. An easy way to solve a problem like this is to plug in 100 for the original price of the book. In 1998, the book cost $100. If the price rose by 25%, it went up $25 to a total of $125. In 2000, the price was $^1/_4$, or 25%, below its 1998 cost. That means that it was $25 below the original $100, or $75.

   Here's where the trap comes in. Reading the question carefully tells you that you want to know the percent decrease from 1999 to 2000, which here is from 125 to 75. The formula (given in the math review) for percent increase or decrease is:

   Number increase or decrease / starting (original) number

   In other words, the denominator is the number you begin with, which in this case is 125 (because the question asks for the change from 1999, not from 1998). The number decrease is 50 (125 – 75 = 50). Finally, $^{50}/_{125} = {^4}/_{10} = 40\%$.

   Choice E traps readers who forget that you are trying to find a percentage decrease and find just the year 2000 price.

12. **J.** A circumference is $2\pi r$ or πd. If $C = \pi d$, which is 10π here, then $d = 10$. As quickly as that, you're done. You almost didn't get your money's worth out of that problem, did you?

   A diameter or a radius does not (as a rule) have π in questions on this test. You can find π in answers for the area and the circumference.

   You should memorize all the common geometry formulas and be able to do them "forward and backward." That is, you need to know how to go from a circumference to an area, and vice versa.

13. A. You have two ways to solve this problem. First, you know that the interior angles of a triangle total 180°. So 85 + 45 = 130. That means that the third angle in the triangle is 180° – 130 = 50. Because angles along a straight line total 180°, subtract again: 180 – 50 = 130.

The second way to do this problem eliminates a few steps. The exterior angle of a triangle is equal to the sum of the two remote interior angles. (***Remote*** just means the two angles are not next to the angle that you're solving for.) You can finish this problem in just one step: 85 + 35 = 130.

This remote-angle rule is one of the less commonly used rules and thus one of the first forgotten. Even if you know the basics of geometry, spend a few minutes looking through Chapter 7 to pick up lesser-known (but still important) tidbits like this one.

14. F. First, square or cube each expression: $(5x^2y^5)(5x^2y^5) = 25x^4y^{10}$ Then $(3x^3y^4)(3x^3y^4)(3x^3y^4) = 27x^9y^{12}$. Next, multiply the products.

Before you go through all the pencil-pushing to find 25 × 27, look at the exponents: $x^4 \cdot x^9 = x^{4+9} = x^{13}$. You've immediately narrowed the answers down to F and J. Because 25 × 27 > 15, eliminate J. What looked like a "pain in the posterior" problem is over with in a flash.

This question is relatively easy if you remember how to work with bases and exponents. To multiple like bases, add the exponents. To work with a "power to a power," that is, with one exponent inside a parenthesis and one outside, multiply the exponents. (If I've totally left you in the dust, go back to the math review section on bases and exponents in Chapter 8. This jazz is easier than it looks.)

15. C. The area of a circle is π radius squared, or 16π for the first circle. Because 16π is $^1/_4$ of 64π, you want a circle with an area of 64π, which means its radius must be 8: $8^2 \times \pi = 64\pi$.

If you chose A, you went backward and didn't think the problem through. If the second circle has a bigger area, it must have a bigger — not smaller — radius. The fact that 1 is $^1/_4$ of 4 is irrelevant. If you chose D, you simply took 4 times the first circle's radius. Remember that you get the ratio of the areas of similar figures by squaring the ratio of their sides (or radii). In other words, if the radii are in a ratio of 1:2, their areas are in a ratio of 1:4.

16. J. The formula for rate, time, and distance is RT = D: *rate* × *time* = *distance*. Plug what you know into the formula: *rate* × 2 hours 20 minutes = 7 miles. Then convert 2 hours 20 minutes to $^7/_3$ hours (because an hour has 60 minutes, 20 minutes is $^1/_3$ hour). Change the 7 miles (distance) to thirds as well: $^{21}/_3$. Now, you have R × $^7/_3$ = $^{21}/_3$ and R = 3.

17. C. Find the ratio of the sides, noting that the dollhouse is in inches while the regular house is in feet. 18 inches = 1.5 feet and 1.5 to 12 = $^{15}/_{120}$ or $^1/_8$. That means the width must be in a $^1/_8$ or 1:8 ratio as well. First, 24 inches = 2 feet. Then $^2/_{16}$ = $^1/_8$.

Did you notice that you can eliminate answers A, D, and E by using common sense? You can eliminate A because the length of the real bedroom is not 18 feet, and the dollhouse is built to scale; the width cannot be 24 feet. Because the floor is wider than it is long (24 inches to 18 inches in the dollhouse), the answer must be more than 12 feet.

18. H. Two figures are similar if their sides (and angles) are in proportion. (See Chapter 7 for a quick refresher on similar figures.) In this case, if the triangles are similar, then the angles of triangle II are also in the ratio 1:2:3, which just happens to be a 30:60:90 triangle. (See Chapter 7 for a refresher on the interior angles of a triangle and on properties of special triangles, like the 30:60:90 triangle.)

The ratio of sides in a 30:60:90 triangle is $\text{side}:\text{side}\sqrt{3}:2\text{side}$. This means that the "$\text{side}\sqrt{3}$" side of triangle I is the $5\sqrt{3}$ side. Therefore, the "side" is 5, and the "2side" is 10. (Check by adding these once more: $5+5\sqrt{3}+10=15+5\sqrt{3}$.) If the shortest side of triangle I is 5 and the shortest side of triangle II is 15, the triangles are in a 1:3 ratio. That means that every side of triangle II is three times as long as every side of triangle I. The sides of triangle II, therefore, are 15, $15\sqrt{3}$, 30. Add these together to get the perimeter $45 + 15\sqrt{3}$.

19. E. On this type of problem, be sure that you note what the question is asking for. It doesn't want the solution to the equation, but rather the equation itself. Often, you will find going backward easier. "Forty percent of everything" means .40 times everything else, eliminating choices A and D. The square of 5 is simply 5^2, but be careful not to take the square root of that answer (eliminating choice B). Because you add $\sqrt{625}$ and 5^2, eliminate choice C. Only E is left.

Read every choice. If you're rushed (and who isn't?), you may do too much work by anticipating what the question is asking for and actually solving out the question. No one here really wants to know Lael's age, just the equation for finding it.

20. H. Add together the number of redheaded children ($^1/_6$) and brown-haired children ($^1/_3$, which can be written as $^2/_6$) to get $^3/_6$ or $^1/_2$. If half the children don't have blond hair, the other half of the children *do* have blond hair. That means that the blondes, 30, are half of the number of children, making the total 60.

21. C. The key to this problem is knowing that any number to the zero power equals one. Therefore, $\frac{9-1}{1-9}=\frac{8}{-8}=-1$.

22. H. The interior angles of any polygon are found by using this formula, discussed in detail in Chapter 7: $(n-2)\times 180°$, where n stands for the number of sides. Here $n = 5$ and $(5-2)\ 180 = 3\ (180) = 540$.

Notice that it makes no difference whether the figure is regular (all sides and angles are the same) or irregular. The exam may give you some truly bizarre-looking figures; don't let them intimidate you. The interior angle formula is the same no matter how grotesque the figure is.

23. C. The total number of tourists is the sum of 200 + 320 + 140 + 180 + 240 = 1,080. The French are $^{180}/_{1080}$ or $^1/_6$ of the total.

Tourists Visiting City M

Japanese

French

Germans

Moroccans

Americans

If you chose E, you fell for the trap and didn't finish working the problem out to answer what the question was asking. A circle has 360°, and $^1/_6$ of 360 is 60°.

24. J. This question tests your ability to reduce square roots. Look for perfect squares in the factors. Follow these steps: $\sqrt{12}=\sqrt{4}\cdot\sqrt{3}$ and $\sqrt{4}=2$, giving you $2\sqrt{3}$. Then $\sqrt{75}=\sqrt{25}\times\sqrt{3}$, which is $5\sqrt{3}$. Finally, $2\sqrt{3}+5\sqrt{3}=7\sqrt{3}$.

25. C. Remove the parentheses: $3x^2y + xy^2 - 2x^2y + 2xy^2$.

The last item is added because of the negative sign in front of the second set of parentheses: $-1(-2xy^2) = 2xy^2$. Confusing signs is one of the most common careless errors in algebra problems.

Combine like terms: $3x^2y - 2x^2y + xy^2 + 2xy^2 = x^2y + 3xy^2$.

26. J. This problem is easy if you remember the basic rule: The ratio of the areas of similar figures is the square of the ratio of their sides. In other words, first you find the ratio of the sides. Here, that is given to you as 3:4. Next, you square that ratio: $3^2 = 9$; $4^2 = 16$. It's as simple as that.

What if you don't remember the rule? You've learned so many geometry rules that it's easy to forget one or two. If you do, draw a picture and plug in numbers. Say that the triangles are sides $3{:}3{:}3\sqrt{2}$. (No, they don't have to be isosceles right triangles, but because those are so easy to work with, why not use them?) Then the sides of the second triangle are $4{:}4{:}4\sqrt{2}$. The area of the first triangle is $^9/_2$ (the area of a triangle is one half base × height). The area of the second triangle is $^{16}/_2$. The ratio $^9/_2$ to $^{16}/_2$ is the same as $^9/_{16}$.

27. C. The difference between 4 and 7 (in the ratio 4:7) is 3. Therefore, an increment of 3 must equal 60, so one increment is 20. First, 20 × 4 = 80. Then 20 × 7 = 140. Finally, 80 + 140 = 220.

28. C. There are two ways to do this problem: The official, gives-you-brain-cramp way, and the easy, Dummies way. Which do you prefer? Me, too. Here's the easy way: Plug in the answer choices. I suggest you start with the middle term. That way, you can see whether the answer is too high or low, and choose your next plug-in accordingly.

If x is 10, then $10 + {}^2/_3(10) = 10 + 6.66$ = about 17, certainly more than 15. The first equation is valid. Try the second. Is $10 + 4 < 15$? Yes. The answer is C.

Just to prove to those Doubting Thomases in the crowd, try another answer. Choose B: $9 + {}^2/_3(9) = 9 + 6 = 15$. The first equation doesn't work; don't even bother with the second. If you take the time to check, you'll see that none of the other answers work.

When you make up your own numbers to plug in, you have to check every single answer, in case more than one can work (if more than one works, plug in something else and try again). But when you plug in the answer choices, you can stop as soon as one works. On the ACT, only one answer can be correct.

29. D. This question tests your ability to convert from English to algebra. Talk it through in your mind: Three less than $2x$ means $2x - 3$. The product of 6 and 4 means 6 × 4. A third of it is $^1/_3(24)$ or 8. Combine $8 = 2x - 3$. Finally, $11 = 2x$ and $x = {}^{11}/_2$.

Did you choose E? Tsk, tsk. You forgot to change your sign and got 8 – 3 = 5 rather than 8 + 3 = 11.

30. K. The only way to roll a 12 is to roll double sixes. The probability of rolling any number on a fair six-sided die (one of a pair of dice) is 1 out of 6, or $^1/_6$. ("Fair" dice are not loaded. The ACT would never corrupt the youth of America by even thinking about cheating!) Multiply consecutive probabilities:

$^1/_6$ (for the first die) × $^1/_6$ (for the second die) = $^1/_{36}$.

Probability is discussed in detail in Chapter 8. ACT-type problems have basically only two probability rules, both easy. I suggest that you learn them and get yourself some quick points. (The probability of your getting a probability question on the ACT is probably 100 percent.)

31. E. A knowledge of basic geometry formulas is essential. (Unlike the SAT I, the ACT does not give you any formulas in the directions to the Mathematics Test. You are expected to have these formulas memorized.) The area of a triangle is $^1/_2$ *base* × *height,* or $^1/_2bh$. If $^1/_2bh = 25$, then $bh = 50$. If $h = 10$, $b = 5$.

Choice B is the trap answer. Although this question is relatively easy, it's not quite as easy as dividing 25 by 10.

32. F. The formula for the volume of a rectangular solid (like a box or a fish tank, for instance) is *length* × *width* × *height* ($l \times w \times h$). The volume of the first tank is 6 × 4 × 10 = 240. The sides of the base of the second tank are half again as long as those of the first tank: If one side of the first tank is 6, the second tank has a side of $6 + {}^1/_2(6)$, or 6 + 3 = 9. If the other side of the first tank is 4, the second tank has a side of length $4 + {}^1/_2(4)$, or 4 + 2 = 6. Multiply these: 9 × 6 = 54. Because the volumes are to be the same, $54 \times h$ = 240. Divide by 54 to get $4.\overline{44}$ or approximately 4.4.

33. A. The area of a triangle is $^1/_2$ *base* × *height,* written as $^1/_2bh$. If Area = 32, then $^1/_2bh = 32$, and $bh = 64$.

Be very careful not to go the opposite way, and say that $bh = 16$. The base is 8, so $8h = 64$, making $h = 8$. Therefore, the figure is an isosceles right triangle. Because similar figures have sides in proportion, DEF is also an isosceles right triangle, making its base 28.

You could use the Pythagorean theorem to say that $a^2 + b^2 = c^2$, or you could remember from Chapter 7 that isosceles right triangles have their sides in the ratio of $\text{side:side:side}\sqrt{2}$. (This theorem is one of the PTs, or Pythagorean triples, that are so useful on this test. They're definitely worth memorizing; see Chapter 7.) That means the hypotenuse DE is $28\sqrt{2}$. To find the perimeter, add all the sides: $28+28+28\sqrt{2}=56+28\sqrt{2}$.

If you chose B, you just added all the numbers and said to heck with that pesky square root sign. No can do. You cannot add roots and nonroots. If you chose C, you kept the square root sign but added everything together anyway. If adding roots and nonroots confuses you, go back to Chapter 8 for a quick refresher.

34. F. The straight lines indicate absolute value, which is always positive. Therefore, $3 - 3a$ must equal 12 or –12. If $3 - 3a = 12$, $|3-3a|=12$ and $-|3-3a|=-12$. If $3 - 3a = -12$, $|3-3a|=12$ and once again $-|3-3a|=-12$. For $3 - 3a = 12$: $-3a = 9$ and $a = -3$, which is not one of the answer choices. For $3 - 3a = -12$: $-3a = -15$ and $a = 5$.

Why not take a simple shortcut? Plug in the answer choices. The ACT is nice enough to give you the answer; all you have to do is plug and chug through the answer choices until you find it. Here, only choice F works.

Note how carefully the question asks which *could* be true. The answer choices never try to trap you by putting in two correct answers. If more than one value works in a problem, the ACT will offer only one as an answer choice.

If you chose H, you forgot to change the sign when you moved the 3 to the other side of the equal sign.

35. D. This problem is much easier than it looks. The sum of the interior angles of any triangle is 180 — whether the triangle is equilateral, isosceles, or scalene (no sides are equal), no matter what the size of the triangle is. The interior angles of a triangle always total 180°, so 180:180 = 1:1.

If you chose A, C, or E, you let yourself be tricked by the areas of the triangle.

36. H. The easy way to do this problem is to plug in numbers. Say the items cost 1 cent each for a total cost of 8 cents. Marcy forked over 2 dimes, for a total of 20 cents. Her change is the difference: 20 – 8 = 12. Go through each answer choice, plugging in 1 for x and 2 for y. Whichever answer comes out to be 12 is the winner. Choice F becomes 2 – 8 = –6. Nope. Choice H is 20 – 8 = 12. That's it.

When you plug in numbers that you choose randomly, you must, absolutely must, go through all the answer choices. Once in a while, more than one answer choice is correct, based on the numbers you've chosen. What do you do then? You choose different numbers and do the problem again with the answer choices that have yet to be eliminated. The chance of the same thing occurring (that is, of having two answers fit with those given numbers) is astronomical.

37. D. Because a circle has 360°, arc AB is $^{10}/_{360}$, or $^1/_{36}$, of the circumference. Make the equation: $3=\frac{1}{36}C$. Cross-multiply (multiply each side by 36): 36 × 3 = C. Finally, C = 108.

Did you fall for the trap answer E? Yes, the circumference of a circle is $2\pi r$ or πd, but in this case, the π is already built into the length of the arc. Don't feel too bad if you missed this question. Most of the time, a circumference (or an area, for that matter) does have a π in it. This was just the exception I put in to drive you nuts.

38. J. If you chose F, I gotcha! Did you think that this was a 5:12:13 triangle, one of the famous PT (Pythagorean theorem) triples? Sorry, not this time (but I like the fact that you thought of the triples, which do show up often on this test). Draw the figure like this:

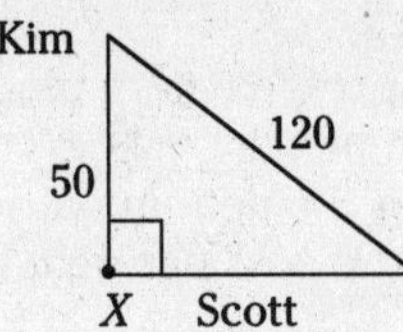

Notice that the 120 is the hypotenuse, which in a 5:12:13 triangle is 13, not 12. No short-cuts here: Do the calculations: $a^2 + b^2 = c^2$. Then $50^2 + b^2 = 120^2$. Then $2{,}500 + b^2 = 14{,}400$. Finally, $b^2 = 14{,}400 - 2{,}500 = 11{,}900$.

If you chose G, you avoided one trap but fell for a second. The 11,900 represents a side *squared.* To find the side, take the square root of 11,900.

39. D. Plug 3 in for x in the equation: $y = 5$ when $x = 3$. The coordinates are (3, 5).

40. F. Use the FOIL method (First, Outer, Inner, Last).

First: $\sqrt{5} \cdot \sqrt{3} = \sqrt{15}$

Outer: $\sqrt{5} \cdot \sqrt{6} = \sqrt{30}$

Inner: $\sqrt{6} \cdot \sqrt{3} = \sqrt{18}$

Last: $\sqrt{6} \cdot \sqrt{6} = \sqrt{36}$

Simplify: $\sqrt{18}$ to $\sqrt{2} \cdot \sqrt{9}$, or $\sqrt{2} \cdot 3$: $3\sqrt{2}$.

Simplify: $\sqrt{36} = 6$

Add: $\sqrt{15} + \sqrt{30} + 3\sqrt{2} + 6$

Even though $\sqrt{30} = \sqrt{2} \cdot \sqrt{15}$, you can't add that $\sqrt{15}$ with the other $\sqrt{15}$. You could add $2\sqrt{15}$ and $\sqrt{15}$ to get $3\sqrt{15}$, but that's definitely not the same as $\sqrt{2} \cdot \sqrt{15}$. Choice K is the trap. If you added everything together, you got $\sqrt{99}$ and then simplified to $\sqrt{9} \cdot \sqrt{11}$, or $3\sqrt{11}$.

If square roots confuse you, go back to Chapter 8. With just a little review, squares and square roots can be some of the easiest types of math questions to answer on the ACT.

If English is not your first language, this problem is a good one to try to solve because it has no English or words involved. The question has only numbers and is very straightforward. One of the most important things you can do is work on the easy-to-*understand* problems first, even if they are not always the easiest to *solve.*

41. D. The easy way to do this problem is to take it one step at a time. After one hour, the pool is at $1/2$. Then after the next hour, it is at $1/4$ (because $1/2$ of $1/2 = 1/4$.) Keep a little chart, as follows:

Hour	***Capacity Left***
1	$1/2$
2	$1/4$
3	$1/8$
4	$1/16$
5	$1/32$
6	$1/64$

Scan the answer choices before you begin solving the problem. Doing so tells you how precise you need to be. Because three of the answers are so close (7, 6, 5), you had to solve the problem exactly. Had the answers been far apart, like 12, 6, 0, you could have estimated.

42. K. The easy way to do this problem is to plug in numbers. Let $m = 5$ and $n = 10$. If five pencils cost ten cents, each pencil costs $^{10}/_{5}$ or two cents. So you know the cost of one pencil is $^{n}/_{m}$. Because m is in the denominator, your answers are already narrowed down to H and K. Multiply the cost per pencil (n/m) by the number of pencils (p) to get $n/m \times p = np/m$.

43. A. First, find out how many 45-minute increments are in $4^1/_2$ hours, or 270 minutes: $^{270}/_{45} = 6$. Faye assembles, therefore, 6 batches of 200 widgets, or 1,200 widgets. Hal assembles 600 in $2^1/_2$ hours, or 1,200 in 5 hours.

Do not bother figuring out how many Hal does in 1 minute, or in 45 minutes, or in any other increment. You're doing too much work. Because 1,200 is 2×600, he works twice $2^1/_2$ hours, or 5 hours. You can talk the problem through instead of heading for Power Math.

44. J. Say that the suit was originally \$100. A 50 percent increase raises the price to \$150. A 20 percent, or $^1/_5$ drop in the price, puts the cost at \$120. First, $^1/_5 \times 150 = 30$. Then $150 - 30 = 120$. A 30 percent decrease from 120 is 84. First, $.3 \times 120 = 36$. Then $120 - 36 = 84$. Now you can easily see what percent of the original (100) the new price (84) is. That's the beauty of starting with 100. Yes, the answer is true no matter what number you choose, but why make life any harder than it already is?

Choice G is the trap answer. Did you simply write down $+50 - 20 - 30 = 0$, meaning there was no change? If so, the new cost would be 100 percent of the old cost, *but*, as explained above, the decreases are not all percentages of the same number.

45. E. A revolution of a wheel is the same as the circumference of a wheel. If the wheel goes 15 revolutions and 300π meters, you divide 300 by 15, and each revolution is 20π. Remember that Circumference = $\pi \times$ diameter. First, $d = 20$. Then $d = 2r$. Finally, $r = 10$.

46. G. A little vocabulary lesson here: ***Prime*** numbers are numbers that have no positive integer factors other than 1 and themselves. Examples are 2, 3, 5, and 7. ***Composite*** numbers do have positive integer factors other than 1 and themselves. Examples are 4, 6, and 9. Because a composite number already has more factors than just 1 and itself, multiplying it by yet another number keeps it composite.

To do a problem of this sort, plug in numbers. Try to plug in numbers that eliminate answer choices, as in this example: 3 (prime) $\times$ 9 (composite) = 27. The answer is not a prime number, nor zero, nor a fraction, nor even, so eliminate answers F, H, J, and K.

47. C. An ***inscribed*** angle (one that has a vertex on the circle) has half the measure of its central angle so that AOC = 12°. (If you forgot this, go back to the circles portion in Chapter 7.) Because a circle has 360°, AOC is $^{12}/_{360}$ or $^1/_{30}$ of the circle. Follow these steps: $120\pi = {}^1/_{30}$ area and $120\pi \times 30$ = area and $3{,}600\pi$ = area.

The ***area*** of a circle is πr^2. Here, $\pi r^2 = 3{,}600\pi$. (When you see a perfect square such as 3,600, you know that you're on the right track.) First, $60^2 = 3{,}600$ and $r = 60$ (not 6 or 600, both easy, careless mistakes to make). Finally, the ***circumference*** of a circle is $2\pi r$, or 120π.

Did I getcha? Did you immediately eliminate choice C because it's the same as the area of the sector? When it comes to the ACT, expect the unexpected. Bizarre is the norm.

48. H. Don't be intimidated if you don't remember anything about circles or their equations. Simply plug the –3 into the equation, and solve for y. First, $-3^2 + y^2 = 25$. Then $9 + y^2 = 25$ and $y^2 = 16$. Then $y = -4, 4$. Either –4 or +4 works.

Now, for those of you who insist on getting excessively paranoid, don't freak out and think that two answer choices would be –44 and +4. You'll get one or the other, not both. The question very carefully asks you which *could* be y, not which *must* be y.

Just as a quick review, the equation of a circle is $(x - h)^2 + (y + k)^2 = r$ where the center is at (h, k) and r is the radius. In this problem, $x^2 + y^2 = 25$ could be written as $(x - 0)^2 + (y - 0)^2 = 5^2$. Therefore, the center is at (0, 0), and the radius is 5. This could be drawn as shown:

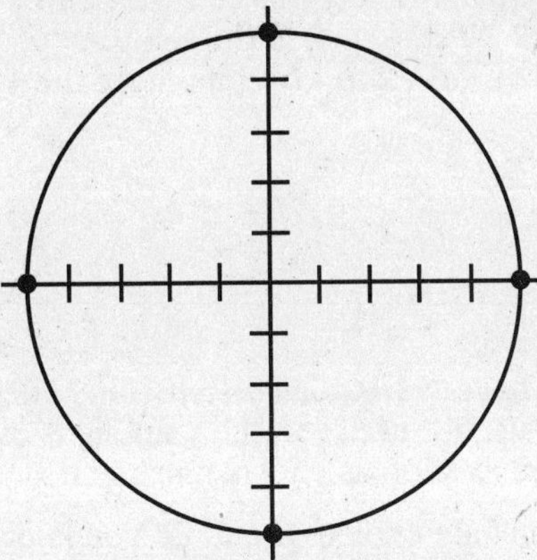

A look at the graph shows that when $x = -3$, $y = 4$ or -4.

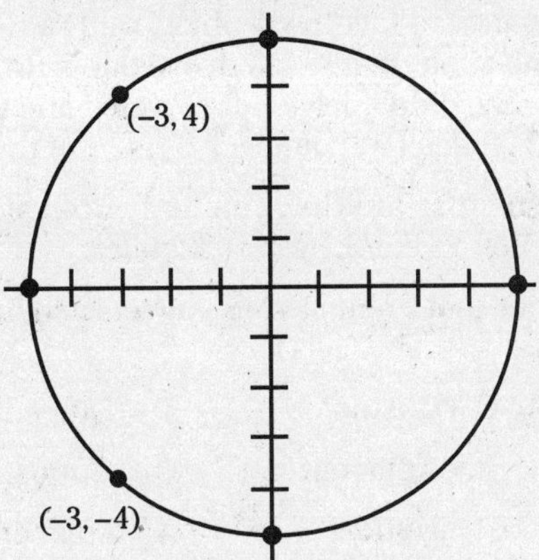

To check this, you can show that the distance from (0, 0) to (–3, 4) is equal to 5, the length of the radius. You can make a 3:4:5 triangle,

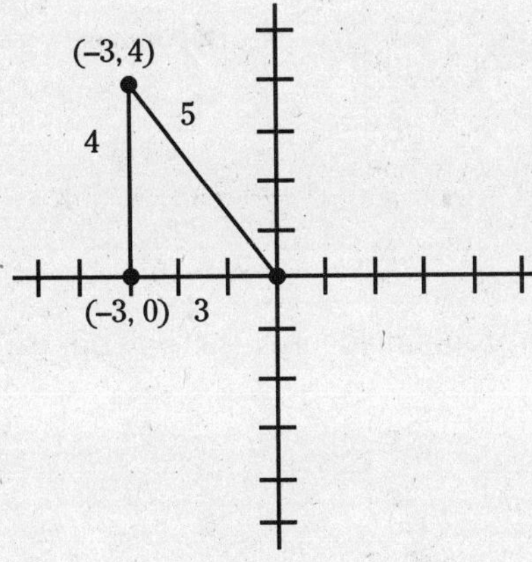

Or you can use the distance formula:

$$\sqrt{(-3-0)^2+(4-0)^2} = \sqrt{-3^2+4^2} = \sqrt{9+16} = \sqrt{25} = 5$$

49. A. You can, of course, FOIL (First, Outer, Inner, Last, as discussed in the algebra portion of Chapter 8). Multiply each expression out, and then add the products. Personally, I refuse to do this much work. If you've been clever enough to pay attention to my suggestions about memorization, you know that $(a + 3)^2$ would follow the same rule as $(a + b)^2$, and automatically know that it is $(a^2 + 2ab + b^2)$, substituting a 3 for the b. That gives you $a^2 + 6a + 9$. Next, $(a - 4)$ is the same as $(a - b)$, which you have (of course) memorized as $(a - b) = a^2 - 2ab + b^2$. Substitute the 4 for the b to get $a^2 - 8a + 16$. Now add vertically:

$$\begin{array}{l} a^2 + \ 6a + \ 9 \\ a^2 - \ 8a + \ 16 \\ \hline 2a^2 - \ 2a + \ 25 \end{array}$$

When the answers have "variations on a theme," such as positive and negative versions of the same numerals, be sure to watch your signs carefully. You should double-check this type of problem as soon as you've finished it.

Did you at least eliminate choices C and D? You know that $a^2 + a^2 = 2a^2$. Don't forget to narrow down the answers as you go, to avoid making a careless mistake.

50. C. Yes, you can set up a chart, and yes, you can do all the pencil-pushing. However, my goal is to show you how to talk the problem out, rather than work it out. This is one easy problem if you think about it. If Helen drove one-fourth of the way, she didn't drive three-fourths of the way. She didn't drive but bicycled and took the subway, for 24 (6 + 18) miles. Therefore, 24 miles (trap answer B) is $^3/_4$ of the total.

First, $^3/_4x = 24$. Then cross-multiply (multiply both sides through by 4) to get $3x = 96$ (trap answer D). Then $x = 96/3$ and $x = 32$ miles.

51. B. Do you remember that great saying you learned in trig: SOH CAH TOA ("soak a toe, uh")? It means

S = Sine	C = Cosine	T = Tangent
O = Opposite	A = Adjacent	O = Opposite
H = Hypotenuse	H = Hypotenuse	A = Adjacent

Here is an illustration:

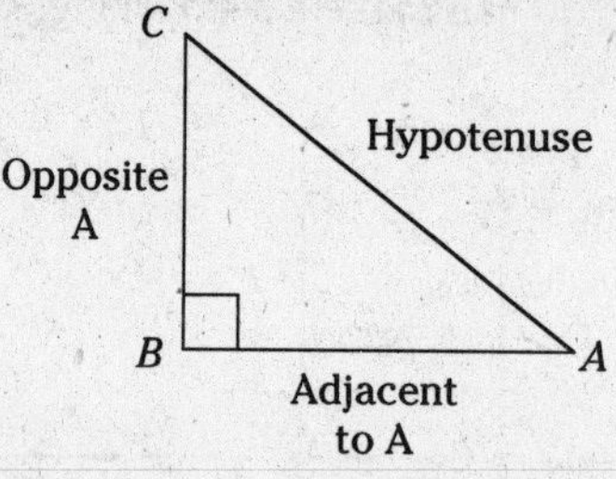

To find tan Z in this problem, identify the side opposite angle Z and the side adjacent to angle Z.

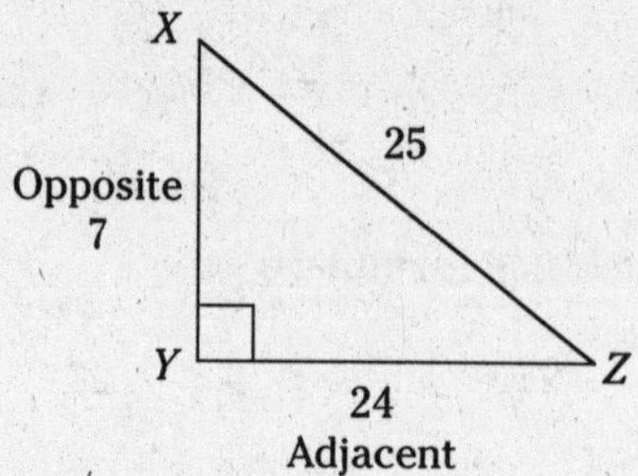

tan Z = Opposite/Adjacent = $^7/_{24}$

52. **D.** The unshaded circle means that point is not included on the graph. Therefore, the –4 is not part of the graph. Eliminate choice C. The shaded circle means that point is included on the graph. Look for an answer that says the graph can be equal to 0. Choice D works well.

    Choice A is far too broad. Numbers greater than –4 are infinite! Choice B is also too broad, for the same reason: Numbers less than –4 are infinite. Choice E is the trap answer. The graph does not go all the way to –5 or all the way to –1. A careless test-taker who didn't take the time to examine this graph closely deserves to miss this question.

53. **D.** Get x and y on one side and all the terms that have nothing to do with x and y on the other side:

    $$4cx - \frac{3d}{e} = 4cy \text{ and } 4cx - 4cy - \frac{3d}{e} = 0 \text{ and } 4cx - 4cy = \frac{3d}{e}.$$

    Factor out $4c$ to leave $x - y$: $4c(x - y) = \frac{3d}{e}$.

    Divide by 4c: $x - y = \frac{3d}{4ce}$.

54. **J.** Remember to use the equation

    slope $\frac{y_2 - y_1}{x_2 - x_1}$. Then $\frac{y_2 - y_1}{x_2 - x_1} = \frac{b-(-b)}{a-(-a)} = \frac{2b}{2a} = \frac{b}{a}$.

    Note: Which point you choose for y_2 doesn't matter, but once you choose y_2 (or b), you must choose the x-coordinate in the ordered pair for x_2 (or a).

55. **E.** To find the angle of depression, first draw a horizontal line from the lookout point. The 14° angle is formed with this line. The horizontal line is parallel to the water's surface. When parallel lines are cut by a transversal, the alternate interior angles are ***congruent*** (the same):

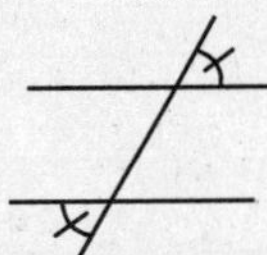

This means that you can draw a right triangle with a 14° angle:

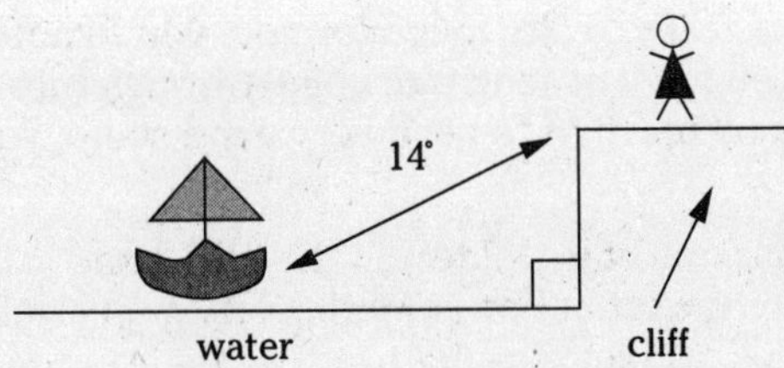

You know the side adjacent to (next to) the 14° angle. You are trying to find the opposite side. The trigonometric function needed is the tangent $\left(\frac{\textit{opposite}}{\textit{adjacent}}\right)$. So $\tan 14° = x/2$. Solve for x by multiplying both sides by 2 to get rid of the fraction: $2 \tan 14° = x$.

56. G. Stop, stop — you don't need to drag out your graphing calculator. This problem requires more common sense than anything else. First, look for a graph showing that nothing was printed for two hours. This narrows the field quickly to choices G and H because the horizontal portion shows that the number of pages (p) remained steady. Choice G is better than choice H because the horizontal portion is longer (representing a longer time) than either of the increasing portions. The computer was broken for two hours, but each printing segment lasted only one hour. Choice G also makes sense in that the second printing phase is steeper than the first. With two computers during the second phase, the segment should have twice the slope of the first.

57. A. The key to answering the question is to remember the equation $\cos^2\theta + \sin^2\theta = 1$. If you have trouble remembering this, think of a right triangle with a hypotenuse of 1, as in $x^2 + y^2 = 1$ (remember the Pythagorean theorem?).

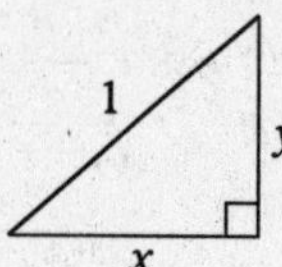

Because $\cos\theta = \dfrac{adjacent}{hypotenuse} = \dfrac{x}{1} = x$ and $\sin\theta = \dfrac{opposite}{hypotenuse} = \dfrac{y}{1} = y$, then $x^2 + y^2 = 1$.

You can just rewrite this as $\cos^2\theta + \sin^2\theta = 1$.

To get back to our problem, use this equation:

$$\frac{\sin^2\theta + \cos^2\theta}{\sec^2\theta} = \frac{1}{\sec^2\theta}$$

$$\sec\theta = \frac{1}{\cos\theta}, \text{ so } \sec^2\theta = \frac{1}{\cos^2\theta}$$

Finally, substitute the following:

$$\sec^2\theta = \frac{1}{\cos^2\theta} = \frac{1}{\sec^2\theta} = \frac{1}{\frac{1}{\cos^2\theta}} = 1 \times \frac{\cos^2\theta}{1}\theta = \cos^2\theta$$

If this problem is really, really tough for you, you're not alone. Many students find this jazz difficult. Keep in mind as you're going through these questions that you don't have to get all the problems right to get a very good score; you can afford to miss several of them.

58. J. This problem is one of the oldest in the books and is included to try to get students to waste time doing a lot of Power Math, setting up algebraic equations full of *p*s and *c*s. Forget it. Talk this problem through.

The first thing you want to do is realize that you can't have a cow and a half, so double that to get three cows. Twice as many cows (three instead of $1^1/_2$) can give twice as much milk (three pints instead of $1^1/_2$) in the same number of hours.

Be very careful not to double all the variables, including the 36 hours, at once. Double two variables at a time.

You now have the right number of cows. You want to double the number of hours ($36 \times 2 = 72$). The same number of cows in double the time can give double the milk: $3 \times 2 = 6$ pints. This problem is much easier than it looks . . . unless *you* made it hard.

59. K. The unknown height is opposite the 21° angle. Because 1,500*m* is the side adjacent to 21°, you can use the tangent=opposite/adjacent. First, tan 21° = $^x/_{1,500}$. Solve for x: 1,500 tan 21° = x.

60. J. If, like most of us, you don't remember anything about the unit circle, draw a right triangle and remember this:

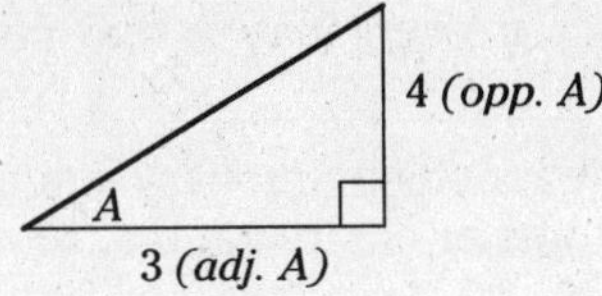

If one leg is 3 and the other is 4, use $a^2 + b^2 = c^2$ to find the length of the hypotenuse: $9 + 16 = 25$ and $\sqrt{25} = 5$.

If you're really on the ball, you remembered the PT (Pythagorean theorem) triple (discussed in detail in Chapter 7) of 3:4:5 triangle to come up with a hypotenuse of 5, without doing any of that busywork.

$$\cos A = \frac{adjacent\ A}{hypotenuse}, \text{ so } \cos A = \frac{3}{5}.$$

To verify that the answer is choice J rather than F or G, draw a unit circle:

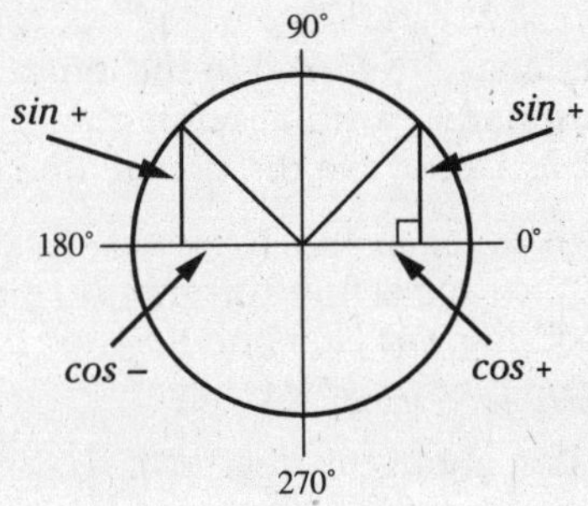

Because $\tan A = \dfrac{opposite\ A}{adjacent\ A}$, $\tan A = \dfrac{\sin A}{\cos A}$ in the unit circle.

Because tan A is positive, sin A and cos A must be both positive or both negative. Between 0° and 90°, sin A and cos A are both positive. But between 90° and 180°, sin A is positive and cos A is negative, ruling out any possibility that A is between 90° and 180° and that cos A is negative.

Depending on what math level you're taking in school, you may not have even learned this in class yet. Don't worry; the ACT has only a few questions like this. And look on the bright side: Quickly guessing on this question frees up more time for you to return to the other questions you could get right — if only you had the time.

Reading Test

Passage 1

1. B. The first paragraph simply introduces blood clots, mentioning fixed and migratory clots. Did you remember that *describe* is one of the Big Three? Three words are often (not always, but frequently enough to merit your attention) the correct answers to a "what is the purpose" question: *discuss, describe, explain.*

2. H. The first paragraph tells you that ***thrombosis*** is clotting; an ***embolism*** is simply a migratory clot. The other answers may or may not be true. The passage doesn't give you that information.

3. A. Lines 32–36 state that, among pulmonary embolism patients, "the great majority suffer no serious symptoms or complications, and the disorder clears up without significant aftereffects."

"Dramatic" words, such as *invariably,* are usually (not invariably) wrong. If you're making a guess (always worth doing, because the ACT has no penalty for wrong answers), eliminate answers with strong, emphatic words (*always, must*) and look for wimpy words (*may, possibly*).

As for choices C and D, the passage did not discuss either children or diet.

4. H. Lines 13–14 state that the site of a pulmonary embolism is often a deep vein of the leg or pelvis.

A question that begins "According to the passage" is usually very straightforward. This type of question is worth an investment of your time. Go back to the passage and find the precise answer.

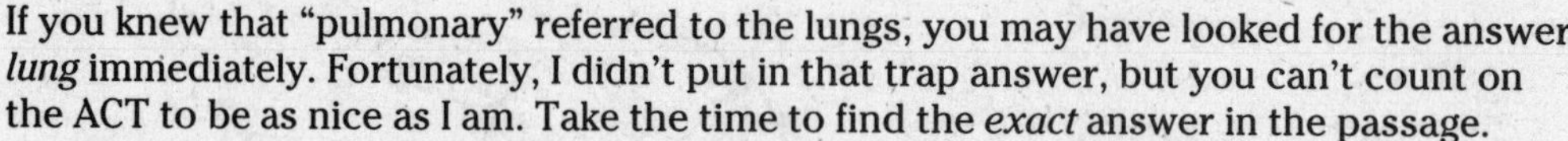

If you knew that "pulmonary" referred to the lungs, you may have looked for the answer *lung* immediately. Fortunately, I didn't put in that trap answer, but you can't count on the ACT to be as nice as I am. Take the time to find the *exact* answer in the passage.

5. B. Although you may have been able to answer this based on common sense, the theme of the first half of the passage is that thrombosis may turn into an embolism. Choice A is outta left field — nothing was said about aiding others. Obviously, this was the cheap trick answer, playing on the word "attendant."

You have no information about the degree of risk (choice C), although the list of disorders is pretty daunting. And although women are classified according to childbirth status, the passage never contrasted women and men (choice D).

6. J. By citing a high percentage of patients who have venous thrombosis after recuperating from hip fractures, the passage implies that the risk of thrombosis is worsened.

In this example, the passage used *exacerbate* in its normal, everyday sense. (The ACT exacerbates, or makes worse, your tension headache.) This will not always be so. A word may have a dozen meanings. Don't be surprised if the ACT uses the least-common of those meanings in a passage.

7. D. The clinical signs refer to the swollen extremity or inflammation mentioned in the preceding sentence.

Every question in a section counts the same. A basic "definition question" like this one is easy to answer quickly. If you're short on time (and who isn't on the reading passages?), this is a good type of question to focus on.

8. J. A "best title" is often the most broad and general statement that is offered. Choice G is mentioned, but only in one brief part of the passage. Choices F and H were never discussed.

You can often predict the answer to a main-idea or best-title question. Pretend that your buddy comes up behind you just as you finish reading the passage and asks you what it was about. Your first reaction is the best title: "Oh, I just read this dull passage about what blood clots are and how to recognize them."

9. **C.** This should have been a very easy question — if you remembered to "expand your search." Often, when a passage sends you to certain lines, the answer isn't there. It's a little above or a little below those lines. Lines 67–68 at the end of the preceding paragraph stated that ". . . other tests may be needed to confirm the diagnosis." The next few paragraphs describe such tests.

This is the third correct answer in this passage that uses the word *describe* (see questions 1 and 8). Many ACT passages, especially science passages, describe a problem or situation. Don't immediately choose *describe* every time you see it, but definitely give *describe* serious consideration. (I like to think of *describe*'s use as being "guilty until proven innocent." I assume that *describe* is correct unless I can find something clearly better.)

To ***lament*** (choice A) is to grieve over. Although you may lament having to take the ACT, few ACT passages themselves lament anything. Choice B has the dramatic word *prove.* Few things are definitively proven in ACT passages. Also, you can probably eliminate choice B by common sense — can *all* of *anything* be diagnosed?

10. **G.** The second-to-last paragraph (the ***penultimate*** paragraph, if you like to use pretentious language) mentions that pulmonary embolisms are difficult to diagnose on the basis of clinical symptoms alone.

You probably could have chosen G based on its wimpy language alone. Dramatic or emphatic answers are rarely correct; hedging or wishy-washy answers are often correct. How can you go wrong saying something like, "should be done cautiously and in conjunction with other tests?" Any physician makes a diagnosis cautiously and usually uses more than one test.

Did you fall for the trap answer, choice J? Lines 94–98 mention a complex test that cannot be done routinely on all patients — but these lines are talking about pulmonary angiography, not clinical symptoms. If you simply skimmed until you found familiar words, you were conned by this cheap trick. Remember: Just because the answer choice is mentioned in the passage does not mean that it is the correct answer to this specific question.

Passage 2

11. **B.** The previous sentence tells you that the young lady made an inquiry. She raised her veil while making this inquiry, or, in other words, asking the question. Choices A and C are there to catch careless readers who use their common sense to answer the question ("Well, obviously, to prefer is to like better, as in 'I'd prefer to be hanging out with my friends than studying for this test'") rather than go back to see how the word is used in context.

12. **H.** This question is slightly harder than number 11. In that question, you are simply asked to define how the term is used. Here, you need to know *why* the author chose that particular word. This is a more subjective question, requiring you to understand the author's feelings about the person in question. Here, Dickens describes the young lady as being slight and delicate and timid (lines 2–3) and neatly and quietly attired (line 13). Therefore, he uses the word *glided* to indicate that quietness.

This type of question is especially difficult for someone whose first language is not English. If you don't understand the passage well enough to "get into the author's head" and know how the author is feeling, guess quickly and go on to the next question. (Don't forget to guess — the ACT has no penalty for wrong answers.)

13. **D.** The author struggles to say tactfully that, while on any other woman, the dress would have looked like what it was ("poor and shabby"), this woman was so attractive and genteel that on her, even low-quality clothing looked good. (Hmmm. . . . I wonder whether I can ever teach my boyfriend to be quite so tactful?)

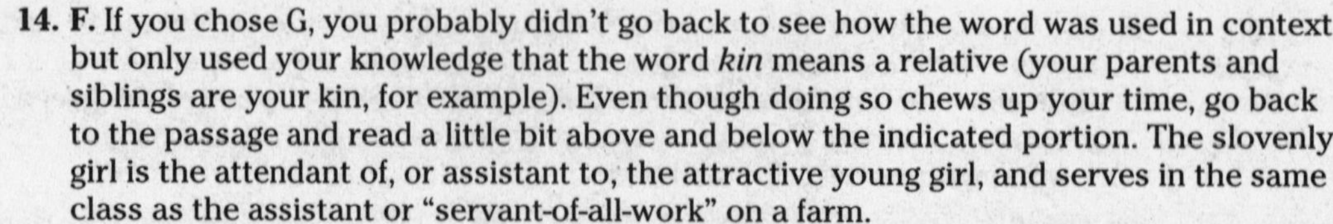

14. F. If you chose G, you probably didn't go back to see how the word was used in context, but only used your knowledge that the word *kin* means a relative (your parents and siblings are your kin, for example). Even though doing so chews up your time, go back to the passage and read a little bit above and below the indicated portion. The slovenly girl is the attendant of, or assistant to, the attractive young girl, and serves in the same class as the assistant or "servant-of-all-work" on a farm.

15. C. First, recognize that *sober* in this sense has nothing to do with being drunk. *Sober* can also mean serious, not frivolous ("consider soberly which college you want to spend four years of your life attending"). Dump the cheap trick answer, choice A.

Dramatic answers, answers with strong, powerful, exclusive words (*all, every, must*) are often wrong. An answer like B, with *obviously,* is rarely right. An answer like D, with *completely,* is almost never right. On the other hand, a wishy-washy answer, with a word like *some* (choice C), is often correct.

In this instance, the author means that Nicholas would have followed the young woman out (to the surprise of others who may have thought more seriously about their conduct and may have acted less impetuously).

16. G. The girl was given a card to get a job, and left — yet Tom indicated that she would be back the next day. From this, you may infer that Tom believes the girl will not take, or will not stay long at, the position. The statement of the fat lady that "She'll have a nice life of it, if she goes there" may be construed as sarcasm, showing that the fat lady agrees that the girl would not like the post.

Nothing in the passage indicates that the girl comes in daily (choice F). It's clear that the girl does not work for Tom and the fat lady, because she was asking about a post of governess. Choice J is tempting (to Nicholas at least), but you get no indication that the girl even noticed that Nicholas was present.

17. C. If you didn't go back to the passage and read this portion in context, you may have chosen A or B. Choice A is exactly wrong; the passage goes on to say that Nicholas was disgusted by Tom's conduct.

Don't choose an answer simply because it is a true statement. Be sure that it answers the specific question asked. Choice B may be a true statement (Tom saw and agreed with Nicholas's admiration of the young woman), but that statement is not the reason for the quote given here. Tom commented and winked at Nicholas in order to flatter him by indicating that Nicholas's skills would be valued by many employers.

18. F. The fat woman makes the comment that Mr. Gregsbury is a Member of Parliament only after saying that she didn't know what the terms of the position were. From this you may infer that the purpose of the comment was to reassure Nicholas that the job would be a good one.

Choice G may or may not be true; you have no way of knowing whether the fat lady's comment is true or false. Choice H seems logical, until you go back to the passage and find that the fat lady (in this excerpt at least) did no boasting whatsoever of any of her clientele. Choice J may have trapped you. True, there was only one listing, but that fact didn't seem to upset the fat lady any.

19. B. Given that the next paragraph discusses Nicholas's going to the building and knocking upon every door until he finds Mr. Gregsbury, you may infer that Nicholas is going to visit the man.

If you chose C, you got careless. Any vocabulary word must be interpreted in context. You have to go back to the passage and see how that word is used there. While "to wait upon" could mean serve, as a waitress waits upon diners, it has no such connotation in this passage.

20. H. If you chose F, you simply focused on the word *chivalrously* and ignored the greater meaning of the sentence. The last paragraph lightly mocks the ideas of chivalry, saying that a "knight" has a duty to knock about anyone who does not praise his lady-love, even if he's never met that lady-love. Therefore, Nicholas had a duty (which he ignored) to defend the young woman's honor.

Passage 3

21. D. A primary purpose is general and broad, not specific. Choice B gives information that is stated in the passage, but only briefly, not as the purpose of writing the passage. Choice C is not mentioned at all. Choice A is the trap answer. The passage does state that bushmasters are poisonous, but not why.

22. J. If you are rushed for time, this is a good question to guess at quickly and come back to later. (The ACT has no penalties for wrong answers, which means that you should never leave an answer blank.) The best way to answer this question is by the process of elimination: Find three questions that were answered, and whatever is left is the correct answer. Paragraph 2 states that the bushmaster's coloring aids in its camouflage. Paragraph 3 tells why the bushmaster has the pits in its head. Paragraph 3 also tells what the bushmaster eats (rodents). Although the passage does talk about the maternal instincts of the bushmaster, it does not discuss mating habits or attracting a mate.

23. C. Paragraph 2 states, "This maternal instinct is quite rare among reptiles."

When a question begins with the words, "According to the passage," it is usually a freebie for you, a complete gift. If you know that you are not going to be able to answer all the questions in time, or if your brain is mush and you are losing focus (I speak from experience!), look for an "According to the passage" question. This is one question that you are almost guaranteed to get correct.

If you chose D, you fell for the trap. Yes, paragraph 1 does state that unlike the rattlesnake, the bushmaster has no rattles on its tail, but nothing is said about this lack of rattles being rare among reptiles. The author is differentiating just two snakes, not making a generalization.

24. F. The first paragraph states that the bushmaster is the largest venomous snake in the *New* World. From this careful distinction (not "the largest snake in the world," but the largest snake "in the New World"), you can infer that there are larger snakes elsewhere in the world.

Choice H is tempting, but is a trap. The bushmaster perhaps attacks humans only when threatened, but the passage implies that the bushmaster does attack its prey for food, even though the prey (like rodents) cannot be considered threatening.

25. B. The third to last paragraph discusses how bushmasters hide from their prey and then ambush it.

You didn't really fall for that piece of lame humor in choice A, did you? "Ambush" has nothing to do with bushes in the Amazon!

26. H. Words have more than one meaning. Much of the ACT reading test asks you to interpret how the author uses the words, not just their straightforward dictionary meanings. To *misplace* does mean to lose, but that's not how the author means the term in this instance. He is saying that people have the wrong idea, that bushmasters are not really fierce.

The key to answering this question is to continue reading. The real answer is in the rest of the paragraph. Careless and lazy readers who go only where they are directed and don't continue will miss this type of question every time.

27. A. The paragraph discusses how the bushmasters' numbers are declining, although the bushmaster is not yet an endangered species. The author implies, without coming right out and stating so, that the bushmaster may become endangered as more and more of its habitat is removed. Choice H is far too dramatic. A common trap on the ACT is offering a very strongly worded answer, which is rarely correct.

28. **F.** The last paragraph states that the hikers step on sleeping snakes, unable to see the snakes because of their coloration or hear them because of the snake's lack of rattles. Choice J is the trap answer. It's true that the bushmaster is nocturnal, out more in the evening than the daytime, but that's not given as the reason the hikers are attacked by the snakes.

Just because something is true does not mean that it is the right answer to the question.

29. **D.** This question is tricky. Choice A states a correct fact; bushmasters do sleep during the day, but that's not the main point of the paragraph. Choice B states a fact that seems logical, based on what we all know about wildlife in general (most animals — including humans — will attack to protect their young and their food), but that's not the main point of the paragraph. Choice C is discussed in the last paragraph, which states that the bushmaster's coloration and silent warning system rarely alert humans to the snake's presence . . . but that's not the main point of the paragraph. The main point (as introduced by the topic sentence of the paragraph) is that the bushmaster is not as ferocious and aggressive as its reputation would make you believe.

When a question asks you for the main idea, whether of the entire passage or of just a paragraph, try to predict an answer before you look at the choices. Pretend that someone just asked you what you're reading. Your response, which in this case may be something like, "People think that this snake is more dangerous than it really is," is the main idea.

30. **J.** If you are rushed for time, a negatively phrased question ("Which was NOT . . .") is a good one to guess at quickly. Answering this question is really like answering three separate questions, as you have to find three questions the passage *does* answer, and then by process of elimination, identify which question it does *not* answer. Paragraph 4 talks about enemies of the bushmaster. Paragraph 3 discusses how a bushmaster locates its prey. The last paragraph explains why some people consider the bushmaster aggressive.

    Choice J can be a little tricky. The author does mention that the bushmaster has a strong maternal instinct that is rare in snakes, but he never tells *why* the bushmaster had that instinct. (If you missed this question, don't feel too bad. Many people miss negatively phrased questions, which is why I suggest that you not invest too much time in them.)

Passage 4

31. **D.** The best title is usually broad and general, encompassing the entire passage. Here, the passage talked about Tanganyika throughout several centuries. Although the passage did mention plants and animals (choice A), those were too specific to be the theme of the *entire* passage. Choice C, on the other hand, is too broad. The Origins of Humanity covers much more territory than just one country. And choice B is totally irrelevant.

32. **F.** Lines 6–7 of the first paragraph state that remnants of the early tribes still exist, making choice F a false statement. All the other statements are mentioned as true in the first paragraph.

Negative or exception questions ("which of the following is *not* true" or "all of the following are true *except*") are among the questions most frequently missed by careless students. Even though the word *not* is already italicized, circle it, draw arrows pointing to it, or call attention to it in some other way.

33. **C.** Something ***nominal*** exists only in name, not in actuality. For example, the Queen of England is the nominal ruler of the country, but she doesn't really have the power to run the nation. If you claim a country, like the Portuguese did, but don't attempt to colonize it, you own it in name only but don't have much involvement with it.

Note that choices A, B, and D are too negative. Correct ACT answers are rarely negative. Besides, you don't know for sure whether the Portuguese control was in fact illegal, incompetent, or vicious. It may or may not have been; the passage gives you no information on the subject.

34. H. If you chose F, you didn't read far enough. Yes, paragraph 3 mention the Persian influence, but only as one of several foreign influences. Choices G and J address topics covered in other portions of the passage, not in these specific lines.

35. C. By putting quotation marks around the word *found,* the author indicates a little sarcasm, as if it were no big deal to locate Dr. Livingstone. From this, you may infer that Dr. L. was not particularly in hiding but there to be found at any time.

This type of question is much more subjective than many others. You don't have the exact answer there in black and white, waiting for you. Often, your best way to answer this question is through the process of elimination. Choice D is definitely out. Nothing was mentioned about destroying Dr. Livingstone's work. Choice A is irrelevant; the passage doesn't tell you the opinions of Mr. Stanley about the slave trade. And choice B is somewhat illogical. Why would a newspaper commission a man to go all the way to Africa to interview someone who had already been interviewed by another paper? Not much of a scoop there.

36. G. This is a pretty straightforward question. Lines 49–53 tell you that the harsh actions of the German administration provoked the rebellion.

One of my goals in this section is to have you learn to recognize which questions are (in fact) very straightforward, requiring that you only go back and skim for the answer, and which require more subjective interpretation and inference. If you are running short of time (and most of us do in this section), head for the direct questions like this one and do them first.

37. D. Lines 71–74 tell you that Tanganyika merged with Zanzibar to become the United Republic of Tanzania. There no longer is an independent, separate nation called Tanganyika.

Note that the other three answer choices all were true of Tanganyika at one point, but not today. These answers were put here to trap students who read only part of the material or who chose the first answer that they remembered as having been mentioned in the passage. Remember that just because something is true and was discussed does not mean that it is the correct answer to this specific question.

38. J. Lines 76–80 specifically discuss Tanzania's judicial structure.

Why did I put in a question this simple? To show you the difference between a *why* question and a *what* question. Many passages *do* answer *what*-type questions: What is the number of crops grown, what is the principal export, and so on. Very few passages answer *why* questions. You do not know *why* the Portuguese destroyed Kilwa, only that they did. You do not know *why* Tanganyika united with Zanzibar, only that it did. The *why* goes to the motivation, which is much less rarely discussed in a passage. Most passages give "just the facts, Ma'am."

39. C. I take it personally if you don't (almost) always get a tone or attitude question correct. Most passages are neutral, unbiased, and objective. They give the facts without passing judgment on them.

Few passages are negative. A passage with a despairing or derogatory tone would be extremely rare. The ACT passages are kind, encouraging, positive, or (at the least) neutral and straightforward. They don't ridicule or criticize people or events. Also, few passages are extreme. An answer like ***effervescent*** (meaning bubbly, joyous) is simply too strong. You may be effervescent while reading the passage (yeah, right; you're more likely to be despairing or derogatory!), but the passage itself is just neutral or objective.

40. H. The last paragraph talks about what the U.S. is doing to help Tanzania. The remainder of the paragraph would probably continue that theme.

Science Reasoning

Passage 1

The ACT often includes descriptive tables, such as Table 1. Don't panic; you are not expected to memorize the appearance descriptions. Remember, the ACT is an open book test. You are allowed to go back and refer to the table as often as you like.

When you read a table like Table 1, be sure to do two things:

- Pay attention to the title and the headings. They give you an overview of the table, telling you what it's all about.
- Try to identify any trends shown in the table and note exceptions to those trends.

A quick look shows you this trend or pattern: The altitude generally goes down as you move down the table. Ice crystals predominate at higher altitudes, water droplets at lower altitudes. But there's a catch: The two clouds at the bottom have both ice crystals and water droplets. How can this situation be? When in doubt, look at the text for a possible explanation. Often, a note given above or below the chart clarifies matters. Sure enough, a note tells you that some clouds may extend upward for quite a distance. It seems logical that cumulus and cumulonimbus clouds are tall enough to reach high altitudes and have ice crystals. The appearance descriptions for these two clouds, especially cumulonimbus, reinforce this conclusion.

Those of you who are really shrewd probably notice one more thing about this table: Certain cloud appearances seem to correspond to certain names. Anything with strato/stratus in its name seems to refer to layer. Anything with a cumulo/cumulus in its name has something to do with ball shapes. Cirro/cirrus clouds are high in altitude. Keeping these thoughts in mind will help you read through the table efficiently and organize your thinking.

1. **C.** Cumulus clouds are characterized by white, puffy balls, not by thin layers. Eliminate statement II, which means that you can cross off answers B and D. If you are making a guess, you're already down to a 50-50 chance of success.

Use the Roman numerals to your advantage. Because you've eliminated B and D, and because both A and C have I in them, you know that statement I must be true. Don't even bother thinking about it. Thin clouds are found at high altitudes. All you have left to do now is to decide whether statement III is true.

The three high altitude clouds are all composed of ice crystals, telling you that statement III is correct.

2. **J.** Answer choices with an extreme or dramatic word (such as *always, never, absolutely, exclusively,* and so on) are often wrong (the ACT is big on wishy-washy answers that it can defend easily). Start by checking those answers.

Choices G and H are dramatic, including the terms *exclusively* and *never.* You can probably dump them quickly. Water droplets clearly appear in some low-altitude clouds, eliminating choice G. Cumulus clouds have water droplets as well as ice crystals, eliminating choice H.

You're down to a 50-50 chance now. If you're short on time, make a quick guess and go on. ***Remember:*** The ACT gives no penalty for wrong answers. Choice J is correct, because the top three clouds are composed of ice crystals, not water droplets. The bottom two clouds can rise to high altitudes, but the table doesn't include anything that suggests that water droplets are found in the high altitude regions of cumulus and cumulonimbus clouds. Most likely, water droplets are in the lower parts of these clouds, and ice crystals are found at higher regions.

3. **D.** Be sure to read and pay special attention to the information found in the note. In this case, the note indicates that the altitude figures are for the bottom of the cloud, and this question asks about the top of the cloud. Don't head for choices A and B simply because they are listed with a higher average altitude. Besides, choosing between A and B is hard. They are both layered clouds with the same bottom altitude. You're better off looking elsewhere for an answer that stands out.

   Stratus clouds (choice C) start at only 500 meters and are flat. Cumulonimbus clouds (choice D) start out low but are described as being tall. These clouds also have ice crystals, suggesting that they extend to high altitudes, which is exactly what you're looking for.

4. **H.** Which clouds are composed exclusively of ice crystals? Look at the first three cloud types mentioned. Why are these clouds at the top of the table? Look at the numbers in the Avg. Altitude column. This information alone should make you lean strongly toward choice H. The clouds composed exclusively of water droplets are lower in altitude than are the clouds composed exclusively of ice crystals.

   The last two clouds on the table also have ice crystals. However, the bottom of a cumulonimbus cloud may be at a low altitude, but the cloud is tall, making it likely that the bottom of the cloud is composed of water droplets while the top is composed of ice crystals. The same is probably also true for cumulus clouds, which start at 500 meters but may extend upwards for several thousand meters. Those puffy balls can be quite large.

   Choices F and G can be eliminated quickly because the table provides no information about evaporation and condensation rates. Don't go overboard and begin thinking about the water cycle and cloud formation. Remember that the ACT is not a test of the specific knowledge you gained in science class. All the information you need to answer the question is given in the chart.

   Choice J doesn't look too promising because both ice crystals and water droplets have their share of clouds with layers. In addition, water droplets vary with regard to the appearance of the clouds. Some of the water-droplet clouds are sheets, some are clumps, and so on. The description of appearances may suggest that ice crystal clouds tend to be relatively thin, but common sense should tell you that composition likely affects appearance more than appearance affects composition. The association between altitude and composition is much clearer, making choice H more logical.

5. **A.** You don't have to be a Latin scholar to answer this question. Look at the appearance descriptions and at the analysis of the table. Stratus appears in five of the ten cloud names. Note the descriptions given for stratus clouds: veil, sheet, layer, ceiling. These words all fit with choice A.

   Heap (choice B) seems to go along with blob, clump, and ball, words that are associated with cumulus. Curl (choice C) is tough to figure out from this table, but cirrus is its root. Cirrus clouds look like curled feathers. Alto means high, choice D.

Passage 2

The important point to understand from the introductory paragraph is that the purpose of the study is to test which drug makes subjects less drowsy.

Although the pharmaceutical company is probably concerned with how effectively its drug alleviates hay fever, this factor is not measured in this study.

The description of Study 1 tells you that drowsiness was tested by counting the number of errors that subjects made on a task that requires alertness. Picture yourself as an experimental subject. If you are drowsy from a pill as you perform a motor task that requires alertness, how do you think you'll do? You'll probably make many mistakes.

The statement that subjects who made fewer errors were judged to be less drowsy concurs with your imagined scenario. The rest of the description of Study 1 tells you that the two drugs were compared at two different times, creating four groups of subjects. Each group had four subjects, making the study symmetrical and straightforward to follow.

As with Data Representation passages, be sure to examine the data and look for major trends. Table 1 reveals that the subjects taking the new drug made fewer errors on the average than those taking the old drug. This difference was far more pronounced for the groups that were tested one hour after ingestion. The errors associated with the old drug were much lower at eight hours than at one hour. This finding makes sense once you realize that the effects of drugs tend to wear off with time. The new drug did not show this decrease in the number of errors, perhaps because it wasn't making its subjects too drowsy to begin with.

How does weight figure in? A scan of Table 1 shows that the heavier subjects made fewer errors than the lighter subjects. The drowsiness caused by the drug seems to be greater in those who are lighter. Some reflection on outside knowledge should help you understand this finding: Who gets a higher dosage of a pain reliever, an adult or a baby? An adult who received a baby's dose would not feel much lessening of the pain.

Now that you've gotten a handle on Study 1 and Table 1, you can readily see what happened in the next two studies. Study 2 was basically a repeat of Study 1 except that the experimenters took out a factor that caused some variability. Table 2 shows much of what Table 1 shows but also indicates that the new drug caused fewer errors than the old drug even at eight hours. The averages of the two eight-hour groups may not seem great (34.75 vs. 30.75), but such a difference is probably significant when the table shows how little variability there is within each group of four.

Study 3 was identical to Study 2 except that the subjects were lighter and female. The number of errors was higher (remember how the lighter subjects made more errors in Study 1), but the trend of the results was virtually identical to that of Study 2.

6. **J.** Note the purpose of the study mentioned in the introduction and the description of Study 1. This study was designed to test the extent to which the drugs make test subjects drowsy. It did not examine how effective the drugs were in relieving hay fever; eliminate choice F. Choice J follows nicely from the analysis of Study 1 presented above. Don't choose answer G just because the numbers decrease. You must remember that lower numbers mean *fewer* errors, or a *better* performance. Choice H is wrong because there are no data showing how well the subjects did on the task before taking the drug. Such information is needed before one can conclude anything about the drug's improving performance.

7. **C.** Once again, the analysis of the results completed before looking at the questions makes answering a question much easier. As stated in that analysis, the researchers eliminated a source of variability by using subjects who were all of the same weight. Choice C expresses this idea. With less variability, researchers can be more confident that any differences observed between drugs or between times is a consequence of the drug taken or the time since ingestion. Small differences between groups don't mean much if the results for both groups range widely. Such small differences may be significant if one group is consistently a little higher than the other group.

   Choice D is the easiest choice to eliminate. Where in this study can anybody learn the weight of typical hay fever sufferers? A comparison of Studies 2 and 3 could provide some information regarding choice A, but such information is already provided in Study 1. Remember that the question is basically asking why the researchers went on to conduct Studies 2 and 3. Choice B is tempting because the subjects in Study 2 were male and the subjects in Study 3 were female, but the description of the studies does not mention the sex of the subjects as something that was of major concern to the researchers. Besides, the way Studies 2 and 3 are designed, it's impossible to look at them and determine whether the greater number of errors in Study 3 came about because the subjects were lighter or because the subjects were female.

8. **H.** Here's your chance to use some common sense. Study 2, as discussed above, may have produced results with less variability, in contrast to what is stated in incorrect choice J, but all Study 2, taken by itself, shows is that the new drug is probably better with regard to producing drowsy side effects only for males of a certain weight. Choice H is correct because it points out that Study 1 used a wider range of subjects. Choice F may look enticing, but you do not know the sex of the subjects used in Study 1. Perhaps the subjects in Study 1 were also all male. Eliminate choice G because the studies were concerned with drowsiness, not the effectiveness of the drug.

9. **C.** Here's a way to save yourself some time. Scan the choices and notice that option II has to be included because it appears in each of the four choices. Don't waste time trying to justify option II.

   Table 3 indicates that the average for the one-hour group was 54.25 while the average for the eight-hour group was 49.75. It is quite reasonable to expect that the average for the two-hour group could be in between these two averages, so option III should be included, and choices A and B are out. You may consider that both options I and IV are within range, but think about the logic of option I. Why would the drug cause fewer errors at two hours than at either one or eight hours? The results suggest that the drug's side effects wear off with time, so it does not seem reasonable that there would be fewer errors at two hours than at eight hours. You may now eliminate choice D because option I is out.

   The only answer left is correct choice C. Move on before you drive yourself crazy trying to understand why the number of errors could be higher at two hours (option IV) than at either one or eight hours. The test-maker has given you a break by the way the options are arranged in the answer choices.

   Okay, okay! You insist upon knowing why option IV is reasonable? The drowsiness produced by the drug may not have peaked at one hour. Perhaps it peaks after one hour before subsiding at eight hours or so. In addition, option IV is closer to the old-drug averages in Table 3 than is option I.

10. **F.** The question tells you that the average you see for the old drug group eight hours after ingestion is probably a bit lower than what would have been obtained had subjects who were not particularly proficient at the motor task been used. With regular, everyday, less-coordinated people, the average would probably be higher than the 41.75 shown. With this higher average, the gap between the new and old drugs would be higher than the current 0.5 and would strengthen the claim, which can be made with Studies 2 and 3, that the new drug produces less drowsiness at eight hours.

    The next two choices have key flaws. To make a case for choice G, you would have to know that the old drug at eight hours normally produces more errors than the old drug at one hour. You may not assume that less-coordinated subjects would make that many additional errors. Another problem with choice G is that it mentions side effects in general while the study simply investigated drowsiness. The best way to get rid of choice H is to realize that the choice mentions the drugs' effectiveness, which was not investigated in these studies.

    Choice J makes some sense. Many studies do use the same subjects for different parts of a study. One advantage of such an experimental design is that different groups are equated for overall ability because the different groups have the same people. One problem with choice J, though, is that the subjects may do better at eight hours not because the drowsiness has worn off but because the subjects already had a chance to practice at one hour.

    A more serious problem with choice J is that it uses the extreme word *require*. Remember that absolute choices are rarely correct on the ACT.

11. **B.** Even if you wanted to be ultraconservative and not recommend the new drug, the reasons given in choices C and D aren't logical. You have no way of knowing what the patients will do, and even if you did, such information doesn't have much to do with the new drug versus the old drug. In fact, the evidence points to the superiority of the new drug at both one and eight hours. If the individual is going to operate dangerous machinery, it's better that he or she do so with the new drug, which doesn't produce as much drowsiness. Choice D doesn't follow from the information in the question or in the studies, so get rid of it because the ACT does not expect you to start using some specialized knowledge of the immune system. In addition, choice D provides no indication as to which drug is superior regarding its effect on the immune system.

    Choice B is consistent with the studies and the information in the question and does not make any outlandish statement such as, "The new drug is vastly superior to the old drug with respect to all short-term and long-term effects." Choice A is out primarily because the ACT does not want you to practice medicine without a license. You would have to know a lot more about the new drug's pharmacological actions before making such a statement. Another point is that the new drug seemed better than the old drug when the dosages of the drugs were equated. Why would you say that the new drug is okay only if the dosage is reduced?

Passage 3

The first two paragraphs and figures provide background information, as is often done on the ACT. Don't worry about understanding all the details. The main point is that when water levels rise, the waves are more likely to hit the bluff. When this happens, the bluff erodes.

Don't waste time thoroughly analyzing each study or Figures 3–5. Often, you can use common sense on these science passages. Study 1 shouldn't shock you; you should expect that precipitation leads to greater lake depth.

Study 2 is somewhat more complex than Study 1. The key is to observe in Figure 4 that higher temperatures are associated with lower water levels (less depth). This relationship makes sense if you reason that high temperatures increase evaporation rate (don't you dry off fast when you get out of a pool on a hot day?), which, as stated, lowers water levels.

The results of Study 3 are similar to those of Study 2. Like high temperatures, strong winds lead to high evaporation, which, as you have seen, lowers water levels. This relationship is illustrated in Figure 5. Link Studies 2 and 3 together in your mind to help you nail down this high temperature, strong wind, high evaporation, less water association.

12. **H.** A quick look at Figure 3 reveals that lake depth goes down as precipitation goes down. Because lake depth is 5.0 m when precipitation is 15 cm/year, choices F and G are unreasonable. Choice J is too precise and is also improbable. A doubling of precipitation from 15 cm/year to 30 cm/year results in only a 0.5 m change in lake depth. The change from 10 cm/year to 15 cm/year is not as great as the 15-to-30 change, so the lake depth changing from 2.5 m to 5.0 m. would not make sense. Choice H, although not certain, is a safe thing to say and is the answer. Such safe answers are good bets on the ACT.

13. **A.** Experimenters conducted Study 2 under the premise that temperature affects evaporation rate. The researchers already know that high evaporation rates lower water levels. Figure 4 shows an association between high temperature and low water levels. If high temperatures result in low water levels, and high evaporation rates result in low water levels, high temperatures probably lead to high evaporation.

    Remember, common sense counts when answering a question in this section. Choice A is logical and fits in with basic science. You have probably observed that liquids disappear faster when the temperature is hot. Also, when evaporating, water changes from a liquid to a gas. Which state is associated with a higher temperature? The gas, so high temperatures and high evaporation go together.

14. F. Although what happens to lake depth cannot be determined with certainty (because several unmentioned factors are involved), the question asks what probably will happen. Therefore, the most obvious choice is safe. Low precipitation is associated with low water levels. High temperatures and strong winds increase evaporation rates, which lower water levels. When all three factors are connected to low water levels, you can safely say that the water level will be low.

15. D. Study 3 provides some evidence that strong winds can be good for the bluff because such winds lower water levels. With low water levels, more waves will hit the beach rather than the bluff. However, the word *definitely* in the question makes choice A incorrect. Other factors, one of which is mentioned in choice D, also exist. Does the fact that powerful waves can lead to erosion on the bluff make sense? Yes, it does, reinforcing choice D as the answer.

As with choice A, choice B is wrong because you can't definitely say things are good. In addition, wind is more likely to erode the soil on the bluff rather than deposit soil on it. Choice C is out because you can't say that wind raises temperatures (which may be good for the bluff).

16. G. The lake depth depends on the temperature and the amount of precipitation and wind. In a cause-and-effect relationship, the cause is the independent variable, and the effect or result is the dependent variable.

Another reason to pick choice G is that the other three choices all work the same way in this investigation. The other choices are all factors that the scientist examines for their effects on lake depth. If you want to select choice F, you would also have to select choices H and J. Because three answers can't all be correct, these choices must all be wrong.

17. A. Because statements I and II mention nothing about the weather, strike them out. Doing so quickly eliminates choices B, C, and D, leaving choice A as the answer. Statement III helps because it is similar to the passage's investigation but more direct; it measures something on the bluff instead of water level, which can affect the bluff. Statement IV is out because tides are the result of gravitational pull from the moon and the sun, which is not a weather factor. Even if you are unsure of this fact, no choice presents III and IV only.

Passage 4

At last, a graph you can actually relate to. You probably know that a compact car gets more miles per gallon than a full-size car does, as shown by the graph. The graph also shows that for each car size, gas mileage is better at slower speeds — which is why, logically enough, speed limits were lowered during the energy crisis of the 1970s.

The information presented before the graph is no big shock. When cars burn gas, they pollute the air. The more gas burned, the more pollution. To put this idea together with the graph, figure that the cars that get better gas mileage use less gas to travel a given distance; therefore, they do not pollute as much as large cars do.

18. J. Reasoning backward from the preceding summary, the car that produces the most pollutants is the one that uses the most gas. Which car uses the most gas? The one that gets the worst gas mileage, choice J.

19. A. When you drive a car faster, you get fewer miles per gallon than when you drive that car slower. This means that you have to use more gas to go a given distance.

Eliminate choice B because time isn't the critical factor in your finding a gas station. The probability of your finding a gas station increases with the distance driven, not the time driven.

You probably eliminated choices C and D as soon as you saw that they began with "Yes." (Good for you!) Choice C looks tricky but is wholly irrelevant. If you are facing being stranded in the middle of the desert, you probably don't care too terribly much whether your car is going to pollute. The key factor is whether you run out of gas. (Besides, just because an environment is relatively unpolluted does not give you license to pollute it.) Choice D is only half true. You will operate your car for less time; however, gas consumption is a function of distance, not time.

20. G. The logical solution is to figure that the answer is in between the miles per gallon for a full-size car driven at 50 mph and 60 mph. These figures are 26 and 24, respectively, making 25 the answer.

Choice F is illogical. That gas mileage is worse than what a full-size car driven at 60 mph gets. Remember, gas mileage should be higher when speed is reduced.

If you chose H or J, you made the test-maker's day. These answers are designed to trap careless readers who didn't notice that the figures are the mileage that midsize and compact (not full-size) cars would get at 55 mph.

21. D. If you got this question right, congratulations — you're thinking like a scientist. Making projections beyond the range of numbers presented in a graph is risky. In the graph, statistics are given for speeds between 50 and 70 mph. The 25-mph figure cited is far outside of this range.

Try hard not to outsmart yourself. You can't simply figure that if slowing down between 70 and 50 mph increases gas mileage, further decreases in speed will improve gas mileage even more. Too many factors that you don't know about are involved (for example, the engine may have to work harder when lower gears are used at lower speeds).

You need to recognize when you may make a reasonable extrapolation and when you may be going too far, right into a trap. In the previous question, you can logically estimate a number (because 55 is between 50 and 60, both of which were on the chart). In this question, you can't logically make an estimate because the chart does not cover the number in question.

22. J. More gas is used when speed increases, which means that more pollutants are emitted when speed increases. Only choice J shows that pollutants increase as speed increases for the entire range of speeds.

Passage 5

Did you take one look at this problem and tell a friend, "Pull the plug; I'm obviously brain dead!"? You don't need to be intimidated by the terms. No one expects you to be a neurosurgeon. All the ACT wants you to understand is that certain parts of the brain control certain muscles in the body. The figures simply indicate the locations of these controlling regions.

23. D. Scan the Roman numeral options. A quick glance at Figure 2 reveals that III is true. Much more of the motor area is dedicated to the hand, for example, than to the trunk, narrowing the field to Choices B and D. If you're in a rush or just want to get this horror over with, make a guess. A 50-50 chance is pretty good odds on this exam.

Now here's where you can use your test-taking skills, rather than using, well, your brain. Did you notice that options I and II are contradictory? As a result, one option, but not both, can be correct. A choice that presents I and III is not available (and remember, you already deduced that statement III is right), so the only thing left is the correct answer, II and III. Statement II, in fact, is correct. You can see how, starting from the inside of the brain, the regions progress from toes, at the bottom of the body, to the head.

Roman numeral questions can be very time-consuming. I often tell my students to skip these questions and to leave them for last. However, if you can immediately say that one statement is either definitely true or definitely wrong, you have narrowed the choices down immensely. Before skipping this sort of question, at least take a look at it. You may be in for one of the few pleasant surprises offered by the ACT.

24. H. One simple way to reason through this question is to see that the hand is much larger than the areas for hip, shoulder, and brow. (If Choice F is the answer, then why not G or J? They're all about the same size.) And don't forget to use your common sense. You can logically think that the more complex areas of the body require more brain control.

25. B. Figure 2 shows that the dot is in the knee area, narrowing the choices to B and C. Because the left half of the brain controls the right side of the body (see the text before Figure 2), the correct answer is Choice B.

In this figure, you see a classic example of how thinking about the diagram and the accompanying notes for a few moments before jumping right into the problems can help. The paragraph below the first figure states that one side of the brain controls the opposite side of the body (left brain, right body, and vice versa). Knowing that fact sends you quickly to the right answer.

26. F. To know what areas H and J do, you would have to have specific science knowledge. Unless you're a brain surgeon, you probably don't have all this info right at your fingertips. Remember that the ACT does not expect you to have specific knowledge but only to deduce information from a chart, table, graph, or picture. The passage tells you nothing about areas H and J.

Area G is near the top of the brain, which, according to Figure 2, is involved with the lower part of the body. Area F is near the face, lips, and jaw area. These parts of the body have more to do with speech (although you've heard of body language, your knees don't really chatter up a storm), making F the more logical choice.

27. D. This question (the entire question set, actually) deals with the motor area of the brain, so focus on choices that mention muscles. Hey! Doing so is a quick process of elimination: Choice D is the only possible answer.

Once again, don't sweat about Choices A, B, and C. Knowing how the brain controls these functions requires too much specialized knowledge for the ACT. The ACT wants to make sure that your brain functions, not that you know how it functions.

Passage 6

The introduction is certainly simple enough. Try to rephrase it in your own words: Pigeons are able to find their way home, but exactly how they do so is not known.

Try to identify one key point in each paragraph. In Paragraph 1 of the sun-compass hypothesis, all you need to understand is that the birds seem to use the sun's position to locate the cup. Don't get hung up trying to figure out more than that.

The main idea of the second paragraph is about internal clocks; when the internal clock provides incorrect information, errors result. This information suggests that the birds use the clock and compare the clock's info with the position of the sun.

This type of question isn't called Conflicting Viewpoints for nothing. Just as you've got the main idea of the first hypothesis, just as you think you've grasped the logic, along comes a second hypothesis. The magnetic-field hypothesis states that pigeons don't always use their internal clocks with the sun. But be careful not to go too overboard with this conclusion. All the findings say is that when the sun is not available, the birds do not compare their internal clocks with the sun to orient themselves. This is not to say that pigeons never use the sun, even though the author of the magnetic-field hypothesis chooses to ignore it. The findings simply suggest that the sun is not essential for orientation. Because the pigeons found their way home, they seem capable of using other information.

Finally, rephrase the gist of the second paragraph. The paragraph presents some evidence that shows that magnetic fields influence pigeon orientation. This evidence suggests that pigeons may use the earth's magnetic field to find their home but does not mean that they must use the field.

28. G. The sun-compass hypothesis says that homing pigeons use the sun. Because the pigeons can see the sun, they will use the sun and fly home. Choices F and H are more consistent with the other hypothesis, which suggests that the magnetic field is a major player in the birds' orientation. Choice J has real problems: It's inconsistent with both hypotheses. If the sun is key, the birds will fly in the correct direction unless their internal clock is altered. If the magnetic field is the most important element, the birds will continue to fly in random directions because the fields are distorted.

29. D. The magnetic-field hypothesis states that pigeons use the earth's magnetic field to orient themselves. A finding that shows that changes in this field change the way pigeons fly is certainly consistent with this hypothesis. The experiments with the magnets and electrical wires produced similar results, which were used to support the magnetic-field hypothesis.

Were you shrewd enough to notice that choices A and B basically say the same thing? Because you can't have two correct answers, both answers must be wrong. Besides, choices A and B are much too extreme. The sun may be overruled by a large disturbance in the magnetic field, but to say that the sun has no effect is going too far. Choice C has the same problem with extremism. The word *only* is too limiting (choices containing *only* are rarely correct). The pigeons still seem to use the sun under normal conditions.

30. F. If you chose J, you were 180 degrees wrong: Choice J is the major piece of support for the magnetic-field hypothesis. Choice H is almost as bad as choice J; this info was also used by the magnetic-field author. Choice G is consistent with the sun-compass hypothesis, but the magnetic-field author can respond by saying that the magnetic field is a factor that is sometimes overruled on sunny days. By process of elimination, F is correct. With no sun, the sun-compass hypothesis would predict that the pigeons would have trouble. On the other hand, the magnetic-field hypothesis would predict that the magnetic field should guide the pigeon, especially on a day when the sun was blocked.

31. A. Because a question like this one is hard to predict an answer for, go through the answer choices. Choice A appears good. The author has to make this assumption because if pigeons were affected by the mere presence of metal, the author could not conclude that the magnets were responsible for throwing the pigeons off. Metal may be disorienting the pigeons. The material may not have to be magnetic.

Choice B is too extreme (remember, a hedging answer is almost always better than a definite answer, so go for the wimpy words) and seems to contradict the author's idea that magnets are important. No information regarding what happens when magnets are worn on sunny days is available.

The downfall of choice C is also extremism. The author may accept that internal clocks may be used on sunny days. What makes this choice particularly bad is that it generalizes to all birds. You have no information regarding other bird species, so you have no way of knowing what the author assumes about this point.

And finally, choice D is wrong because the author may accept that the sun can be used under certain conditions. The author's main point is that magnetic fields are used.

32. G. Here's a case where opposites don't attract. If two statements are contradictory, they can't both be right. Eliminate choices F and J immediately because they include both I and II together. Doing so means that statement III has to be correct (because the remaining answer choices, G and H, both contain statement III). Don't strain any brain cells trying to think about it. (Okay, if you insist: Statement III is consistent with the magnetic-field discussion. When the sun is wiped out as a factor, the magnetic field plays an important role.)

Option I looks good because of its similarity to the sun-compass evidence cited in the passage. Option II is out because the beginning of the passage rules out landmarks. With I in and II out, only choice G can be the answer.

33. D. A major idea to get from this passage is that the two hypotheses present factors that homing pigeons may use. The evidence does not suggest that the sun or the earth's magnetic field is essential. (Both hedging and looking for exceptions when dealing with science passages are a good idea. Very rarely will you see an absolute, something that must be true. Note the very safe, wimpy language in the correct answer, choice D.) Evidence that brings up another possible factor does not contradict either hypothesis. This reasoning eliminates choices A and B. Choice C is easily dumped. If barometric pressure is consistent with one hypothesis, it has to be consistent with the other.

34. J. According to the sun-compass hypothesis, clock-shifted pigeons should make mistakes when light is present. The pigeons did not make mistakes, so choices F and G are out. The magnetic-field hypothesis, on the other hand, uses evidence of clock-shifted pigeons' not making errors to build up support for its claim. Choice G is wrong because pigeons did not respond correctly to the light, when you consider that a clock-light calculation should have pointed them in another direction. The pigeons did respond correctly, but they did not use the light to do so. If they had, they would have gone another way. Choice J, the correct answer, is similar to what is presented in the first paragraph of the magnetic-field hypothesis.

Passage 7

Start off by summarizing to yourself the passage's main idea, which tells you why the passage was written. Although the introduction may seem long and complicated, all it is saying is that the concentration of what you start with affects how fast you get a product as the chemical reaction takes place.

When looking at the experiments, don't get hung up on the chemical formulas. You can skim over them for the moment. (And remember: You are not required to have any background science to answer these questions. You do not need to memorize the Periodic Table or know anything about chemistry.) Just try to identify the information the tables give and the conclusions you can draw from the tables.

The key factor to note is that an increase of any reactant increases the formation rate. Increases in H^+ lead to larger increases in formation rate than do increases in the other two reactants.

35. C. H_3AsO_3 is the product, so the change that increases the formation rate the most is the change that produces more H_3AsO_3 in a given amount of time. As you deduced from your analysis of the introduction, increases in H^+ lead to the largest increases in formation rate.

36. G. The chemists varied only one concentration at a time, so you can easily observe how each reactant affects the formation rate. For example, Table 1 shows that doubling the concentration of H_3AsO_4 doubles the formation rate, while Table 3 shows that doubling the concentration of H^+ quadruples the formation rate. If both these reactants are doubled, the formation rate is eight times the original rate, but without knowing anything beforehand, scientists are not able to tell which reactant, if any, has a greater effect on the rate.

In general, you can interpret experiments more easily when the experimenters change only one factor at a time. This type of experimental methodology question is a frequent one on the ACT.

The other choices do not make sense. Why would an explosion occur (choice F)? No explosion occurs even when the concentration of a given reactant is four times the original amount. You can reasonably think that changing the concentration of a couple of reactants by small amounts would not lead to any calamities. This type of reasoning also rules out choice J. In Experiment 3, scientists measure a rate that is almost 20 times the original rate. Even if measuring greater rates is difficult, the scientists can take care not to change the concentrations of two or three reactants by too great an amount.

Choice H is not at all PC (politically correct). The ACT will not have you believe that scientists are not up to a task. Even if measuring two or more concentrations is difficult, you can rest assured that the scientists will find a way. Besides, who said that the concentrations had to be measured at the same time? Why not measure each concentration separately and then dump all the reactants in at once?

37. D. How do the concentrations compare with the original concentrations, the concentrations that appear in the top line of each table? The concentrations of the first reactants are doubled, while the concentration of H^+ is the same. Table 1 shows that when the concentration of H_3AsO_3 is doubled, the formation rate doubles from 2.8 to 5.6 rate units. Table 2 reveals that doubling the concentration of I^- also doubles the formation rate. When each concentration is doubled, as in Table 2, the formation rate will be 2×2 or four times the rate obtained when the original concentrations are used ($4 \times 2.8 = 11.2$).

38. F. With two liters of solution instead of one and the same amounts of reactants, the concentration of each reactant decreases. In each experiment, increasing concentration increases formation rate, so decreasing concentration decreases formation rate.

39. D. Get rid of choices A and B immediately. Why would the rate go down when the concentration of H^+ goes up? Throughout Table 3, the rate increases. A sudden reversal makes no sense.

Don't fight the ACT. Rarely, very rarely, does the Science Reasoning Test contain traps (as opposed to some other tests, such as the mathematics). The logical conclusion is usually correct; the reasonable interpretation of a table or chart or graph is usually the right one.

Did you choose Choice C? Don't feel bad. It is tempting to think that doubling the concentration of H^+ from 0.40 moles/liter to 0.80 moles/liter would double the formation rate, but look at Table 3. Did doubling the concentration from 0.10 to 0.20 merely double the rate? No, doubling the concentration quadrupled the rate, making choice C too low. The answer is Choice D, which is quadruple the rate when the concentration of H^+ is only 0.40 moles/liter.

40. J. Uh-oh: Where did H_2O come from? Don't panic. The equation written in the introduction indicates that H_2O is formed when H_3AsO_3 is formed. Well, what happens to the formation rate of H_3AsO_3 when reactant concentration increases? All the experiments show that this formation rate increases. Because H_2O is also formed when H_3AsO_3 is formed, the increase in the formation rate of H_2O makes sense.

Don't think that questions in this test necessarily follow the same order of the passage. That is, question one doesn't have to come from the introduction and question six from the last paragraph. As you just saw, the last question can be from the first part of the passage. That's one reason I suggest that you jot down your thoughts — your summary of the passage — in the margin of the test booklet. You may need to go back and refer to your notes a few times.

Chapter 16

Practice Exam 2: Questions

You are now ready to take a sample ACT. The following exam consists of four tests: a 45-minute English Test, a 60-minute Mathematics Test, a 35-minute Reading Test, and a 35-minute Science Reasoning Test. You probably are familiar with the format of each test by now.

Please take this test under normal exam conditions. (This is serious stuff!)

1. **Sit where you won't be interrupted (even though you'd probably welcome any distractions).**
2. **Use the answer grid provided.**
3. **Set your alarm clock for the intervals indicated at the beginning of each test.**
4. **Do not go on to the next test until the time allotted for the test you are taking is up.**
5. **Check your work for that test only.**
6. **Do not take a break during any test.**
7. **Give yourself one ten-minute break between tests two and three.**

After you've completed the entire test, check your answers with the answer key at the end of this chapter. A section explaining your score precedes the answer key.

Chapter 17 gives detailed explanations of the answers. Go through the answer explanations to *all* the questions, not just the ones that you missed. You will find a plethora of worthwhile information, material that provides a good review of everything that you've learned in the other chapters of the book. I've even tossed in a few good (?) jokes to keep you somewhat sane.

Answer Sheet

Begin with number 1 for each new section.

English Test

1. (A) (B) (C) (D)
2. (F) (G) (H) (J)
3. (A) (B) (C) (D)
4. (F) (G) (H) (J)
5. (A) (B) (C) (D)
6. (F) (G) (H) (J)
7. (A) (B) (C) (D)
8. (F) (G) (H) (J)
9. (A) (B) (C) (D)
10. (F) (G) (H) (J)
11. (A) (B) (C) (D)
12. (F) (G) (H) (J)
13. (A) (B) (C) (D)
14. (F) (G) (H) (J)
15. (A) (B) (C) (D)
16. (F) (G) (H) (J)
17. (A) (B) (C) (D)
18. (F) (G) (H) (J)
19. (A) (B) (C) (D)
20. (F) (G) (H) (J)
21. (A) (B) (C) (D)
22. (F) (G) (H) (J)
23. (A) (B) (C) (D)
24. (F) (G) (H) (J)
25. (A) (B) (C) (D)
26. (F) (G) (H) (J)
27. (A) (B) (C) (D)
28. (F) (G) (H) (J)
29. (A) (B) (C) (D)
30. (F) (G) (H) (J)
31. (A) (B) (C) (D)
32. (F) (G) (H) (J)
33. (A) (B) (C) (D)
34. (F) (G) (H) (J)
35. (A) (B) (C) (D)
36. (F) (G) (H) (J)
37. (A) (B) (C) (D)
38. (F) (G) (H) (J)
39. (A) (B) (C) (D)
40. (F) (G) (H) (J)
41. (A) (B) (C) (D)
42. (F) (G) (H) (J)
43. (A) (B) (C) (D)
44. (F) (G) (H) (J)
45. (A) (B) (C) (D)
46. (F) (G) (H) (J)
47. (A) (B) (C) (D)
48. (F) (G) (H) (J)
49. (A) (B) (C) (D)
50. (F) (G) (H) (J)
51. (A) (B) (C) (D)
52. (F) (G) (H) (J)
53. (A) (B) (C) (D)
54. (F) (G) (H) (J)
55. (A) (B) (C) (D)
56. (F) (G) (H) (J)
57. (A) (B) (C) (D)
58. (F) (G) (H) (J)
59. (A) (B) (C) (D)
60. (F) (G) (H) (J)
61. (A) (B) (C) (D)
62. (F) (G) (H) (J)
63. (A) (B) (C) (D)
64. (F) (G) (H) (J)
65. (A) (B) (C) (D)
66. (F) (G) (H) (J)
67. (A) (B) (C) (D)
68. (F) (G) (H) (J)
69. (A) (B) (C) (D)
70. (F) (G) (H) (J)
71. (A) (B) (C) (D)
72. (F) (G) (H) (J)
73. (A) (B) (C) (D)
74. (F) (G) (H) (J)
75. (A) (B) (C) (D)

Mathematics Test

1. (A) (B) (C) (D) (E)
2. (F) (G) (H) (J) (K)
3. (A) (B) (C) (D) (E)
4. (F) (G) (H) (J) (K)
5. (A) (B) (C) (D) (E)
6. (F) (G) (H) (J) (K)
7. (A) (B) (C) (D) (E)
8. (F) (G) (H) (J) (K)
9. (A) (B) (C) (D) (E)
10. (F) (G) (H) (J) (K)
11. (A) (B) (C) (D) (E)
12. (F) (G) (H) (J) (K)
13. (A) (B) (C) (D) (E)
14. (F) (G) (H) (J) (K)
15. (A) (B) (C) (D) (E)
16. (F) (G) (H) (J) (K)
17. (A) (B) (C) (D) (E)
18. (F) (G) (H) (J) (K)
19. (A) (B) (C) (D) (E)
20. (F) (G) (H) (J) (K)
21. (A) (B) (C) (D) (E)
22. (F) (G) (H) (J) (K)
23. (A) (B) (C) (D) (E)
24. (F) (G) (H) (J) (K)
25. (A) (B) (C) (D) (E)
26. (F) (G) (H) (J) (K)
27. (A) (B) (C) (D) (E)
28. (F) (G) (H) (J) (K)
29. (A) (B) (C) (D) (E)
30. (F) (G) (H) (J) (K)
31. (A) (B) (C) (D) (E)
32. (F) (G) (H) (J) (K)
33. (A) (B) (C) (D) (E)
34. (F) (G) (H) (J) (K)
35. (A) (B) (C) (D) (E)
36. (F) (G) (H) (J) (K)
37. (A) (B) (C) (D) (E)
38. (F) (G) (H) (J) (K)
39. (A) (B) (C) (D) (E)
40. (F) (G) (H) (J) (K)
41. (A) (B) (C) (D) (E)
42. (F) (G) (H) (J) (K)
43. (A) (B) (C) (D) (E)
44. (F) (G) (H) (J) (K)
45. (A) (B) (C) (D) (E)
46. (F) (G) (H) (J) (K)
47. (A) (B) (C) (D) (E)
48. (F) (G) (H) (J) (K)
49. (A) (B) (C) (D) (E)
50. (F) (G) (H) (J) (K)
51. (A) (B) (C) (D) (E)
52. (F) (G) (H) (J) (K)
53. (A) (B) (C) (D) (E)
54. (F) (G) (H) (J) (K)
55. (A) (B) (C) (D) (E)
56. (F) (G) (H) (J) (K)
57. (A) (B) (C) (D) (E)
58. (F) (G) (H) (J) (K)
59. (A) (B) (C) (D) (E)
60. (F) (G) (H) (J) (K)

Reading Test	Science Test
1. Ⓐ Ⓑ Ⓒ Ⓓ	1. Ⓐ Ⓑ Ⓒ Ⓓ
2. Ⓕ Ⓖ Ⓗ Ⓙ	2. Ⓕ Ⓖ Ⓗ Ⓙ
3. Ⓐ Ⓑ Ⓒ Ⓓ	3. Ⓐ Ⓑ Ⓒ Ⓓ
4. Ⓕ Ⓖ Ⓗ Ⓙ	4. Ⓕ Ⓖ Ⓗ Ⓙ
5. Ⓐ Ⓑ Ⓒ Ⓓ	5. Ⓐ Ⓑ Ⓒ Ⓓ
6. Ⓕ Ⓖ Ⓗ Ⓙ	6. Ⓕ Ⓖ Ⓗ Ⓙ
7. Ⓐ Ⓑ Ⓒ Ⓓ	7. Ⓐ Ⓑ Ⓒ Ⓓ
8. Ⓕ Ⓖ Ⓗ Ⓙ	8. Ⓕ Ⓖ Ⓗ Ⓙ
9. Ⓐ Ⓑ Ⓒ Ⓓ	9. Ⓐ Ⓑ Ⓒ Ⓓ
10. Ⓕ Ⓖ Ⓗ Ⓙ	10. Ⓕ Ⓖ Ⓗ Ⓙ
11. Ⓐ Ⓑ Ⓒ Ⓓ	11. Ⓐ Ⓑ Ⓒ Ⓓ
12. Ⓕ Ⓖ Ⓗ Ⓙ	12. Ⓕ Ⓖ Ⓗ Ⓙ
13. Ⓐ Ⓑ Ⓒ Ⓓ	13. Ⓐ Ⓑ Ⓒ Ⓓ
14. Ⓕ Ⓖ Ⓗ Ⓙ	14. Ⓕ Ⓖ Ⓗ Ⓙ
15. Ⓐ Ⓑ Ⓒ Ⓓ	15. Ⓐ Ⓑ Ⓒ Ⓓ
16. Ⓕ Ⓖ Ⓗ Ⓙ	16. Ⓕ Ⓖ Ⓗ Ⓙ
17. Ⓐ Ⓑ Ⓒ Ⓓ	17. Ⓐ Ⓑ Ⓒ Ⓓ
18. Ⓕ Ⓖ Ⓗ Ⓙ	18. Ⓕ Ⓖ Ⓗ Ⓙ
19. Ⓐ Ⓑ Ⓒ Ⓓ	19. Ⓐ Ⓑ Ⓒ Ⓓ
20. Ⓕ Ⓖ Ⓗ Ⓙ	20. Ⓕ Ⓖ Ⓗ Ⓙ
21. Ⓐ Ⓑ Ⓒ Ⓓ	21. Ⓐ Ⓑ Ⓒ Ⓓ
22. Ⓕ Ⓖ Ⓗ Ⓙ	22. Ⓕ Ⓖ Ⓗ Ⓙ
23. Ⓐ Ⓑ Ⓒ Ⓓ	23. Ⓐ Ⓑ Ⓒ Ⓓ
24. Ⓕ Ⓖ Ⓗ Ⓙ	24. Ⓕ Ⓖ Ⓗ Ⓙ
25. Ⓐ Ⓑ Ⓒ Ⓓ	25. Ⓐ Ⓑ Ⓒ Ⓓ
26. Ⓕ Ⓖ Ⓗ Ⓙ	26. Ⓕ Ⓖ Ⓗ Ⓙ
27. Ⓐ Ⓑ Ⓒ Ⓓ	27. Ⓐ Ⓑ Ⓒ Ⓓ
28. Ⓕ Ⓖ Ⓗ Ⓙ	28. Ⓕ Ⓖ Ⓗ Ⓙ
29. Ⓐ Ⓑ Ⓒ Ⓓ	29. Ⓐ Ⓑ Ⓒ Ⓓ
30. Ⓕ Ⓖ Ⓗ Ⓙ	30. Ⓕ Ⓖ Ⓗ Ⓙ
31. Ⓐ Ⓑ Ⓒ Ⓓ	31. Ⓐ Ⓑ Ⓒ Ⓓ
32. Ⓕ Ⓖ Ⓗ Ⓙ	32. Ⓕ Ⓖ Ⓗ Ⓙ
33. Ⓐ Ⓑ Ⓒ Ⓓ	33. Ⓐ Ⓑ Ⓒ Ⓓ
34. Ⓕ Ⓖ Ⓗ Ⓙ	34. Ⓕ Ⓖ Ⓗ Ⓙ
35. Ⓐ Ⓑ Ⓒ Ⓓ	35. Ⓐ Ⓑ Ⓒ Ⓓ
36. Ⓕ Ⓖ Ⓗ Ⓙ	36. Ⓕ Ⓖ Ⓗ Ⓙ
37. Ⓐ Ⓑ Ⓒ Ⓓ	37. Ⓐ Ⓑ Ⓒ Ⓓ
38. Ⓕ Ⓖ Ⓗ Ⓙ	38. Ⓕ Ⓖ Ⓗ Ⓙ
39. Ⓐ Ⓑ Ⓒ Ⓓ	39. Ⓐ Ⓑ Ⓒ Ⓓ
40. Ⓕ Ⓖ Ⓗ Ⓙ	40. Ⓕ Ⓖ Ⓗ Ⓙ

English Test

45 Minutes — 75 Questions

DIRECTIONS: Following are five passages with underlined portions. Alternate ways of stating the underlined portions are to the right of the passages. Choose the best alternative; if the original is the best way of stating the underlined portion, choose NO CHANGE.

You also have questions that refer to the passage or ask you to reorder the sentences within the passage. These questions are identified by a number in a box. Choose the best answer and blacken in the corresponding oval on your answer grid.

Passage 1

A Short History of Banking

When the United States were established (1) in 1776, the 13 colonies had separate banking systems. There was hardly no (2) common standard of currency among the colonies. Each jealously guarded its (3) independence, and governmental involvement was not encouraged. It wasn't until 1791 that the First Bank of the United States was created in Philadelphia. It had a 20-year charter and closed in 1811. In 1863, the National Banking Act, being the first to establish national banks. (4) It adopted the dollar as the national currency and forbade states to printing their own money (5). Just two years later, checks became a standard means

1. A. NO CHANGE
   B. were establishing
   C. was established
   D. was being established

2. F. NO CHANGE
   G. There wasn't hardly no
   H. There was hardly any
   J. There was, hardly, any

3. A. NO CHANGE
   B. it's
   C. it is
   D. their

4. F. NO CHANGE
   G. Banking Act, and it was being the first to establish national banks.
   H. Banking Act; being the first to establish national banks.
   J. Banking Act first established national banks.

5. A. NO CHANGE
   B. from being printing their own money
   C. to print their own money
   D. which printed, each one, its own money

Go on to next page

of payment. However, it wasn't until the Federal Reserve Act of 1913 that the FRS (Federal Reserve System) was established as the central bank, with authority to regulate and supervising [6] state member banks and collect and clear checks for banks.

There is one more thing you need to know. [7] Many people have heard of the Great Depression, this is the common name given to the period that followed the stock market crash of 1929. [8] Farm prices and steel production both fallen [9]. By four years later, unemployment had reached a high of 25 percent. The national income had dropped 50 percent below that of 1929. [10] The stock market was 75 percent below what it had been during its high of 1929, and bank closings were common [11]. A recovery program was obvious and needed. [12]

6. F. NO CHANGE
   G. to be regulating and supervising
   H. to regulate and supervise
   J. regulating and to supervise

7. A. NO CHANGE
   B. One more thing it is necessary for your knowing.
   C. You should be knowing one more thing.
   D. OMIT the underlined portion.

8. F. NO CHANGE
   G. Many people have heard of the Great Depression, the common name given to the period that followed the stock market crash of 1929.
   H. Many people have heard of the Great Depression, which periodically followed the stock market crash of 1929.
   J. Many people, having heard of the Great Depression, the common name given to the period that followed the stock market crash of 1929.

9. A. NO CHANGE
   B. both fell
   C. fell, both of them
   D. both felled

10. F. NO CHANGE
   G. below 1929.
   H. below that of 1929's.
   J. OMIT the underlined portion.

11. A. NO CHANGE
   B. it's high of 1929, with common bank closings.
   C. its 1929, and closing banks commonly
   D. the 1929 bank closings.

12. F. NO CHANGE
   G. obvious, needed.
   H. obviously needy.
   J. obviously needed.

Go on to next page

The Federal Home Loan Bank Act of 1932 was part of that program, as was the Banking Act of 1933. [13] The Banking Act of 1933 established the FDIC as the authority to relegate and supervise state non-member banks. [14] It prohibited banks from paying interest on checking accounts (a prohibition that was not overturned until many years later). [15]

13. A. NO CHANGE
    B. the Banking Act of 1933 was too.
    C. and also the 1933 Banking Act.
    D. as was banking in 1933.

14. At this point, the author is considering adding the following sentence:

    Most of the banks were, in fact, non-member banks, and had been excluded from the important banking acts by virtue of this fact.

    Would this addition be logical and useful in the rest of the passage?

    F. Yes, because it addresses a point the author introduced but forgot to follow up.
    G. Yes, because it provides essential background information.
    H. No, because the passage doesn't distinguish between member and non-member banks.
    J. No, because the non-member banks are outside the scope of the Act.

Item 15 poses a question about the passage as a whole.

15. The author needs to eliminate a paragraph to save space. Which of the following would be the best paragraph to eliminate, and why?
    A. Paragraph 1, because it provides non-essential introductory material.
    B. Paragraph 2, because it doesn't address the history of banking.
    C. Paragraph 3, because it depresses the readers by focusing on the negatives of banking.
    D. Paragraph 4, because it fails to draw a conclusion to the underlying question of the passage.

Go on to next page

Passage 2

Native American Government

The question has been asked how Native American tribes, <u>whom govern themselves</u> [16] do so. Most tribal governments are <u>organized democratic,</u> [17] that is, with an elected leadership. The governing body is referred to as a <u>council, it is</u> [18] composed of persons elected by vote of the eligible adult tribal members. The presiding official is the chairman, although some tribes use other titles, <u>such as principal chief</u> [19], president, or governor. An elected tribal council, recognized as such by the Secretary of the Interior and the people working for him, <u>have</u> [20] authority to speak and act for the tribe and <u>to represent it</u> [21] in negotiations with federal, state, and local governments.

Just what do tribal governments do? They generally define conditions of tribal membership, <u>regulate</u> [22] domestic relations of members, prescribe rules of inheritance for reservation property not in trust status, levy taxes, regulate property under tribal jurisdiction, control conduct of members by tribal ordinances, <u>and they administer</u> [23] justice.

16. F. NO CHANGE
    G. who govern themselves,
    H. governing them
    J. whom, governing themselves,

17. A. NO CHANGE
    B. organized democratically
    C. organized in a democracy
    D. OMIT the underlined portion

18. F. NO CHANGE
    G. council; however, it is
    H. council, but is
    J. council, and is

19. A. NO CHANGE
    B. such as a principle
    C. like a principle
    D. like principle

20. F. NO CHANGE
    G. had
    H. has
    J. having

21. A. NO CHANGE
    B. be representing it
    C. to represent them
    D. representing them

22. F. NO CHANGE
    G. regular
    H. regulating
    J. having regulated

23. A. NO CHANGE
    B. and administering
    C. and administer
    D. and to be administering

Go on to next page

What role do Native Americans have in the American political system? They have the same obligations for military service as do other U.S. citizens. <u>They have fought</u> (24) in all American wars since the Revolution, they served on both sides in the Civil War. Eli S. Parker, a Seneca from New York, was at Appomattox as an aide to General Ulysses S. Grant when Lee surrendered, and the unit of Confederate Brigadier General Stand Watie, a Cherokee, was the last to surrender. It was not until World War I <u>that Native American's demonstrating</u> (25) patriotism (6,000 of the more than 8,000 who served were volunteers) moved Congress to pass the Indian Citizenship Act of 1924. One reads <u>in your history books</u> (26) <u>about using the Navajo Marines of their language</u> (27) as a battlefield code, the only such code that the enemy could not break. Today, one out of every four Native American men is a military veteran, and 45 to 47 percent of tribal leaders <u>is a military veteran</u> (28). [29]

24. **F.** NO CHANGE
G. They did fight
H. It has fought (the tribal)
J. Fighting

25. **A.** NO CHANGE
B. when the Native Americans, who demonstrated
C. that the Native Americans' demonstrated
D. when the Native Americans'

26. **F.** NO CHANGE
G. in history books
H. in their history books
J. in one of their history books

27. **A.** NO CHANGE
B. about the use by Navajo Marines of their language
C. about Navajos using their Marine language
D. , the Navajo Marines' language use

28. **F.** NO CHANGE
G. is military veterans
H. are military veterans
J. are a military veteran

Question 29 refers to the entire passage.

29. Which of the following best describes the author's purpose in writing this passage?

A. to argue the need for governmental withdrawal from Native American affairs
B. to explain tribal structure and Native American military participation
C. to hypothesize causes of racial tension between Native Americans of warring tribes
D. to predict the roles of Native Americans in future wars

Go on to next page

Passage 3

Mountains and Volcanoes

[1]The theory of plate tectonics hold that as (30) the expanding oceanic crust is thrust beneath the continental plate margins; it penetrates (31) deep enough into the Earth to be partly remelted. [2]Pockets of molten rock (magma) result. (32) [3]Before Lassen Peak was emplaced, Mount Tehama had collapsed, but its caldera was breached, and no large lake ever developed as did Crater Lake in Oregon. [4]About 500,000 years ago, Mount Tehama gradually building up here throughout countless (33) eruptions. [5]These become the feeding chambers for volcanoes, like (34) the great Pacific Ring of Fire stratovolcano, Mount Tehama; remnants of its caldera flanks are Brokeoff Mountain, Mount Diller, Pilot Pinnacle, and Mount Conard.

[6]If you connect these peaks in a circle on the map, you can envision Mount Tehama's base, which was more than 18 kilometers (11 miles) wide. [7]The park's plant life mixes species of the Sierra Nevada to the south from (35) those of the Cascade Range. [8]The result is more species than you can break a stick over (36). The park boast some (37) 715 plant species, but nearby Mount Shasta has

30. **F.** NO CHANGE
G. hold when
H. holds that whichever
J. holds that as

31. **A.** NO CHANGE
B. margins, it penetrates
C. margins; however, it penetrates
D. margins and penetrating

32. **F.** NO CHANGE
G. resulting
H. results
J. resulted

33. **A.** NO CHANGE
B. was bilt up here, going through countless
C. had built up here throughout uncounted
D. built up here through countless

34. **F.** NO CHANGE
G. as
H. as if
J. likely

35. **A.** NO CHANGE
B. with
C. form
D. to

36. **F.** NO CHANGE
G. more species than you can shake a stick at
H. as many species as you can find in two shakes of a stick
J. so many species that they break the sticking point

37. **A.** NO CHANGE
B. boasts and has
C. boasts some
D. boast some more of the

Go on to next page

only 485 species. Of 38 transitional species, about 24 Sierran species are at the northern limit of their range here; therefore, about 14 Cascadian species are at their southern limits. [39] [40]

38

What was life like on these peaks? Sometimes historians have difficulty determining that. The Lassen area, for example, was a meeting point for four groups of Native Americans: Atsugewi, Yana, Yahi, and Maidu. Because of its weather and snow conditions, generally high elevation, and seasonally mobile deer populations, the Lassen area was not conducive to year-round living. These Native American groups encamped here in warmer months for hunting and gathering. The Native Americans left few artifacts. History generally describes the period from 1840 on, even though mountain man Jedediah Smith passed through in 1828 on his overland trek to the West Coast. Two pioneer trails, developed by William Nobles and Peter Lassen, are associated with the park. [43]

41

42

38. **F.** NO CHANGE
G. , therefore;
H. ,
J. : and

Question 39 refers to the entire passage.

39. Using a cliché in sentence 8 does which of the following?
A. It changes the meaning of the passage.
B. It introduces a new concept.
C. It forestalls an opposing argument.
D. It inserts inappropriate humor into a serious discussion.

40. Which of the following would be the correct order of sentences in the first paragraph?
F. 3 — 5 — 4 — 2 — 1
G. 2 — 3 — 4 — 5 — 1
H. 2 — 5 — 3 — 1 — 4
J. 1 — 2 — 5 — 4 — 3

41. **A.** NO CHANGE
B. Since
C. Therefore,
D. OMIT the underlined portion

42. **F.** NO CHANGE
G. have few artifacts.
H. with few artifacts left.
J. leaving few artifacts.

43. Which of these best describes the effect of the last paragraph?
A. It summarizes the information given in the previous paragraphs.
B. It presents a personal opinion that contradicts the beginning of the passage.
C. It introduces a new concept.
D. It supports the author's hypothesis.

Go on to next page

Passage 4

One Boy's Role Model

As a young boy, I having dreamed of [44] following in the footsteps of explorer Richard Halliburton, who it is fair to say [45] has been my hero since childhood. Let other boys dream of being Viking warriors or knights in shining armor. I have always wanted to be a world-famous explorer, going places no one has ever been, or returning to places where civilization flourished long ago. Richard Halliburton lived the life I always wanted to live and wrote about it in ways that motivated me as a youngster and still have the power to thrill me as a man. I am especially fascinated by [46] his stories of his trip to Pompeii, which he calls the city that rose from the dead. A few miles past Naples, Italy, along the slopes of Vesuvius. This city is found, [47] which is much the same as it was in A.D. 79, with wine jars still lying [48] in place and the ruts in the streets from the passing chariots still visible.

[1]He calls these chilling effects the volcano's "tantrums" and mentions that while the locals treat them causally, [49] he himself cannot help but think of what future explorers would think if they found his body, complete with tourist guide, wristwatch, and toothbrush. [2]My favorite is, "Good health to anybody who invites me to dinner [50]." [3]Neither too wordy or too concise, [51] the explorer's writing

44. F. NO CHANGE
G. As a young boy, I dreamed of
H. As a young boy, I am dreaming of
J. Dreaming, as a young boy, of

45. A. NO CHANGE
B. who fairly says
C. who, its' fair to say
D. of whom it is fairly said

46. F. NO CHANGE
G. enslaved with
H. captivated to
J. enriched of

47. A. NO CHANGE
B. Vesuvius, is found this city,
C. Vesuvius: This city is found,
D. Vesuvius, finding this city

48. F. NO CHANGE
G. laying
H. being to lay
J. lain

49. A. NO CHANGE
B. whereas the locals treat them causally
C. although the locals treat them causally
D. while the locals treat them casually

50. F. NO CHANGE
G. invite me to dinner
H. invite him to dinner
J. OMIT the underlined portion

51. A. NO CHANGE
B. or concise, too,
C. nor too concise
D. nor concisely

Go on to next page

appeals to the secret fears of all of us by mentioning that as he sat in his hotel room that evening <u>and looked out over</u> [52] the landscape, he could see flashes of red light shooting up from the summit of Vesuvius. [4]Halliburton <u>makes his writing breathing</u> [53] by showing the homey points that we all can <u>relate to. The graffiti on the walls.</u> [54] [5]He also mentions the signboards and posters <u>in very perfect condition</u> [55] that show the announcements of new plays and the contests of the <u>gladiators. Sure to</u> [56] inspire every young boy's imagination to feats of daring and bravery. [57] [58] [59]

52. **F.** NO CHANGE
G. and looks out over
H. and is looking out over
J. , having looked

53. **A.** NO CHANGE
B. makes his writing vivid
C. , making lively writing,
D. made his writing breath

54. **F.** NO CHANGE
G. relate with — the graffiti on the walls.
H. relate to, one example is the graffiti on the walls.
J. relate to, such as the graffiti on the walls.

55. **A.** NO CHANGE
B. in perfect condition
C. , which are in completely perfect condition,
D. — perfect —

56. **F.** NO CHANGE
G. gladiators, they're sure to
H. gladiators and sure to
J. gladiators, which are sure to

57. Which of the following represents the best order of the first four sentences for the second paragraph to make the most sense?

A. 1 — 2 — 3 — 4
B. 4 — 3 — 1 — 2
C. 4 — 2 — 3 — 1
D. 2 — 3 — 1 — 4

Questions 58 and 59 refer to the entire passage.

58. In which of the following places would you be most likely to find this passage?

F. an encyclopedia
G. a newspaper editorial
H. a memoir
J. a geography textbook

59. Why did Halliburton mention a toothbrush (paragraph 2, sentence 1)?

A. to show how far hygienic practices have come
B. to add a touch of humor to the prospect of having his body found in a lava flow
C. to ridicule the idea of treating a volcano casually
D. to emphasize the completely destructive effects of volcanoes

Go on to next page

Passage 5

Lizards

The lizard is a cold, bloody reptile [60] that cannot keep its body temperature much higher or lower than its [61] surroundings. Although it often basks [62] in the sunlight to regulate its temperature. Although other related animals are also cold-blooded, they usually avoid [63] direct sunlight. Lizards are often found on or in the ground, especially in deserts or dry regions, fewer in the trees [64].

Lizards come in above [65] 3,000 species of all sizes and shapes. Some lizards resemble large crocodiles calling [66] Komodo dragons. These are indigenous to Komodo, Indonesia. The Komodo dragons may grow as large as seven feet and measure around to [67] 200 pounds. They eat most kinds of meat, stalking live prey. Smaller tree-dwelling lizards — called geckos, [68] may measure only three inches and weigh only a few ounces.

60. F. NO CHANGE
G. is a cold-blooded reptile
H. is a reptile and has cold blood
J. is a reptile (cold-blooded)

61. A. NO CHANGE
B. than that of its
C. then its
D. than that of its'

62. F. NO CHANGE
G. Basking often
H. It often basks
J. Although, often, it basks

63. A. NO CHANGE
B. it usually avoids
C. usually avoiding
D. it has usually been avoiding

64. F. NO CHANGE
G. lesser in the trees
H. but few in the trees
J. although a few are found in the trees

65. A. NO CHANGE
B. are over
C. come in more than
D. , numbering above

66. F. NO CHANGE
G. so therefore they are called
H. and are called
J. OMIT the underlined portion

67. A. NO CHANGE
B. come in about
C. weigh up to
D. weight around

68. F. NO CHANGE
G. lizards, called geckos —
H. lizards — called geckos —
J. lizards — (called geckos) —

Go on to next page

The majority of lizards are egg-laying (ovoviviparous) reptiles. Some species keep the eggs within the female's body. Until they are hatched, [69] causing the young to be born alive. Ovoviviparous species are rare to care for [70] their offspring or nourish them after birth. Although most lizards eat live prey (such as ants and other insects), some are vegetarians.

Color is important to lizards, especially during courtship rituals. Normally dull lizards can develop bright red, orange, or blue splotches of color for the attraction of [71] females or to warn off other males. The color is due to pigment cells called chromatophores, in which pigment granules migrate. These color changes can be very dramatic, sometimes even allowing a lizard to have the two halves [72] of its body be entirely different colors.

Few lizards are harmful to humans, although they may look threatening. The American horned lizards have spines that some mistake for stingers. Although no lizards can sting, most will bite if threatened. Some lizard bites are venomous, but most are not life-threatening. Children's fairy tales and stories told around campfires in lonely deserts on starry nights often imply [73] nearly mystical qualities to what are basically harmless creatures. [74] [75]

69. **A.** NO CHANGE
B. female's body until they hatched,
C. female's body until hatching,
D. bodies of the females until they have been hatching,

70. **F.** NO CHANGE
G. rarely care for
H. , rarely caring for
J. , rare and caring for

71. **A.** NO CHANGE
B. to attract
C. in order for attracting
D. by attracting

72. **F.** NO CHANGE
G. to halve the two halves
H. to half the two halfs
J. to have the two hafes

73. **A.** NO CHANGE
B. infer
C. impute
D. describe

Questions 74 and 75 refer to the entire passage.

74. If the author were to add a description of lizards' mating rituals, he would most likely place it in paragraph

F. 1, because it discusses the lizards' habits.
G. 3, because it discusses reproduction.
H. 4, because it mentions attracting mates.
J. 5, because it talks about the appearance of spines.

75. If a student studying for a biology exam were to read this passage, which of the following might she consider to be a weakness of the material?

A. It does not discuss the various types of lizards.
B. It neglects to mention lizard habitats.
C. It fails to differentiate lizards based on their size and appearance.
D. It does not describe a lizard's place in the chain of evolution.

STOP
END OF TEST 1
DO NOT TURN THE PAGE UNTIL TOLD TO DO SO.
DO NOT RETURN TO A PREVIOUS TEST.

Mathematics Test

60 Minutes — 60 Questions

DIRECTIONS: Each question has five answer choices. Choose the best answer for each question and shade the corresponding oval on your answer grid.

---

1. Five cheerleaders and ten football players contributed to a coach's retirement party. Each cheerleader gave the same amount of money, exactly twice as much as each football player gave. If together the 15 friends donated \$480, how much money did each football player give?

A. \$5
B. \$15
C. \$22
D. \$24
E. \$26

2. What is .01% of 1,000,000?

F. 10
G. 100
H. 1,000
J. 10,000
K. 100,000

3. Let $x = -3$. Which of the following is equal to $2x - (3y - 3x) + 4y$?

A. $y + 15$
B. $y + 12$
C. $y - 12$
D. $y - 15$
E. $7y - 15$

4. What is the measure of angle *LMX*?

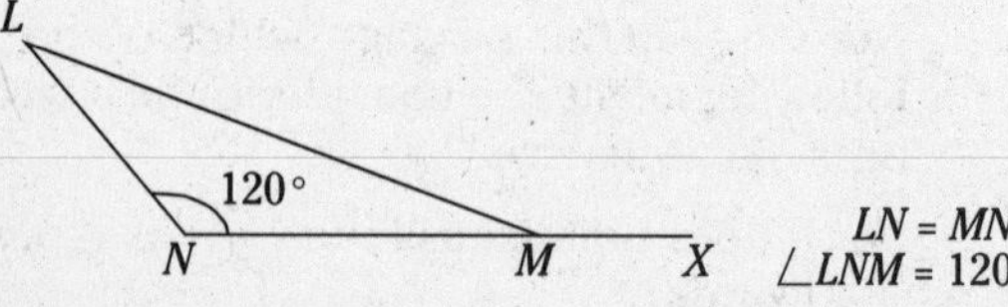

F. 150°
G. 120°
H. 100°
J. 60°
K. 30°

5. Jarnelle can assemble 300 widgets in an hour. To be eligible for a raise, she must be able to raise her rate of assembly by 25 percent. At the new rate, how many widgets could Jarnelle assemble in 8 hours? (Assume a steady rate with no breaks.)

A. 6,125
B. 3,000
C. 375
D. 300
E. 75

6. The angles of a right triangle are in the ratio 1:2:3. If the longest side of the triangle is 30 units, what is the number of units in the perimeter of the triangle?

F. 15
G. 45
H. $45\sqrt{3}$
J. $45+15\sqrt{3}$
K. $60\sqrt{3}$

7. What is the number of square units in the area of an isosceles right triangle with a hypotenuse $5\sqrt{2}$?

A. $2\sqrt{2}$
B. 25
C. $12.5\sqrt{2}$
D. 12.5
E. $10 + 5\sqrt{2}$

8. Which of the following is another way of expressing $6a - [(a - 3) - a]$?

F. $4a + 3$
G. $5a - 3$
H. $6a - 3$
J. $5a + 3$
K. $6a + 3$

9. Veronica buys a car on sale for 25 percent off the original price but has to pay a 5 percent luxury tax on the sale price. If the before-sale price of the car is \$18,000, how much does Veronica pay for the car?

A. \$18,900
B. \$14,400
C. \$14,175
D. \$13,500
E. \$4,500

Go on to next page

10. A floor with a length three times its width has a perimeter of 640 feet. What is its area in square feet?

F. 100,000
G. 19,200
H. 14,400
J. 8,800
K. 6,000

11. If $a = 3$; $b = 10$, which of the following is the closest approximation to

$$\frac{a+b(a-b)^2(a^2-b)}{b(a^2+b)}?$$

A. 10
B. 2.5
C. –1
D. –2.5
E. –8

12. Three angles, x, y, and z, lie along a straight line. If $x = \frac{1}{2}y$, and $y = \frac{2}{3}z$, how much is $z - x$?

F. 90°
G. 85°
H. 80°
J. 70°
K. 60°

13. What is the answer when $5a^3b^4 + 3a^2b^3$ is subtracted from $a^3b^4 - 2a^2b^3$?

A. $-4a^3b^4 - 5a^2b^3$
B. $-4a^3b^4 + a^2b^3$
C. $6a^3b^4 + a^2b^3$
D. $4a^3b^4 + a^2b^3$
E. $4a^3b^4 + 5a^2b^3$

14. If a 30:60:90 triangle has a perimeter of $30 + 10\sqrt{3}$, what is its area in square units?

F. $2000\sqrt{3}$
G. 2000
H. $100\sqrt{3}$
J. $50\sqrt{3}$
K. $10\sqrt{3}$

15. $ab - ba = 0$. $ab \neq 0$. What is $\frac{ab}{ba}$?

A. –1
B. 0
C. $\frac{1}{2}$
D. 1
E. 2

16. What is the area of trapezoid *ABCD* in square units?

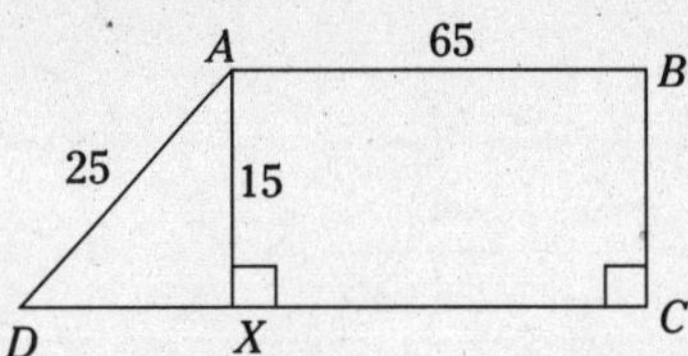

F. 1,400
G. 1,200
H. 1,125
J. 1,050
K. 975

17. $(.240 \times 10^4) + (7.01 \times 10^2) = ?$

A. 9.41×10^4
B. 3.01×10^{-3}
C. 9.41×10^2
D. 3.101×10^3
E. 14.1×10^8

18. For all x and y, $(3x^2y + xy^2) - (2x^2y - 2xy^2) = ?$

F. $x^2 - x$
G. $x^2y - xy^2$
H. $x^2y + 3xy^2$
J. $5^2y - xy^2$
K. $x^4y^2 + 3x^2y^4$

19. What is the number of square units in the total surface area of this cylinder, including both ends?

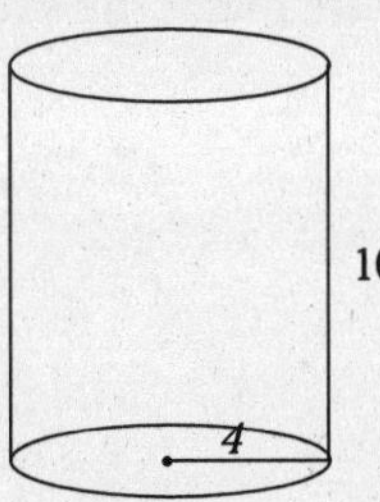

A. 16π
B. 40π
C. 100π
D. 104π
E. 112π

Go on to next page

20. What is the area in square units of trapezoid ABCD shown below?

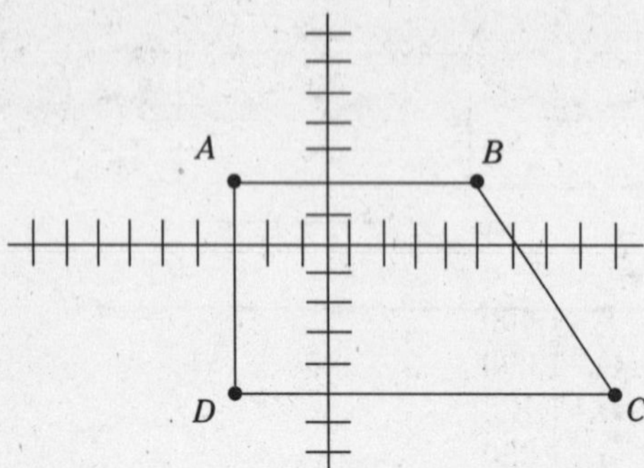

NOTE: Each tick mark represents one unit.

F. 80
G. 70
H. 52
J. 50
K. 7

21. What is $(2a^2 + ab - 8) - (3a^2 - 2ab + 8)$?

A. $ab + a^2$
B. $3ab + a^2 - 16$
C. $3ab + a^2$
D. $3ab - a^2 - 16$
E. $ab - a^2 - 16$

22. Liz takes six tests during the semester and gets scores of 81, 90, 74, 79, and 92 on the first five tests. If she wants her overall average to be 85, what grade does she need on the sixth test? (All tests count the same toward the average.)

F. 95
G. 94
H. 93
J. 85
K. 83

23. Simplify $2y - (4 - 3y) + 3$.

A. $-y - 12$
B. $-y + 7$
C. $5y - 7$
D. $5y - 1$
E. $5y + 1$

24. If the area of the square is 144 square units, what is the number of square units of the shaded area?

F. $144 + 36\pi$
G. $144 - 36\pi$
H. $144 - 12\pi$
J. $144 - 16\pi$
K. $144 - 144\pi$

25. Solve for the number of degrees in x.

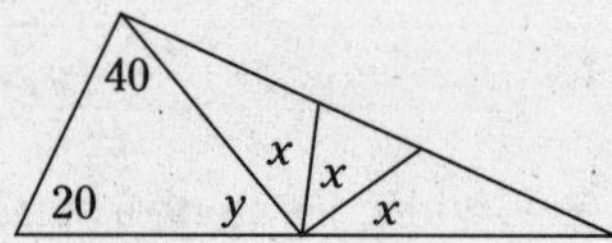

A. 10°
B. 20°
C. 30°
D. 40°
E. 50°

26. A machine sorts ball bearings. Due to a mechanical problem, the machine drops half the ball bearings per cycle. If the machine finishes its fifth cycle with 11 balls still remaining in the machine, how many balls were in the machine at the beginning of the first cycle?

F. 704
G. 352
H. 176
J. 88
K. 44

27. $a = 3 + b$

$16a = 20 - 4b$.

What is the value of a?

A. $-7/5$
B. $7/5$
C. $9/5$
D. $11/5$
E. $22/5$

Go on to next page

28. If $\frac{1}{a} = 4$ and $\frac{1}{b} = 5$, how much is $\frac{1}{ab}$?

F. $\frac{1}{20}$
G. $\frac{1}{9}$
H. 9
J. 20
K. 200

29. The area of circle *O* is 25π. What is the area of triangle *ABC* in square units?

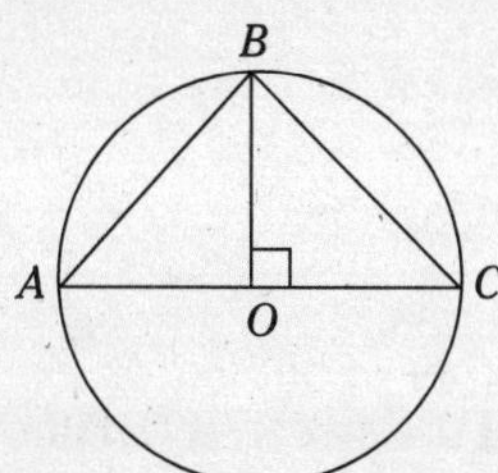

A. 10
B. 15
C. 20
D. 25
E. 20π

30. $4^{-x} = 64$. What is the value of x?

F. –4
G. –3
H. 0
J. 3
K. 4

31. In the right triangle *XYZ* below, what is the value of tan *Z*?

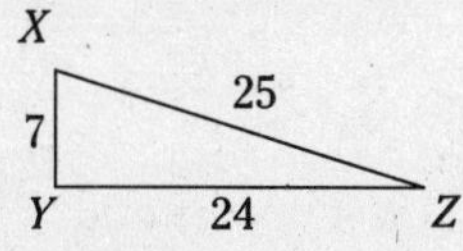

A. $\frac{7}{25}$
B. $\frac{7}{24}$
C. $\frac{24}{25}$
D. $\frac{25}{24}$
E. $\frac{24}{7}$

32. After a slow reader increased her speed by 25 percent, she was still 50 percent slower than a fast reader. *Before* the slow reader increased her speed, the fast reader's speed was what percent of the slow reader's speed?

F. 300
G. 250
H. 225
J. 200
K. 125

33. The current pushes a swimmer back 2 feet for every 2 yards she swims. If she needs to cover 500 yards and each stroke takes her 5 yards, how many strokes must she take?

A. 1,000
B. 700
C. 500
D. 150
E. 100

34. A farmer can plow *x* rows in *y* minutes. Which of the following represents the number of rows the farmer can plow in *w* hours?

F. $60xyw$
G. $\frac{x+y}{60} \cdot w$
H. $\frac{w}{60} \cdot x$
J. $\frac{w+x+y}{60}$
K. $60\frac{x}{y} \cdot w$

35. If $f(x) = 1 + x^3$, what is $f(-5)$?

A. 126
B. 124
C. –124
D. –125
E. –126

36. Three interior angles of a hexagon sum up to 360°. What is the average measure of each of the remaining interior angles?

F. 360
G. 300
H. 280
J. 180
K. 120

Go on to next page

37. Square ABCD has an area of 36. If R, S, T, and U are midpoints of their respective sides, what is the area of square RSTU?

A. $36\sqrt{2}$
B. 36
C. $18\sqrt{2}$
D. 18
E. $9\sqrt{2}$

38. The formula for interest on a bank account is PRT = I, where Principal (the money invested) × Rate × Time = Interest. If an investor earns $28.50 interest in one year at 9.5 percent simple annual interest, how much principal did he invest?

F. $550
G. $450
H. $400
J. $390
K. $300

39. The diameter of Circle *O* has the same length as the diagonal of square *ABCD*. If the area of Circle *O* is 36π, what is the number of units in the area of square *ABCD?*

A. 144
B. 72π
C. 36π
D. 72
E. 36

40. If $x \neq 4$, solve for $\frac{\sqrt{x}+2}{\sqrt{x}-2}$.

F. -1
G. $\frac{x+4}{x-4}$
H. $-\sqrt{x}-1$
J. $\frac{x+4\sqrt{x}+4}{x-4}$
K. $-\sqrt{x}+4$

41. $64^{\frac{2}{3}} = ?$

A. 0
B. 4
C. 8
D. 16
E. 32

42. Let *a* @ *b* be defined as the sum of the prime factors of the sum of *a* and *b*. For example, 3 @ 5 = 6 because 3 + 5 = 8; 8 = 2 × 2 × 2. Finally, 2 + 2 + 2 = 6. Solve for 10 @ 21.

F. 17
G. 19
H. 31
J. 32
K. 40

43. A tool drawer in a workbench has five nuts, four bolts, and six nails in it. A worker pulls out and throws away three nuts and two nails. What is the probability that on his next reach into the drawer he'll pull out a bolt?

A. $62\frac{1}{2}\%$
B. 50%
C. 40%
D. $33\frac{1}{3}\%$
E. 25%

44. A street has a number of billboards. Starting at the beginning of the street, the billboard advertising milk is the 13th; from the other end of the street, the billboard is the 14th. How many billboards are there along the street?

F. 24
G. 25
H. 26
J. 27
K. 28

45. The trinomial $x^2 + 7x - 8$ can be factored as the product of two linear factors, in the form $(x + a)(x + b)$. What is the polynomial sum of these two factors?

A. $2x - 7$
B. $2x + 7$
C. $2x - 6$
D. $2x + 6$
E. $2x - 8$

46. $3a + 5b = 10$. Solve for *b* in terms of *a*.

F. $5-\frac{5}{2}a$
G. $2-\frac{3}{2}a$
H. $2-\frac{3}{5}a$
J. $2a-\frac{3}{2}$
K. $2a-\frac{3}{5}$

Go on to next page

47. If $-4mx - \frac{3b}{c} = 4my$, then $x + y$ = ?

A. $\frac{-3b}{4mc}$

B. $\frac{-3b}{8mc}$

C. $\frac{-3b}{16m^2c}$

D. $\frac{-6b}{4m^2c}$

E. $\frac{-3b}{c} - 4m$

48. What is the solution set of $a(a + 4) = 12$?

F. {6, –2}
G. {–6, 6}
H. {–6, 2}
J. {12, 0}
K. {4}

49. What is the simplified form of $x[(3 + x)(4x) + 2]$?

A. $4x^3 + 12x^2 + 2x$
B. $2x^3 + 12x^2 + 2x$
C. $12x^3 + 4x^2 + 2x$
D. $4x^3 + 2x^2 + 4x$
E. $4x^3 + 4x^2 + 12$

50. A car passed a designated point on the freeway and traveled for 2 hours at 80 km/hr. Then, in an effort to save gas, the driver slowed to 70 km/hr for 1 hour. The driver stopped for gas and lunch for 1 hour and then traveled 80 km/hr for 1 hour. The graph of the driver's distance *(d)* from the designated point as a function of time *(t)* would most resemble which of the following?

F.
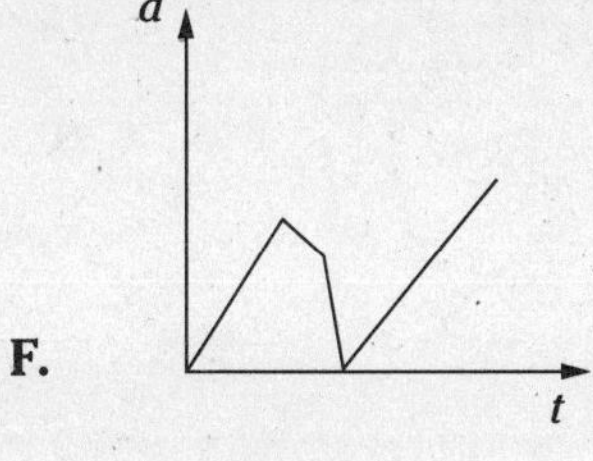

G.
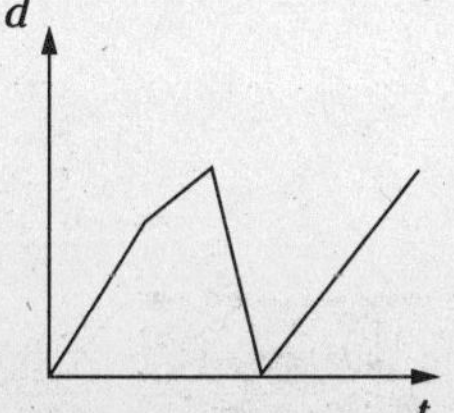

H.
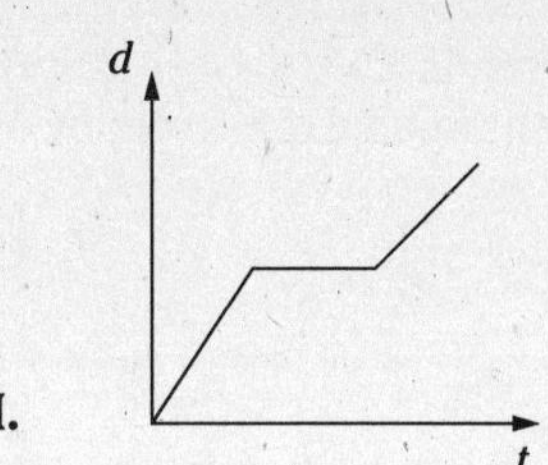

J.
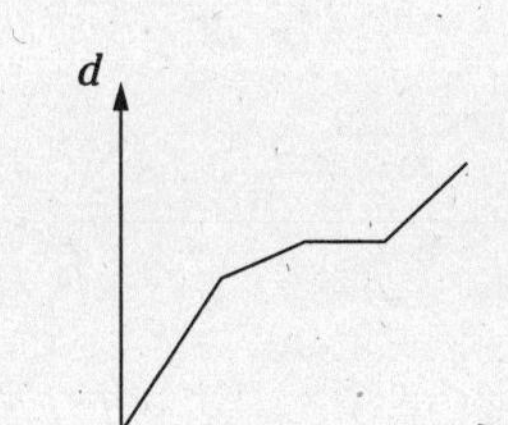

K.
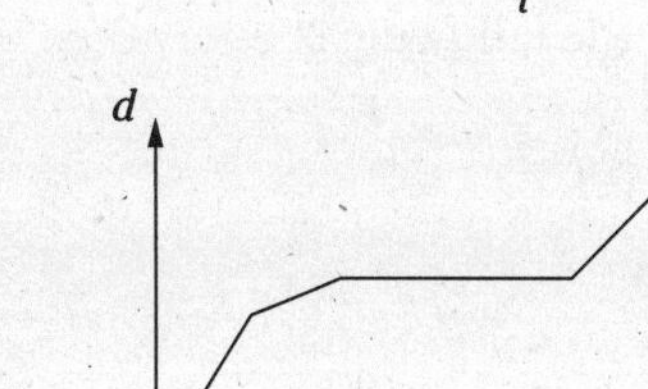

51. What is the sum of the two solutions to the equation $x^2 - 5x + 6 = 0$?

A. –5
B. –1
C. 1
D. 5
E. 6

52. Which of the following represents the graph of the solution set of $x + 1 \leq 8$?

F.
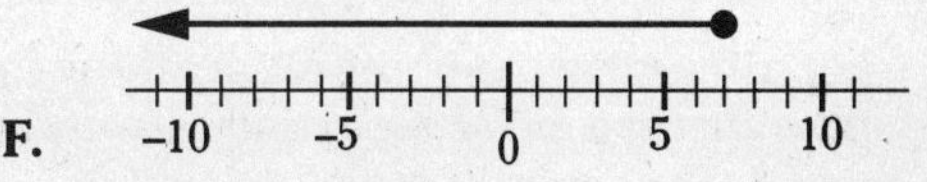

G.
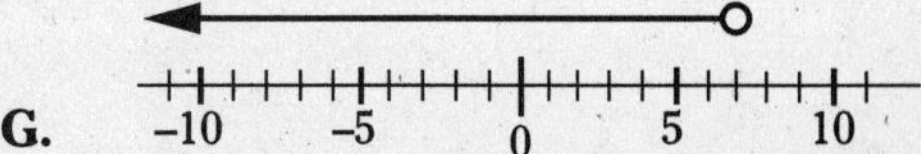

H.
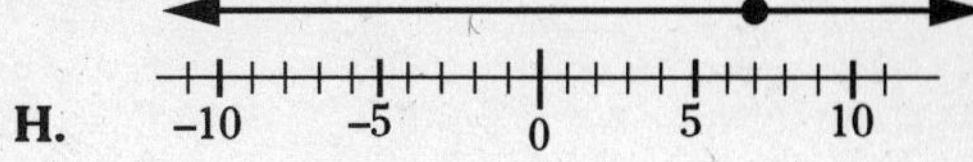

J.
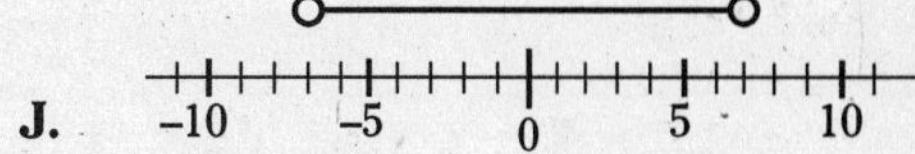

K.

Go on to next page

53. A line's equation is $x + 2y = 4 - (x + y)$. Its equation may also be expressed as y = ?

A. $\frac{3}{4}+\frac{2x}{3}$
B. $\frac{4}{3}+\frac{2x}{3}$
C. $\frac{4}{3}-\frac{2x}{3}$
D. $\frac{1}{4}-\frac{2x}{3}$
E. $\frac{2x}{3}$

54. Which of the following is equivalent to $\frac{\sin^2\theta+\cos^2\theta}{\sec^2\theta}$?

F. $\cos^2\theta$
G. $\sin^2\theta$
H. $\tan^2\theta$
J. $\frac{1}{\cos^2\theta}$
K. $\sin^2\theta + 1$

55. What is the simplified form of $\frac{7}{2+\sqrt{3}}$?

A. 21
B. $7+\sqrt{3}$
C. $7-7\sqrt{3}$
D. $14+7\sqrt{3}$
E. $14-7\sqrt{3}$

56. For all $a \neq 0$, what is the slope of the line passing through $(2a, -b)$ and $(-a, -b)$ in the usual (x, y) coordinate plane?

F. 0
G. $\frac{2b}{3a}$
H. $\frac{3a}{2b}$
J. 3a
K. Undefined

57. Three painters take ten hours to paint four rooms. How many hours will 9 painters take to paint 12 rooms?

A. $1\frac{1}{3}$
B. $3\frac{1}{3}$
C. 6
D. 10
E. 30

58. Which of the following is equal to $\frac{10.8(10^{-3})}{400(10^{-5})}$?

F. $.027(10^2)$
G. $.0027(10^2)$
H. $.27(10^{-2})$
J. $.0027(10^2)$
K. $27(10^{-2})$

59. Georgia buys q quarts of milk at d dollars per quart and b boxes of cereal at $d + 1$ dollars per box. Which of the following expressions represents the total amount spent?

A. $qd + bd + 1$
B. $(q + b)(d + 1)$
C. $(q + b)(2d + 1)$
D. $d(q + b) + b$
E. $bd(q + b)$

60. Find the area of rectangle ACEG.

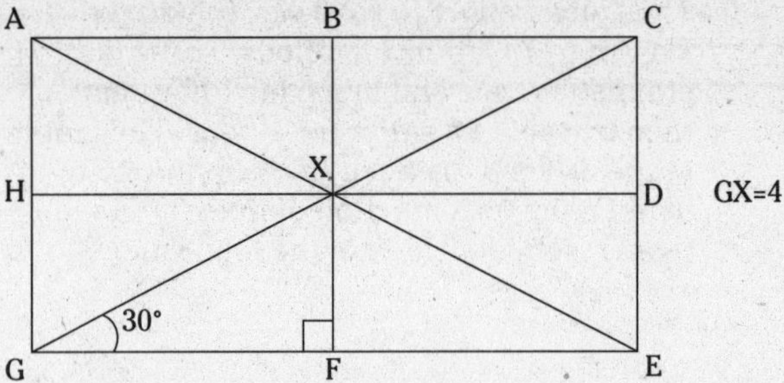

F. $8\sqrt{2}$
G. $8\sqrt{3}$
H. 16
J. $16\sqrt{2}$
K. $16\sqrt{3}$

STOP

END OF TEST 2

DO NOT TURN THE PAGE UNTIL TOLD TO DO SO.
DO NOT RETURN TO A PREVIOUS TEST.

Reading Test

35 Minutes — 40 Questions

DIRECTIONS: Each of the four passages in this section is followed by ten questions. Answer each question based on what is stated or implied in the passage, and shade the corresponding oval on your answer grid.

Passage 1

Natural Science

A cave is a natural opening in the ground extending beyond the zone of light and large enough to permit the entry of man. Occurring in a wide variety of rock types and caused by widely differing geologic processes, caves range in size from single small rooms to interconnecting passages many miles long. The scientific study of caves is called *speleology* (from the Greek words *spelaion* for cave and *logos* for study). Speleology is a composite science based on geology, hydrology, biology, and archaeology.

Caves have been natural attractions since prehistoric times. Abundant evidence of early people's interest has been discovered in a plethora of caves scattered throughout the world. Fragments of skeletons of some of the earliest humanlike creatures (Australopithecines) have been discovered in cave deposits in South Africa, and the first evidence of primitive Neanderthal Man was found in a cave in the Neander Valley of Germany. Cro-Magnon people created their remarkable murals on the walls of caves in southern France and northern Spain, where they took refuge more than 10,000 years ago during the chill of the Ice Age.

A simple classification of caves includes four main types and several other relatively less important types. Solution caves are formed in carbonate and sulfate rocks such as limestone, dolomite, marble, and gypsum by the action of slowly moving ground water that dissolves the rock to form tunnels, irregular passages, and even large caverns. Most of the caves in the world, including the largest, are of this type. Lava caves are tunnels or tubes in lava formed when the outer surface of a lava flow cools and hardens while the molten lava within continues to flow and eventually drains out through the newly formed tube. Sea caves are formed by the constant action of waves that attack the weaker portions of rocks lining the shores of oceans and large lakes. Such caves testify to the enormous pressures exerted by waves and to the corrosive power of wave-carried sand and gravel. Glacier caves are formed when water excavates drainage tunnels through the ice.

Of entirely different origin, and not to be included in the category of glacier caves, are so-called "ice caves," which usually are either solution caves or lava caves within which ice forms and persists through all or most of the year.

In desert areas, some shallow caves may be formed by the sandblasting effect of silt or fine sand being blown against a rock face. These eolian caves, some of which are spectacular in size, are surpassed in number by caves of other origins in most deserts. More common even in the driest deserts are sandstone caves eroded in part by water, particularly if the sandstone is limy. Caves commonly known as "wind caves" are named not for the mode of origin of the cave but for the stronger air currents that alternately blow in or out of the cave as the atmospheric pressure changes. Most wind caves are, in fact, solution caves.

Solution caves are formed in limestone and similar rocks by the action of water; they can be thought of as parts of a huge subterranean plumbing system. After a rain, water seeps into cracks and pores of soil and rock and percolates beneath the land surface. Eventually, some of the water reaches a zone where all the cracks and pores in the rock are already filled with water. The term *water table* refers to the upper surface of this saturated zone. Calcite (calcium carbonate), the main mineral of limestone, is barely soluble in pure water. Rainwater, however, absorbs some carbon dioxide as it passes through the atmosphere and absorbs even more as it drains through soil and decaying vegetation. The water, combining chemically with the carbon dioxide, forms a weak carbonic acid solution. This acid slowly dissolves calcite, forms solution cavities, and excavates passageways. The resulting calcium bicarbonate solution is carried off in the underground drainage system.

Go on to next page

Recent studies of movement and chemistry of ground water have shown that the first stage in cave development — the dissolving of carbonate rocks and the formation of cavities and passageways — takes place principally just below the water table in the zone of saturation where continuous mass movement of water occurs.

A second stage in cave development occurs after a lowering of the water table (the water table normally sinks as the river valleys deepen). During this stage, the solution cavities are stranded in the unsaturated zone where air can enter. This leads to the deposition of calcite, which forms a wide variety of dripstone features.

1. You may infer that the author uses "zone of light" in line 2 to refer to

- **A.** the distance that light penetrates into a cave.
- **B.** the weight of the rocks around the entrance to a cave.
- **C.** the number of light years that a cave has existed.
- **D.** the latitude and longitude of a cave.

2. "Greeks were the first to study caves." Can you infer this as an established fact from the passage?

- **F.** Yes, because speleology, the study of caves, is from the Greek words *spelaion* (cave) and *logos* (study).
- **G.** Yes, because the Greeks were the first to develop the scientific process.
- **H.** No, because evidence of earlier interest in caves has been found in the caves themselves.
- **J.** No, because each language has its own name for cave study.

3. The main purpose of the second paragraph is to

- **A.** describe the long-standing human interest in caves.
- **B.** contrast caves from different areas.
- **C.** dismiss as unimportant caves of less than 10,000 years.
- **D.** prove the commonality of cave paintings throughout the world.

4. You may infer that Neanderthal Man got his name from

- **F.** the region in which evidence of his existence was found.
- **G.** the Greek term for "first man."
- **H.** the style of cave paintings he left behind.
- **J.** the unusual structure of his skeleton.

5. The author uses the term *plethora,* line 14, to mean

- **A.** attraction.
- **B.** hypothesis.
- **C.** unscientific statement.
- **D.** abundance.

6. Caves are classified

- **F.** by the process that formed them.
- **G.** by their location.
- **H.** by the era in which they were created.
- **J.** by the name of the peoples who first discovered them.

7. According to the passage, the largest type of cave is

- **A.** solution.
- **B.** lava.
- **C.** sea.
- **D.** glacier.

8. Which of the following is the distinction between a glacier cave and an ice cave?

- **F.** None; they are the same.
- **G.** A glacier cave is older than an ice cave.
- **H.** An ice cave contains no dirt or rock.
- **J.** An ice cave is a solution or lava cave.

9. Which of the following was *not* mentioned as possibly being a solution cave?

I. ice caves
II. lava caves
III. wind caves

- **A.** I only
- **B.** II only
- **C.** III only
- **D.** I and III only

10. The dripstone features of a cave

- **F.** are composed of ice.
- **G.** are composed of calcite.
- **H.** occur as a result of a rising water table.
- **J.** cannot occur in caves without decaying vegetation.

Go on to next page

Passage 2

Prose Fiction. This passage is adapted from George Eliot's *Middlemarch.*

The human soul moves in many channels, and Mr. Casaubon, we know, had a sense of rectitude and honorable pride in satisfying the requirements of honor, which compelled him to find other reasons for his conduct than those of jealousy and vindictiveness. The way in which Mr. Casaubon put the case was this:

"In marrying Dorothea Brooke I had to care for her well-being in case of my death. But well-being is not to be secured by ample, independent possession of property; on the contrary, occasions might arise in which such possession might expose her to the more danger. She is ready prey to any man who knows how to play adroitly either on her affectionate ardor or her quixotic enthusiasm; and a man is standing by with that very intention in his mind — a man with no other principle than transient caprice, and who has a personal animosity towards me — I am sure of it — an animosity which he has constantly vented in ridicule, of which I am as well assured as if I had heard it. Even if I live I shall not be without uneasiness as to what he may attempt through indirect influence. This man has gained Dorothea's ear; he has fascinated her attention; he has evidently tried to impress her mind with the notion that he has claims beyond anything I have done for him. If I die — and he is waiting here on the watch for that — he will persuade her to marry him. That would be calamity for her and success for him. She would not think it calamity; he would make her believe anything; she has a tendency to immoderate attachment which she inwardly reproaches me for not responding to, and already her mind is occupied with his fortunes. He thinks of an easy conquest and of entering into my nest. That I will hinder! Such a marriage would be fatal to Dorothea. Has he ever persisted in anything except from contradiction? In knowledge he has always tried to be showy at small cost. In religion he could be, as long as it suited him, the facile echo of Dorothea's vagaries. When was sciolism ever disassociated from laxity? I utterly distrust his morals, and it is my duty to hinder to the utmost the fulfillment of his designs."

The arrangements made by Mr. Casaubon on his marriage left strong measures open to him, but in ruminating on them his mind inevitably dwelt so much on the probabilities of his own life that the longing to get the nearest possible calculation had at last overcome his proud reticence and had determined him to ask Lydgate's opinion as to the nature of his illness.

He had mentioned to Dorothea that Lydgate was coming by appointment at half past three, and in answer to her anxious question, whether he had felt ill, replied, "No, I merely wish to have his opinion concerning some habitual symptoms. You need not see him, my dear. I shall give orders that he may be sent to me in the yew-tree walk, where I shall be taking my usual exercise."

When Lydgate entered the yew-tree walk he saw Mr. Casaubon slowly receding with his hands behind him according to his habit, and his head bent forward. It was a lovely afternoon; the leaves from the lofty limes were falling silently across the somber evergreens, while the lights and shadows slept side by side; there was no sound but the cawing of the rooks, which to the accustomed ear is a lullaby, or that last solemn lullaby, a dirge. Lydgate, conscious of an energetic frame in its prime, felt some compassion when the figure which he was likely soon to overtake turned around and in advancing towards him showed more markedly than ever the signs of premature age — the student's bent shoulders, the emaciated limbs, and the melancholy lines of the mouth.

"Poor fellow," he thought, "some men with his years are like lions; one can tell nothing of their age except that they are full grown."

"Mr. Lydgate," said Mr. Casaubon with his invariably polite air, "I am exceedingly obliged to you for your punctuality. We will, if you please, carry on our conversation in walking to and fro."

"I hope your wish to see me is not due to the return of unpleasant symptoms," said Lydgate, filling up a pause.

11. Which of the following best expresses the same idea as that given in the first sentence of the passage?

A. Mr. Casaubon is justifiably proud of not being jealous or vindictive.
B. Mr. Casaubon justified his actions to himself in a way that didn't make him seem jealous or vindictive.
C. Mr. Casaubon was ashamed of his jealousy and vindictive toward those who pointed it out to him.
D. Mr. Casaubon is afraid of his wife's jealousy and vindictiveness.

Go on to next page

12. Mr. Casaubon feels that leaving his money to Dorothea in case of his death
    - F. would be unfair to his children from a previous marriage.
    - G. would leave her vulnerable to fortune-hunters.
    - H. would be the right and proper thing to do.
    - J. would be fair because getting his money was the only reason that Dorothea married him in the first place.

13. Which of the following may you infer about the animosity of the man whom Mr. Casaubon fears is "standing by" to take Dorothea after Mr. Casaubon's death (line 16)?
    - A. He has never directly expressed any animosity toward Mr. Casaubon.
    - B. He has valid reasons for his animosity, which Mr. Casaubon is uneasily aware of.
    - C. His intentions toward Dorothea are not honorable.
    - D. He was a rival of Mr. Casaubon's for Dorothea long ago.

14. In lines 8–45, you learn that Mr. Casaubon
    - F. is afraid of the other man's corrupting Dorothea.
    - G. has convinced himself that frustrating the other man is his responsibility.
    - H. hopes to avoid a confrontation with the other man.
    - J. is uneasily aware that Dorothea prefers the other man to him.

15. The sentence, "The arrangements made by Mr. Casaubon on his marriage left strong measures open to him . . ." emphasizes that
    - A. Mr. Casaubon believed that Dorothea was marrying him only for his money.
    - B. Dorothea was unaware of Mr. Casaubon's fears and neuroses.
    - C. Mr. Casaubon was a cautious man and may have had his concerns over Dorothea's remarriage from the start.
    - D. Dorothea demanded that Mr. Casaubon divulge his arrangements to her before she agreed to marry him.

16. ". . . his mind inevitably dwelt so much on the probabilities of his own life that the longing to get the nearest possible calculation . . ." (lines 48–51). Which of the following expresses most nearly the same thought as in this quotation?
    - F. He worried about his success at gambling and wanted advice from an outside expert.
    - G. He regretted his past actions and sought to find out what repercussions they may have.
    - H. He wondered how long he had left to live and wanted an estimate of his time remaining.
    - J. He was obsessed with himself and cared for no one else.

17. Which of the following attitudes best describes Lydgate's feelings upon seeing Mr. Casaubon?
    - A. confusion
    - B. embarrassment
    - C. self-pity
    - D. ebullience

18. You may infer which of the following was the author's reason for describing the loveliness of the day (lines 65–70)?
    - F. to show Lydgate's tranquil frame of mind
    - G. to contrast the beauty of his surroundings with the unattractiveness and frailty of Mr. Casaubon
    - H. to foreshadow impending doom to Mr. Casaubon and his wife
    - J. to emphasize Mr. Casaubon's wealth in comparison to his ill health

19. The author indicates that Lydgate's comment (lines 85–87)
    - A. was a professional pleasantry with which he always began a visit.
    - B. was intended to encourage Mr. Casaubon to discuss his illness.
    - C. was designed to make Mr. Casaubon conscious of his infirmity.
    - D. was made to end an awkward silence.

20. Which of the following most likely happens to the reader's attitude toward Mr. Casaubon as he goes through this excerpt?
    - F. It changes from contempt toward the man to pity for him.
    - G. It becomes progressively less tolerant of the man and more disgusted with his behavior.
    - H. It becomes indifferent, as the reader no longer cares what happens to Mr. Casaubon but focuses on Lydgate.
    - J. It becomes more understanding, finally seeing the reasons Dorothea married her husband.

Go on to next page

Passage 3

Social Science. This passage is adapted from *How to Develop Self-Esteem in Your Child* by Dr. Bettie Youngs (copyright 1991 Bettie Youngs).

What is the work of childhood? Each stage of a child's development presents its own set of tasks and demands, all focused on gaining self-knowledge: selfhood. The work of each stage is pretty well-defined.

Until the age of two, a child primarily views himself as part of his mother (or father, if he is the primary caretaker). Upon reaching two, he develops the ability to be aware that he is in reality separate from her. This situation presents him with the task of establishing autonomy — separateness. The two words that best describe his new-found selfhood, that he is in fact a separate person, are *no* and *mine*. Possession is the tool he uses to enforce that sense of separate self.

Having realized his separateness, the three-year-old goes on to master his environment. Mastery plays an important role in his perception of self. It influences his feelings of being capable or not capable. His need for success in his endeavors at this stage is crucial. He labors over each of his accomplishments. He is slow and methodical and takes forever to do each task. Needing feedback to know if he has been successful, he strives for recognition of these achievements. ("Watch me, Mommy! Watch me, Mommy!") That he has something to offer nurtures his sense of competence and proves his value.

Parents are the name of the game for the five-year-old. At this age, the mother is the center of the child's world. He not only wants to please her, but he also wants to be near her, wants to talk with her, wants to play with her, and wants to help her around the house. The five-year-old's adoration of his parents is unquestionably heartwarming. The result is almost totally parent-pleasing behavior. In his determination to do everything just right, he'll ask permission for the simplest thing, even when he needn't; and he will then beam with pleasure when the parent smiles and gives permission.

Age six can be described as the stage of "me-ness." Self-centeredness comes before other-centeredness. While children were in the preschool stage, they discovered that they were separate from their parents, although they still kept their parents as the center of their existence. At six, they must shift the focus from their parents to themselves. They now place themselves at the center of their world instead of parents or others. Although they may appear to be excessively self-centered and unconcerned with the needs and feelings of others, this is an important milestone in their development. They are now ready to undertake the task of being receptive to their own interests and attempting to understand them.

At age 16, it is not uncommon for a child to experience feelings of being confused, embarrassed, guilty, awkward, inferior, ugly, and scared, all in the same day. In fact, a teenager can swing from being childish and petulant to being sedate, or from acting rational to irrational, all in the same hour. It's a time of confusion and uncertainty. The goal is to experience intimacy; he needs to belong. This is a time of duality. The 16-year-old wants to be with others, yet he wants to be alone; he needs his friends, but he will sabotage them if they appear to outdo him; he'll root for a friend out loud, but he'll secretly wish for his friend's failure. Age 16 is a time when he wants total independence, but he is not capable of it. He doesn't really want to live without his parents, although he believes that they are roadblocks hindering his life.

The final stage of development in childhood is establishing total independence. In changing from being dependent on others to being self-dependent, children confront some pretty big (and frightening) issues. They have three tasks. Their first task is to determine vocation. A child needs to ask what he is going to do with his life. Underlying this task is the self-esteem need to be somebody, to experience positive feelings of strength, power, and competence. Second, he needs to establish values. The goal is to sort out his own values and to decide which ones to keep and which ones to discard. Following this step is the only way that he can develop integrity. Perhaps most striking is his need to establish a workable and meaningful philosophy of life. Reevaluating his moral concepts will mean searching for his own personal beliefs, complete with facing religious, ethical, and value-laden ideologies. Developing personal convictions will be influenced by his level of self-esteem, especially if a conflict exists among what he believes, what his family believes, and what his friends find acceptable. Third, he needs to establish self-reliance.

Go on to next page

21. The author's primary purpose in writing this passage is

A. to show the importance of early childhood learning, which provides the foundation for life.
B. to analyze the causes behind low self-esteem in children.
C. to denounce child psychologists.
D. to discuss the various behaviors associated with the ages of children.

22. According to the author, the ultimate goal of children is

F. recognition.
G. selfhood.
H. praise.
J. competence.

23. The author uses the comment "Watch me, Mommy! Watch me, Mommy!" to make the point that three-year-olds

A. recognize they are individuals, separate from their parents.
B. do tasks in order to please their parents.
C. need outside acknowledgment of their accomplishments at a specific age of development.
D. are prone to repeating themselves.

24. Which of the following is another way of stating "Parents are the name of the game" (line 29)?

F. Parents design games and activities to entertain and stimulate their children.
G. The names parents give their children determine their sense of self-worth.
H. Parental gamesmanship influences children's development.
J. Parents are of prime importance to their children.

25. You may infer from paragraph five that the author considers a lack of sensitivity in six-year-olds

A. abnormal and rare.
B. unacceptable in adults, but cute in small children.
C. precocious; such egotism doesn't usually begin until the teenage years.
D. vital in order for children to recognize their separateness from their parents.

26. Which of the following phrases from paragraph six best expresses the idea of the paragraph?

F. "The goal is to experience intimacy."
G. "This is a time of duality."
H. "Age 16 is a time when he wants total independence."
J. "He believes that [his parents] are roadblocks hindering his life."

27. As used in line 79, *vocation* means

A. rest and relaxation.
B. geographical area.
C. romance.
D. career.

28. Which of the following does the author *not* mention as a factor in the development of convictions?

I. educational level
II. age group
III. self-esteem

F. I only
G. II only
H. II and III only
J. I, II, and III

29. Which of the following best describes the organization of the passage?

A. from most-important to least-important concepts
B. from theories to proven facts
C. chronological
D. from beliefs to predictions

30. You may infer that all stages of childhood have as their ultimate goal

F. fiscal security.
G. recognition.
H. independence.
J. parental respect.

Go on to next page

Passage 4

Humanities

The months are familiar to everyone. Nearly any small child can rattle off the twelve months of the year. When students learn foreign languages, one of the first exercises they practice is saying the names of the months. Despite all that familiarity, however, one important piece of knowledge is still missing: an explanation of how and why the names of the months came into existence. Who decided on the names? Were the months named after people? Did the months always have the same names throughout history? The story of the months is a fascinating one and deserves more attention.

Every month's name tells a story. January is named after Janus, a Roman god who was depicted as having two faces, one looking forward and one looking back. *Janus* is the Latin term for an arch or gate (*janua* is door). The god Janus needed both of his faces. As the guardian of doors or gateways, he had to be vigilant for friends and foes coming from either direction. Of course, January is the first month of the year, but it wasn't always so. Until around 150 B.C., January was the eleventh month of the year.

February is one of the few months not named after a person. February is a form of *februare,* which was the Latin word for "to purify." This month's name came from the February 15 feast of purification. On that feast day, people attempted to atone for their sins and, by so doing, hoped to appease the gods sufficiently to ensure healthy children and abundant crops in the next year.

March is named for Mars, whom many people have read about as the god of war. Few people realize that originally Mars was the god of springtime and new blossoms. Warriors would "take the winter off" from fighting, resting while the weather was too bad for battle. In the spring — around what we now think of as March — battles would resume. From this time line, Mars soon became more well-known as the god of war than of springtime.

Not every month's name has a definitive provenance. Scholars debate the origins of the name of April. Some writers and researchers claim that the word is from the Latin term *aperire,* meaning to open. The buds of new plants opened at this time of year. Other scholars believe the name April is perhaps the namesake of the Greek goddess Aphrodite (abbreviated to Aphro). Aphrodite and Ares — whose Latin name was Mars — were a couple. Romantics prefer to think that as April follows March, Venus/Aphrodite followed Mars.

May is also named after a goddess, Maika. She was the goddess of plants. Because plants often blossom in May, naming the month after the goddess has an indisputable logic. Not much else is known about Maika.

Not every month retained its original name over the years. For example, July and August weren't always known by those names. The original name for July was Quintilis, "fifth month." (Previously, the Latin calendar began with what is now March. Therefore, the month of July was originally the fifth month: March, April, May, June, July.) August was previously called Sextilis, "sixth month." Likewise, September, October, November, and December were the seventh, eighth, ninth, and tenth months. (The roots *sept, oct, nov,* and *dec* are common in many other words we use today. A septuagenarian is a person in his seventies; an octogenarian is a person in his eighties, and so on.) How did July and August get their new names? When Julius Caesar was assassinated, Mark Anthony ordered the Roman senate to rename the fifth month, when Caesar was born, after him. Quintilis became Julius, or July. Almost forty years later, Julius Caesar's relative, Augustus Caesar, had August named after him. Augustus was born in September but chose to give August his name because that was the month in which he had made several of his most important conquests.

The number of days in the months has changed throughout the years as well. It was a Roman superstition that even numbers were unlucky. Therefore, all months in the Roman calendar had an odd number of days, usually 31 or 29. Even the number of days in the year has changed. In order to bring the Roman calendar back into sync with the solar year, one memorable year, 46 B.C., actually contained 445 days! The calendar of 365 days officially began on January 1, 45 B.C. Even that, however, was not sufficient to make the year balanced and equivalent with nature. To remedy the discrepancy, in 1582, Pope Gregory XIII stated that the day after October 4 should be October 15!

Of course, not every year has exactly 365 days. Some, known as leap years, have 366 days. A trivia question that many people believe they can answer is, "When do leap years occur?" Most people answer, "Every four years." They gloss over one very important fact, however. Not every fourth year is a leap year. The century years — 1600, 1700, 1800, 1900, and 2000 — are not leap years unless they are evenly divisible by 400. For example, 1600 and 2000 are leap years, but 1700, 1800, and 1900 are not.

Go on to next page

31. As it is used in line 2, "rattle off" most nearly means
   A. shake until it drops off.
   B. recite quickly.
   C. eliminate.
   D. upset.

32. The main purpose of the passage is
   F. to explain how the months got their names.
   G. to show why there are twelve, not just ten, months.
   H. to explain the role of superstition in the naming of the months.
   J. to suggest new, alternate names for the months.

33. The passage states that Janus needed both of his faces for which of the following reasons?
   A. He was the caretaker of warriors in battle.
   B. He was the god of the beginning of the year.
   C. He had to look in both directions as the god of doors and gateways.
   D. He had more days in his month than in the other months.

34. According to the passage, which of the following months was named for a feast?
   F. February
   G. March
   H. April
   J. May

35. With which of the following statements would the author most likely agree?
   A. Many people have misconceptions about the origin of the name of March.
   B. Many people believe that all the months are named after gods and goddesses.
   C. Scholars agree on the origins of the names of the months.
   D. The number of days in any month is determined by its lunar cycle.

36. As it is used in line 88, the expression "into sync" most nearly means
   F. within the receptacle
   G. in line
   H. politically correct
   J. into the future

37. The passage discusses all of the following EXCEPT
   A. how July and August got their names
   B. why July changed its name
   C. how the calendar is balanced with the natural cycle
   D. why Romans considered even numbers unlucky

38. Which of the following is the main idea of the seventh paragraph?
   F. Roman emperors had the power to change the calendar.
   G. The Roman calendar was different from the calendar we have today.
   H. Extra months were necessary to make the Roman calendar consistent with the calendars of the rest of the world.
   J. The names of the months of the Roman calendar have changed over time.

39. The author of the passage states which of the following about leap years?
   I. They are every fourth year.
   II. No century year is a leap year.
   III. Century years are leap years if they are also millennium years.
   A. None
   B. I only
   C. II and III only
   D. I, II, and III

40. In line 100, the author uses the phrase "gloss over" to mean
   F. polish
   G. finish
   H. ignore
   J. shine

STOP

END OF TEST 3

DO NOT TURN THE PAGE UNTIL TOLD TO DO SO.
DO NOT RETURN TO A PREVIOUS TEST.

Science Reasoning Test

35 Minutes — 40 Questions

DIRECTIONS: Following are seven passages and then questions that refer to each passage. Choose the best answer to each question and blacken in the corresponding oval on your answer grid.

Passage 1

In the pole vault, the pole acts to convert the energy generated by an athlete running down a runway into a force that lifts the athlete over a crossbar. The most advanced vaulters use stiff poles that quickly convert the horizontal energy into the lifting force. Beginning vaulters are not strong, fast, or skillful enough to bend a stiff pole as needed to generate substantial vertical lift. Beginning vaulters must use more flexible poles.

To test the suitability of two materials for use in poles, scientists subjected three miniature poles to two laboratory tests. Pole No. 1, made of fiberglass, is 50 cm long, with a diameter of 1 cm and a mass of 1 kg. Pole No. 2, also made of fiberglass, is also 50 cm long but has a diameter of 1.5 cm and a mass of 2.25 kg. Pole No. 3, made of carbon fiber, is 50 cm long, 1.5 cm in diameter, and has a mass of 1 kg.

Study 1

Scientists tested the three poles to determine how much force is required to bend the poles to an 85-degree angle. Table 1 shows the results.

Table 1 Results of Bent-Pole Test

Pole	*Force in Newtons (N)*
1	4.9
2	5.8
3	6.3

Study 2

Scientists bent each pole to an 85-degree angle and then allowed the pole to snap back to a straight position. Table 2 shows the time required for each pole to snap back.

Table 2 Results of Snap-Back Test

Pole	*Time in Milliseconds (msec)*
1	733
2	626
3	591

1. According to the results, what is the relationship between the force required to bend a pole and the time needed for the pole to snap back to its regular position?

A. The greater the force required to bend the pole, the more time required for the pole to snap back.
B. The greater the force required to bend the pole, the less time required for the pole to snap back.
C. For only the fiberglass poles, the greater the force required to bend the pole, the more time required for the pole to snap back.
D. For only the fiberglass poles, the greater the force required to bend the pole, the less time required for the pole to snap back.

2. On the basis of Study 1, what is the relationship between pole mass and stiffness?

F. The greater the mass, the stiffer the pole.
G. For a fiberglass pole, the greater the mass, the stiffer the pole.
H. The less the mass, the stiffer the pole.
J. Mass and stiffness have no relationship.

3. Which of the following is a controlled variable in this study?

A. pole diameter
B. force required to bend poles
C. time for poles to return to vertical
D. force generated when poles return to vertical

Go on to next page

4. Kinetic energy results from the actual motion of an object, while potential energy is a measure of the energy that results if an object moves from a certain location. During a pole vault, at which times is virtually all the energy in the form of potential energy?

   F. when the vaulter is running down the runway
   G. when the pole is bent
   H. as the pole unbends and sends the vaulter upward
   J. as the vaulter falls into the pit

5. Ideally, vaulters like to use long poles because the poles reach closer to the crossbar. If a pole is too long, though, a vaulter has difficulty carrying it down the runway because of its mass. Given these considerations, which material is best suited for a very long pole?

   A. Fiberglass, because it snaps back relatively slowly.
   B. Fiberglass, because it has a relatively high mass-to-volume ratio.
   C. Carbon fiber, because it's hard to bend.
   D. Carbon fiber, because it has a relatively low mass-to-volume ratio.

6. On the basis of the entire study, which poles, if they were proportionately enlarged for use by a vaulter, are most appropriate for a beginning and experienced vaulter, respectively?

   F. Pole No. 1, Pole No. 2
   G. Pole No. 1, Pole No. 3
   H. Pole No. 1, either Pole No. 2 or Pole No. 3
   J. Pole No. 2, Pole No. 3

Passage 2

Very few humans live to the age of 100. Another way of saying this is that almost all members of the human population who were born in a given year will die within 100 years. Scientists, health professionals, and life insurance agents are interested in examining how many people in a population will live to be a certain age. One way to measure this information is to look at how much of the population has died after a certain number of years. This information is presented in Figure 1.

7. According to Figure 1, approximately what percentage of the human population lives to at least 80 years of age?

   A. 10 percent
   B. 40 percent
   C. 60 percent
   D. 80 percent

8. The increase in percentage of deaths is highest for which of the following intervals?

   F. 0 to 20 years
   G. 20 to 40 years
   H. 40 to 60 years
   J. 60 to 80 years

9. Suppose infant mortality (children dying at birth or very shortly thereafter) is eliminated. How will the graph change?

   A. The quick rise that is seen just after 0 years will disappear.
   B. The graph will be higher at 20 years.
   C. The graph will be less steep between 60 and 80 years.
   D. The graph will rise until past 120 years.

10. According to the graph, by what age do the largest number of people die?

   F. 25 years
   G. 45 years
   H. 75 years
   J. 95 years

11. For a person born the same year this population started, what is the maximum number of years he could live and still observe an 80 percent chance of still being alive?

   A. 15 years
   B. 35 years
   C. 55 years
   D. 80 years

Go on to next page

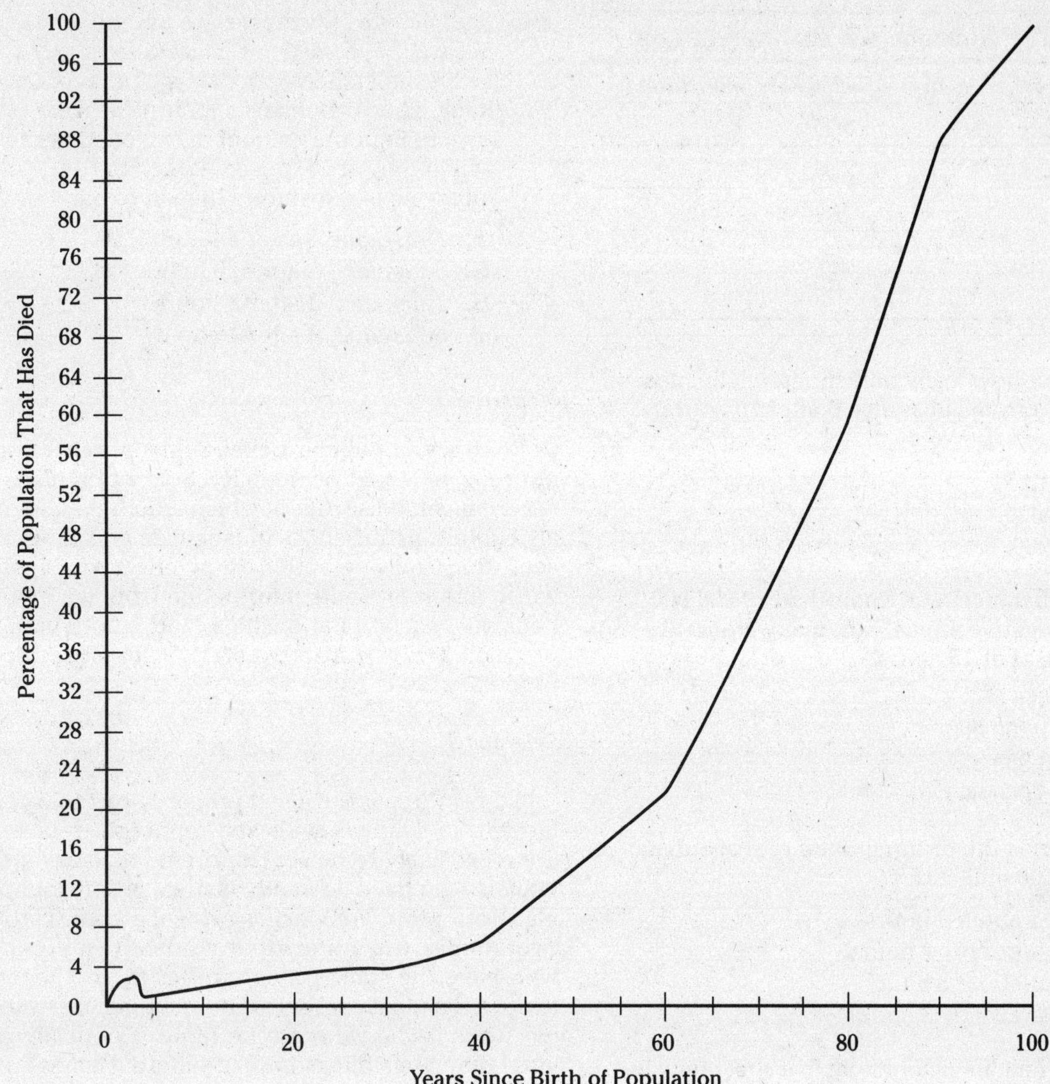

Figure 1: Human deaths as a function of time.

Passage 3

A radioactive substance is one that contains atoms whose nuclei change into other types of atomic nuclei. For example, a uranium nucleus can lose two protons and two neutrons and become a thorium nucleus. Atoms of some radioactive substances change more frequently than others. Over time, the rate of change for any substance slows as a greater percentage of atomic nuclei change to a final, more stable state.

Devices can measure the number of atomic changes that take place at a given time. Each of these changes is commonly called a disintegration. Table 1 and Table 2 show the disintegration rates for two unknown substances.

Table 1 Substance A Disintegrations

Time (hours)	*Disintegration Rate (millicuries)*
0	200
5	100
10	50
15	25
20	12.5

Go on to next page

Table 2 Substance B Disintegrations

Time (hours)	*Disintegration Rate (millicuries)*
0	2000
4	1000
8	500
12	250
16	125

12. About how many millicuries will be measured from Substance B after 20 hours?

F. 0
G. 12.5
H. 62.5
J. 200

13. If Substance A originally had 10,000,000 radioactive atoms, how many atoms are present at 15 hours?

A. 666,667
B. 1,250,000
C. 3,333,333
D. 5,000,000

14. When is the disintegration rate of Substance B 1,500 millicuries?

F. at about 2 hours
G. at exactly 2 hours
H. at about 3 hours
J. at exactly 3 hours

15. The half-life of a radioactive substance is the time it takes for half of the radioactive atoms to disintegrate. Which substance has a shorter half-life?

A. Substance A, because only 50 millicuries are present after 10 hours
B. Substance A, because it will all be gone after 25 hours
C. Substance B, because the disintegration rate fell to half its original value in only 4 hours, instead of 5 hours
D. Substance B, because it was measured for only 16 hours instead of 20

16. Radioactive substances are potential health hazards. The particles emitted from radioactive substances can damage parts of the human body. Humans should take great care to limit the amount of radioactivity to which they are exposed. Which of the following is safest for a human to handle?

F. Substance A after 5 hours
G. Substance A after 20 hours
H. Substance B after 8 hours
J. Substance B after 16 hours

Passage 4

Contrary to popular belief, schizophrenia does not refer to a split personality. Schizophrenia is a severe mental disorder in which afflicted individuals exhibit disturbances in language and thought, sensation and perception (how one takes in the world and represents information from it), motor behavior, social relationships, and emotional expression. Two scientists debate the causes of schizophrenia.

Scientist 1

Schizophrenia is caused primarily by biological factors. Individuals with schizophrenic relatives are more likely to be schizophrenic than are individuals who have no family history of schizophrenia. Even more convincing evidence comes from twin studies, which show that identical twins (twins who have the same genes) are far more likely to share a diagnosis of schizophrenia than are fraternal twins (twins who are no more genetically related than are siblings born at different times).

Furthermore, adopted children who have at least one schizophrenic biological parent have a higher incidence of schizophrenia than do adopted children whose biological parents are not schizophrenic. In all cases, the adopted children were removed from their biological parents at a very young age, long before the parents could transmit schizophrenia through any child-rearing practices.

Scientist 2

Environmental, rather than biological, factors are responsible for schizophrenia. The high occurrence of schizophrenia seen in some families can be explained by noting that child-rearing techniques are similar throughout an extended family. Several studies show that as they develop, identical twins share more experiences than do fraternal twins. In

Go on to next page

other words, when compared to fraternal twins, identical twins are more likely to be influenced by the same environmental conditions.

The adoption studies do not provide convincing evidence for a biological cause. First of all, the majority of children with schizophrenic biological parents did not develop schizophrenia, showing that the way children are brought up is key. Furthermore, some of the children were not removed from their biological parents until one month, which is enough time for parents to influence a behavior such as schizophrenia. In addition, some of the adoptive parents knew of a family history of schizophrenia and may have, by trying to compensate for what they perceived as a predisposing factor, caused their adopted children to develop schizophrenia.

17. Which of the following could Scientist 1 use as evidence against Scientist 2's explanation that environmental similarities, rather than genetic similarities, account for the data found with relatives and identical twins?

- **A.** Siblings born at different times are less likely to share a diagnosis of schizophrenia than are fraternal twins.
- **B.** Siblings born at different times are less likely to share a diagnosis of schizophrenia than are identical twins.
- **C.** Identical twins reared in separate households are just as likely to share a diagnosis of schizophrenia as are identical twins raised together.
- **D.** Most families have no schizophrenic individuals.

18. What would Scientist 2 say will occur when a child with no family history of schizophrenia is placed in a foster home with schizophrenic foster parents and foster siblings?

- **F.** The child will definitely develop normally.
- **G.** The child will probably develop normally.
- **H.** The child is at high risk for developing schizophrenia.
- **J.** The child will definitely become schizophrenic.

19. Both scientists assume that

- **A.** most people are schizophrenic.
- **B.** most people are not schizophrenic.
- **C.** the studies cited in the passage are accurate.
- **D.** mental disorders in general run in families.

20. Studies have shown that excessive amounts of dopamine, a chemical that is found in the brain, are associated with schizophrenia. How would Scientist 1 probably respond to these studies?

- **F.** These studies disprove my claim because it is unclear how brain chemicals are inherited.
- **G.** These studies are irrelevant because it must be shown that dopamine causes schizophrenia.
- **H.** These studies support my claim because the environment causes changes in brain chemicals.
- **J.** These studies support my claim because brain chemistry is a biological factor.

21. Parents of schizophrenics typically act differently than do parents of non-schizophrenics. Does this definitively establish that environmental factors are responsible for schizophrenia?

- **A.** No, because parents of schizophrenics may act differently as a response to their child behaving abnormally.
- **B.** No, because child-rearing behavior is inherited.
- **C.** Yes, because children pick up on everything their parents do.
- **D.** Yes, because children must protect themselves from such parenting techniques by acting in a schizophrenic manner.

22. The majority of children born to and raised by at least one schizophrenic do not develop schizophrenia. This evidence casts the most doubt on the claim of which scientist?

- **F.** Scientist 1, because schizophrenia is a recessive trait, one that requires two genes to be expressed.
- **G.** Scientist 1, who claimed that inherited factors are sufficient to cause schizophrenia.
- **H.** Scientist 2, who would point out that these children were raised normally.
- **J.** Scientist 2, because the evidence weakens her conclusion about the majority of adopted children with schizophrenic biological parents.

Go on to next page

23. How would Scientist 1 respond to the fact that the majority of adopted children who had schizophrenic biological parents developed normally?

A. The environment is more important than genetics.
B. The children were given corrective medications at an early age.
C. The children underwent extensive psychotherapy.
D. Genetics is a necessary, but not sufficient, cause of schizophrenia.

Passage 5

Angiosperms, or flowering plants, typically produce flowers seasonally. The various angiosperm species produce their flowers at different times of the year. For example, some flowers bloom in early spring, while others bloom in the summer. Research has shown that these flowering plants respond to changes in day length. A cocklebur, for example, does not produce flowers during the time of year that has days longer than 15.5 hours. When the length of day drops below this figure, flowering occurs. This type of flower is known as a short-day (SD) plant. Long-day (LD) plants do the opposite. These plants do not flower until the length of day exceeds a certain critical value. Plants that do not respond to changes in day length are called day-neutral (DN) plants. The following experiments investigate what aspect of changing day length is responsible for the plants' responses.

Experiment 1

Botanists raise both SD and LD plants in a greenhouse under long-day conditions. As expected, SD plants do not flower, and the LD plants do flower. When a brief period of darkness interrupts a long day, the plants continue to flower.

Experiment 2

Scientists raise both SD and LD plants in a greenhouse under short-day conditions. The SD plants do flower, and the LD plants do not flower. When a brief flash of light interrupts the long night, the SD plants stop flowering, and the LD plants began to flower.

Experiment 3

Experimenters perform a yearlong study in which they raise both SD and LD plants in several greenhouses. The light/dark cycle corresponds to the day length changes that occur over the course of a year. Daytime temperatures differ in each greenhouse. All SD plants flower at the same time of year. As expected, all LD plants flower at a different time than the SD plants do, but the LD plants all flower at the same time when compared to one another.

Experiment 4

Conditions are identical to those of Experiment 3, except that daytime temperatures are the same across greenhouses, while nighttime temperatures vary. SD and LD plants still flower at different times of the year, but the plants vary considerably as far as when each plant begins to flower. For example, SD plants in greenhouses with warmer nighttime temperatures flower at a different time than do SD plants in cooler greenhouses.

24. On the basis of Experiments 1 and 2, which of the following is the most critical factor in determining whether SD and LD plants will flower?

F. the total number of daytime hours
G. the total number of nighttime hours
H. the number of uninterrupted daytime hours
J. the number of uninterrupted nighttime hours

25. Cocklebur, an SD plant, and spinach, an LD plant, are both raised on an 8-hour day, 16-hour night cycle. If a brief flash of light is presented in the middle of the 16-hour night, what is the most likely result?

A. Neither plant will flower.
B. Cocklebur will flower; spinach will not.
C. Spinach will flower; cocklebur will not.
D. Both plants will flower.

26. Which of the following variables is not directly controlled by the experimenters?

F. type of plant
G. flowering
H. amount of light
J. temperature

27. Are the results of Experiments 3 and 4 consistent with the results of Experiments 1 and 2?

A. No, because Experiments 3 and 4 use a wider variety of plants.
B. No, because the temperature is not changed in Experiments 1 and 2.
C. Yes, because both sets of experiments suggest that the plants respond to a night factor rather than a day factor.
D. Yes, because both SD and LD plants are used in all the experiments.

Go on to next page

28. Which of the following best represents the shape of a graph plotting flowering activity as a function of day length for an LD plant that starts to flower when day length exceeds 15 hours?

F.

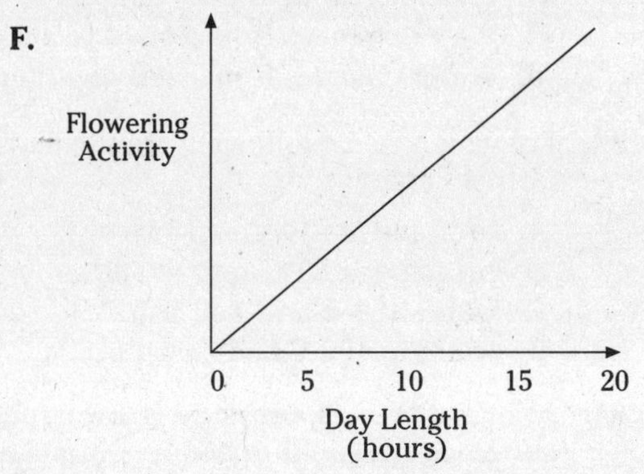

G.

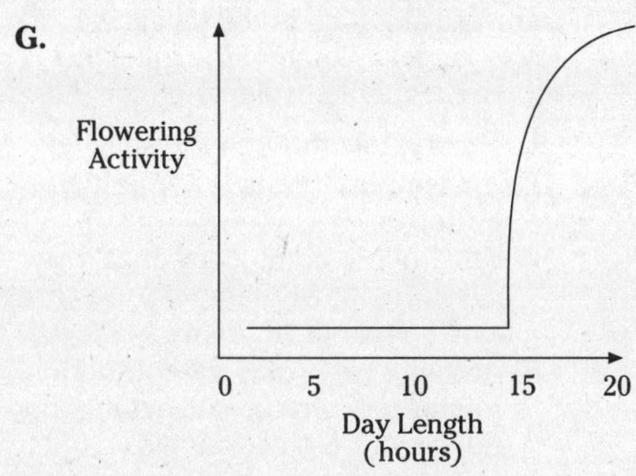

H.

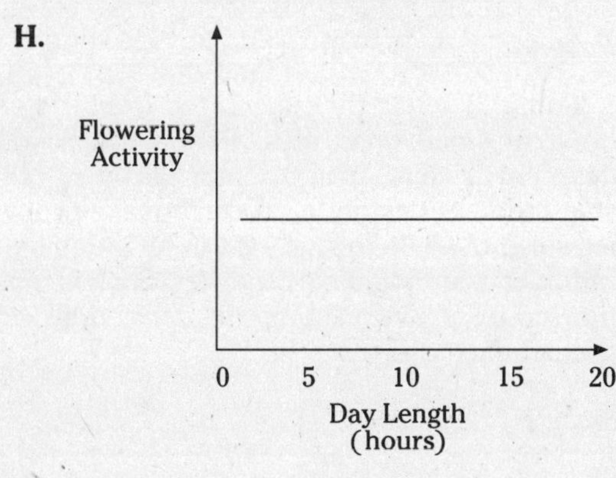

J.

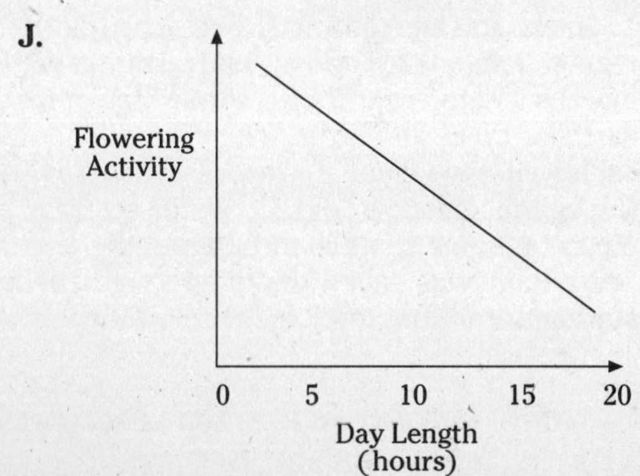

29. Near the equator, day length varies little throughout the year. That is, days and nights are close to 12 hours each during every season. Which of the following plants would most likely flower (assuming proper soil, water, and other essential conditions) if grown near the equator?

I. an LD plant that flowers only when the day length exceeds 12 hours
II. an SD plant that flowers only when the day length falls below 12 hours
III. an SD plant that flowers only when day length falls below 8 hours
IV. a DN plant

A. IV only
B. I, II, and III
C. I, II, and IV only
D. I, II, III, and IV

Passage 6

Matter exists in three phases: solid, liquid, and gas. In general, these phases are defined by how far apart the particles in the substance are. Particles are typically closest together in a solid and farthest away from one another in a gas.

Temperature is clearly related to phases. When temperature rises, particles move faster and away from one another. As temperature increases, matter changes from a solid to a liquid to a gas.

Pressure also affects phases of matter. A substance that is a gas at a certain temperature and low pressure may become a liquid at the same temperature if pressure is increased.

Go on to next page

The following figures summarize the relationship among temperature, pressure, and phase for both bromine and water:

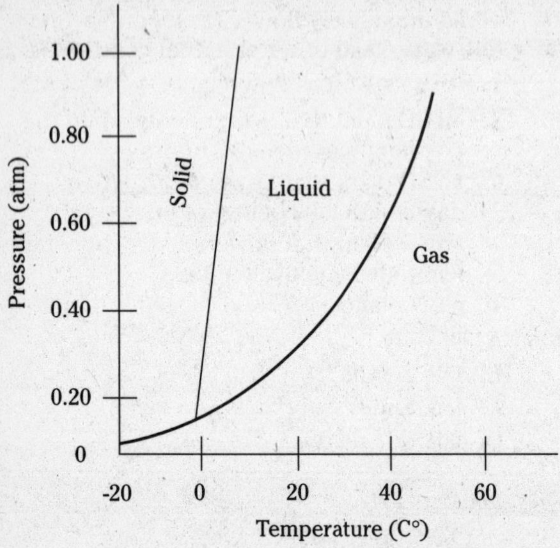

Figure 1: Bromine phases.

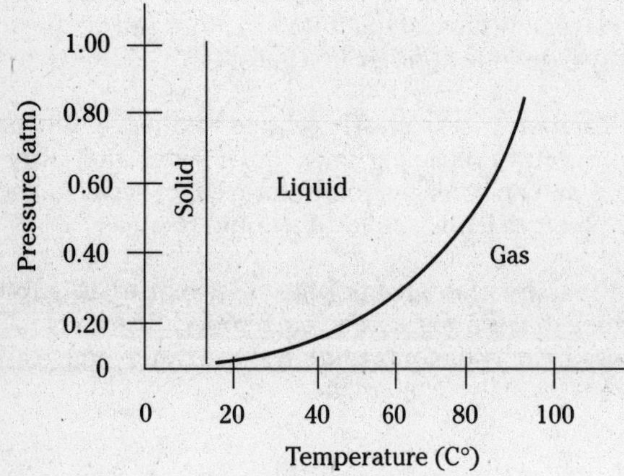

Figure 2: Water phases.

30. At 60°C and 1.00 atm, water is

F. a solid.
G. a liquid.
H. a gas.
J. melting (changing from a solid to a liquid).

31. Sublimation occurs when a solid changes to a gas without going through a liquid phase. Under which of the following conditions can sublimation occur?

A. bromine at –20°C and 0.05 atm
B. bromine at 0°C and 0.80 atm
C. water at 0°C and 0.80 atm
D. water at 80°C and 0.50 atm

32. At 30°C, as pressure is decreased from 0.6 atm to 0.3 atm, which of the following is true?

F. Bromine changes from a gas to a liquid.
G. Bromine changes from a liquid to a gas.
H. Water changes from a solid to a liquid.
J. Water changes from a gas to a liquid.

33. For which of the following are the particles farthest apart?

A. bromine at –10°C and 1.00 atm
B. bromine at 50°C and 0.80 atm
C. water at 0°C and 0.40 atm
D. water at 100°C and 0.60 atm

34. At high altitudes, pressure is lower, and softening spaghetti in boiling water (temperature at which liquid changes to a gas) takes longer. Which of the following is the most reasonable explanation for this effect?

F. Ice crystals form on the spaghetti.
G. Air temperature is lower at high altitudes.
H. The boiling point is lower at lower pressure. Lower temperatures are not as effective in softening spaghetti.
J. At lower pressure, water boils at a higher temperature. Reaching this temperature takes longer.

Passage 7

Radon is a gas that is emitted from the earth's crust in small quantities. Radon can readily be detected in wells. An accidental discovery of excessive radon emission in an earthquake-prone area led seismologists to study the association between radon emission and earthquakes. Such an association could prove valuable in perfecting ways to predict earthquakes.

Study 1

Scientists selected four sites that had experienced recent earthquakes and measured radon emissions in wells located near the epicenter (the point on the earth's surface above the focus of an earthquake). At each well, the scientists recorded the percent that the radon emission exceeded the average radon emission found in wells throughout the world. This percentage was called the differential. These measurements are depicted in Figures 1 through 4.

Go on to next page

Figure 1

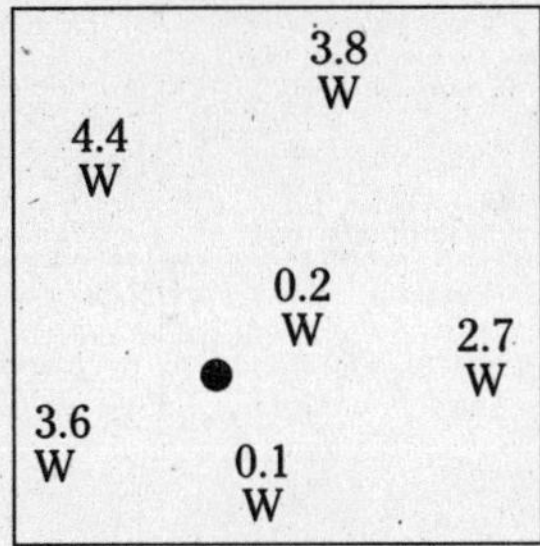

China
Magnitude - 7.9
Average Differential - 2.5

Figure 2

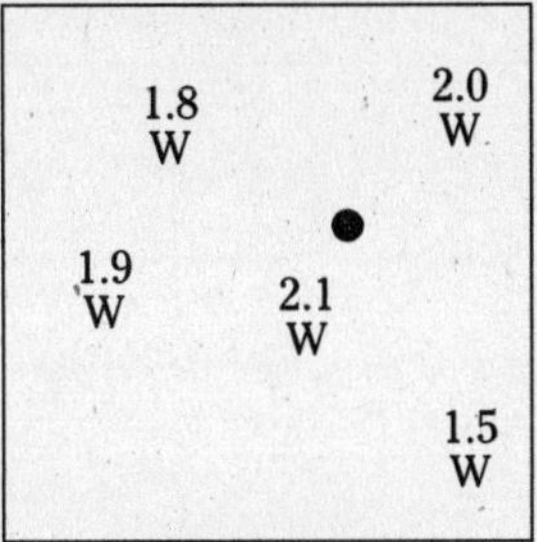

Iran
Magnitude - 6.9
Average Differential - 1.9

Figure 3

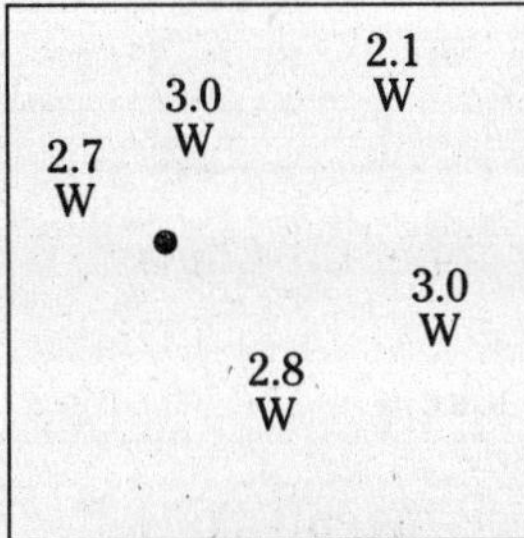

California, USA
Magnitude - 7.2
Average Differential - 2.7

Figure 4

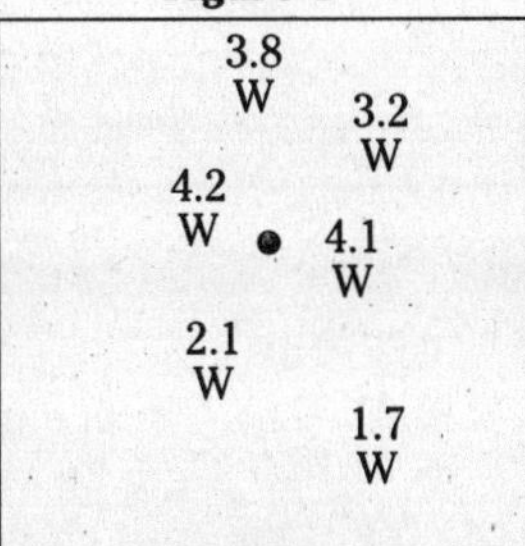

Chile
Magnitude - 7.5
Average Differential - 3.2

Legend for all figures

● - epicenter

Number - percent that radon emission is greater than normal (differential)

W - well

Scale: 1 cm = 100 km

Study 2

To study whether the differential varied with the magnitude of an earthquake, seismologists made a scatter plot of the average differential against earthquake magnitude for each site. Figure 5 (see next page) shows this scatter plot.

35. Which of the following is the most reasonable conclusion that can be drawn from Study 1?

A. No association is present between earthquakes and increased radon emissions.
B. Some evidence suggests an association between earthquakes and increased radon emissions.
C. Radon emissions of wells more than 1,000 km from the epicenter did not increase.
D. The radon emission right at the epicenter is more than 5 percent greater than normal levels for the entire earth.

36. Which of the following would strengthen the claim that increased radon emissions are associated with earthquakes?

I. more well sites in the vicinity of each epicenter showing higher than normal radon emissions
II. a location that had a 7.9 magnitude quake and an average emission differential of 3.6
III. more earthquakes at the epicenters depicted in Figures 1 through 4

F. II only
G. III only
H. I and II only
J. I and III only

37. Can it be determined from the results that radon emissions cause earthquakes?

A. No, because the results merely suggest that earthquakes and increased radon emissions occur at about the same time.
B. No, because the differentials would have to exceed 4 percent at all well sites to make such a condition.
C. Yes, because every well site had higher-than-normal radon emissions.
D. Yes, because the radon comes from beneath the earth's surface.

Go on to next page

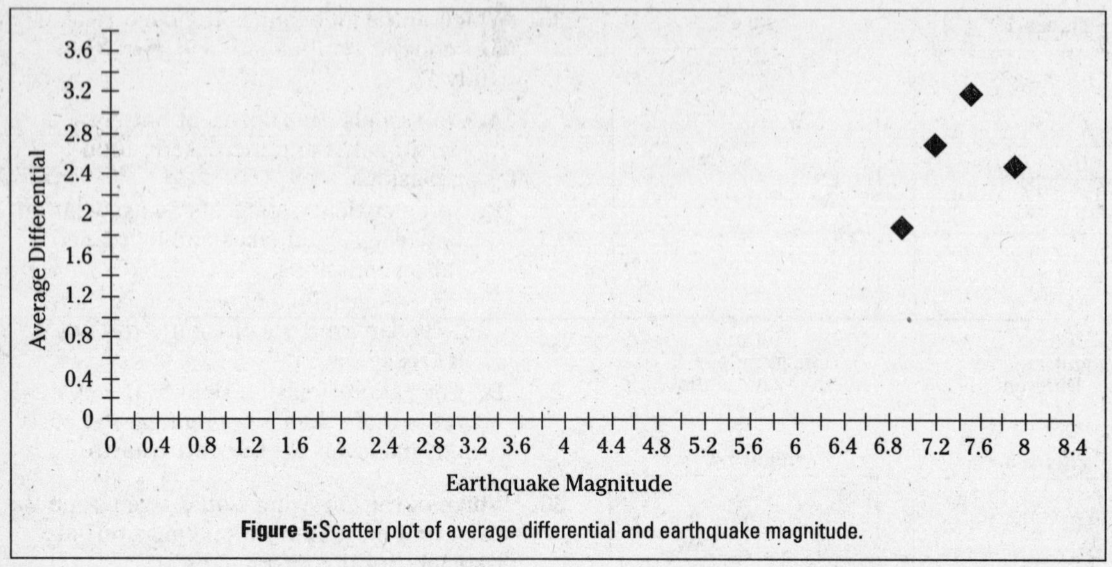

Figure 5: Scatter plot of average differential and earthquake magnitude.

38. Which of the following is an important control condition that is lacking in the studies?

F. radon emissions from a well very distant from the epicenter

G. radon emissions from sites that experienced earthquakes of magnitude greater than 8.0

H. radon emissions from sites that haven't had an earthquake in over 400 years

J. radon emissions from the Study 1 sites when no earthquake took place

39. What type of study needs to be done to help determine whether radon emissions can be used to predict earthquakes?

A. measuring radon emissions before an earthquake takes place

B. measuring radon emissions as an earthquake takes place

C. measuring radon emissions around epicenters for quakes weaker than 6.9

D. measuring radon emissions around epicenters for quakes stronger than 7.9

40. What is most puzzling about the China results?

F. The China earthquake was the strongest earthquake studied.

G. One well showed a differential of 4.4, higher than that of any other well in the studies.

H. The wells closest to the epicenter had lower differentials than those farther away.

J. Readings were taken from six wells.

STOP

END OF TEST 4

DO NOT TURN THE PAGE UNTIL TOLD TO DO SO.
DO NOT RETURN TO A PREVIOUS TEST.

Getting Down to the Nitty-Gritty: Subscores

Three of the tests of the ACT feature subscores as an added bonus (think of these as a "gift with purchase"). In 20-plus years of tutoring for the ACT (I started when I was a mere child, you see), I have had very few students care about the subscores. By the time you get through this book, you should know very well which sections are your best and which are your weakest. However, you'll see subscores on your score report, so a few words about them are necessary.

English Test

The English test has 40 questions in the Usage/Mechanics subscore area and 35 questions in the Rhetorical Skills subscore area — a total of 75 questions. (See Chapter 2 for more info on the types of questions on the English Test.) Because I wrote these practice exams to give you more practice with the types of questions that my experience shows students have the best chance of getting correct with practice, this breakdown is not really applicable to the practice exams in this book. Besides, students get headaches trying to understand the fine distinctions between what is rhetorical and what is not. Don't worry about it.

Mathematics Test

The actual ACT Mathematics Test usually has 24 prealgebra/elementary algebra problems, 18 intermediate algebra/coordinate geometry problems, and 18 plane geometry/trig problems — a total of 60 questions. Good news! The ACT has only four trig questions, so if you haven't had the subject yet, don't panic.

However, because this book is a *teaching* book and not the actual ACT (hey, you can get a free copy of an actual ACT just by walking into your guidance counselor's office and picking one up; you don't need that, but instruction on *how* to take the ACT), I'm not going to put you through the trauma of subscores. Besides, there are a lot of "gray" areas in which one person is convinced that a problem is elementary algebra, while another will argue that it is intermediate algebra or worse. Here's the simple solution: Be able to do all the problems (easy for *me* to say!), and don't worry about typecasting and labeling them.

Reading Test

The Reading Test subscores couldn't possibly be any easier. You get a subscore for questions in social studies/sciences (20 questions, based on 2 passages) and arts/literature (20 questions, based on 2 passages).

Science Reasoning Test

The Science Reasoning test has no subscores.

Score One for Our Side: The Scoring Key

The ACT scoring may be weird (Why a 36? Why not a 21 or a 49 or a 73?), but it is very straightforward. Follow these simple directions to score your practice exam.

1. **Count the number of correct responses in each of the practice tests: English, Mathematics, Reading, and Science Reasoning. Do *not* subtract any points for questions you missed or questions you didn't answer. Your score is based only on the number of questions you answered correctly. That number is called your *raw score.***
2. **Locate your raw score on the following table. Move to the left or right and find the scaled score that corresponds to your raw score. (For example, a raw score of 50 on the English Test gives you a scaled score of 21.)**
3. **Add your four scaled scores. Divide that sum by 4. The resulting number is your *composite score.* (For example, if your scaled scores were 23, 31, 12, and 19, your composite score would be 85 ÷ 4 = 21.25, or 21.)**

	Raw Scores				
Scale Score	***English***	***Mathematics***	***Reading***	***Science Reasoning***	***Scale Score***
1	0-1	0	0	0	1
2	2	-	1	-	2
3	3	1	2	1	3
4	4-5	-	3	-	4
5	6-7	-	4	-	5
6	8-9	2	5	2	6
7	10-11	3	6	3	7
8	12-13	-	7	4	8
9	14-16	4	8	5	9
10	17-19	5	9	6	10
11	20-22	6-7	10	7	11
12	23-25	8	11-12	8-9	12
13	26-28	9-10	13	10	13
14	29-31	11-12	14	11-12	14
15	32-35	13-14	15	13-14	15
16	36-37	15-17	16	15	16
17	38-40	18-19	17	16-17	17
18	41-43	20-22	18-19	18-19	18
19	44-45	23-24	20	20-21	19
20	46-48	25-26	21	22	20
21	49-50	27-29	22	23-24	21
22	51-53	30-32	23	25	22
23	54-55	33-34	24	26-27	23
24	56-57	35-37	25	28	24
25	58-59	38-40	26-27	29	25
26	60-62	41-42	28	30	26
27	63-64	43-45	29	31	27
28	65-66	46-48	30	32	28
29	67	49-50	31	33	29
30	68-69	51-53	-	34	30
31	70	54-55	32	35	31
32	71-72	56	33	36	32
33	73	57	34	37	33
34	-	58	35	38	34
35	74	59	36	39	35
36	75	60	37-40	40	36

Answer Key

English Test

1. C	39. D
2. H	40. J
3. A	41. A
4. J	42. F
5. C	43. C
6. H	44. G
7. D	45. A
8. G	46. F
9. B	47. B
10. F	48. F
11. A	49. D
12. J	50. F
13. A	51. C
14. G	52. F
15. A	53. B
16. G	54. J
17. B	55. B
18. J	56. J
19. A	57. C
20. H	58. H
21. A	59. B
22. F	60. G
23. C	61. B
24. J	62. H
25. C	63. A
26. G	64. J
27. B	65. C
28. H	66. H
29. B	67. C
30. J	68. H
31. B	69. C
32. F	70. G
33. D	71. B
34. F	72. F
35. B	73. C
36. G	74. H
37. C	75. D
38. F	

Mathematics Test

1. D	31. B
2. G	32. G
3. D	33. D
4. F	34. K
5. B	35. C
6. J	36. K
7. D	37. D
8. K	38. K
9. C	39. D
10. G	40. J
11. D	41. D
12. K	42. H
13. A	43. C
14. J	44. H
15. D	45. B
16. H	46. H
17. D	47. A
18. H	48. H
19. E	49. A
20. G	50. J
21. D	51. D
22. G	52. F
23. D	53. C
24. G	54. F
25. B	55. E
26. H	56. F
27. E	57. D
28. J	58. F
29. D	59. D
30. G	60. K

Reading Test

1. A	21. D
2. H	22. G
3. A	23. C
4. F	24. J
5. D	25. D
6. F	26. G
7. A	27. D
8. J	28. F
9. B	29. C
10. G	30. H
11. B	31. B
12. G	32. F
13. A	33. C
14. G	34. F
15. C	35. A
16. H	36. G
17. B	37. D
18. G	38. J
19. D	39. A
20. F	40. H

Science Reasoning Test

1. B	21. A
2. G	22. J
3. A	23. D
4. G	24. J
5. D	25. C
6. G	26. G
7. B	27. C
8. J	28. G
9. A	29. C
10. H	30. G
11. C	31. A
12. H	32. G
13. B	33. D
14. F	34. H
15. C	35. B
16. G	36. H
17. C	37. A
18. H	38. J
19. C	39. A
20. J	40. H

Chapter 17

Practice Exam 2: Answers and Explanations

Now you've done it! You've completed the practice exam, checked your answers against the key, and found your score on the Raw Score chart.

Hang on! Invest another hour or so to go through this chapter, reading why one answer was correct and the others weren't. Along the way, you'll find tons of tips and traps — valuable information that you'll be able to use when you face the Big One.

English Test

Passage 1

1. **C.** Even though States is plural, the United States is one country, singular. Use the singular verb *was.* Choice D unnecessarily uses the dreaded word *being,* which is often found in trap, wrong answers.

2. **H.** The word *hardly* is negative, making *hardly no* a double negative.

Double negatives are wrong in English. (In some other languages, like Spanish, they are correct. If English is your second language, you may need to be especially careful to note this sort of error.)

Choice J adds commas that are not necessary. A good general rule is: "When in doubt, leave it out." Don't change the sentence any more than you absolutely need to in order to correct the error.

3. **A.** *Its* (with no apostrophe) is the possessive form of *it. It's* (with an apostrophe) means *it is.* In this sentence, *its* refers to each colony, requiring the possessive. ***Note:*** The Grammar Review has a good discussion of *its/it's* and other commonly confused word duos.

4. **J.** Although the word *being* is not wrong 100 percent of the time, it is used incorrectly so often that you should be paranoid and neurotic about it. In many instances, *being* is unnecessary and adds nothing to the sentence. Here, the more straightforward "first established" is much better than "being the first" or "was being the first." (If you missed this question, you probably forgot to go back and reread the sentence with your answer choice inserted. Just listening to how the question sounds can get you the correct answer many times.)

5. **C.** The past tense of forbid, *forbade,* requires the infinitive — *to print,* in this case. An *-ing* word is often used incorrectly on this exam and should be checked very suspiciously. If you chose A, chances are that you automatically corrected the error by reading the sentence the way you wanted it to be, rather than the way it really is.

6. **H.** Parallelism means that items in a series must be in parallel, or equal, form. In this instance, that means that the two verbs must be in the same form: to regulate and to supervise. Yes, choice G has the verbs in the same form, both *-ing* verbs, but choice H says the same thing in a more concise, straightforward manner. Often, *-ing* verbs indicate overly casual (okay, sloppy!) grammar.

7. **D.** This sentence is just filler. It doesn't add anything to the passage, and can easily be omitted.

As a private tutor, I've noticed that many students fall into the habit of choosing OMIT every single time they see it. Bad habit. In this instance, OMIT is correct; the next time, it may not be. Judge every case on its own merits.

8. **G.** The original sentence is a run-on, two sentences incorrectly joined. The "this" begins a complete second sentence. Eliminate it and make the second clause a subordinate clause, one that can't stand on its own. Choice J is a fragment, an incomplete sentence that goes nowhere. Choice H is tempting but changes the meaning of the sentence entirely.

9. **B.** The sentence requires the simple past tense, *fell.* Choice C has the correct verb but is unnecessarily wordy.

10. **F.** The sentence compares the drop in income of 1929 to the drop in income of 1933. The word *that* is required, to refer to the income. Choice G sounds as if it is comparing a drop in income to a year. Comparisons must be between equivalent concepts. Choice H goes overboard. Use either the *that* or the *'s* to show possession (the *'s* indicates "that of 1929"), but not both.

11. A. Even though this version of the sentence seems a little wordy, it is the best of a sorry lot. Choose A by the process of elimination. Choice B incorrectly uses *it's.* (*It's* with an apostrophe means *it is.* If you confuse *it's* and *its,* go back to the grammar review.) Choice C makes no sense when reinserted into the sentence.

If you chose D, you fell for a trap. You cannot correct the grammar only to change the meaning of the sentence! Be sure to invest a few minutes to reread the entire sentence with your new choice, to make sure that you haven't altered the concept of the sentence.

12. J. The original sounds as if the recovery program were obvious, clear to everyone. In the context of the passage, it's more likely that the author means not that the program itself was clear, but that the program was clearly needed. Choice H is wrong because the program itself cannot be needy (having needs).

13. A. The sentence is clear as written. Choice B has the "too" stuck on the end of the sentence like an afterthought, weakening the sentence. Choice C sounds awkward.

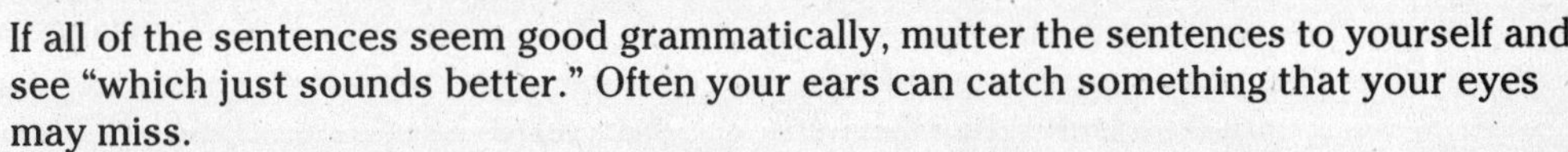

If all of the sentences seem good grammatically, mutter the sentences to yourself and see "which just sounds better." Often your ears can catch something that your eyes may miss.

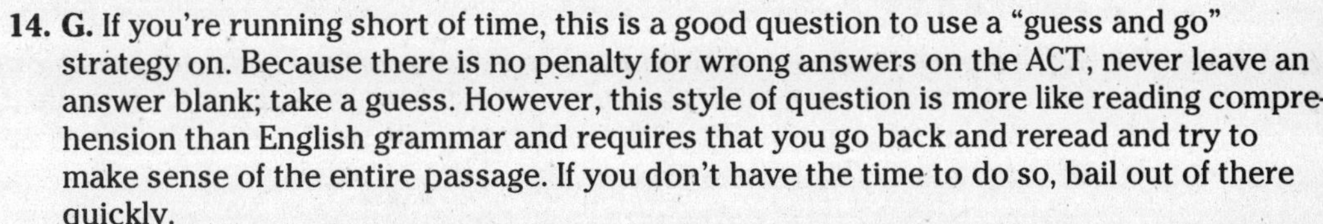

14. G. If you're running short of time, this is a good question to use a "guess and go" strategy on. Because there is no penalty for wrong answers on the ACT, never leave an answer blank; take a guess. However, this style of question is more like reading comprehension than English grammar and requires that you go back and reread and try to make sense of the entire passage. If you don't have the time to do so, bail out of there quickly.

If you decide to answer the question, first predict whether you need a Yes or a No answer. Does the answer fit? Here, it does because the previous sentence talks about supervising non-member banks. As quickly as that, you have narrowed the answers down to F or G. Now, answering is more a matter of subjective opinion (in other words, I would consider this an "acceptable" miss. The answer is based not on definitive grammar rules, but on Your Opinion versus Their Opinion.) The question does give background information that is important and relevant, giving G a slight edge over choice F.

15. A. This would be a *grrrrreat* question to guess at quickly. (Never leave an answer blank because the ACT, unlike the SAT, does not penalize you points for a wrong answer.) To answer this question, you really need to go back and reread the entire passage, as if it were a Reading Comprehension passage, not an English passage. Who has time for that? If you're rushed for time (and nearly everyone is in this section), just make a quick guess.

Use your common sense. Eliminate choice B because paragraph 2 does discuss the history of banking (the whole passage discusses that topic). Eliminate choice C, which is the kinda-sorta-almost-funny answer. You don't delete a paragraph because it "depresses the readers." And choice D is illogical: There was no "underlying question" in the passage.

Passage 2

16. G. This question primarily tests *who* versus *whom. Who* is a subject and does the action of the sentence. In this case, *who* is doing the governing. *Whom* is an object and receives the action. For example, you may say, "Whom do they govern?" In that case, the *whom* would be the ones being governed or receiving the action of the governing.

Again, if you confuse *who* and *whom,* substitute *him,* with an *m,* for *whom* with an *m.* If *him* works, *whom* is necessary. If *him* does not work, use *who.* Knowing that *who* is required eliminates choices F and J. Choice H does not fit when reinserted into the sentence.

17. B. An adverb, which usually ends in *-ly,* answers the question *how.* How are most tribal governments organized? Democratically. Choice C is tempting. Choice C *is* grammatically correct, but choice C is also unnecessarily awkward and prolix. (No, *prolix* isn't an expensive brand of watch. ***Prolix*** just means wordy.) It is not necessary to say a government is organized in a democracy, but rather, democratically. Choice D makes no sense. Omitting the underlined portion makes the sentence read, "Most tribal governments are, that is, with an elected leadership."

Many students fall into a bad habit on this exam. They choose the *OMIT* answer every time that they see it. OMIT has no better or worse chance of being correct than does any other answer choice.

18. J. The original is a run-on sentence, two sentences (independent clauses) incorrectly joined. The ability to use a period instead of a comma is a good hint that the sentence is a run-on. Eliminating the subject of the second sentence, *it,* makes the second portion subordinate and thus part of one complete sentence. Choice G sounds tempting, but it changes the meaning of the sentence. The conjunction *however* indicates that the second sentence is changing (or in some way contradicting) the first sentence. This situation is not the case here. The same error eliminates choice H. The sentence does not need a *but.*

19. A. This question tests the distinction between *principal* and *principle.* ***Principal*** (with a *-pal*) means main or primary. (You may have learned in about sixth grade that "The principal is your pal, your buddy.") ***Principle*** (with an *-le*) is a rule. Eliminating the *-le* option immediately narrows the choices down to only one.

This type of question is one that you should always be able to get right. It tests a diction error, two commonly confused words. Diction errors are discussed at length in the Grammar Review. Be sure that you have these diction twosomes memorized before the exam. Correcting a diction error is, in general, much easier than correcting, for example, a verb-tense error or answering a question on the meaning of the passage.

20. H. If you missed this easy question, pack your bags — you're going on a guilt trip. This situation is a typical subject-verb agreement problem. The subject of the sentence is "an elected tribal council." Council is singular and requires the singular verb *has.*

Did you let yourself get bamboozled by the prepositional phrase? "Of the Interior and the people working for him" is a prepositional phrase (*of* is a preposition). Prepositional phrases do not affect subject-verb agreement (this concept is covered in the Grammar Review).

21. A. *Tribe* is singular. You say "the tribe *is*" not "the tribe *are.*" (Tribe is a collective noun. Collective nouns look plural, but they are always singular. Collective nouns are discussed in the Grammar Review.) Because *tribe* is singular, it requires a singular pronoun, *it,* rather than *them.* Eliminate choices C and D because of the plural pronoun *them.*

Have you noticed how often you may use a diction rule or a "twosomes" concept to narrow the answers quickly down to two? Be sure that you have *memorized* all the twosomes discussed in the Grammar Review.

Choice B has an *-ing* verb, always a suspicious character. If you insert it back into the sentence, you'll see that "be representing" changes the flow of the sentence: ". . . authority to speak and act for the tribe and be representing it. . . ." Verbs in a series must be in parallel forms: *to speak, to act,* and *to represent.*

22. F. The sentence is satisfactory as is. Verbs in a series must have parallel forms. "Tribal governments define . . . regulate . . . prescribe . . . levy," and so on.

Did you notice the error in Choice G? *Regular* is not the same word as *regulate.* Be careful not to anticipate, to read the word you expect to see rather than the word that's actually on the page.

23. C. No need to break into a cerebral sweat for this pretty simple question. Verbs in a series must be in parallel form. This very long sentence has a number of verbs, and all are in the simple present: *define, regulate, prescribe, levy, regulate,* and *control.* The last verb must be in the same form as well: *administer,* eliminating choices B and D immediately. The original unnecessarily adds a subject, *they.*

24. J. Ahh, did you immediately eliminate J because of the *-ing* verb? If so, I gotcha! You know that *-ing* verbs are almost always wrong — but not always. In this case, the original looks correct until you read the entire sentence. "They have fought . . . , they served." Because the "they served" portion is not underlined, it cannot be changed. The beginning of the sentence must become a subordinate clause (one that cannot stand alone). Subordinate clauses often begin with *-ing* verbs: "Fighting in all wars . . . , they have served. . . ." Besides that, F, G, and H are run-ons.

Beware of taking my tips as gospel and using them automatically. The tips and tricks you are learning in this book are not chiseled in stone. They are *tips,* not rules. Personally, I think of *-ing* words as guilty until proven innocent. They're probably wrong, but at least give them a chance and check them out.

25. C. *Demonstrated* patriotism caused Congress to pass the Indian Citizenship Act. "Demonstrating patriotism" has an *-ing* verb and should be looked at with suspicion. Choice D leaves out the verb entirely.

This situation presents a persnickety grammatical point, one that is difficult even for native English speakers. If all of the answers sound correct to you, just make a quick guess and go on. (Remember that the ACT does not subtract penalty points for wrong answers. Guessing is always to your advantage.)

26. G. The original, using both *one* and *you,* is all mixed up. Use either one selection or the other, but do not use both. Choice J is tempting because it has the word *one,* but this choice is actually using the plural pronoun *their,* which is incorrect. *One* does not read in *their* books. Eliminate H for the same reason.

27. B. Choice C is tempting, but it changes the meaning of the sentence. The Navajos did not use the Marine language; they used the Navajo language. Getting so involved in the grammar that you forget the reading comprehension concepts is very easy. Be sure, when you correct a grammatical mistake, that you have not introduced a new mistake in the meaning of the sentence. Choice A is totally awkward (if it's hard to read aloud, it's probably the wrong answer). Choice D doesn't fit when reinserted into the sentence.

28. H. You need to use a plural verb: "Forty-five to forty-seven percent of tribal leaders *are* . . . ." Although the word *percent* looks singular, you have to determine what the percent is. This example presents one of the rare instances in which a prepositional phrase *does* affect subject-verb agreement. (Sometimes you have to look at the object of the preposition. For example, 50 percent of the *house is* infested with termites, but 50 percent of the *houses* in the neighborhood *are* infested with termites.) Because "of tribal leaders" is plural, use a plural verb, *are,* and a plural noun, *veterans.*

And speaking of termites, a quick joke: What did the termite say when he walked into the saloon?

"Is the bar tender here?"

29. B. This question is like the main idea question that you would find after a regular reading comprehension passage. In order to answer this question, you probably have to reread the entire passage, ignoring the grammar concepts and focusing on the meaning of the passage.

Before you make a wild guess, look at the answer choices; look especially at the verbs. You can eliminate choice A based on the verb *to argue.* Very few passages are passionate enough to *argue* a point of view. In choice C, *to hypothesize* is wrong. Nothing about this passage is theoretical; it simply gives the facts. In choice D, *to predict* is wrong. The passage tells you what has been and what is, not what will be.

The main idea of a passage is often described by one of three words: *discuss, describe,* or *explain.* The primary purpose of a passage is to discuss something, to describe something, or to explain something. If you're making a wild guess, choose one of those verbs.

Passage 3

30. J. The subject of the sentence is *the theory. Theory* is singular, requiring a singular verb, *holds.* This narrows the answers down to H and J. In H, *whichever* makes no sense when reinserted into the sentence.

An underlined portion that features a verb often tests subject-verb agreement. Go back and identify the specific subject, ignoring (in most cases) the prepositional phrase.

31. B. A simple comma indicating a pause is sufficient. A semicolon separates independent sentences. In other words, the part before the semicolon and the part after the semicolon must each be a complete sentence. The part before the semicolon here would be a fragment, an incomplete sentence. Choice D introduces an unnecessary *-ing* verb (always be suspicious of *-ing* verbs) that would ruin the parallelism of the sentence *(is thrust . . . penetrating).*

32. F. The subject of the sentence is *pockets,* which is plural, requiring a plural verb, *result.* If you thought the subject was *rock,* you fell for the trap answer, choice H. Prepositional phrases, such as "of molten rock," rarely affect subject-verb agreement. Choice J unnecessarily changes the tense of the sentence. Be careful that your change makes your new sentence fit within the paragraph. The rest of the paragraph here is in the present tense.

33. D. The original is a fragment, an incomplete sentence. When you read it, you expect to hear something more at the end. Alter the *-ing* verb (often an indication of an error) to *built* to change the sentence to the simple past tense.

I hope that you didn't fall for choice B. The English language has no such word as *bilt. Bilt* is not the past tense of *build.* The past tense of *build* is *built.* (Come, come now, don't leave in a huff over that cheesy answer. As Groucho Marx would say, "Wait a minute and a huff!")

34. F. *Like* compares similar objects. That is, *like* usually connects two nouns. *As* compares situations or actions. Eliminate choices G and H. Choice J changes the meaning entirely. *Likely* means probably; *like* means similar to.

35. B. The correct expression is "to mix one thing *with* another" not "to mix one thing *from* another."

36. G. This question tests whether you know a cliché, a common saying such as "more (something) than you can shake a stick at." For example, Chapter 4 has more good rules than you can shake a stick at. If you didn't know this saying, you would have been well advised to skip (or just guess at) this question.

Occasionally this exam expects you to know a proverb, a quotation, or a saying that is in common usage in English. If the saying is completely foreign to you (pun fully intended, I'm sorry to say), make a quick guess and go on.

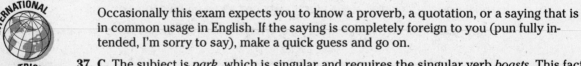

37. C. The subject is *park,* which is singular and requires the singular verb *boasts.* This fact eliminates choices A and D. Did you fall for the trap I set? "Boast some," when read aloud, sounds like "boasts some," because of the *s* in *some.* Whenever a verb is underlined, check that the subject agrees with the verb. Choice B is wrong because it sounds as if the park is doing some boasting. The expression ***boasts some of the*** simply means *is proud to have.* You and your friends can boast some of the highest ACT scores around if you learn the tricks and the traps of the exam.

38. F. The correct construction is semicolon, coordinating conjunction, and comma, as used in the original. Choice G is backward. The semicolon should come before the comma. Choice H would make the sentence into a run-on with a comma splice (a comma is not strong enough to join independent sentences). Choice J has the colon used incorrectly. A colon usually indicates a sequence or series of items to follow. For example: Please learn the following rules: 1 . . . ; 2 . . . ; and so on.

(I can never see a punctuation problem without remembering a really smart student who informed me, "Punctuation exacerbates my clinomania." As soon as he left, I looked up the word: ***Clinomania*** is an overwhelming desire to stay in bed!)

39. D. This passage is very straightforward. It discusses a certain geographical area, how that area was built, and what species of plants and animals and people live in that area. The passage is objective and neutral (as most passages are on this test), and the passage does not need humor. A cliché or slang expression, such as "more . . . than you can shake a stick at," is inappropriate (although you personally may be relieved to find even a glimmer of comic relief at this point).

If you had trouble choosing an answer, use the process of elimination. Choice A is wrong because nothing in this sentence changes the meaning of the passage. The passage discusses species; this sentence talks about more species. Choice B is wrong; nothing new was introduced. Choice C can sound confusing. To ***forestall*** an opposing argument means to anticipate an objection and address it directly. No objections were discussed or anticipated here.

This question is a good one to guess on. Fill in something, anything, because the ACT does not penalize you for wrong answers (random guesses). You just can't afford the time to go back through the whole passage and try to figure out this sentence's role in it.

40. J. Don't invest a lot of time and effort in this type of question; make a wild guess and go on. If English is not your native tongue, reading the passages is hard enough to do when the sentences are in the correct order and nearly impossible to do when the sentences are all jumbled up.

If you decide to do this sort of question, the best place to begin is with the *topic* or *main idea* sentence. The subject of the paragraph is "the theory of plate tectonics," meaning that sentence 2 should come first. This positioning of sentence 2 eliminates choices F and J. Now, if you're really shrewd, you will simply look at choices G and H to determine which second sentence would come next. In choice H, the second sentence is number 5, which begins with "These become. . . ." Because nothing appears in sentence 2 for *these* to refer to, sentence 5 must not be second. Look at choice G. Sentence 3 says "pockets of molten rock result." Result from what? Sentence 2: "It penetrates deep enough into the earth to be partly remelted."

This type of question is a major time-waster and is one of the most frequently missed questions. Unless you are very confident of your answer, you're better off not destroying any brain cells unnecessarily, but just guessing.

41. A. "Because of" is correct when used to mean "due to." Choices B, C, and D turn the sentence into a fragment. If you selected any of these three choices, you didn't take the final, critical step: Reread the entire sentence with the new answer inserted. If you're going to answer a question, take enough time to do it right.

42. F. The sentence means to say that the Indians didn't leave many artifacts behind. Choice G changes the meaning (and the tense). Choices H and J turn the sentence into a fragment.

43. C. This last paragraph starts an entirely new train of thought. Previously, the passage gave a physical description of the land and discussed its plant life. This paragraph is the first time that you learn that humans inhabited the area.

Passage 4

44. G. Read a little bit ahead in the paragraph to learn that the writer is no longer a young boy. Therefore, the simple past tense *dreamed* is required. Choice J turns the sentence into a fragment.

Remember, *-ing* words often make complete sentences into incomplete sentences or fragments. If you decide to choose an *-ing* verb, be sure to reinsert it into the sentence and reread the entire sentence.

45. A. You can immediately eliminate choice C because the English language has no such word as *its'*. *It's* means *it is,* and *its* is the possessive of *it,* but no *its'* exists. Choice D looks tempting because *of whom* is a proper formation (*of* is a preposition; *whom* is the object of the preposition). However, choice D, when reinserted into the sentence, destroys the structure of the sentence, as does choice B.

46. F. This question tests the use of prepositions. You can be fascinated by, enslaved by, captivated by, or enriched by something, but you are not enslaved *with,* or captivated *to,* or enriched *of* something. Choice J does not work when reinserted into the sentence (as an *-ing* word, it was dubious from the start).

And speaking of enriching, did you ever hear John D. Rockefeller's three rules for becoming rich? (1) Go to work early. (2) Stay late. (3) Find oil.

47. B. This question is an interesting one because all of the answer choices are pretty bad. Your job is to choose the least-awful among them. (Hmm: Sounds rather like a mixer dance, doesn't it?) The original creates a fragment: "A few miles past Naples, Italy along the slopes of Vesuvius." This fragment doesn't finish the thought. The same is true for the next part: "This city is found, which is much the same it was in A.D. 79. . . ." Choice B, even though it is in the passive voice *(is found)* rather than the active voice *(we find),* makes a complete sentence. (Active voice is usually preferable to passive voice because active voice is usually more concise, less wordy.) Choice C has an unnecessary colon. The colon usually introduces items in a series, as in "I want you to learn the following: . . . ." Choice D lacks a subject for the sentence (*who* finds the city?) and is a fragment.

48. F. For the ACT, you need to be very comfortable with all of the forms of the verbs *lie* and *lay. Lie* requires no object. You do not *lie something.* For example, you can say, "Studying for the ACT makes me so sleepy that I want to lie down." *Lay* requires an object. You'd say, "Now I lay *me* down to sleep." In this question, no object is supplied for the verb, meaning that the correct form is a conjugation of *lie.* This lack of an object eliminates choices G, H, and J.

Can you list the conjugations of *lie* and *lay*? They are as follows:

lie, lay, have lain

lay, laid, have laid

49. D. If you got this question correct, congratulate yourself. Most people immediately misread *causally* as *casually.*

Anytime you think that the sentence has no error, read *every* word carefully to ensure that you haven't automatically, subconsciously corrected the errors. If you selected NO CHANGE for 30 out of 75 questions, this automatic correction is probably a habit of yours.

50. F. *Anybody* is singular and requires a singular verb, *invites*. Eliminate choices G and H immediately. Choice J is tempting, but omitting this portion destroys the meaning the author is trying to get across and deletes necessary punctuation.

Many students fall for the trap of choosing "OMIT the underlined portion" every time they see it. Sometimes an omission creates havoc with the sentence. If you decide to omit the underlined portion, be sure to reread the entire sentence with the portion omitted.

51. C. *Neither* is teamed with *nor* (and *either* is teamed with *or*). Whenever you see the word *neither,* be sure that *nor* follows hard upon its heels.

When you find a simple grammar or diction error, change only that part and leave the rest of the sentence alone. In general, it's good to change as little of the sentence as possible.

52. F. Because the nonunderlined portion uses the past tense *sat* ("as he sat in his hotel room"), the underlined portion also requires the past tense *looked.*

Trivia: Most of us have heard about the ruins of Pompeii, but did you know that the courthouse was found full of arms and legs? Yeah, now that's clear evidence that the people had paid their lawyers' bills!

53. B. The original sounds as if Halliburton earns money simply by breathing and writing at the same time! (Only John Grisham, Tom Clancy, and Stephen King can do that!) The sentence means to say that the writing comes alive. However, it does not literally start to breathe; it simply becomes ***vivid,*** or lively.

54. J. The correct expression is "to relate to," not "to relate with," eliminating choice G immediately. Choice H becomes a run-on sentence. The comma is not sufficiently strong punctuation to separate independent clauses. The original is definitely a fragment. This portion has no conclusion, no verb, no complete thought.

Fun Fact: Do you know the singular form of the word graffiti? It's graffito. I read all the graffiti on the walls regularly. My all-time sicko favorite graffito is "Join DAM: Mothers Against Dyslexia.")

55. B. *Perfect* is an absolute adjective. Something either is perfect or is not perfect. Perfect cannot be modified; for example, nothing can be *very* perfect or *completely* perfect, eliminating choices A and C. Choice D disrupts the flow of the sentence.

Although the shortest answer is often the best answer (because lengthy, verbose answers tend to be redundant or to add superfluous terms), if you decide to choose the shortest answer, check to be sure that it doesn't make the sentence awkward or difficult to read. This "flow" is one reason that I suggest rereading the sentences aloud. Of course, during the test you will not be able to shout out your answers, but you can always mutter under your breath.

56. J. The portion "Sure to inspire every young boy's imagination to feats of daring and bravery" is a sentence fragment, an incomplete sentence. Adding it to the previous noun *(gladiators),* which the clause modifies, eradicates this problem. Choice G makes a run-on sentence. A comma splice is not sufficiently strong to separate independent sentences. Choice H does not fit when reinserted into the sentence.

57. C. The easiest way to answer an "order-of-sentences" question is to identify the topic sentence or the main idea. The main idea of this passage is Richard Halliburton, his writing, and his travels. It makes sense to begin the passage with Halliburton. Doing so immediately narrows the answers down to choices B and C. Next, look only at choices B and C to determine whether the second sentence should be sentence 3 (choice B) or sentence 2 (choice C). Because the first sentence talks about the graffiti at its end, logic dictates that the next sentence should talk about the graffiti at its beginning, as does sentence 2.

58. H. The best way to answer this question is through the process of elimination. The article is too personal to be in an encyclopedia. It doesn't express an idea or argue an opinion as an editorial would. Although choice J is tempting, the article discusses very little actual geography. The writing is more reminiscent, as if a man were writing of what influence Halliburton had on him.

Personal Aside: I've always wanted to write a travel memoir. I even have a title ready for the chapter about my trip through Egypt: *Ankhs for the Memories!*

59. B. Immediately eliminate choices C and D as negative. This passage is lightweight and charming, not somber and macabre. The purpose of questions is rarely to ridicule or to emphasize a negative point. Choice A is inane: Who cares about dental hygiene when you're dealing with a volcano?

Riddle: How do you know that a dentist is sad?

Answer: He's always looking down in the mouth!

Passage 5

60. G. *Cold-blooded* is a compound adjective. This compound adjective is commonly expressed with a hyphen between *cold* and *blooded.* Knowing that you need the hyphen eliminates choice F. Choices H and G are unnecessarily wordy and awkward. Put the adjective before the noun, not after.

In many languages, the adjective comes after the noun. If this practice is true in your tongue, you need to be especially alert to this situation.

61. B. This sentence contains an incorrect comparison. It compares the body temperature of the lizard to the surroundings. The sentence means to compare the body temperature of the lizard to the *temperature* of the surroundings. Using the word *that* (". . . much higher or lower than *that* of its surroundings") eliminates the problem.

Choice D has a trap in it. No such word as *its'* exists. *It's* means *it is. Its* is the possessive form of *it.* Choice C required careful reading. Did you notice the word *then* rather than *than*?

If you think that two answer choices are identical (for example, if in this problem you thought that both choices A and C said *than*), go back over the words letter by letter to catch your mistake.

62. H. The original is a fragment, an incomplete sentence. The word *although* supposes that a second clause will follow. This sentence has no second clause. Eliminate *although* to solve the problem. Choices G and J turn the sentence into a fragment.

63. A. First, check the pronoun (always double-check a pronoun to make certain that it has the same number — singular or plural — as the word that it replaces). The plural *they* correctly refers to the plural *animals.* Eliminate choices B and D, which have the singular pronoun *it.* Choice C turns the sentence into a fragment.

Did you notice that this sentence features the word *cold-blooded* with a hyphen between the two adjectives? Because *cold-blooded* in this sentence is not underlined, you must assume that this compound adjective is correct. You can use this information to go back to question 60 and correctly answer it. Would the ACT ever be this nice? You never know.

64. J. This question is very unusual in that the longest answer is the correct answer. Normally, shorter is better, and you can eliminate the lengthy, verbose answers. Here, however, the extra words are necessary to make sense of the sentence. The comparatives, *fewer* and *lesser* (choices F and G), indicate that the sentence compares the lizards in the trees to the lizards on the ground. This sentence is not doing that. The sentence is simply saying that some lizards are found on the ground, but a few are found in the trees.

If you are not certain of the distinction between *fewer* and *lesser,* go back to the diction portion of the Grammar Review. *Few* refers to countable units, such as few lizards. *Less* refers to measurable bulk, such as less weight of the lizards. But the word *lesser* does not mean the same as *fewer.* ***Lesser*** means of a lower degree or quality (a lesser woman would not have put in this trap).

65. **C.** This expression is an *idiomatic* expression. You don't say that something is *above* 3,000 species, but rather *more than* 3, 000 species. Choice D changes the sentence to a fragment. Choice B sounds as if the lizards are hovering in the air, flying above the 3,000 species.

66. **H.** When you read this sentence, you probably predicted that you would need the word *called:* ". . . resemble large crocodiles called Komodo dragons." Alas, your prediction was not among the answer choices. Choice H is the closest that you're going to get. Choice G is unnecessarily wordy. *So* and *therefore* express the same idea; use one or the other, but do not use both. Choice F is awkward. Choice J eliminates material that is necessary later.

67. **C.** Something doesn't *measure* 200 pounds, but *weighs* 200 pounds. (If I don't cut down on the doughnuts, I'll weigh 200 pounds, too. I don't want to say I'm fat, but my driver's license picture was taken with a panoramic camera!) Narrow the answer choices down to C and D. In choice D, *weight* is a noun. You are looking for the verb, *weigh.*

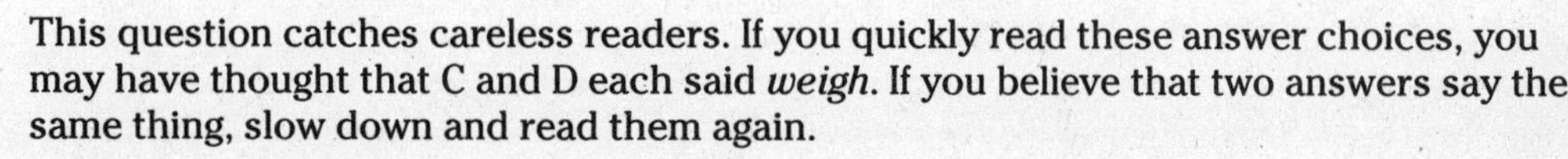

This question catches careless readers. If you quickly read these answer choices, you may have thought that C and D each said *weigh.* If you believe that two answers say the same thing, slow down and read them again.

68. **H.** Either use a comma before *and* after an expression to set it off or use a dash before *and* after an expression to set it off. You may not use a comma in one place and a dash in another place to mix and match. Knowing this fact narrows the answer choices down to H and J. Choice J unnecessarily uses both dashes and parentheses; use one or the other, but not both.

69. **C.** The second sentence in the original, "Until they are hatched," is not a complete sentence. Add it to the previous sentence without any comma or other punctuation. Choice B is tempting if you read it quickly, but this choice is missing the helping verb *are.* The sentence should say ". . . female's body until they *are* hatched." Choice D is unnecessarily long and wordy and uses the wrong verb tense.

Choice C has an *-ing* word, *hatching.* Normally, *-ing* words are traps, but not always. Do not become so enamored of the tips and traps that I give you that you immediately eliminate answer choices. The purpose of the tips is to make you paranoid, neurotic, and suspicious enough to double-check, not to make you immediately dismiss what can turn out to be correct answers.

70. **G.** Use the adverb *rarely* to answer the questions *how* or *when.* How or when do the species care for their offspring? Rarely. Eliminate choices F and J. Choice H includes an-*ing* verb *(caring)* that doesn't match the word *nourish,* which parallels it in the sentence ("rarely caring . . . or nourish").

71. **B.** Choices A and C are unnecessarily wordy. Choice D changes the meaning of the sentence. The colors are not developed *by attracting* females, but in order *to attract* females.

Query: What did one chameleon say to another?

Answer: "You make my thoughts so bright and colorful — are you just a pigment of my imagination?"

72. **F.** This type of problem can drive you crazy if you say it out loud. *To have,* meaning *to possess,* is the correct verb. The plural of *half* is *halves.* Eliminate choices H and J because of the incorrect word *halfs;* eliminate choice G because of the incorrect verb *to halve.*

73. **C.** To ***imply*** is to suggest, as in, "How dare you imply that I didn't know this rule!" To ***infer*** (choice B) is to deduce. "I can only infer that you don't believe that I've studied the Grammar Review." Eliminate both of those choices. Choice D is tempting; however, one does not describe qualities *to,* but describes qualities *of.* Because the phrase "nearly mystical qualities to" is not underlined, you cannot change it, but must work with it. The correct answer, ***impute,*** means to ascribe or give to, as in, "I impute a high intelligence to students smart enough to buy this book."

74. H. The mating rituals have to do with attracting, and then bonding with, a mate. Paragraph 4 discusses how mates are attracted (through the use of color). Choice G is a trap answer. Although Paragraph 3 discusses reproduction, it actually discusses the birth aspects rather than the bonding or mating aspects of reproduction.

This question is a built-in time-waster. In order to answer it correctly, you have to go back and practically reread the entire passage. To spend your time better, make a quick guess on this question (remember that the ACT does not penalize you for wrong answers) and double-check your earlier work.

75. D. This question looks harder than it really is. You can answer it by the process of elimination. The passage does discuss various types of lizards (choice A) including Komodo dragons and geckos. It does (choice B) mention habitat (in trees and on the ground and in Indonesia). It does (choice C) differentiate lizards based on size and appearance (some grow up to seven feet; some measure only three inches). The only thing that the passage does not do is describe the lizards' place in the chain of evolution (as if you care!).

Mathematics Test

1. **D.** The official, algebraic way to do this is to let the amount each cheerleader gave be c and the amount each football player gave be f. Then $c = 2f$. Because there are five cheerleaders, their total amount was $5c$ or $10f$. The ten football players also gave $10f$. The final equation is $10f + 10f = 480$. $20f = 480$. $f = 24$.

After you have finished the problem, double-check it by plugging in your answer and talking through the problem. This takes only a few seconds and can save you from yourself. If each football player gave 24, then the ten of them gave 240. Each cheerleader gave twice as much as each football player, or 48. First, $5 \times 48 = 240$. Then $240 + 240 = 480$.

The ACT was nice enough to give you answer choices; why not take advantage of them? You can do this whole problem without algebra by simply plugging in the answer choices. Start with the middle value. If the middle value doesn't work, you'll know whether the number must be greater or lesser than that choice. First, $22 \times 10 = 220$ and $44 \times 5 = 220$ and $220 + 220 = 440$. Because 440 is not enough, go to the next higher number, choice D. Begin with $10 \times 24 = 240$. Then $5 \times 48 = 240$. Finally, $240 + 240 = 480$.

2. **G.** To convert a percentage to a decimal, move the decimal point two places to the left. For example, 50% = .50. Here, .01% = .0001. To multiply by a million, move the decimal point six places to the right: 100.

3. **D.** First, plug in –3 for x. Then $2x = 2(-3) = -6$ and $-3x = -3(-3) = 9$.

The minus sign outside the parentheses changes the +9 to –9. (Remember that you have to distribute the minus sign through the parentheses.) You now have $-6 + -9 = -15$. The answers are narrowed down to D or E. Next, solve for y: $-3y$ plus $+4y = y$.

Make a habit of eliminating answers as you go. This method can prevent your working through an entire problem and then choosing the wrong answer because you forgot the first part of the problem by the time you did the second part.

4. **F.** If two sides of a triangle are equal, their angles are equal as well. Because all three angles of a triangle total 180°, the two unmarked angles must be 60° total (180 – 120 = 60) or 30° each ($^{60}/_{2} = 30$). Angles along a straight line are *supplementary,* or total 180°. Therefore, 180 – 30 = 150. The exterior angle measures 150°.

The measure of an exterior angle is equal to the sum of the measures of its two remote interior angles. Here, the *remote* (in other words, "not next to") interior angles are NLM, which is 30, and LNM, which is 120, for a total of 150.

Did you notice that F is the only possible answer? It is the only choice greater than 120. Because exterior angle = the sum of two remote interior angles, it must be $120 + x$; x is not equal to 0. Therefore the exterior angle is greater than 120.

5. **B.** First, use your common sense to eliminate choices C, D, and E. If she can already assemble 300 widgets in one hour and is going to raise her rate and work eight hours, she certainly is going to assemble a lot more widgets than these answers show. Quickly narrow the answers down to choices A and B.

Next, find that 25% or $^{1}/_{4}$ of 300 is 75 — trap choice E, which you have already eliminated. (One good reason to eliminate choices as you go is to avoid falling for cheezy traps like this one.) If she increases her rate by 75, Jarnelle can now assemble 375 widgets in one hour (trap choice C). In eight hours, she can assemble 375×8 or 3,000 widgets.

Another way to estimate is to say that 375 is about 400 and $400 \times 8 = 3{,}200$. Only choice B is remotely close.

6. **J.** The interior angles of a triangle sum up to 180°. If the ratio of those angles is 1:2:3, think of them as 1x:2x:3x. Add the numbers in the ratio: 6x = 180. Solve for x: 180/6 = 30. If x = 30, the angles of the triangle are 30:60:90. (Ratios are explained in detail in Chapter 8 of the math review.)

A 30:60:90 triangle has a special formula for the sides (triangles are also discussed in Chapter 7 of the math review): **side:side $\sqrt{3}$:2 side.** The longest side is the "2 side" which here you are told is 30. That means that $s = 30/2 = 15$. The sides of the triangle, therefore, are 15:15$\sqrt{3}$:30. Add them together to get $45 + 15\sqrt{3}$.

Choice H is the trap answer. You can't add the $\sqrt{3}$ side to the non-$\sqrt{3}$ sides. That's like adding apples and oranges. You can add the sides with no roots (15 + 30 = 45), but the side with the root stands alone. If you are confused on working with roots, please return to the math review, Chapter 8.

7. **D.** The sides of an isosceles right triangle are in the ratio **side:side:side $\sqrt{2}$**. The side $\sqrt{2}$ is the hypotenuse. (If you forgot this formula, go back to Chapter 7.) Each side or leg of the triangle, therefore, is 5. The area of a triangle is $^1/_2bh$, one half *base* × *height.* In an isosceles right triangle, the two legs are the base and the height, making the area of this triangle $^1/_2$ (5) (5) = $^1/_2$ (25) = 12.5.

Choice B traps students who forget to multiply by $^1/_2$. Choice E is the perimeter, not the area. Because answer choices often have such "variations" to trap a careless test-taker, circle what the question is asking for. Before you fill in the oval on the answer grid, refer to that circled info again to be sure that you're answering the right question.

Did the term "square units in the area" confuse you? Not to worry. Just think of it as the area.

8. **K.** Distribute the negative: When I was in school, I always inserted a 1 in front of parentheses. You can use that principle here and distribute the negative 1. A negative 1 times a is $-a$. A negative 1 times a is $-a$. A negative 1 times –3 is +3 (which immediately eliminates choices G and H). A negative 1 times $-a$ is $+a$. Combine like terms: $6a - a + a = 6a$.

When the answers are all "variations on a theme" like this, double-check that you are keeping your positive and negative signs correct.

9. **C.** First, find 25% or $\frac{1}{4}$ of 18,000: $\frac{18{,}000}{4} = 4{,}500$ (trap choice E). Because that's the discount, subtract it from $18,000 to get $13,500 (trap choice D). Then take 5% of $13,500, which is $675. That's the luxury tax, so add it to $13,500 to get $14,175.

If you chose A, you added the sales tax to the original cost, not to the sales cost. If you chose B, you assumed that a discount of 25 percent and a tax of 5 percent is the same as a discount of 20 percent. The logic is superficially plausible, but wrong because the percentages are percentages of different *wholes* (in the first case, the percent is of the original price; in the second case, the percent is of the sale price). Keep in mind, whenever you deal with percentages, that a percentage is part of a whole, and double-check that you have started with the correct "whole."

10. **G.** This is a relatively simple problem — easier than it looks. Draw a rectangle of width x and length $3x$ (because the problem tells you that length is 3 × width). Add all the sides to find the perimeter: $x + 3x + x + 3x = 8x$. The perimeter is 640, so $8x = 640$. $x = 80$. If x, the width, is 80, then $3x$, the length, is 240. The area of a rectangle is *length* × *width*: 80 × 240 = 19,200.

Did you see where you could estimate instead of doing all the division? Say that the numbers are 80 × 200, giving you 16,000. Because you are multiplying by "more than 200," the final answer must be "more than 16,000." That eliminates choices H, J, and K. Common sense tells you that the answer is nowhere near as large as 100,000 (again, because 80 × 200 = 16,000), allowing you to eliminate choice F.

11. **D.** First, circle the words "closest approximation." That's a clue that the problem is going to be a pain in the posterior — that you will probably have some very weird numbers. More importantly, it's a clue that you don't have to work the problem through to the bitter end but that you can estimate a final answer.

Next, plug and chug. Put the numbers in and work the problem through.

$$\frac{3+10(3-10)^2(9-10)}{10(9+10)}$$

$$\frac{3+10(49)(-1)}{190}$$

$$\frac{3-490}{190}$$

$$\frac{-487}{190}$$

Here's where you estimate. –487 is about –500; 190 is about 200. $\frac{-500}{200}=-2.5$

This type of problem is great to do if the word problems are hard for you. This question consists of numbers, numbers, and more numbers. However, this problem also lurks to catch those who are prone to making careless errors. The more calculations you do, the greater the chance of a careless error. Double-check work like this.

12. **K.** Angles along a straight line total 180°. Forget about all the fraction jazz; start off by plugging in nice, simple numbers. Say, for example, that $x = 1$ part. Then $y = 2$ parts and $z = 3$ parts. See how neatly things work out? You are often rewarded for plugging in simple numbers. Then you have $x + y + z = 180$, or $1 + 2 + 3 = 180$; 6 parts = 180; 1 part = 30. Then $x = 30$, $y = 60$, and $z = 90$. Yes, it works. Now just go back and answer the question: $z - x = 90 - 30 = 60$.

13. **A.** This problem looks a lot harder than it is; don't let yourself be intimidated. First, be sure that you get the wording straight. You're subtracting the first term from the second term. Think of this as "second term minus first term." If you overlook this wording, you may have fallen for trap choices D or E.

    Second, check that the variables are the same and are to the same power, or else you can't subtract them. For example, you can subtract $5a^3 - 3a^3$, but you cannot subtract $5a^3 - 3a^2$ (unless, of course, you know the value of a). Because the variables and exponents (powers) are the same, you can ignore them and just subtract the *numerical coefficients* (the numbers in front of the variables). $1 - 5 = -4$. (Because no number is in front of the a^3b^4, you assume a 1.) Now your answers are narrowed down to choices A and B. Subtract the coefficients in front of the a^2b^3: $-2 - 3 = -5$.

14. **J.** The sides of a 30:60:90 triangle are in the ratio **side:side$\sqrt{3}$:2side.** (If you forgot this ratio, go back to the triangles section of the Geometry Review in Chapter 7.) Draw the figure like this:

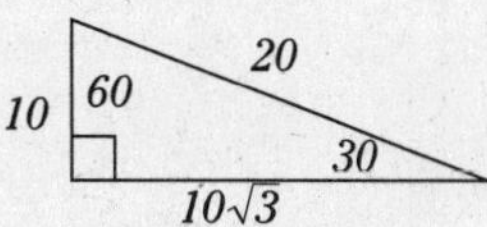

You know the "side$\sqrt{3}$" side is the base, opposite the 60° angle, and the "side" side is the height, opposite the 30° angle. The area of a triangle is $^1/_2$ *base* × *height*.

$$\frac{1}{2}(10)(10\sqrt{3})=50\sqrt{3}$$

15. **D.** Did you complain as you read this problem that the first statement gave you no information? Remember that ab always equals ba. Any number minus itself equals zero. Any number divided by itself equals 1. This problem is an easy one unless you have what I call "Smart Students' Disease" and try to make it harder than it really is. If you thought this question was too good to be true (and I applaud your paranoia, which is useful in general on this exam), just plug in numbers and work through the problem: $a = 1$ and $b = 2$. Then $1 \times 2 = 2$ and $2 \times 1 = 2$. Finally, $2 - 2 = 0$. $^2/_2 = 1$.

16. H. The area of a trapezoid is $^1/_2$ (*base one* + *base two*) × *height*. The top base is given as 65. (Because you are adding the terms, it makes no difference whether you consider the top *base one* or *base two*. The adding gives you the same answer, either way.) Because of the right angles, you know that ABCX is a rectangle, making CX 65. The height, AX, is 15. All you have to find is DX, so that you can add it to CX to find base two.

You could use the Pythagorean theorem to say $a^2 + b^2 = c^2$, such that $a^2 + 15^2 = 25^2$, but who wants to work with such big numbers? Whenever you see a right triangle, check whether it could be one of those fabulous PT triples, especially 3:4:5, which is the most common. (These PT triples are covered in detail in the Math Review.) $15 = 3 \times 5$; $25 = 5 \times 5$. That means you are missing the "4:" side, or $4 \times 5 = 20$. Add $20 + 65 = 85$. Now plug the numbers into the formula: $^1/_2 (65 + 85) \times 15 = {}^1/_2 (150) \times 15 = 75 \times 15 = 1{,}125$.

If you chose K, you forgot to use the entire bottom base but used

$^1/_2 (65 + 65) \times 15 = 65 \times 15 = 975$.

17. D. This problem is harder — or at least trickier — than it looks. You cannot just add the digits to get 7,250. Work out each parenthetical expression: $.240 \times 10^4$ means to move the decimal point four places to the right: 2,400. Next, 7.01×10^2 means to move the decimal point two places to the right: 701. Now you can add: $2{,}400 + 701 = 3{,}101$. Eliminate choices A, C, and E.

If you chose B, you got careless. Choice B would be .003101, moving the decimal three places to the left. You want 3.101 with the decimal moved three places to the right, to get 3,101.

Whenever you see that the answers have the same digits, double-check the decimal.

18. H. Remove the parentheses: $3x^2y + xy^2 - 2x^2y + 2xy^2$.

The last term is added because of the negative sign in front of the second set of parentheses. Remember to distribute the negative sign throughout the parentheses.

$-1(-2xy^2) = +2xy^2$. Confusing signs is one of the most common careless errors in algebra problems.

Combine like terms: $3x^2y - 2x^2y + 2xy^2 = x^2y + 3xy^2$.

19. E. The key to this problem is knowing the formula for the TSA (total surface area) of a cylinder: $2\pi r^2 + 2\pi rh$. This formula is explained in detail in the Math Review in Chapter 9.

The $2\pi r^2$ represents the areas of the top and bottom circles: Here, $4^2\pi = 16\pi$. Add top and bottom: $16\pi + 16\pi = 32\pi$. The $2\pi r$ represents the circumference of the cylinder, which, if cut, would be the length of the base of a rectangle, like this:

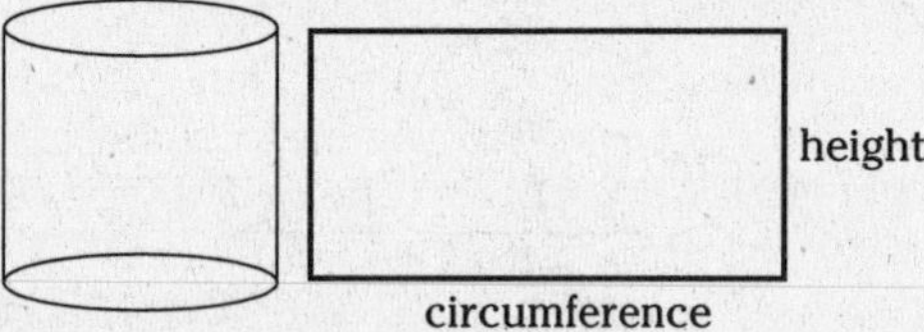

The area of a rectangle is *length* × *width*. Here, that is $2\pi r$ times *height*, which is $(2)4\pi \times 10 = 80\pi$. Finally, add: $32\pi + 80\pi = 112\pi$.

20. G. The area of a trapezoid is $^1/_2$ (*base one* + *base two*) × *height*. Because you add the bases, you don't care which is *base one* and which is *base two*. The top of the trapezoid goes from –3 to 5, a distance of eight units. The bottom goes from –3 to 9, a distance of 12 units. The height goes from 2 to –5, a distance of seven units. Plug the numbers in to the equation: $^1/_2 (8 + 12)\, 7 = {}^1/_2 (20)\, 7 = 10 \times 7 = 70$.

21. D. First, distribute the negative sign from outside the parentheses, making the second expression $-3a^2 + 2ab - 8$. Then combine like terms: $2a^2 - 3a^2 = -a^2$. Immediately your answers are narrowed down to choices D and E. If you're in a big hurry, quickly make a 50/50 guess.

Next, $ab + 2ab = 3ab$. Because you've already narrowed the answers down to choices D and E, only D works. (Finish up the problem: –8 –8 = –16.)

22. G. The algebraic (that is, hard, tedious, and official) way to do this problem is to say $\frac{81+90+74+79+92+x}{6} = 85$, letting x be the score on the sixth test. Combine the terms and get $\frac{416+x}{6} = 85$. Then cross-multiply (multiply each side by 6): $85 \times 6 = 416 + x$.

Finally, $510 = 416 + x$ and $x = 94$.

The shortcut way — which prevents you from making a careless error — is to find out how many points above or below the average each test is. (Chapter 9 discusses this technique in full. If the following explanation goes too fast for you, return to the averages portion of the Math Review.)

81 = –4 (4 points below an 85)

90 = +5 (5 points above an 85)

74 = –11 (11 points below an 85)

79 = –6 (6 points below an 86)

92 = +7 (7 points above an 85)

Add the pluses and minuses together to get –9 points. This student is nine points below where she wants to be. She'll have to gain back those nine points to balance out: 85 + 9 = 94.

23. D. Remove the parentheses. Remember that the minus sign in front means that you write the opposite of 4, which of course is –4, and the opposite of $-3y$, which is $+3y$. That means that $2y - (4 - 3y) + 3$ becomes $2y - 4 + 3y + 3$. Combine the $2y$ and the $3y$ to get $5y$. Then –4 + 3 = –1. All together now, you have $5y - 1$.

This is a great problem for students whose first language is not English. This question has no confusing words and no tricky phrasing — it's just straightforward numbers. But be especially careful to keep the – and + signs straight.

24. G. The area of a square is side squared. $s^2 = 144$; $s = \sqrt{144}$ or 12. If the side of the square is 12, the diameter of the circle is 12 and the radius is 6. The area of a circle is πr^2. Here, that's 36π. To find the shaded area, subtract the total area minus the unshaded area: $144 - 36\pi$.

If you're lucky enough to get a totally stupid answer among the answer choices, eliminate it quickly. Choice K here is the ridiculous answer. Because π is approximately 3.14, $144\pi > 144$, making choice K negative. The ACT does not test "negative areas," so eliminate that answer pronto. Even if you don't have a clue how to solve the problem (shaded area questions are discussed in the Math Review in Chapter 7), eyeball the answer choices and eliminate any illogical ones.

25. B. First, solve for angle y inside the triangle. Because the angles of a triangle total 180°, $y = 180 - (20 + 40)$ or 120. Next, the three xs and this y angle total 180° because they form a straight line. Therefore, $120 + 3x = 180$ and $3x = 60$ and $x = 20$.

Did you see the shortcut to completing this problem? An exterior angle of a triangle is equal to the sum of the two remote interior angles. In other words, this outside angle is the same as the sum of the two interior angles that are not adjacent to it. The exterior angle is actually $3x$, and $3x = 60$. So $x = 20$.

26. Sometimes the hardest part of a math problem is knowing where to start. I suggest that you use the answer choices, working backwards from there. If there were 704 ball bearings in the first cycle, there were 352 in the second cycle, 176 in the third cycle, 88 in the fourth cycle, and 44 in the fifth cycle. Nope, that's too big. Try a smaller number. Skip down to choice C (which good test-takers should have tried first, as per the suggestion in the math lecture) and try it. If there were 176 ball bearings in the first cycle, there were 88 in the second cycle, 44 in the third cycle, 22 in the fourth cycle, and 11 in the fifth cycle. That's exactly what the problem says; we have a winner!

The ACT rewards "unusual" problem-solving strategy. Did you see another way to solve this problem? You could also have worked it the opposite way. If there were 11 balls at the end of the fifth cycle, there were 22 in the fourth cycle, 44 in the third cycle, 88 in the second cycle, and 176 in the first cycle.

27. **E.** This is a relatively hard problem. Use substitution, putting "3 + b" in for a in the second equation. This gives you:

$16(3 + b) = 20 - 4b$. Multiply the 16 by each term in the parentheses.

$48 + 16b = 20 - 4b$. Move the 20 to the left and the $16b$ to the right, remembering to change the signs. (Forgetting to change the signs is one of the most common errors students make.)

$48 - 20 = -16b - 4b$. Combine terms.

$28 = -20b$. Divide both sides through by the number next to the variable.

$28/-20 = -20b/20$

$-7/5 = -b$

$b = {}^7/_5$

Notice that ${}^7/_5$ is the trap answer, choice B. If you fell for that, hang your head in shame! You're not done with the problem yet. The question wants to know the value of a. Stick the value for b back into the equation and solve for a.

$a = 3 + b$

$a = 3 + {}^7/_5$

$a = {}^{22}/_5$

If you chose A, you probably made a careless error. If you forgot to divide both sides through the *negative* 56, you got ${}^7/_5 = -b$, and thought $b = -{}^7/_5$.

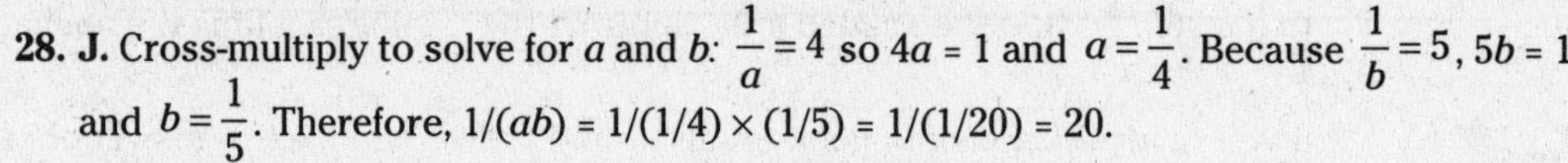

28. **J.** Cross-multiply to solve for a and b: $\frac{1}{a} = 4$ so $4a = 1$ and $a = \frac{1}{4}$. Because $\frac{1}{b} = 5$, $5b = 1$ and $b = \frac{1}{5}$. Therefore, $1/(ab) = 1/(1/4) \times (1/5) = 1/(1/20) = 20$.

If you chose F, you forgot to invert (turn upside down) and multiply. If you chose G or H, you added the 4 and 5 instead of multiplying them.

29. **D.** The area of a circle is πr^2. If $\pi r^2 = 25\pi$, $r^2 = 25$, and $r = 5$. The diameter of the circle (which is $2r$ or 10) is the base of the triangle ACB. The radius of the circle, 5, is the height of the triangle. The area of a triangle is ${}^1/_2\ bh$: ${}^1/_2(10 \times 5) = {}^1/_2(50) = 25$.

Choosing E would have been illogical. You usually don't have π in the area of a triangle, only in the area of a circle.

30. **G.** You know that $4^3 = 64$, but if you chose J, you fell for a cheap trick. Choice J would have 4^{-3}, or $\left(\frac{1}{4}\right)^3$ or $\frac{1}{64}$. You need x to be -3, such that (two negatives make a positive) $4^{-(-3)} = 4^3$, or 64.

31. B. Do you remember that great saying that you learned in right triangle trig: SOH CAH TOA ("soak a toe uh")? This means

S = Sine	C = Cosine	T = Tangent
O = Opposite	A = Adjacent	O = Opposite
H = Hypotenuse	H = Hypotenuse	A = Adjacent

Here is an illustration:

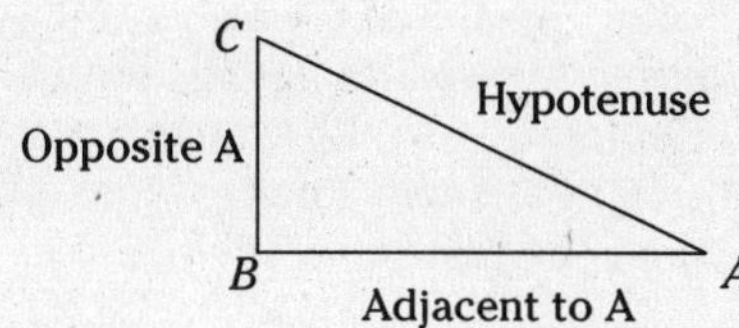

To find tan Z in this problem, identify the side opposite angle Z and the side adjacent to angle Z.

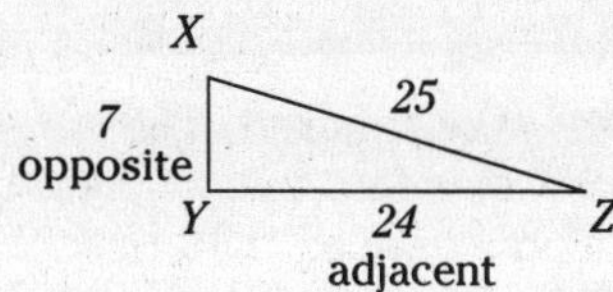

$$\text{Tan Z} = \frac{\text{opposite}}{\text{adjacent}} = \frac{7}{24}.$$

32. G. When you deal with percentages, start by plugging in 100. Say that the slow reader originally read at 100 words per minute. Then when she increased her speed by 25 percent, she read at 125 words per minute (because 25 is 25% of 100). If she is only 50 percent, or half as fast as the fast reader, the fast reader reads 250 words a minute. The fast reader's speed, 250, is what percent of the slow reader's original speed, 100? Make the is/of fraction (250 *is* what percent *of* 100): $\frac{250}{100}$ = 2.5 = 250%.

If you chose D, you got careless and found what percentage the fast reader's speed is of the slow reader's *increased* speed rather than of her original speed. Circle precisely what the question is asking you so that you don't fall for traps like this one.

33. D. For every 2 yards (6 feet) that she swims, the swimmer actually progresses only 4 feet (because she loses 2 feet for every 2 yards). That means 1 yard swum = 2 feet covered. If 1 stroke is 5 yards, she goes 10 feet in that one stroke. The swimmer needs to cover 500 yards, or 1,500 feet, meaning that she has to take 150 (that is, $\frac{1500}{10}$) strokes.

This is a great problem to skip if English is not your primary language. The wording is quite confusing. In addition, the best way to solve this problem is not to use an equation but to talk it through. Word problems of this sort are very hard to get correct for native English-speakers and nearly impossible for others.

34. K. One easy way to do this problem is to plug in numbers. Let $x = 5$ and $y = 10$. The farmer can plow five rows in ten minutes or one row every two minutes. Therefore, the farmer can plow 30 rows in one hour (because one hour = 60 minutes). Let $w = 2$, such that the farmer works for two hours. If he can plow 30 rows in 1 hour, he can plow 60 rows in 2 hours. The answer to the problem is 60. Go through all the answer choices, plugging in your values for *x, y,* and *w,* to find which one works out to 60 (choice K).

$$\frac{60(5)}{10} \times 2 = \frac{300}{10} \times 2 = 30 \times 2 = 60$$

35. C. The only way to miss this problem is to intimidate yourself, to make the problem look harder than it really is. Even if you haven't studied functions in school (that's what the little *f* stands for, functions), you can solve this problem by "following directions." Talk your way through the problem. Say to yourself, "I have something in parentheses. That means I cube the something, then add one." In this case, the "something," the *x*, is given as –5. So cube –5 to get –125. Then add 1 to get –124. That's all there is to it!

The answer choices are full of traps for the careless student. If you cubed –5 and got positive 125, then added 1, you got answer A. If you correctly cubed –5 and got –125, then added 1 and got –126 (!), choice E was waiting for you. And if you got choice B, you combined both mistakes, cubing –5 to get the wrong answer of +125, then subtracting rather than adding 1. Remember: Just because the answer you got is in front of you does not mean it is the right answer. The test-makers are aware of commonly-made mistakes and put them on the test to tempt you.

36. K. A hexagon has six sides. (An easy way to remember this is to think of the *x* in *hex* and the *x* in *six*.) You can find the total interior angles of any polygon with the following formula: $(n - 2)\ 180$ where *n* is the number of sides. The interior angles of a hexagon are $(6 - 2)\ 180 = (4)\ 180 = 720$. If three of the angles total 360, the remaining three total $720 - 360$, or 360. The average measure of three angles that total 360 is $^{360}/_{3} = 120$.

37. D. The *area* of a square is side squared. If $36 = s^2$, $s = 6$. Each side of square ABCD = 6. The midpoint breaks each side into two segments of 3 each. If AR = 3 and AU = 3, then UR is the hypotenuse of an isosceles right triangle of sides 3 and 3. The hypotenuse is $3\sqrt{2}$. (Remember the Pythagorean triples: **side:side:side**$\sqrt{2}$. If you forgot this, go back to the Geometry Review in Chapter 7). If the side of square RSTU is $3\sqrt{2}$, the area is $3\sqrt{2}$ squared. $3\sqrt{2} \times 3\sqrt{2} = 9\sqrt{4}$ or $9 \times 2 = 18$. (If you are confused on how to multiply radicals, go back to Chapter 8.)

38. K. Plug the numbers you are given into the formula you are given: $.095P = 28.50$. Notice that because the investment is for one year, the *T*, for time, becomes irrelevant. Divide both sides through by .095: $P = 300$.

Did you see the shortcut in this problem? (As soon as you find out that you have to do some "real" arithmetic, like long division, look for a shortcut somewhere. The purpose of the ACT is to test your thinking and reasoning, not your pencil-pushing abilities.) Estimate that the interest is $30 rather than $28.50 and estimate that the percent interest is 10, instead of 9.5. Then you can talk your way through this: 30 is $^1/_{10}$ of what number? 300. The other answers are obviously too large.

39. D. The area of a circle is πr^2. Because $36\pi = \pi r^2$, $r^2 = 36$; $r = 6$. If the radius of the circle is 6, the diameter is 12 (because $2r = d$). The square, therefore, has diagonal 12.

The diagonal of a square divides it into two isosceles right triangles, as shown.

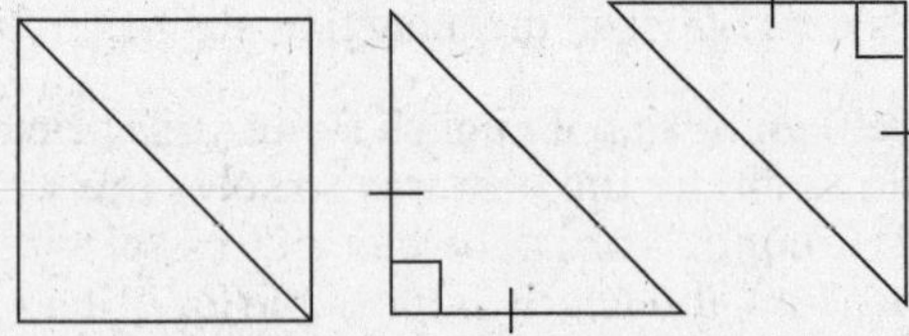

You could use the Pythagorean theorem:

$\text{side}^2 + \text{side}^2 = 12^2$. $2s^2 = 144$; $s^2 = 72$; $s = \sqrt{72}$.

The area of a square is side squared: $\left(\sqrt{72}\right)^2 = 72$.

40. J. Does this problem make you think of Egyptian hieroglyphics? Join the crowd. Instead of just saying, "That's history, Babe!" and guessing at this problem, make it easy to work through by plugging in numbers. Choose a number that has an easy square root. Make $x = 9$ (because $\sqrt{9} = 3$). Now solve the question:

$$(\sqrt{9}+2)\div(\sqrt{9}-2)=(3+2)\div(3-2)=\frac{5}{1}=5.$$

Keep in mind that 5 is the answer to the problem. It is not the value of x. Jot down the 5 to the side, draw a circle around it, put arrows pointing to it — do whatever it takes to remind yourself that the answer you want is 5. Now go through each answer choice, seeing which one comes out to be 5. Only choice J works:

$$(9+4\sqrt{9}+4)\div(9-4)=(9+4\times3+4)=(9+12+4)\div5=\frac{25}{5}=5$$

Be very, very careful not to put 3 in for x in the problem because $x = 9$ and $\sqrt{x} = 3$. I suggest that you make a chart to the side simply writing down $x = 9$ and Answer = 5.

When you plug in numbers, go through every single answer choice, ***soporific*** (sleep inducing) though that may be. If you started with choice K, for example, and made a careless mistake, you would find that choices J, H, and G didn't work either . . . and probably choose F by process of elimination. If you take just a second to work out F, you'll see that it too is wrong, alerting you to the fact that you made a careless mistake somewhere.

41. D. Begin the steps for this problem with $64^{\frac{2}{3}} = (\sqrt[3]{64})^2$. The cube root of 64 is 4, and $4^2 = 16$.

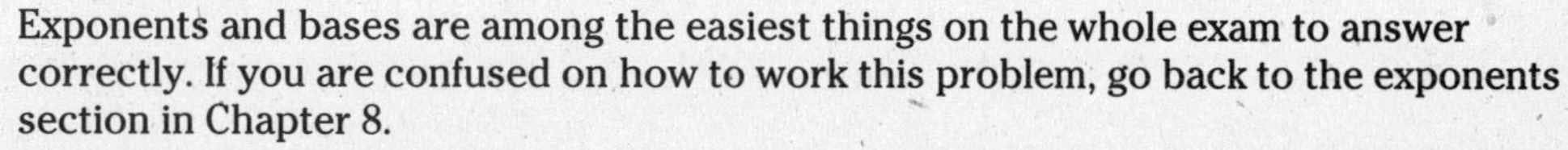

Exponents and bases are among the easiest things on the whole exam to answer correctly. If you are confused on how to work this problem, go back to the exponents section in Chapter 8.

This type of problem, because it involves only numbers and no words, is perfect for students who get headaches just looking at some of those lengthy word problems.

42. H. Take this one step at a time. First, find the sum of the a and b terms, which are 10 and 21. Then $10 + 21 = 31$. The only prime factor of 31 is 31. There are no other prime factors of 31; therefore, the answer is just 31.

If you chose J, you fell for the trap. Remember: 1 is not a prime number! If you added 31 + 1, you forgot this important point. By definition (which is mathematical jargon for "because we say so, that's why"), 0 and 1 are neither prime nor composite. Both terms are defined in Chapter 9.

43. C. Probability is often expressed as this fraction:

$$\frac{\text{The number of possible desired outcomes}}{\text{The number of total possible outcomes}}$$

Because the worker wants a bolt and there are still four bolts in the drawer, 4 is the numerator, "The number of possible desired outcomes." The total number of items in the drawer, ten (two nuts, four bolts, and four nails), is the denominator. $4/10 = 40\%$.

44. H. I sincerely hope that you didn't make an equation to solve this problem. There is a much easier way: Draw yourself a simple diagram. Put dashes so that the 13th dash has a billboard, like this:

—	—	—	—	—	—	—	—	—	—	—	—	B
1	2	3	4	5	6	7	8	9	10	11	12	13

Then counting backwards with the billboard as the 14th, make a second diagram:

B __ __ __ __ __ __ __ __ __ __ __ __ __

14 13 12 11 10 9 8 7 6 5 4 3 2 1

Put the two together and count:

__ __ __ __ __ __ __ __ __ __ __ __ __ __ B __ __ __ __ __ __ __ __ __ __ __ __ __

If you were careless and thought that you could just add, you probably chose J, 27. Invest a few moments to make a simple diagram and get the problem right.

45. B. Take this problem step by step. First, factor. You know, via FOIL (First, Outer, Inner, Last), that the first two terms have to come out to x^2, making them (x) and (x). You know that when you multiply the last two terms, you must get –8, which means that one term is positive and one is negative.

The middle two terms have to total +7. How about +8 and –1? That gives you $(x + 8)(x - 1)$. Quickly remultiply this to be absolutely sure that it equals the original, $x^2 + 7x - 8$. It does. All is well. Now that you know that $x^2 + 7x - 8$ factors into $(x + 8)(x - 1)$, add the two expressions: $(x + 8) + (x - 1) = x + 8 + x - 1 = 2x + 7$.

46. H. The wording "in terms of" can be very confusing — ignore it. You are simply solving for b. Do this problem the same way that you do any other algebra problem. First, get all the bs on one side and all the non-bs on the other: Subtract $3a$ from each side. $5b = 10 - 3a$. Next, divide both sides by what is next to the b:

$$\frac{5b}{5} = \frac{10-3a}{5}$$

$$b = 2 - \frac{3}{5}a$$

(Don't forget that $\frac{10}{5} = 2$.)

47. A. Get all the terms with x and y on one side of the equation and all the terms without x and y on the other side of the equation. You do this by first adding $4mx$ to each side:

$-4mx - \frac{3b}{c} = 4my$. Next, $-4mx + 4mx - \frac{3b}{c} = 4mx + 4my$. $-\frac{3b}{c} = 4mx + 4my$.

To solve for x and y, factor out the $4m$ on the right. $-\frac{3b}{c} = 4mx + 4my$. Next, divide by $4m$: $\frac{-3b}{4mc} = x + y$.

If your English isn't up to solving word problems or story questions, this type of math problem should make your day. It's all numbers and variables without any confusing phrasing or terminology. If you're running short on time or patience, head for this type of question first.

The most common mistake that I see students making on this type of problem is confusing their – and + signs. As soon as you get an answer, turn around and double-check it *immediately.* You can be pretty sure that the test-makers will include, as one of the answer choices, whatever you get if you mess up the – and + signs.

48. H. First, multiply through the parentheses: $a(a + 4) = 12$, so $a^2 + 4a = 12$. Next, make everything equal to zero by moving the +12 to the other side of the equal sign, remembering to make it –12 (forgetting to change the sign is a common mistake): $a^2 + 4a - 12 = 0$. Next, factor the expression down into $(a + 6)(a - 2) = 0$. Finally, make the parenthetical expressions equal to 0 and solve, $a = -6$ or $a = 2$.

49. A. First, multiply through the parenthetical expressions: $(3 + x)(4x) = 3 \times 4x = 12x$ and x times $4x = 4x^2$. Add 2 to get $4x^2 + 12x + 2$. Next, multiply everything by the x outside the brackets: x times $4x^2 = 4x^3$. Then x times $12x = 12x^2$. Next, x times $2 = 2x$. Finally, $4x^3 + 12x^2 + 2x$.

This problem is great to do if you are running short of time. It doesn't take much effort to understand what you are expected to do, nor much time to do it. The only mistake you are likely to make is a careless one, so be sure to double-check your work.

50. J. Get rid of choices F and G right away. These choices show that the distance equals 0 at one time beyond the starting time. The car never moves back to the initial designated point. Choice H does not feature an interval in which the car slows to 70 km/hr. Choice H shows that the car moved forward at a constant speed, stopped, and then resumed the constant speed. Choice J is correct. Choice K is close, but the gas/lunch interval (horizontal line) lasts too long.

51. D. To solve, factor $x^2 - 5x + 6$ by thinking of FOIL (First, Outer, Inner, Last) in reverse: $x^2 - 5x + 6 = 0$

$(x \_\_\_\_)(x \_\_\_\_) = 0$

The missing numbers need to add to –5 and multiply to 6.

$(x - 2)(x - 3) = 0$

Check with FOIL: $(x - 2)(x - 3)$

$= x^2 - 3x - 2x + 6$

$= x^2 - 5x + 6$

To solve for x, make either expression inside the parentheses equal to 0.

$x - 2 = 0$ when $x = 2$

$x - 3 = 0$ when $x = 3$.

The solutions are $x = 2$ and $x = 3$. Check this:

$(2 - 2)(2 - 3) = 0$

$(3 - 2)(3 - 3) = 0$

These are okay. The sum of the solution is $2 + 3 = 5$ (choice D).

52. F. If $x + 1$ is less than or equal to 8, then x is less than or equal to 7 (subtract 1 from both sides).

If you chose choice G, you fell for the trap. You neglected to account for the "or equal to" portion of the inequality.

53. C. First, put the equation in slope-intercept form: $y = mx + b$. Then $x + 2y = 4 - x - y$ (distribute the – sign). Next, $3y = 4 - 2x$ (move the xs and ys to different sides of the equation). Then $y = \frac{4-2x}{3}$ (divide everything through by 3 to isolate the y). Finally, $y = \frac{4}{3} - \frac{2x}{3}$.

54. F. The key to answering the question is to remember that $\cos^2\theta + \sin^2\theta = 1$.

If you have trouble remembering this, think of a right triangle with a hypotenuse 1:

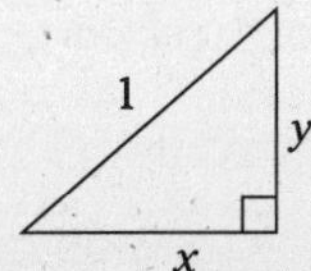

$x^2 + y^2 = 1$ (remember the Pythagorean theorem?).

Because $\cos\theta = \frac{adjacent}{hypotenuse} = \frac{x}{1} = x$ and $\sin\theta = \frac{opposite}{hypotenuse} = \frac{y}{1} = y$, then $x^2 + y^2 = 1$.

You can just rewrite this as $\cos^2\theta + \sin^2\theta = 1$

To get back to our problem,

$$\frac{\sin^2\theta + \cos^2\theta}{\sec^2\theta} = \frac{1}{\sec^2\theta}$$

$$\sec\theta = \frac{1}{\cos\theta}, \text{ so } \sec^2\theta = \frac{1}{\cos^2\theta}$$

Finally, substitute $\sec^2\theta = \frac{1}{\cos^2\theta} = \frac{1}{\sec^2\theta} = \frac{1}{\frac{1}{\cos^2\theta}} = 1 \cdot \frac{\cos^2\theta}{1}$

If this problem is really, really tough for you, you're not alone. Many students find this jazz difficult. Keep in mind as you're going through these questions that you don't have to get all the problems right to get a very good score; you can afford to skip or miss several of them.

If you are an international student having a tough time with the word problems, brush up on your trig to be sure that you get this type of problem correct. If you can do this hard problem that's all numbers and symbols, you don't have to worry so much about the easy and medium story problems that are so confusing to you because of the wording.

55. E. Multiply both the top and the bottom of the fraction by $2 - \sqrt{3}$ (known as the conjugate of the denominator, just in case you care). Doing so makes the denominator equal to 1, so you can just ignore it from that point on.

This problem is great to do if you are short on time. It looks incredibly complicated, but all you have to do is multiply both top and bottom by the conjugate of the denominator.

56. F. The most straightforward way to approach this problem is to remember that *slope* is change in rise over change in run, or $\frac{y_2 - y_1}{x_2 - x_1}$. In this case, $y_2 - y_1 = -b - (-b)$. That comes out to be $-b + b = 0$. Next, $x_2 - x_1 = -a - 2a$, which comes out to be $-3a$. Substitute and you get slope $= \frac{0}{-3a} = 0$.

If you did this problem upside down, and got $\frac{3a}{0}$, you thought that it was undefined (because division by 0 is undefined) and chose choice K. You may have recognized that $y = -b$ in both points. This means that y is constant and the line is horizontal.

y
x
y = –b
(0, –b)

Horizontal lines have a slope of 0, reinforcing choice F as the answer.

57. D. Choice E is a sucker bet. Just because the problem multiplied both the number of painters and the number of rooms by 3 does not mean that you multiply number of hours by 3.

If three times as many painters are working, they can do the job in $^1/_3$ the time just one painter takes. If you are confused, reword the problem in your own terms. Suppose that you take three hours to mow a lawn. If your two friends chip in and help you, the three of you can work three times as fast and get the job done in just one hour. The same is true here. Three times the number of painters (from 3 to 9) means that the job can be done in $^1/_3$ the time: $^{10}/_3 = 3^1/_3$.

If you chose $3^1/_3$, you didn't finish the problem. Nine painters would do the same job — that is, paint four rooms — in $3^1/_3$ hours. But the number of rooms is three times what it was, so this factor triples the amount of time needed. Triple $3^1/_3$ to get ten hours. Yup, you're back to the original amount of time, which unfortunately was probably the first answer your "common sense" told you to eliminate.

Think about this logically. The painters take $^1/_3$ the time, but they do three times the work. The $^1/_3$ cancels out with the 3 to get you right back where you started from.

58. F. First, write out each expression: 10.8 (10^{-3}) means to move the decimal point three places to the left. (***Remember:*** A negative power means the number gets smaller, shifting the decimal point to the left, not to the right.) That gives you .0108. Do the same for the denominator: 400 (10^{-5}) means to move the decimal point 5 places to the left, giving you .004. Next, divide .0108 by .004 to get 2.7. Finally, figure out which of the expressions is equal to 2.7. The expression .027 (10^2) means to move the decimal point two places to the right (a positive exponent makes the number larger, meaning the decimal point shifts to the right, not the left): 2.7.

This question is probably the easiest one to make a careless mistake on in this whole exam. If you are going to do a problem of this sort, be sure that you can commit the time to the problem. Do the problem carefully, double-checking your decimal point as you go, and then triple-checking it after you have finished.

59. D. Okay, you can make this easy, or you can make it hard. You want to do it the easy way, you say? Great: Plug in numbers. You can choose any numbers that your heart desires, but I suggest that you keep them small. Why waste time on a lot of multiplication? Let $q = 1$. Georgia buys 1 quart of milk. Let $d = 2$; the milk costs 2 dollars a quart. (It doesn't have to make fiscal sense; maybe this is rare yak's milk. You have better things to worry about.) Let $b = 3$. She buys 3 boxes of cereal at 3 dollars a box $(d + 1 = 2 + 1 = 3)$. Now you can easily figure the total: 1 quart of milk at 2 dollars a quart equals 2 dollars. Three boxes of cereal at 3 dollars a box equals 9 dollars. Add them up to get 11 dollars. Plug the values for q, d, and b into the answer choices and see which one equals 11.

Keep two important concepts in mind when you plug in numbers: First, keep the numbers small and easy to work with. Second, jot down the numbers as you create them. That is, write to the side: $q = 1$, $d = 2$, and $b = 3$. It's very easy to get the numbers confused in the pressure of the exam and say that $d = 3$ or $b = 1$. Take just a nanosecond to put down the assigned values and refer to them constantly.

Here's the algebraic way to solve this problem: The amount spent for milk is (q quarts) (d dollars/quart) = Cancel the "quarts" and get qd. Then the amount spent for cereal is (b boxes) ($d + 1$ dollars/box) = cancel the "boxes" = $b(d + 1) = bd + b$. Add these together: $qd + bd + b$. Take out the d: $d(q + b) + b$.

If you think the algebra is straightforward, you're right . . . as long as you set up the original equation correctly. Unfortunately, too many people have no idea how to set up the equation and do it upside down, inside out, or whatever. If you plug in numbers, you can talk your way through this relatively difficult problem in just a few seconds.

60. K. The interior angles of any triangle sum up to 180°. You are given two of the three angles of triangle GFX, 30 and 90. Solve 180 – (30 + 90) = 60. A 30:60:90 triangle has a special ratio for its sides: **side:side$\sqrt{3}$:2side**. The side GX here is the "2side" part (the hypotenuse or side opposite the 90° angle). That means that the other sides are 2 and $2\sqrt{3}$. (If this ratio is confusing to you, return to the triangles section of the math review.) If FXS is 2, then XB is 2, and FB sums up to 4. The height of the rectangle is 4. If side GF is $2\sqrt{3}$, then FE is also $2\sqrt{3}$, and the length of the rectangle is $2(2\sqrt{3})$ or $4\sqrt{3}$. The area of a rectangle is base times height (also called length times width): $4\times4\sqrt{3}=16\sqrt{3}$.

Reading Test

Passage 1

1. **A.** This is really a commonsense question. The natural opening cannot extend beyond the *weight* of something (choice B) or a number of years (choice C). To think that the zone of light *of a cave* extends beyond the latitude and longitude *of a cave* is also illogical.

2. **H.** If you chose F, you fell for the trap. Just because the word we use today for the study of caves is the Greek word doesn't mean that the Greeks were the first to study caves. Probably other races used other words for cave study. Evidence of early man has been found in caves, leading us to infer that people studied caves before the Greeks did so.

3. **A.** Three words are often correct for the main idea of a passage (or in this case, of a paragraph): *discuss, describe,* and *explain.* The purpose of a passage is usually *to discuss* something (for example, the importance of studying for the ACT), *to describe* something (the types of questions on the ACT), or *to explain* something (how to answer the ACT questions). Although those three words aren't automatically correct, you should check them out carefully. Here, the paragraph simply describes the areas in which caves have been found.

Negative and dramatic words are rarely correct. Almost never is the main purpose of a passage to "dismiss as unimportant" some topic, or to "prove" something. (Few things in life can be definitively proven; the word *proven* is much too strong.)

Choice B may have been tempting. Yes, the paragraph talks about the different places, but it doesn't particularly *contrast* them, pointing out their differences.

4. **F.** Lines 18–20 tell you that the first evidence of Neanderthal Man was found in a cave in the Neander Valley of Germany.

Over the years, I've had students go ballistic on me arguing about the difference between *infer* and *state.* For some reason, many students have gotten the idea that, if the question asks you what you may *infer,* the answer cannot be given directly. Well, this situation is all a matter of interpretation. Some students think that, because the Neander Valley was specifically mentioned, it can't be right because no *inference* is required. Others think that this *is* an inference. I think that it makes no difference at all and that the students are driving themselves crazy for nothing. Go back and look for the answer and don't make life harder than it already is.

5. **D.** The author mentions several caves and emphasizes that they are "throughout the world." From this, you may deduce that ***plethora*** means an abundance. You have a plethora of ACT questions scattered throughout this book.

6. **F.** Paragraph three discusses the various types of caves, mentioning how each was formed (solution caves by dissolving rock, sea caves by the action of waves, and so on).

Choice G is the trap answer. You learned earlier that Neanderthal Man was named after the area in which he was found, but that does not mean that the caves were named after the areas in which they were found. Don't transpose information from one statement to another.

7. **A.** This question was very simple, almost a freebie for you. All you had to do was go back and read paragraph three. Lines 32–33 tell you that solution caves are the largest.

This type of question is an excellent one to head for if you are running out of time. When a question begins "According to the passage . . . ," the answer is usually given word for word. Invest a few moments of your time to find the precise answer; don't just hope you remember it from your reading.

8. **J.** Lines 45–49 tell you that ice caves are different from glacier caves and, in fact, are solution or lava caves. If you chose F, you fell for the trap. The last line of paragraph three tells you that "glacier caves are formed by water which excavated drainage tunnels through the ice," which may have led you to believe that glacier caves are, in fact, ice caves. (Common sense would also make you think this, because most people think of glaciers as ice.)

When you *think* that you've found the correct answer in the passage, extend your search. Read a little above and a little below, to be absolutely sure. Had you done so here, you would have found the exact answer just waiting for you in the next paragraph.

9. **B.** Lines 47–48 tells you that an ice cave may be a solution cave. Lines 61–62 tell you that most wind caves are, in fact, solution caves.

If you chose D, you fell for the trap. You didn't notice that the question asks which of these was *not* mentioned as possibly being a solution cave. When a question is phrased in the negative, be sure to circle the negative word *(not, never,* or *except)* to call it to your attention. I never cease to be amazed at how many students — even the best and brightest, like you — miss this type of question.

10. **G.** The answer is given in lines 96–97.

Choice H is the trap answer. Yes, the final paragraph starts off by talking bout the water table — but about the *lowering* of it, not the *rising*. Careless readers may have been trapped by this answer.

Passage 2

11. **B.** By rereading the first sentence carefully, you note that Mr. Casaubon in fact *was* full of jealousy and vindictiveness himself, eliminating choices A and D. The phrase "which compelled him to find other reasons for his conduct" tells you that he was trying to justify his jealousy and vindictiveness, sugarcoating them or calling them by other names.

12. **G.** Lines 11–13 say that "occasions might arise in which such possession might expose her to the more danger." The next few sentences talk about how men might prey upon her, allowing you to deduce that it is the money that turns Dorothea into the prey.

    Choice F is such a '90s answer, don't you think (1990s, that is)? Nothing in the passage talks about Mr. Casaubon's having had a previous marriage or having had children. Choice H is exactly wrong. Mr. Casaubon argues to himself that his responsibility, in fact, is not to give Dorothea money, but to keep it from her, in order to keep her safe. If you chose J, you really are a cynic, aren't you? Although this brief excerpt makes us wonder what Dorothea ever saw in the man that she married, we have no real reason to assume that she was a gold digger, after only his money.

13. **A.** Lines 16–22 have an amusing sentence containing the following passage: "an animosity which he has constantly vented in ridicule, of which I am as well-assured as if I had heard it." If you read that carefully, you see that Mr. Casaubon has, in fact, not heard the man express any animosity at all. The sentence implies that this so-called animosity is all in Mr. Casaubon's head.

    The other answers may or may not be true statements. For example, perhaps Mr. Casaubon has given the other man ample reason for animosity. (Just from reading this little bit, don't you get the idea that Mr. Casaubon is that type of man?) Maybe the other man, who wants to marry Dorothea, has dishonorable motives for doing so (he's after only her money). Maybe the other man vied with Mr. Casaubon for Dorothea's affections long ago. All those things may or may not be true; you just don't know. Be very careful not to read too much into the material.

14. G. By such sentences as "Such a marriage would be fatal to Dorothea" and "it is my duty to hinder to the utmost the fulfillment of his designs," Mr. Casaubon makes it clear that he believes — or at least wants to believe — that the responsibility to foil the other man's intentions in order to protect Dorothea is his. (You already learned in question number 2 how easily Mr. Casaubon could convince himself that he is doing everything from the loftiest of motives, not out of petty jealousy and spite.)

Choice F may be a true statement. Maybe Mr. Casaubon believes the other man will "corrupt" Dorothea, given Mr. Casaubon's low opinion of the person. However, the primary theme of the indicated lines is not Mr. Casaubon's fears (those were expressed earlier) but his determination to hinder such an attachment. Be very careful not to choose an answer simply because the statement is true. Check that the answer directly answers the question.

15. C. All the other answers are too strong and include information that you have no way of knowing. Maybe Mr. C did believe Dorothea was marrying him only for his money. Maybe Dorothea was unaware of Mr. C's fears. (It sounds as if she'd have been crazy to marry the guy, had she known what he was really like!) Choice C seems logical; a man who has made "arrangements" that leave "strong measures open to him" sounds quite cautious.

In fiction passages, try to get a sense of the overall moral worth of the character and then answer questions based on that impression. For example, you can tell from a quick reading of the passage that Mr. C is a cantankerous old coot (at least in this excerpt). Most of the answers involving him will show him in a bad light. Dorothea is spoken of highly by the author. Therefore, anything said about her will probably be positive. Using this very simplistic "good guy/bad guy" concept can help you to eliminate at least a few of the answers, such as choices A and D (the passage sounds as if Dorothea were a pushover, a passive person, not one likely to "demand" anything).

16. H. You must take the sentence in the context of the entire passage, not just read it alone. The passage talks about Mr. C's concern over what will happen to his money — and incidentally, to his wife — when he dies. He therefore wants to have some idea of how much longer his life will be.

Choice F is the cheesy answer. Just because the quote has the word *probabilities* in it does not mean the man is a gambler. Nothing in the passage even hints at such a possibility. While choice J is possible (the man cared more for how people would mock him than for his wife's future happiness, it seems), the answer is too strong, using dramatic words like "obsessed" and "no one else." Moderate, more temperate answers are more likely to be correct than emphatic answers.

17. B. This was a rather difficult question. Lydgate was "conscious of an energetic frame in its prime," meaning that he knew what an energetic frame in its prime was. Lydgate is obviously a physician — this is the source of his knowledge — and he contrasted his vitality with the weakness of the man coming toward him.

Choice C is the trap answer. Yes, Lydgate felt pity, but pity for Mr. Casaubon, not for himself. And if you chose D, you went for the big, hard word on the principle of "if I don't know it, it must be the right answer" (we all have those feelings of insecurity, believe me). Usually, the most difficult word is merely a trap answer. Unless you can absolutely, positively eliminate the rest of the answers, don't choose a word you can't define.

18. G. The paragraph primarily describes how weak Mr. Casaubon is, contrasting that condition with both Lydgate's vitality and the beauty of the surroundings.

A *why* question like this one can be very difficult for international students. You are asked to understand not just the passage itself, but the motivation of the writer. If the correct answer doesn't immediately jump out at you, don't waste a lot of time on this sort of question. Make a quick guess (wrong answers are not penalized on the ACT) and go on to the next question.

Choice H is the trap answer. The paragraph talks about a ***dirge,*** which is a hymn sung at a funeral. If you knew that, you may have thought the purpose of this description was to predict a death. However, that may be going too far. If you have a choice between a moderate answer, such as contrasting *fit* versus *unfit,* and a dramatic answer — predicting death! — go for the more moderate of the two.

19. **D.** Eliminate choice C immediately. Very rarely is the correct answer negative in an ACT question. In this case, Lydgate is filled with compassion at seeing Mr. Casaubon and would be unlikely to be malicious. Choices A and B are possible, but D is more directly related to what the author specifically says: ". . . said Lydgate, filling up a pause." One fills up a pause by saying something when the silence becomes awkward.

20. **F.** The first half of the passage shows Mr. Casaubon in a very bad light, discussing how petty and jealous and vindictive he is. The last half of the passage elicits a feeling of compassion for a prematurely old man.

    Choice G is exactly wrong. The reader becomes more tolerant of Mr. Casaubon when learning of his problems. Choice H is unlikely. Although Lydgate is introduced at the end of the passage, the focus is still definitely on Mr. Casaubon. Choice J goes too far. The reader may feel sorry for Mr. Casaubon but is even less likely than before to understand why Dorothea married him (the man is not only nasty but also unattractive and prematurely old).

If two answers are direct opposites, the chances are good that one of them will turn out to be the correct answer choice. Here, choices G and F are opposites, indicating that one of them is likely to be the correct answer. You have a 50-50 guess, almost a present from the test-makers.

Passage 3

21. **D.** The primary purpose of many passages is to describe, discuss, or explain something. Those three words are so often the correct answer to a "main idea" or "primary purpose" question that you should immediately give them serious consideration. (They're not *always* right, of course — but almost always.)

    You should have dumped choice C right away. The ACT is not going to write a passage whose primary purpose is to trash (***denounce*** means to put down, to bad-mouth) someone, especially a professional such as a child psychologist. Main-idea, primary-purpose, or best-title answers are almost always positive or neutral, not negative.

    Choice B is tempting. The passage does mention self-esteem (and for those of you smart enough to look at the attribution, you'll see that the excerpt, in fact, comes from a book on self-esteem), but it never mentions anything about *low* self-esteem.

    Choice A is also tricky. It just sounds so pompous and correct: "provides the foundation for life." La-di-da. However, the passage discusses children up to the age of 16, well beyond "early childhood."

22. **G.** This question was an absolute gift to you. The answer is given specifically in the second sentence of the passage.

If you chose J, you fell for the trap. Yes, children work to achieve competence at various tasks throughout the stages of childhood, but all the tasks lead to the ultimate goal of selfhood. Don't choose an answer simply because it was mentioned in the passage. Be sure that the answer that you choose refers to the specific question asked.

23. **C.** Paragraph three mentions this cry of a child to make the point that he needs feedback, recognition of his achievements.

Choice A is a true statement, and it was discussed in the passage. However, choice A is not the answer to this specific question. Be careful that you don't choose a statement merely because it was true and was mentioned in the passage. Doing so is like saying, "There are 360 degrees in a circle," when the teacher asks you for the capital of Romania. Sure, the statement is true, but what does it have to do with the matter at hand?

Choice B is tempting, but parent-pleasing behavior was discussed later (in paragraph four) as typical of 5-year-olds.

24. J. This question traps rushed students who don't go back and see how the statement is used in the context of the passage. Lines 30–31 say that "the mother is the center of the child's world." True, the other answers mention games, but the phrase "the name of the game" was used metaphorically in this instance. To say that something ***is the name of the game*** means that it's the main idea, the point of the whole activity. For example, getting into college is the name of the game when studying for the ACT. If you didn't need a good ACT score to get into school, would you really go through all this mind-numbing studying? (You would? Just for my jokes? I'm flattered, but whoa — get a life!)

If it appears that a question depends on your understanding of a slang phrase or saying, you may want to make a quick guess. Such phrases are especially difficult to non-native speakers because such phrases are not literally translated. Don't waste a lot of time trying to understand the phrase; guess and go. Remember that the ACT does not penalize you for wrong answers, so guessing is always to your advantage.

25. D. The author states that this separateness is an important milestone in the children's development, indicating that this separateness is vital. (A ***milestone*** is an event marking a significant stage in life. For example, getting a driver's license is a milestone to teenagers.)

Did you notice that all the wrong answers were negative, and only the correct answer was positive? If you are guessing (and the ACT has no penalty for wrong answers, so a guess is always worthwhile), dump the negative answers and go for the positive. The ACT rarely trashes anyone or anything and is all sweetness and light.

26. G. The theme of the passage is the confusion between wanting two opposite things, such as demanding to have freedom from parents but being afraid to let go of them.

Every answer, obviously, comes right from the passage itself, so they all look familiar and "sound right." In a question like this one, I suggest that you ignore the answer choices at first. Reread the passage and identify its main idea to yourself. Then go back and find which answer best expresses that idea. If you look at the answer choices, every one looks good. Try to predict the answer first.

27. D. This should have been a pretty easy question. You want to examine more than just the indicated sentence; read the few sentences surrounding it. The next sentence tells you that, "He needs to ask what he is going to do with his life."

You didn't fall for the cheap trick in choice A, did you? A *vocation* is not the same thing as a *vacation.* And if you fell for choice B, you confused a *vocation* with a *location.* (Occasionally, I'll have a student come back after the test and exclaim, "There was a typographical error in the ACT, but I corrected it." Wrong. Although you may find a typo or two in this book — because I'm not perfect like the ACT — the ACT itself has none. If you think that you found a typo, you probably fell for the trap.)

28. F. Lines 92–96 mention that the convictions (which are developed at specific ages, statement II) will be influenced by the level of self-esteem (statement III), especially if a conflict exists among what a child believes, what he was raised with, and what his friends find acceptable. Nothing was mentioned about educational level.

When doing Roman numeral questions, focus first on the statement that you are most sure of. In this example, the author does, in fact, mention self-esteem. This fact means that you can eliminate any answer with III in it, choices H and J. As quickly as that, you've gotten the choices down to two. (You should *always* guess, because the ACT has no penalty for wrong answers; but a 50/50 guess is a real luxury.)

29. C. The passage discusses the various stages of children by their ages. ***Chronological*** means in order of time. If you didn't get this question, you outsmarted yourself and tried to make matters more difficult than they really were. Believe it or not, not every single question on the ACT is out to get you.

30. H. You could answer this question based on either the last paragraph or the first paragraph. The final paragraph discusses how the final stage of development is establishing total development. If that's the final stage, then the ultimate goal is that independence. The first paragraph also discusses how the purpose of childhood development is to achieve selfhood or self-knowledge.

Passage 4

31. B. The easy way to answer this question is to "plug 'n' chug." Plug each answer choice into the sentence and chug, or read through it. It makes sense to say, "Nearly any small child can recite quickly the twelve months of the year."

Choices A and D are traps. Yes, when you rattle something, you can shake it, or you can rattle someone and upset her, but those uses are not appropriate in this particular sentence. Words have more than one meaning. Your job is to identify which meaning works best in the context of the sentence.

32. F. The first paragraph specifically states that a piece of information is missing: how the names of the months came into existence. The majority of the rest of the passage explains the names.

If you chose G or H, you fell for the "But I know I read that!" trap. Just because something is mentioned in the passage does not mean that it is the main idea of the passage. A main idea is a general, underlying theme that runs through most of the passage. A good way to identify a main idea is to pretend that you are answering a buddy's question: "Hey, what did you just read?" In this case, you would respond with something like, "Oh, I read a passage about how the months got their names." Often, you can predict the correct answer to a main idea question before you ever read the answer choices.

33. C. Lines 19–21 state, "As the guardian of doors or gateways, he had to be vigilant for friends and foes coming from either direction." This should have been a very easy question for you. It is called a detail or fact question and simply asks you to find one fact from the passage. You don't have to interpret anything or draw a conclusion. It's important to recognize this type of question. If you are running short on time, or your brain cells are so scrambled that you know that you are missing most of the questions, this type of question is worth investing time in, because you can almost always get it correct.

34. F. When a question begins with the words, "According to the passage," it is usually quite simple. The answer is given, almost word for word, in lines 27–29, which state, "This month's name came from the February 15 feast of purification." If you missed this question . . . well, hang your head in shame.

35. A. Paragraph 4 implies that because people know Mars was the god of war, they assume that the month of March got its name from warfare. Instead, the author states, the origin of the name actually referred to the fact that war was postponed until the springtime, and that Mars was also the god of springtime.

Choice B is close but not quite right. The author discusses that most of the months are named after gods and goddesses but never states or implies that most people believe that *all* months are named for gods and goddesses. (Be careful not to read too much into the answer.) Choice C is definitely wrong. Paragraph five talks about how not every month's name has a definite ***provenance,*** or known origin. And choice D is off the wall: Nothing is mentioned in the entire passage about lunar cycles.

36. G. This question should have been relatively easy (unless you were too lazy to go back and look at how the expression is used in the passage). Plug the answer choices into the sentence and see which one works best. Here, it is logical to say, "In order to bring the Roman calendar back in line with the solar year . . . ."

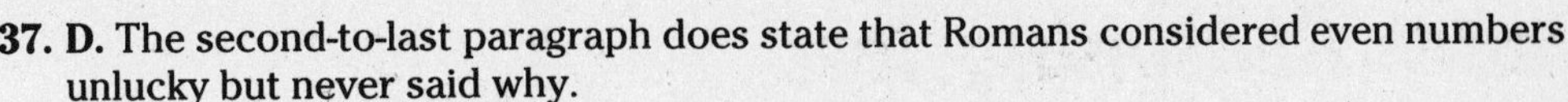

37. D. The second-to-last paragraph does state that Romans considered even numbers unlucky but never said why.

Often, when a question asks which of the following is *not* discussed, the answer has a "why" in it. Passages often state facts but may not give the why and wherefore behind those facts.

TIP

38. J. Because the question asks for a main idea, look for the most general answer. Choices F and G are mentioned in the paragraph but are not its main point. A main idea is usually given in the topic, or opening sentence of the paragraph, which here states, "Not every month has retained its original name over the years."

39. A. The author states that most people believe every fourth year is a leap year, but that's not the case. The century years are not leap years unless they are evenly divisible by 4. For that reason, statements I and II are wrong. Statement III takes a little more thought. If the millennium year were 1000 or 2000, both of which are divisible by 4, it would be a leap year. But if the millennium year were 3000, which is not evenly divisible by 4, it would not be a leap year. Therefore, statement III is not correct. (Give yourself a pat on the back if you got this question right.)

40. H. This is a very typical "vocabulary in context" question. Sure, you know what *gloss* normally means, but the ACT rarely uses a word in its normal sense. In fact, the normal sense of the word is usually the trap. (Choice F and choice J here are the trap answers.)

The key is to insert every answer choice into the sentence and see which one makes the most sense. The author is discussing how people don't realize something (that not every fourth year is a leap year), which means that they ignore a fact.

Did you notice that choices F and J are basically the same? Because you can't have two right answers, both must be wrong.

Science Reasoning Test

Passage 1

Did you remember to slow down and think about the introductory material and examine the tables before you headed to the questions? You're normal if you want to get right down to business, but spend at least a minute going over the material you are given. You don't have to understand that material perfectly, but do at least identify what the study is about and the basic results.

You've probably watched pole vaulting on television, right? When you're reading through this problem, try to visualize a pole-vaulter, running down the runway, planting the pole, zooming skyward, clearing (or crashing into) the bar, and finally, falling into the pit. The main point to get out of the intro to this problem is that the pole, as it unbends, forces the vaulter up.

Looking at the second paragraph and Table 1, you should note that a thick fiberglass pole is harder to bend than a thin fiberglass pole (logically enough), but the carbon fiber pole is harder to bend than a fiberglass pole.

Tables 1 and 2 combine to show that the more force required to bend a pole, the faster the pole bends back. Think of this relationship in another way: as a spring. You know that the harder a spring is to stretch, the more forcefully the spring recoils when released.

Okay, you now have the picture in mind and have evaluated the tables. Time to go on to the questions.

1. **B.** The answer to this question follows from the major relationship noted in the next-to-last paragraph of the analysis of this passage. Remember that the harder a spring is to stretch, the faster it will snap back to its regular position once it's released. Look at the two tables: Pole 3 requires the most force to bend but the least amount of time to snap back. Pole 1 requires the least force to bend but the greatest amount of time to snap back. Pole 2 is intermediate for both force and snap-back time. Choice B follows very cleanly from the numerical relationship shown in the two tables. The more force/less time relationship holds for all three poles, so you cannot justify choice D.

2. **G.** More force is required to bend a stiffer pole, as you are told in Table 1. In the introductory material before the tables, you find out that poles No. 1 and No. 3 have the same mass (no, you don't have to calculate mass; the mass is just given to you right out, as a gift) and that pole No. 2 has the greatest mass. Therefore, pole No. 3, the carbon fiber pole, which is one of the least massive poles, is the stiffest. Eliminate choice F. When looking at fiberglass compared to carbon fiber, this relationship doesn't hold. Eliminate choice H because with poles No. 1 and No. 2 , the more massive pole is stiffer. To choose between choices G and J, look at poles No. 1 and No. 2, the two fiberglass poles. Because the table indicates that the most massive pole is the stiffest, G is the right answer.

3. **A.** This type of question is common in Research Summaries (the name of this style of passage). This question requires you to understand some fundamentals of experimental design. A controlled variable (also known as an independent variable) is a factor that the experimenter can directly control (duh!). Because you are often asked about controlled variables, you may want to identify them as you are reading through the experimental data up front. In other words, as you read the problem, say to yourself, "Okay, what's different here? The two factors that are being fiddled with are the size of the pole and the material it's made of. Those, therefore, are the controlled variables."

   In this study, pole dimensions and material (fiberglass or carbon fiber) are controlled variables. The experimenter can easily change the diameter or length of a pole to a specific value, or he can change the pole's material. Choices B, C, and D mention factors that result from the experiment, not factors that can be changed going into the experiment.

4. **G.** Don't despair; this question is not as tough as the terminology initially suggests. In fact, you can answer this question pretty much by using your common sense. What is "potential"? Potential is something that can happen but hasn't happened yet. (You have the potential to enjoy these questions . . . but that hasn't happened yet!)

   The pole acts to transfer the energy produced while the vaulter runs into energy that lifts the vaulter upward. When bent, the pole has stored the energy gained from the running, but has not yet moved upward. At this point, the pole has the potential to move with much energy, but is not moving at the moment. Therefore, the pole has potential energy, but no kinetic energy.

5. **D.** The question tells you that the vaulter needs a pole that isn't too massive when it is very long. Home in on choices B and D because they focus on mass. Because low mass is the objective, D is correct.

6. **G.** This passage's introduction tells you that beginning vaulters need poles that are relatively easy to bend. Therefore, pole No. 1 is best for beginners, and choice J is out. The ideal advanced pole is one that quickly returns to a vertical position. That is, the pole quickly transfers the energy to a lifting force. Study 2 reveals that the best pole to transfer energy quickly to a lifting force is pole No. 3.

   Bonus! Did you see the second way to identify pole No. 3 as best for an experienced vaulter? The pole has a low density, meaning that the pole can be longer. If you remember question 5, vaulters like longer poles because they allow a vaulter to get closer to the crossbar.

Passage 2

Always begin by summarizing to yourself just what exactly the graph (or table, chart, or picture) indicates. This graph shows that the percentage of deaths grows with time. Well, duh! This relationship, of course, is what happens. The total number of deaths can never decrease. Fewer people may die in certain years, but when people die, the overall number of deaths goes up until 100 percent of the people are deceased.

Be careful not to interpret the graph as showing that more people die at the age of 100. Because the total number of deaths keeps growing, not only the number — but also the percentage — has to be higher at 100 years.

To get an idea of when most people die, look at where the graph makes the steepest climb. This increase appears to be between about 55 and 85 years. The percentage of people who have died grows from about 20 percent to about 80 percent over this time, so more than half the population dies between the ages of 55 and 85. Not too many people die at 100 because not that many people are left by that time. (They probably took too many ACTs, SATs, and various other agents of neurocellular destruction.)

The graph shows that a typical human being lives to be about 75. (Don't get too depressed. The mere fact that you bought this test prep book rather than a more serious tome shows that you are definitely not typical.) Half the population dies in 75 years. The remaining half of the people die after more than 75 years pass.

7. **B.** Not to worry. This question is a basic test of graph reading skills, with a little twist thrown in. First, find 80 years on the horizontal axis. Go straight up from this year (your ACT answer grid can serve as a straight edge) until you hit the plotted curve. Next, go straight to the left to find the percentage of people who have died. But watch out: If you chose choice C, you fell right for the trap. The question is asking for the percentage alive after 80 years. You must subtract 60 percent from 100 percent to get 40 percent.

Get into the habit of circling precisely what the question is asking for. In this case, circle the word "alive," so that you keep in mind that the percentage alive is what the question wants.

8. **J.** The percentage climbs from 0 percent to only 10 percent or so from 0 to 40 years, so choices F and G are out. A good look at later intervals shows much bigger increases in later intervals. The graph climbs from about 10 percent to 25 percent (an increase of 15 percent) between 40 and 60 years and from about 25 percent to 70 percent (an increase of 45 percent) between 60 and 80 years. (Just looking at the slope of the graph quickly provides the answer for this question.)

9. **A.** With no infant mortality, nobody dies just after 0 years. The graph will stay at 0 for a year or so and then start rising when children start dying from accidents, childhood diseases, brain explosion (from taking the ACT), and so on.

   For choice B to be correct, more people would have to die in the first 20 years. With fewer people dying soon after birth, more people will likely be alive at 20 years, so the graph should be lower. Even if all the people who would have died as infants die before 20, the graph would be the same at 20. Additional people would have to die to make the graph higher.

   Choice C is out because with more people surviving infancy, more people will have to die at later ages. The graph will be more, not less, steep in later years.

   Choice D is unreasonable because those who survive past 1 year of age are almost certain to die before they reach 100. Most people survive infancy but still don't make it to 100. (Yes, of course, some people do live past 100, but you are not expected to think of remote possibilities. Curb your argumentative tendencies and go for the logical, commonsense scenario, unless a question specifically says otherwise.) Another reason to eliminate choice D is that it mentions a figure, 120 years, that is far beyond the range shown on the graph. For the graph to get to 120, a significant number need to live to 100. Only a small percentage of people die before 1. Why would keeping these people alive swell the number surviving past 100?

10. **H.** You can answer this question by process of elimination. The graph tells you that choices F and G are out. A clear majority of people live past 45, which means that the largest number of people have yet to die.

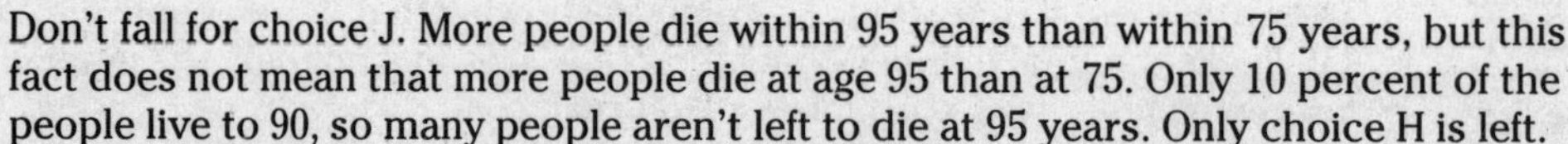

   Don't fall for choice J. More people die within 95 years than within 75 years, but this fact does not mean that more people die at age 95 than at 75. Only 10 percent of the people live to 90, so many people aren't left to die at 95 years. Only choice H is left.

11. **C.** At 15 years (choice A), less than 5 percent have died, so more than 95 percent are still alive. Just because a statement is correct doesn't make it the right answer choice. Note that the question asks you for the *maximum* number of years. Keep going to find out whether a larger number can be correct. At 35 years (choice B), over 90 percent are still alive. This larger number eliminates choice A. Keep going. At 55 years (choice C), 20 percent have died, so 80 percent are still alive. This number is mentioned in the question. At 80 years (choice D), 60 percent have died, so this choice is out.

   Did you see the word *maximum* and immediately choose the largest number? Do you really think the ACT is that easy? By all means, check the largest number, but don't automatically assume that that number is right.

Passage 3

No, nuclear physics is not a required course for the ACT. Although this topic may seem incredibly advanced, the reading and interpretation are relatively straightforward. All you have to do is to realize that the radioactive substances change in a way that can be measured and that the rate of change slows down with time. The tables show these relationships: You can see that the disintegration rates consistently slow down as time goes on.

Be sure to notice that the time frames used for the two substances differ. Don't assume that Table A and Table B use the same frame of reference. Treat each table separately.

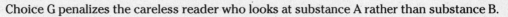

12. H. You can dump choice J immediately. If the substance is down to 125 after 16 hours, how can there be 200 after 20 hours? Use your common sense to eliminate illogical answers.

Choice G penalizes the careless reader who looks at substance A rather than substance B.

The most important thing to notice is that the disintegration rate is cut in half every four hours. After 20 hours (which is only one 4-hour segment after 16 hours), you can expect that the rate will be half of what it was at 16 hours. Half of 125 is 62.5.

13. B. The disintegration rate goes down because the number of radioactive atoms goes down as the substance disintegrates. (Actually, that's what "disintegration" is all about.) When fewer atoms are available to disintegrate, the disintegration rate naturally decreases.

So what does all this information mean to you? The number of atoms decreases in the same way that the disintegration rate decreases. At 15 hours, the disintegration rate is only $^{25}/_{200}$ or $^{1}/_{8}$ of what the rate was when measuring began. The number of atoms must be only $^{1}/_{8}$ of the original 10,000,000. A little simple multiplication finishes the problem: $^{1}/_{8} \times 10{,}000{,}000 = 1{,}250{,}000$.

14. F. Because wimpy or wishy-washy answers are usually better than dramatic or precise answers, eliminate choices G and J. Think about the choices as follows: If G is correct, the test-maker also has to accept choice F, which really wouldn't be wrong. However, choice F can be correct without choice G being correct. The same thing is true for choices H and J. If you are going to make a guess, guess F or H, the safer answers.

Just because 1,500 is halfway between 2,000 and 1,000 does not mean that the time has to be halfway between the times that are associated with 2,000 and 1,000. Take a look at Table 2. You'll notice that for every 4-hour interval, the decrease in millicuries is less. For example, the millicuries decrease 1,000 during the first 4 hours but decrease only 500 during the next 4 hours and decrease only 250 during the next 4 hours. You can conclude that more of a decrease occurs during the first 2 hours than during the second 2 hours. At 2 hours, the number of millicuries will be closer to 1,000 than to 2,000. You can conclude that 1,500 was reached a little before 2 hours, making choice F the safe bet.

Although this question is tough, thinking logically about how the test is constructed can help you narrow the field. Remember: The test-makers don't want to have to defend their answers. They're usually going to leave themselves some leeway by choosing less-precise answers.

15. C. The key is to look for which substance took less time for the disintegration rate (which is directly related to the number of radioactive atoms) to fall to one half of the original value. Substance A went from 200 to 100 in 5 hours, while substance B went from 2,000 to 1,000 in only 4 hours. Therefore, substance B has a shorter half-life, which narrows the field to choices C and D. Choice D is full of irrelevant garbage (just because the scientists decided to go home after 16 hours does not affect the half-life), while choice C actually reinforces the definition of half-life.

Choice A is misleading because the key is not the absolute amount of substance present but the amount of substance present relative to the starting amount. Choice B is simply wrong. The amount present after 25 hours is half the amount after 20 hours; the amount does not all disappear.

16. G. Hey, don't do too much work on this question. All you have to do is look at both tables and find the substance that has the lowest disintegration rate (which means a lower emission rate). You do not have to be concerned with the rate relative to the starting rate.

Because the disintegration rate is always lower after more time, knock out choices F and H right away. Table 1 shows that the rate for substance A after 20 hours is only 12.5 millicuries, while Table 2 shows 125 millicuries for substance B after 16 hours.

Passage 4

What is most interesting about this passage is that the two scientists do not dispute the results of the studies cited. They agree that schizophrenia runs in families; is often shared by identical twins; and among adopted children, is more common when a biological parent is schizophrenic. (Scientist 2 mentions an additional result regarding the adopted children, but nothing suggests that Scientist 1 would dispute this finding.) The disagreement revolves around how the information is interpreted, which is what frequently happens on the ACT.

Scientist 1 stresses genetic similarity and tries to rule out environmental factors. Scientist 2, on the other hand, points out that, despite genetic similarities, everything can be explained by looking at the environment.

17. C. A study would shed light on this issue if it used the same environment but different genetics. For example, if unrelated children reared by schizophrenic parents or guardians were all found to be free of schizophrenia, a case could be made that environment has little effect. Also helpful would be a study in which the genetics are the same, but the environment is different (choice C). The results were similar to what was found when twins were reared together, suggesting that environment is not very critical.

Choice A would actually support Scientist 2. Fraternal twins are no more genetically similar than are siblings born at different times; but fraternal twins, because they are the same age, are more likely to experience the same environment. If fraternal twins share a diagnosis of schizophrenia, the environment may be the reason.

Choices B and D are compatible with both scientists' views. Choice B is implied in both passages. The scientists agree on this finding but disagree on the cause. Regarding choice D, nothing in either passage addresses how common schizophrenia is in the general population. No matter how common it is, the two scientists could agree on the numbers and disagree on what causes schizophrenia.

18. H. Besides questioning the wisdom of the social worker who made such a placement, what do you think as you read the question? Scientist 2 claims that environment is key. The foster home is rife with schizophrenia, which, according to an environmental advocate, greatly increases the probability that a child would develop schizophrenia.

Choice J is too extreme. Dramatic or extreme answers are rarely correct. A good wishy-washy answer that hedges its bets as skillfully as a cornered politician is more likely correct.

Choices F and G are more in accordance with the views of Scientist 1, who would look at the apparently normal genes and predict normal development.

19. C. Without this assumption, the scientists would probably cite other studies instead of discussing how to interpret the findings mentioned.

Choices A and B can be eliminated quickly. Neither study touches on the prevalence of schizophrenia. Choice B is probably true, but the scientists don't have to assume that. Their arguments would still stand even if almost everybody were schizophrenic. Choice D overgeneralizes. The scientists discuss schizophrenia, a specific mental disorder. You have no way of knowing what they may assume about mental disorders in general.

20. J. Brain chemistry certainly qualifies as a biological factor (chemicals make up living organisms). Choice J also makes sense because it is likely that Scientist 1 would try to support her argument.

Choice H is wrong because the reason mentioned in that choice is more in line with what Scientist 2 would say. Choice G does hint at a shortcoming of studies that simply find an association: They do not prove a cause. However, saying that the studies are irrelevant is unjustified. Think of a real-life example. Studies on smoking show a high association between smoking and health problems but do not prove that smoking directly causes such problems. Nevertheless, the smoking studies are relevant.

Choice F is knocked out because when something is unknown, some claims may be questioned, but they are not disproved. How brain chemicals are inherited may be unclear, but Scientist 1 claims that biology is key and is likely to let an unknown factor wipe out her claim.

21. **A.** Home in on choices A and B. The word *definitively* makes choices C and D too extreme. (Good scientists are cautious; they don't hastily jump to conclusions.) The children could be schizophrenic because of genetics or some other biological factor. Parents may start acting differently in an attempt to correct the schizophrenia or because they are upset by what they observe in their children. Choice B is out because even if this statement were true about child-rearing (which it probably isn't), an environmental link between child-rearing and schizophrenia is not ruled out. The word *no* in choice B and the reason given are inconsistent.

22. **J.** If you follow the method Scientist 2 uses to support her argument, you will have an easier time with this question. In her reasoning, Scientist 2 points to the finding that the majority of adopted children who were born to schizophrenics develop normally. She concludes that the way they are brought up is key, implying that a normal upbringing by the adoptive parents is enough to overcome a genetic background of schizophrenia. The evidence presented in this question, however, points out that most children born to schizophrenics develop normally no matter who brings them up. Scientist 2's conclusion that upbringing is the key factor is weakened, so choice J is the answer. Choice H is out because the reason given would actually strengthen Scientist 2's argument.

As mentioned in the introductory analysis of this passage, Scientist 1 would not dispute Scientist 2's mention of adopted children who were born to schizophrenics. Scientist 1 never claimed that a genetic history of schizophrenia means it is certain that one will become schizophrenic. Scientist 1 claims that when schizophrenia occurs, biological factors are responsible, but she never said that these factors were sufficient to cause schizophrenia. Eliminate choice G. Choice F is out not only because Scientist 1 has no problem with normal development despite schizophrenic parents but also because the reason given is something that Scientist 1 could use to explain why schizophrenia does not always result when at least one parent is schizophrenic.

You can also eliminate choice A based on a tip you have learned throughout these materials: Outside knowledge is not required to answer a question. In other words, everything you need to answer the question is stated or implied in the passage and graphs. Choice F requires too much outside knowledge. Because the ACT does not expect you to know anything about recessive traits, an answer that hinges on such knowledge can't be correct.

23. **D.** This statement is a good way for Scientist 1 to play it safe. She said that schizophrenia is caused primarily by biological factors but never claimed that biology was all that mattered.

Choice A is something that Scientist 2 would say. In conflicting-viewpoints types of passages, often a wrong answer is wrong only because it would be supported by the wrong scientist. For example, if a question asks you which statement would most support Scientist 1's point of view, a typical wrong answer would give a statement that is true and valid but would support Scientist 2's point of view. Choice C is also in line with Scientist 2. Psychotherapy deals a lot with environmental factors. You can eliminate both choices C and B based on the fact that too much is read into the passage. Be careful to answer questions based only on what is stated or implied in the passage, and not to extend the reasoning.

Passage 5

Did you look at this experiment and mutter to yourself, "What a blooming mess!" If so, congratulate yourself: Your humor is becoming almost as sorry as mine. That aside, this passage isn't too bad. This passage doesn't shock the senses by introducing concepts unfamiliar to you. You've seen plants produce flowers at only a certain time of year. You know that the length of daylight is different throughout the year (longer days in summer, shorter days in winter).

After you've got the topic of this passage (the effect of the length of day on plants), you're ready to summarize each experiment. (You may want to write your brief synopsis in the margin.) Experiment 1 shows that interrupting the day has no effect.

Experiment 2 shows that interrupting the night changes the plants' responses, indicating that the plants may actually respond to the length of night rather than the length of day. An SD plant is actually a long-night plant, whereas an LD plant is a short-night plant.

Experiment 3 may sound complicated, but the gist is that, as with Experiment 1, manipulating the day has no effect on the plants.

In Experiment 4, as in Experiment 2, changing a nighttime factor affects the plants.

Taken together, these experiments suggest that the plants are sensitive to changes in the length of night, rather than the length of day. Don't economize on time here. Wanting to jump right into the questions is natural, but take a minute or two to think about what you just read. You don't have to be able to quote chapter and verse; you just have to know a little bit of what's going on. If you get confused here, you're likely to miss nearly every question.

24. J. Experiments 1 and 2 showed that only interruptions that occur during the night affect the flowering response. Eliminate choices F and H, which mention daytime hours. Choice J makes more sense than choice G because if the total number of hours are critical, a brief interruption would have very little effect. On the other hand, if the plants are somehow measuring the number of continuous nighttime hours, a brief interruption would affect the plant.

25. C. One major point of this passage is that SD and LD plants show opposite responses. This difference makes choices A and D unlikely. You can make a good guess at this point by choosing between choices B and C. Remember, the ACT does not subtract points for wrong answers, so guessing is always justified. Having a 50/50 choice is a real treat.

When the light is presented in the middle of the 16-hour night, the plants are exposed to only 8 hours of uninterrupted night hours. The plant that flowers when nights are short will start flowering. Which plant meets this criteria? The LD plant, which is spinach in this passage, flowers when days are long and nights are short.

Some of you are probably saying, "Yes, but what if . . ." Ah, Smart Students' Disease (in which you make things harder than necessary) is back. Don't be too concerned with the exact number of uninterrupted nighttime hours that spinach requires to flower. Although some LD plants may not flower until the number of uninterrupted night hours falls to, say, seven hours, the ACT will not pull this type of trick on you. The ACT does not expect you to memorize such obscure facts. What the ACT is testing is your understanding that a nighttime interruption effectively shortens the night and therefore leads to LD flowering.

The information presented in the first part of the passage reinforces choice C. The passage mentions that cocklebur does not flower until day length is less than 15.5 hours. This statement means that nighttime must exceed 8.5 hours (24 – 15.5 = 8.5) for cocklebur to flower. When the light is flashed in the middle of the 16-hour night, the night is effectively only 8 hours long, which means that the cocklebur will not flower.

26. **G.** The experimenter can easily choose another plant, keep the lights on or off at a certain time, or change the temperature. Whether the plants flower, on the other hand, has to do with how the plants respond to the conditions presented in the experiment. Flowering depends on what happens to the other variables. Such dependent variables are a step removed from the direct control of the experimenter.

27. **C.** In both sets of experiments, changing day conditions has no effect on the plants' responses, although changing night conditions does. Choice D acknowledges this consistency, but the reason focuses on how the experiments are set up, not on the results. In many biological experiments, the same organisms are used, but doing so does not guarantee similar results. (Imagine, for example, if you and your friend both had colds and both were given aspirin. The aspirin does not guarantee that both of you would have the same response to the medication.)

    Choices A and B, besides being flat-out wrong from the start, also provide reasons that focus on the experimental conditions rather than the results. In addition, choice A may not even be correct because you have no information regarding the variety of plants used in Experiments 1 and 2. Choice B points out a key way that the sets of experiments differ, but the results are similar.

28. **G.** On the horizontal axes, day length increases to the right. The LD plant flowers during long days. This information means that high vertical values are associated with the right side of the graph. Eliminate choices H and J, in which flowering does not increase with the increasing day length.

    Choice G is better than choice F because with LD plants, no flowering occurs until a critical day length is reached. (The experiments actually show that the LD plant responds when the length of night falls below a certain value, but associating an LD plant's flowering with long days is still okay.) In choice F, the graph continually rises, implying that flowering increases as day length increases from 0 hours. Choice G correctly shows that flowering does not occur when the day length is less than 15 hours.

29. **C.** So many questions are about SD and LD that you may have forgotten the third actor in this play, a DN plant. Look at the introduction, which defines a DN plant as one that is not sensitive to changes in day length. This type of plant should flower in any environment, including near the equator. (So you shouldn't be surprised that some weeds are DN plants.) Because IV is part of the answer, choice B is out.

    Plants that require very long or very short days will probably not flower near the equator because the day length stays close to 12 hours and will not approach the number of hours necessary for flowering. This means that III is out. Such an SD plant will flower when days are less than 8 hours (and nights are more than 16 hours), which never happens near the equator. With III out, you can eliminate choice D, leaving you with only choices A and C.

    Do I and II seem reasonable? Yes, because the day length does vary slightly from 12 hours near the equator. Such changes are enough to produce flowering in plants that don't require much different from a 12-hour day/night. With statements I and II acceptable, you can eliminate choice A.

Passage 6

Even though you do not need outside knowledge to answer these questions, information you have gained over the years (along with just plain common sense) can be very helpful. The ACT does not try to trap or trick you by giving wrong science. What you have learned in school or from experience will remain valid and useful for the ACT.

Use your own knowledge. What's more spread out: a solid, such as a block of ice, or oxygen gas as it is sprayed from a tank into a room? You know or can visualize that in a gas, particles quickly spread out as much as possible.

Continue using your own knowledge. What happens when you heat ice? The ice melts and turns into liquid water. Further heating leads to boiling, and the water evaporates. These thoughts should help you grasp what's being stated in paragraph two.

The third paragraph is probably less familiar to you, but the figures should help. You can see from Figure 2, for example, that at 60°C and 0.20 atm, water is a gas, but at 60°C and 0.80 atm, water is a liquid. Try to summarize the information to get the gist or main point. The main point is that pressure affects phases.

The figures re-emphasize that high temperature is associated with a gas and that low temperature is associated with a solid. When pressure is high, a relatively high temperature is needed to turn a liquid into a gas.

30. **G.** This straightforward question simply tests your ability to read a graph. Look at Figure 2, which deals with water. Locate 60°C on the horizontal axis and then go straight up until you are even with 1.00 atm (on the vertical axis). You are in the liquid region.

31. **A.** You are looking for a point on one of the figures where a solid is next to a gas. Choice A looks good. In Figure 1 (bromine), –20°C and 0.05 atm is near the lower-left corner, where a solid and a gas are next to each other. Liquid is out of the way, up and to the right.

    Choice B is wrong because at 0°C and 0.80 atm, bromine is near the solid-liquid boundary. Water is also near that boundary at 0°C and 0.80 atm, so choice C is out. Choice D is way off because water is nowhere near a solid at 80°C and 0.50 atm.

32. **G.** The easiest way to do this question is to take a straightedge (your answer grid will work) and, on each figure, draw a vertical line from the 30°C mark. Now, for each figure, mark 0.6 atm and 0.3 atm on the line. On the bromine graph (Figure 1), 0.6 atm is in the liquid region, and 0.3 atm is in the gas region when the temperature is 30° C, so choice G is the answer. Don't be careless and pick choice F. The pressure is going down, so you are moving from the liquid to the gas, not from a gas to a liquid. The liquid region is generally higher than the gas region. On the water graph (Figure 2), you can see that both of your marks are in the liquid region, eliminating choices H and J.

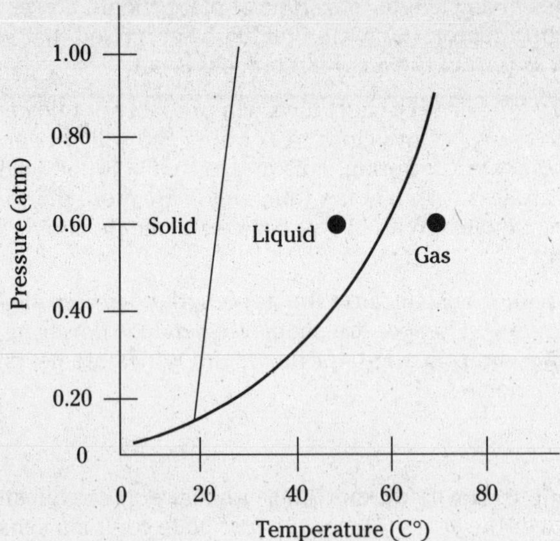

Figure 1: Bromine Phases

33. D. Your gut instinct should attract you to choices B and D because higher temperatures move particles further apart. If you are running out of time, go ahead and make a guess; 50/50 odds aren't that bad on this test, and remember: The ACT has no penalty for wrong answers. Choice D is correct because water at 100°C and 0.60 atm is a gas, while bromine at 50°C and 0.80 atm (choice B) is a liquid. Just to be certain, (good test-takers are always paranoid, but are you paranoid *enough?*), check choices A and C. In choice A, bromine is a solid. In choice C, water is also a solid.

34. H. You can probably eliminate choice F by using common sense: Higher altitudes don't necessarily mean your pasta freezes! When an answer seems illogical or even amusing, put it aside for a moment. If none of the other answer choices are correct, you can always come back to it. (For those of you who love Sherlock Holmes, you will recognize this strategy as a variation on his famous saying, which roughly goes, "When you have eliminated the impossible, whatever remains, however improbable, must be true.")

Go through the rest of the choices without wasting any time on choice F. Choice G is out because the water temperature (the spaghetti is in the water) is important, not the air temperature. A look at Figure 2 confirms the first part of choice H: At 1.00 atm, water becomes a gas. At 0.80 atm, water becomes a gas at about 90°C. With the water boiling at a lower temperature, there's less heat available to soften the spaghetti. The answer is probably choice H, but double-check choice J just to be sure. Choice J is contradicted by Figure 2 (think of how you analyzed choice H). Besides, in this problem, the water is already boiling, so the length of time required to boil water is irrelevant.

Passage 7

First of all, don't panic if the terminology is not familiar to you. You don't have to know what radon is to understand the introduction. Remember that the ACT does not presuppose any specific scientific knowledge on your part. Simply note that radon may have something to do with earthquakes and that scientists are going to check out this possibility.

Spend a minute or two looking at the charts. You don't have to understand the charts perfectly, and you certainly don't want to start memorizing the information given. Just realize that Figures 1 through 4 are basically maps. You can see the epicenters and note that wells around the epicenters have higher-than-normal amounts of radon emission.

Figure 5 shows a systematic relationship (called a correlation) between earthquake magnitude and the differential, which is a measure of how much the radon emission exceeds normal. The rightmost point is the only one that bucks the trend. When you see something abnormal, something that doesn't follow the same pattern as the others, pay special attention to it. The chances are good that you will be asked a question about this aberration. Which earthquake site is represented by the rightmost point? The site had a magnitude of 7.9 and an average differential of 2.5. Scan Figures 1 through 4 and you will see that the point in question represents China. Note that China has two wells near the epicenter that were not much above normal. Perhaps these wells were measured inaccurately. Whatever the case, these wells may have something to do with why China is a little off in regard to Figure 5.

35. B. Choice A doesn't look right. All four sites had radon emissions that were greater than the normal amount found over the earth, making choice B look good.

You should have been leaning toward choosing B as soon as you saw the wishy-washy, wimpy language. A correct answer often has language that is not extreme, language that hedges a little bit. A conclusion that stated that an association is *definitely* present would be too strong unless a lot more data were collected.

None of the figures show wells that are 1,000 km (10 cm) away from the epicenter, so you can determine nothing about choice C.

The conclusion stated in choice D is also unjustified. For the most part, wells near the epicenters show higher emissions, but the numbers are not very close to 5 percent and no measurement was taken right at the epicenter.

36. H. The results of the studies indicate some association between earthquakes and radon emissions. Results that go along with the trend found in the studies strengthen the results and any claim derived from the results. Option I is one such result. You can already see that a higher-than-normal emission from all the well sites shown exists. With more evidence, the case becomes more compelling. Because statement I is true, you can immediately narrow the answers down to choices H or J. If you're in a huge rush, guess and go. ***Remember:*** The ACT does not subtract points for wrong answers. Guessing is always to your advantage.

Does statement II look good? It does if you remember the introductory analysis about China. The one point that is off in Figure 5 is the one from China. The finding cited in statement II would produce a point that would fall in line with the points from the other three sites. Because statement II is valid, choice J has been eliminated.

On the real test, you wouldn't even need to look at statement III. However, for you skeptics in the audience, I'll examine III. It does not provide enough information. What is needed are more quakes associated with high radon emissions. Simply having more quakes doesn't shed any light on the association between earthquakes and radon emissions.

37. A. You've got to be careful when dealing with data that show an association (a correlation in more mathematical terms). Just because two things go together does not imply that one causes the other. For example, the number of skyscrapers in a city and the number of children who live in that city have a correlation. That is, in general, cities that have more skyscrapers also have more young people. Does this mean that young people are building the skyscrapers? Of course not. A more reasonable explanation is that when a city is large, it has many skyscrapers and youngsters. An underlying cause, namely overall city size, exists. Children do not cause skyscrapers or vice versa.

This study simply measured a correlation. This study was not designed to investigate any possible mechanism that would convert radon emissions into earthquakes, which knocks out choices C and D and narrows the field to choices A and B. Choice B is out because nothing in the study points to 4 percent as a magic number. This fact is not true, but even if it were, you would not have to know this information from some specialized outside study, which is not required on the ACT.

38. J. When experimental results are obtained, the responsible factor is often unclear. For example, if a scientist wanted to study whether a new drug could increase ACT scores, he could give the drug to a group of students and then look at the scores. If the scores are high, the scientist could conclude that the drug had an effect. But what if the group studied included many people who have a history of scoring well on tests similar to the ACT? What if the students did better simply because they believed the drug would help them? By including a control condition, experimenters can rule out these possibilities. Experimenters can find a group that was equal to the drug group on previous test scores and then give these control students a placebo (a fake pill) but tell them that this pill is supposed to help raise ACT scores. If the drug group scores higher, experimenters can be more confident that the high scores weren't simply the result of using a high-achieving group or a psychological belief in the drug because the two groups were matched in terms of these factors. In this case, the chemicals in the drug more likely had something to do with the higher scores. The control condition helped rule out other possible factors.

In the earthquake studies, radon emissions were measured after earthquakes. The researchers obtained high values, but such values can occur even in the absence of an earthquake. Scientists would need to know the radon emission level that normally occurs in the sites studied.

In a sense, choices F and H mention conditions that are included in the studies. The studies did compare the wells near the epicenters to worldwide values. Sites far from the epicenters or in virtually earthquake-free areas are included in the worldwide averages.

All choice G would do is add more data to what has already been found. Clearing up the graph in Figure 5 would be particularly helpful, but the condition is not a control condition.

39. A. Use common sense! If you want to predict an earthquake, you have to measure something *before* the earthquake occurs. The problem with the current studies is that scientists measured emissions after the earthquakes. Maybe the earthquakes caused the emissions, making radon pretty useless as a predictor. Choices B, C, and D wouldn't help unless measurements were taken before.

You are not required to have specific science knowledge to answer an ACT question, but the test-makers do assume a level of common sense. The ACT does not teach or test false science (for example, you won't have an experiment with totally illogical results). This small act of kindness means that you can trust your common sense and general knowledge. The science portion of the ACT has very few traps or tricks in it. The science is pretty straightforward, as are the questions. Don't make these questions harder than they have to be.

40. H. What's so puzzling about choice F? One site had to have the strongest earthquake, so why not China? Choice G is logical. It's not surprising that the highest differential would be found near the epicenter of the strongest earthquake, given the trend shown in Figure 5.

Choice H is the strange one. At the other three sites, the wells closest to the epicenter had differentials that were among the highest found in the area. In China, the two closest wells had far lower differentials. Choice J is not puzzling. Why not measure from as many wells as possible? Besides, readings were taken from six wells in Chile as well as China.

Part IX
The Part of Tens

The 5th Wave
By Rich Tennant
It didn't help that the ACT proctor also happened to be Kevin's dentist.
Well, I don't like the looks of that. You keep working– I'm going out to the car for some Novocaine.

In this part . . .

Party time! You've finished the tough stuff, all that learning and exercising your mind. Reward your new, leaner and meaner brain cells with these fun chapters. Sure, you actually learn a few things, like the answers to some of the most important questions about college applications. But you also get a warning about ten of the — ahem — least brilliant (okay, boneheaded!) things you can do to mess up your score.

Chapter 18

Ten Wrong Rumors about the ACT

In This Chapter

- You can't study for the ACT
- Different states have different ACTs
- The ACT has a passing score
- The ACT tests IQ
- If you don't know the answer, choose A or F
- You should never guess
- The ACT is easier than the SAT
- The ACT is the same as the Achievement Exam
- You have to write an essay
- You can't take both the SAT and the ACT

They're whispered in the bathrooms, they're written in notes passed in the classroom. What are they? They're the vile and vicious rumors about the ACT, rumors that seem to grow with each telling.

"You can't use a calculator." (Wrong. You may use a calculator, just as you may use one on the SAT.)

"They make you write an essay." (No. You write an essay on the SAT II but not on the ACT.)

The Friday night before the ACT, my phone rings off the hook. I spend hours reassuring students and their parents that the latest rumors they've heard about the ACT are completely false. Here are ten of the rumors you may have heard.

You Can't Study for the ACT

If you really thought that, why did you buy this book (not that I don't appreciate your purchase, mind you)? The ACT tests grammar; you can certainly refresh your memory of the grammar rules. The ACT has algebra, geometry, and arithmetic questions on it; you can certainly study formulas and rules in those areas. In addition, a little preparation can make you very comfortable with the format and timing of the test, helping to reduce test anxiety and ultimately improve your score. This book, in particular, discusses tricks and traps that are built into the exam — *gotchas!* that I want you to be prepared for.

Different States Have Different ACTs

This rumor is based on the fact that the score sheet compares your performance to that of other students who have taken the ACT in your state. When you get back your ACT score, you are told your percentile rank nationally and within your state. However, all students in all states take the exact same ACT on any one test date. (Of course, the ACT changes from one date to the next; otherwise, you could keep retaking the same test. You'd be surprised how many students don't realize this and merrily say to me, "Oh, I remember the questions from last time, so I'll do great next time." Duh.) It will do you no good to fly to Rhode Island or Nebraska, thinking that you can get an easier exam there.

The ACT Has a Passing Score

There is no such thing as a passing or failing score on the ACT. By looking at the college bulletins of the schools you are interested in, you can deduce your minimum entrance score based on your GPA. If you have a high GPA, your ACT score can be lower than if you have a low GPA. In fact, you may be pleasantly surprised how low your ACT score can be. Scoring on the ACT is not like scoring on high school exams, in which a 65th percentile is failing. If you score in the 65th percentile on the ACT, you may still be able to get into the college of your choice.

The ACT Tests IQ

The ACT is a college entrance exam. It tests your potential for doing well in college. If you are the type who normally studies hard for an exam, you will probably study hard for the ACT and do well on it, and then study hard for college exams and do well on them, too. The key is in the preparation. You have the same opportunity to do well on the ACT regardless of whether you are a SuperBrain or as cerebrally challenged as the rest of us. With this book, you can learn to improve your ACT scores with all sorts of tricks, tips, and techniques, something that is *much* harder to do on IQ exams.

If You Don't Know the Answer, Choose A or F

I'm constantly amazed at how many people tell me that they've heard this rumor. The answer choices on the ACT are A, B, C, D, and F, G, H, and J. (***Note:*** The one exception is the Mathematics Test. In that section, the answer choices are A, B, C, D, E and F, G, H, J, and K.) Students tell me repeatedly that they have been told to guess an A or an F if they don't know the answer. This is ridiculous. Every answer choice has the same possibility: one out of four (or in the math section, one out of five).

You Should Never Guess

Wrong, wrong, wrong. You should *always* guess on the ACT. *That exam has no penalty for guessing.* Never leave an answer blank. Fill in something, anything, on the chance that you may get lucky and get the question correct.

For those of you who are also taking the SAT I, notice that the two exams are different in this respect. The SAT I *does* penalize you (either 1/4 or 1/3 point, depending on the type of question) for each wrong answer so that random guessing on that test is discouraged (except on the grid-in math portion). Random guessing on the ACT can only help you.

The ACT Is Easier than the SAT I

Maybe. Maybe not. The ACT has no vocabulary on it, only English grammar. Obviously, if you are better at grammar than vocabulary, the ACT is easier for you. The math questions on the ACT are all straightforward multiple choice with none of the tricky QC (Quantitative Comparisons) or grid-in questions featured on the SAT I. However, the ACT does feature a few trigonometry questions (only about four; don't sweat 'em), which are not on the SAT I. The ACT reading passages, both in the Reading Test and in the Science Reasoning Test, tend to be slightly longer than some of those on the SAT I but not necessarily more difficult.

The ACT Is the Same as the Achievement Test

Many people, especially parents, confuse ACT with ACH. The Achievement Test used to be referred to as ACH. To confuse everyone totally, the test-makers have renamed the Achievement Test the SAT II. Got that? The regular old SAT is the SAT I; the former Achievement Test is the SAT II. Neither is connected to the ACT. ACT stands for American College Testing. SAT II consists of single-subject tests that require you to actually know things like Chinese verbs or botany rules. The ACT does not test single subjects, but general knowledge and reasoning skills.

You Have to Write an Essay

No. You do not have to write an essay during the ACT. The ACT has a section called English, but it features multiple-choice questions. (The SAT II, formerly known as the Achievement Test or ACH, does require an essay.)

You Can't Take Both the SAT I and the ACT

Wrong, wrong, wrong. *Many* students take both exams. Usually, the ACT is offered a week or two after the SAT I. You may be burned out, taking two exams this closely, or have trouble *studying* for both of them, but you certainly may *take* both tests. Some colleges require the SAT I. Other colleges will accept either the ACT or the SAT I. A few colleges accept the ACT only. When I tutor students, I suggest that they take both exams.

Chapter 19

Picking the Expert's Brain: Ten Things That Colleges Want

In This Chapter

- What's the number one thing that colleges look for?
- How important is the ACT, really?
- Do schools care whether I repeat the ACT?
- Can I take the ACT instead of the SAT?
- If I mess up big time on the ACT, what can I do to compensate?
- What classes do you recommend that I take as a senior? junior? sophomore?
- How helpful are charity work and sports?
- What should I say on the college essay?
- What will they ask me in the interview, and what should I say?
- How can I decide which school is best for me?
- What's the biggest mistake most students make in college planning?
- Anything else I should know?

The number one question that I'm asked by my students is, "What do colleges want outta me?" I took that question to an expert, Jill Q. Porter, M.S., of La Jolla, California. An independent college counselor, Jill has helped thousands of students get into the schools that best meet their needs and fulfill their dreams. She visits dozens of colleges every year, talks with the admissions officers, and knows what's important to them. She's great at debunking some of the rumors that make the rounds. Here are her answers to 12 of the most important questions a student recently posed in an interview.

What's the Number One Thing That Colleges Look For?

"Grades and the level of coursework. If you get straight *A*s but you take basket weaving and lint picking, schools aren't going to be impressed. If you take five solids, like physics, calculus, Spanish, history, and English lit, and get a few *A*s and a few *B*s, schools are going to be very impressed. It's not just the grades but the difficulty level of the classes that's important."

How Important Is the ACT, Really?

"The ACT is crucial. Do you think the colleges would spend so much time and money separating students by their ACT scores if the schools didn't consider the scores important? The colleges need to have some universal measure of skills, something that can put all students on an equal footing. Some kids don't have the chance to take calculus in their high schools, or they go to schools that just plain don't offer AP (Advanced Placement) classes. By having everyone take the same test, schools have a more fair and equitable frame of reference."

Do Schools Care Whether I Repeat the ACT?

"The answer to this depends on the college. The very top-tier colleges don't expect you to take the ACT six or seven times and may be dubious if you do so. Twice is enough for the top schools. The second-rung schools don't mind if you take the ACT three or four times. Check directly with the individual school to find out its policy."

Can I Take the ACT instead of the SAT I?

"Many schools in the Midwest will accept ACT scores in lieu of SAT I scores. Other schools will let you take both exams and will evaluate both scores. My suggestion is that you plan to take both exams. You want to keep your options open. What if you suddenly decide you want to go to a different college, one you hadn't considered before? By the time you realize you need an SAT score, it may be too late to take the test. Automatically plan on taking both tests, if possible."

It just so happens that your friendly neighborhood bookstore has copies of *The SAT I For Dummies* (IDG Books Worldwide) to help you prepare for that exam. Could life *get* any better?

If I Mess Up Big Time on the ACT, What Can I Do to Compensate?

"Adjust your expectations. Reality is the name of the game when it comes to college planning. While we'd all love to go to Status U., most of us will have to settle for less. If you do very badly on the ACT and don't have time to take it again, there's nothing you can do but look at another school. You always have the option of transferring after your first or second year.

"Keep in mind that schools do get last-minute openings. Even if you think your ACT score absolutely disqualifies you from your Dream School, send in the application and try to get on a wait list. You never know how lucky you can get."

What Classes Do You Recommend That I Take as a Senior? Junior? Sophomore?

"In general, the more challenging and complete your course load, the more likely you are to get accepted by a good college. And let me warn you: You can't slack off your senior year. Many students tell me that they work super-hard their junior year and then take easy classes their senior year because it's too late for the colleges to get those grades. Wrong. Some schools don't send out confirmation notices until the end of March of the senior year. That means they get the first semester grades and know if you've signed up for and then dropped classes your senior year. Remember, the application form is a legal contract. If you write that you're taking a bunch of hard classes which you actually stayed in for a day and then dropped, you're lying to the college, and that's called fraud.

"Enough of scaring you. Here's what most colleges are looking for: three years of math (four is even better); four years of English; two to three years of language (any language is fine; you won't get extra points for taking a 'classy' language like Latin); two to three years of science; and two years of social studies. As far as the math goes, you don't have to take calculus unless you are trying to get into a math, engineering, or architecture program. And physics isn't required by all colleges either."

How Helpful Are Charity Work and Sports?

"Colleges *expect* you to have some sort of community involvement. The key is doing something you enjoy. Don't sign up to work at a preschool if you don't have patience with small children, for example. The newspaper is always full of organizations requesting volunteers; somewhere, there's a perfect match for you. In my opinion, it's more important to be very involved with one charity than to sign up for ten different charities just to have them on your application form. The schools aren't dumb; they'll know what you're doing.

"As for sports, they show you're well rounded. You don't have to play varsity sports, just be involved in something, even intramurals. A word of caution: Sports are *not* more important than grades. Don't let your athletics stand in the way of your academics."

What Should I Say on the College Essay?

"I stress individuality. Show the colleges who you really are. College admissions officers read hundreds, maybe even thousands, of essays every year. They don't award points when you say what you obviously think the college wants to hear. They're impressed when you let your personality shine through. If you are archconservative and take pride in campaigning for right-wing candidates, mention your experiences. If you are really into pyramid power, channeling, and New Age stuff, talk about that. The key is to write about something you enjoy.

"And it goes without saying that your writing should be well organized and grammatically correct. With spell-checkers (both mechanical and that type called 'parents'), there's no excuse to turn in a sloppy essay."

What Will They Ask Me in the Interview, and What Should I Say?

"Colleges have two basic types of interviews, those done by alumni and those done by college staff. The alumni interviews tend to be a little less formal, but that doesn't mean you don't have to take them seriously.

"In both types of interviews, the most important thing is to show you are seriously interested in *this* school. Demonstrate that you've done your homework. By that, I don't mean bring in your algebra scratch paper, but indicate that you've done your background reading on the college. Mention some programs you find impressive or something about the history of the school. Above all, be very careful not to annoy the interviewer by asking some trite question that's already been answered in the promotional literature. For example, asking 'How many students are on campus?' is lame when that number is given in the school bulletin. Ask questions that relate to your personal goals in college."

How Can I Decide Which School Is Best for Me?

"This is the big question. First, be realistic. As I've said before, we all want to go to the best schools in the country, but we can't all get accepted there. While you should have one Dream School just for fun, be prepared by having several more realistic schools as backups.

"Next, look at affordability. Be absolutely sure that you can afford a school before you go through all the visitations and applications (which cost money). You may think you'll get a scholarship and financial aid, but they are getting harder and harder to acquire and rarely cover all the costs. Figure out just exactly how much you have to contribute, and then have a realistic talk with your parents about how much they can help. Yes, you can get a job during school as well, but that money usually goes towards daily expenses and fun, not tuition and books. You may be able to work only part-time, remember.

"Of course, the physical comfort of a school is vital. By that I mean, would you enjoy living in that particular city and on the campus? If you are a big-city sophisticate, you may not want to live in a small college town in the Midwest that has few of the extras you grew up with. If you are a laid-back, small-town type, life in the big city may be so distracting that you don't concentrate on your studies. And you have to like the campus, too, as you'll probably live on it for at least a few years.

"And last, I always recommend thinking about long-range internships and job opportunities. If you want to be a schoolteacher, for example, does the college have a good student-teaching program? Are there jobs in the community for teachers after you graduate? Many students fall in love with the city in which their school is located and want to stay there after they graduate. You're only in high school now and may not be thinking as far ahead as graduation and job hunting, but they should be a vital part of your decision on colleges."

What's the Biggest Mistake Most Students Make in College Planning?

"Relying on misinformation. The school grapevine and rumor mill are always working. I have students come to me who are convinced that they can have a mediocre ACT score and still get into their Dream School 'because a friend of a friend at school, this guy who plays water polo, did it.' Check your facts. You may want to believe what you hear, but trust me, much of it will be wrong. Read the school bulletin. Talk to the admissions office or to an alumna of the school. Talk to your high school guidance counselor, or get help from an independent counselor.

"The second biggest mistake is choosing a college based solely on how much money it will give you in scholarships or financial aid. While money is critical, as I discussed earlier, it should not be your *only* reason for attending a school. Somewhere out there, you can find a school you love, one that fits you to a *T*. You don't have to settle for the first school that offers you money, thinking that you won't find anything better. Your college experience is something you'll remember forever. It will affect your friendships, your career, and the rest of your life. Don't just settle for 'good enough'; look for 'just right.'"

Anything Else I Should Know?

"Colleges are getting more and more competitive. The proportion of children who are reaching college age is always growing, yet relatively few new colleges and universities are being built. Simple logic tells you that the current schools are getting more and more selective. Do everything you can to do well in your classes and absolutely everything you can to get a great ACT score. It may be annoying now to give up your afternoons and weekends to study, but you'll greatly increase your options by doing so. The higher your grades and ACT scores, the more colleges will want you. Good luck!"

Chapter 20

Ten Dumb Things You Can Do to Mess Up Your ACT

In This Chapter

- Losing concentration
- Panicking over time
- Messing up numbering on the answer grid
- Rubbernecking
- Cheating
- Worrying about previous sections
- Worrying about the hard problems
- Transferring information from problem to problem or section to section
- Forgetting to double-check
- Looking back and playing "coulda-shoulda"

Throughout this book, you've learned techniques for doing your best on the ACT. I'm sorry to say, however, that there are just as many techniques for messing up big time on this test. Take a few minutes to read through them now to see what dumb things people do to blow the exam totally. By being aware of these catastrophes, you may prevent their happening to you.

And no — no booby prize is awarded to the student who makes the greatest number of these mistakes.

Losing Concentration

When you're in the middle of an excruciatingly boring reading passage, the worst thing you can do is to let your mind drift off to a more pleasant time (last night's date, last weekend's soccer game, the time that you stole your rival school's mascot and set it on the john in the principal's private bathroom). Although visualization (picturing yourself doing something relaxing or fun) is a good stress-reduction technique, it stinks when it comes to helping your ACT score. Even if you have to pinch yourself to keep from falling asleep or flaking out, stay focused. The ACT is less than five hours of your life. You've probably had horrible blind dates that lasted longer than that and managed to survive them. This too shall pass.

Panicking Over Time

Every section on the ACT begins with directions and a line that tells exactly how many questions are in the section and, therefore, how many minutes you have per question. It's not as if this is some big mystery. You can waste a lot of time and drive yourself crazy if you keep flipping pages ahead, counting up how many more questions you have to do. You can do what you can do; that's all. Looking ahead and panicking only wastes time and is counterproductive.

Messing Up Numbering on the Answer Grid

Suppose that you decide to postpone doing question number 11, hoping that inspiration will strike. But now you accidentally put the answer to question 12 in question 11's blank . . . and mess up all the numbers from that point on. After you answer question 30 and suddenly realize that you just filled in bubble number 29 and have one bubble left — *aaargh!* Stroke City! It's easy for me to say, "Don't panic," but chances are that your blood pressure will go sky-high, especially when you eyeball the clock and see that only one minute remains.

If you have a good eraser with you (which is one of the things I suggested in Chapter 1 that you bring with you), the wrong answers on the answer grid should take only a few seconds to erase. But how on earth are you going to resolve all those problems and reread and reanswer all the questions? You're not; you're going to thank your lucky stars that you bought this book and took the following advice: When you choose an answer, *circle that answer in your test booklet first* and *then* fill in the answer on the answer grid. Doing so takes you a mere gigasecond and helps you not only in this panic situation, but also as you go back and double-check your work.

Throughout this book, I remind you that random guesses can't hurt you on the ACT because there is no penalty for wrong answers. Never leave a bubble blank. Make a random guess. Fill in the bubble; then put an arrow in the margin of the test booklet (*not* on the answer grid) to remind yourself to review that question. Because you have all the bubbles filled in, you won't make a numbering error like that described earlier.

Rubbernecking

Rubbernecking is craning your neck around to see how everyone else is doing. Forget those bozos. You have too much to do on your own to waste precious seconds checking out anyone else. You don't want to psych yourself out by noticing that the guy in front of you is done with his section and is leaning back whistling while you're still sweating away. Maybe the guy in front of you is a complete moron and didn't notice that the booklet has yet another page of problems — so he did only half the section. After the exam booklet is put in front of you, don't look at anything but it and your watch until time is called.

Try not to sit by the clock in the classroom. Because everyone looks at the clock constantly, you may become self-conscious, thinking that *you're* being checked out. People staring at you every few seconds can be quite distracting. You need to keep your mind entirely on what you're doing, not continually look up and catch someone's eye.

Cheating

Dumb, dumb, *dumb!* Cheating on the ACT is a loser's game — it's just plain stupid. Apart from the legal, moral, and ethical questions, let's talk practicality: You can't predict what types of grammatical mistakes will show up in the questions; what are you going to do, copy a textbook on the palm of your hand? All the math formulas that you need can't fit onto the bottom of your shoe. Copying everything that you *think* you may need would take more time than just learning it. Besides, the ACT tests critical reasoning skills, not just rote memorization. The test never asks a question as straightforward as, "How many degrees in a triangle?" The questions require thinking and reasoning, not just copying down a formula. Short of having a brain transplant, cheating is impractical.

Worrying about the Previous Sections

Think of the ACT as four separate lifetimes. You are reborn three times and so get three more chances to "do it right." Every time the proctor says, "Your time is up. Please turn to the next test and begin," you get a fresh start. The ACT rules are very strict: You cannot go back to a previous section and finish work there or change some of your answers. If you try to do so, the proctor will catch you, and you'll be in a world of hurt. But suppose that you're too ethical even to consider going back to earlier material. There's still the problem of *worrying* about the previous test. If you're now working on math, you shouldn't be racking your brain trying desperately to remember what that frustrating, it's-on-the-tip-of-my-tongue grammar rule was. Forget one test as soon as you enter the next. Think of it as you would think of a new boyfriend or girlfriend in your life: out with the old, in with the new.

Worrying about the Hard Problems

As you've learned throughout this book, the ACT contains some incredibly hard problems and questions. Forget about 'em. Almost no one gets them right, anyway. A ridiculously few total 36s are scored every year, and if you get into the 30s, you are in a super-elite club of only a few percent of the thousands and thousands of students who take the ACT annually. Just accept the fact that you either won't get to or can't answer a few of the hard questions, and learn to live with your imperfection. If you do go fast enough to get to the hard questions, don't waste too much time on them. Scan them; if you can't think of how to begin, choose an answer at random. Then go back and double-check your easy questions. Keep reminding yourself that every question counts the same in a section, whether that question is a simple $1 + 1 = 2$ or some deadly word problem that may as well be written in Lithuanian.

Transferring Information from Problem to Problem or Section to Section

Each question exists in its own little world. If $x = 17$ in question number 15, it does not necessarily equal that in question number 16 (unless a note says something like, "Questions 15 and 16 refer to the following information"). Now that sounds incredibly simplistic, but it's surprising how many people transfer information from problem to problem. This practice is especially prevalent in dealing with symbolism questions. If you learn in a symbolism question that $\triangle x = 25$, it is highly unlikely that it will be equal to 25 in another triangle problem.

Forgetting to Double-Check

If you finish a test early, go back and double-check the *easy* and *medium* questions. Don't spend more time trying to do the hard questions. If a question was too hard for you five minutes ago, it's probably still too hard for you. Your brain capacity probably hasn't doubled in the last few minutes. If you made a totally careless or dumb mistake on an easy question, however, going back over the problem gives you a chance to catch and correct your error. You're more likely to gain points by double-checking easy questions than by staring openmouthed at the hard ones. ***Remember:*** Every question counts the same. A point you save by catching a careless mistake is just as valuable as a point you earn, grunting and sweating, by solving a mondo-hard problem.

Looking Back and Doing "Coulda-Shoulda"

Don't discuss the questions with your friends in the bathroom during break. They don't really know any more than you do. Your friends may all tell you that they got answer A for question five — but maybe answer A was the trap answer and they all fell for it. If you get depressed because you chose answer B, you're only hurting yourself. Maybe B was right all along, and you alone brilliantly recognized and circumnavigated the trap. Why put yourself through this grief? The same is true after the exam. Forget the postmortem. You did what you did; no sense fretting about it until you get your scores back.

Chapter 21

Ten Points You Should Always Double-Check

In This Chapter

- Exponents
- Commonsense connections
- Decimal places
- Operations signs
- Political correctness
- *–ing* and other *beware!* words
- Context
- Fill in the blank
- Completed answer grid

My father's favorite thing to say to me before I take a test is, "Always double-check! If your mother and I had double-checked before we left the hospital with you, we might have brought home a *normal* child. . . ."

Mental and emotional child abuse aside, Dad has a point. Double-checking is integral to getting what you want. The test-makers know what types of careless mistakes students make, so they build those mistakes into the test. The following are some of the most common areas in which people get sloppy.

Exponents

Make sure that as you multiplied like bases, you added the exponents ($x^5 \times x^5 = x^{10}$), and that as you divided like bases, you subtracted the exponents ($x^9 \div x^3 = x^6$). Forgetting this and just multiplying ($x^5 \times x^5 = x^{25}$) or dividing ($x^9 \div x^3 = x^3$) instead of adding or subtracting is all too easy to do.

Commonsense Connections

Think about what a math question is asking. If you are asked to find the weight of a child and your answer is 400 pounds, something went haywire somewhere. If McCaela is bicycling and you deduce that she bikes at a rate of 220 mph, sign that woman up for the Olympics!

Decimal Places

If a question has two or more answers with the same digits, you know that the decimal point is being tested. If the choices are .05, 0.5, 5, 50, and 500, double-check that your decimal point is in the right place.

Operations Signs

Double-check all operations signs (+, –, ÷, and ×) when you move from one side of the equal sign to the other side.

Political Correctness

The verbal portion of the ACT contains very few correct, negative-sounding answers. If a passage talks about people, especially those in a minority group, it never says nasty things about them. The entire ACT is sweetness and light; if your answer is petty and mean-spirited, it is probably wrong.

-ing and Other Beware! Words

Always double-check the words that give you trouble: *lie* or *lay* and *affect* or *effect,* for example. Pay close attention to the *-ing* words as well.

Context

When you're taking the English and Reading tests, read a few sentences before and after the sentence you're working on. You won't get tripped up by an answer choice that seems correct in the sentence but isn't because of text that precedes or follows the sentence.

Fill in the Blank

To double-check your work, insert your answer in the question and complete it again. Does your answer still make sense?

Completed Answer Grid

If you've read through this book, you've seen the following information a gazillion times, but it bears repeating: *Wrong answers on the ACT are not penalized.* You lose no points for a mistake. Therefore, it behooves you to answer every question, even if you have to make wild guesses to do so. When you see that you have only a minute or two left, fill in an answer for every question left in the test. You may pick up several points for lucky guesses.

Chapter 22

Ten Stress-Busters to Help You Survive the ACT

In This Chapter

- Breathe deeply
- Rotate your head
- Hunch and roll your shoulders
- Cross and roll your eyes
- Shake out your hands
- Extend and push out your legs
- Relax your eyes
- Rotate your scalp
- Curtail negative thoughts
- Before the test or during the break, visualize

Most people are tense before a test, with butterflies dancing in their stomachs. The key is to use relaxation techniques that keep your mind on your test and not on your tummy.

Breathe Deeply

Breathing is grossly underrated. Breathing is good. Take a deep breath until your belly expands, hold your breath for a few counts, and then expel the air through your nose. (Be careful not to blow anything but air, especially if your boyfriend/girlfriend is sitting next to you.) Try not to take short, shallow breaths, which could cause you to become even more anxious, as your body is deprived of oxygen. Try breathing in and out deeply while reciting something in your mind, such as your favorite line from a movie or a totally stupid, mindless rhyme.

Rotate Your Head

Try to see behind your head. Move your head as far as possible to the right until you feel a tug on the skin on the left side of your neck. Then reverse it and move your head all the way to the left until you feel a tug on the skin on the right. Move your head back, as if you're looking at the ceiling, and then down, as if looking at your feet. You'll be surprised how much tension drains out of you as you do this a few times.

Be careful that you perform this exercise with your eyes closed and make what you're doing obvious. You don't want a suspicious proctor to think that you're craning your neck to look at someone else's answer grid.

Hunch and Roll Your Shoulders

While breathing in, scrunch up your shoulders as if you're trying to touch them to your ears. Then roll them back and down, breathing out. Arch your back, sitting up super-straight, as if a string is attached to the top of your head and is being pulled toward the ceiling. Then slump and round out your lower back, pushing it out toward the back of your chair. These exercises relax your upper and lower back. They are especially useful if you develop a kink in your spine.

Cross and Roll Your Eyes

Look down at your desk as you're doing this so that people won't think that you're even stranger than they already know you are. Cross your eyes and then look down as far as you can into your lower eyelids. Look to the right and then up into your eyelids and then look to the left. After you repeat this sequence a few times, your eyes should be refreshed.

Shake Out Your Hands

You probably do this automatically to try to get rid of writer's cramp. Do it more consciously and more frequently. Put your hands down at your sides, hanging them below your chair seat, and shake them vigorously. Imagine all the tension and stress going out through your fingers and dropping onto the floor.

Extend and Push Out Your Legs

While you're sitting at your desk, straighten your legs out in front of you; think of pushing something away with your heels. Point your toes back toward your knees. You feel a stretch on the backs of your legs. Hold for a count of three and then relax.

Relax Your Eyes

Cup your hands, fingers together. Put them over your closed eyes, blocking out all the light. You're now in a world of velvety-smooth darkness, which is very soothing. Try not to let your hands actually touch your eyes. (If you see stars or flashes of light, your hands are pushing down on your eyes.)

Rotate Your Scalp

Put your open hand palm-down on your scalp and move your hand in small circles. You feel your scalp rotate. Lift your hand and put it down somewhere else on your scalp. Repeat the circular motions. You're giving yourself a very relaxing scalp massage.

Curtail Negative Thoughts

Anytime you feel yourself starting to panic or thinking negative thoughts, make a conscious effort to say to yourself, *"Stop!"* Don't dwell on anything negative; switch over to a positive track. Suppose that you catch yourself thinking, "Why didn't I study this math more? I saw that formula a hundred times but can't remember it now!" Change the script to, "I got most of this math right; if I let my subconscious work on that formula, maybe I'll get it, too. No sense worrying now. Overall, I think I'm doing great."

Before the Test or During a Break, Visualize

Don't do this *during* the test; you just waste time and lose concentration. Before the exam, however, or at the break, practice visualization. Close your eyes and imagine yourself in the test room, seeing questions that you know the answers to, cheerfully filling in the bubble grids, happily finishing early and double-checking your work. Picture yourself leaving the exam room all uplifted and then, five weeks later, getting your scores and rejoicing. Think of how proud your parents are of you. Imagine the acceptance letter you get from the college of your dreams. Picture yourself driving a fire-engine-red Ferrari ten years from now, telling the *Time* magazine reporter in the passenger seat that your success started with your excellent ACT scores. The goal is to associate the ACT with good feelings.

Index

• A •

• B •

• C •

• D •

• Q •

• R •

• S •

• T •

• U •

• V •

• W •

• X •

• Z •

Notes

Notes

Notes

Notes

Notes